敦煌文化·译丛（汉英对照）

Dunhuang Culture in Translation: A Series

主编 姜秋霞

副主编 [美]安瑞 柳菁

丝路明珠

敦煌

Dunhuang：Pearl of the Silk Road

郑炳林 李军 著 贾慧 赵粉琴 马凌飞 译

甘肃教育出版社

图书在版编目（CIP）数据

丝路明珠：敦煌 = Dunhuang:Pearl of the Silk Road：汉英对照 / 郑炳林，李军著；贾慧，赵粉琴，马凌飞译. -- 兰州：甘肃教育出版社，2021.11
（敦煌文化·译丛 / 姜秋霞主编）
ISBN 978-7-5423-5144-9

Ⅰ. ①丝… Ⅱ. ①郑… ②李… ③贾… ④赵… ⑤马… Ⅲ. ①敦煌—概况—汉、英 Ⅳ. ①K924.23

中国版本图书馆 CIP 数据核字(2021)第 133354号

丝路明珠——敦煌

Dunhuang: Pearl of the Silk Road

郑炳林　李军　著　　贾慧　赵粉琴　马凌飞　译

责任编辑　王露莹
封面设计　石　璞
内文设计　方　圆
图片支持　敦煌研究院

出　版　甘肃教育出版社
社　址　兰州市读者大道 568 号　730030
网　址　www.gseph.cn　E-mail　gseph@duzhe.cn
电　话　0931-8436105（编辑部）　0931-8773056(发行部)
传　真　0931-8773056
淘宝官方旗舰店　http://shop111038270.taobao.com

发　行　甘肃教育出版社　印　刷　山东新华印务有限公司
开　本　787 毫米 × 1092 毫米　1/16　印　张　28　字　数　399 千
版　次　2021 年 11 月第 1 版
印　次　2021 年 11 月第 1 次印刷
书　号　ISBN 978-7-5423-5144-9　定　价　98.00 元

“丝绸之路·敦煌文化翻译”工程

编 委 会

“丝绸之路·敦煌文化翻译”工程是甘肃文化翻译中心在甘肃省委宣传部的领导下所实施的文化翻译工程，旨在助力共建“一带一路”，弘扬丝路文化和敦煌文化，推进敦煌文化国际交流与传播，推动中国文化“走出去”。

“敦煌文化·译丛”为“丝绸之路·敦煌文化翻译”工程系列成果之一。

玉门关(王　玫　摄)
Yumen Pass (Photo by Wang Mei)

"敦煌文化·译丛"简介

近年来,在"中华文化走出去""讲好中国故事"与共建"一带一路"的大背景下,充分展示了中华民族文化自信的敦煌文化,以其丰富的内涵和独特的魅力吸引着全世界的目光。越来越多的海内外人士渴望掀起敦煌文化神秘的面纱,走近敦煌,从而走进敦煌。"敦煌文化·译丛"的编纂,以"敦煌文化走出去"为目标,以"讲好敦煌故事"为原则,对外传播敦煌文化,交流敦煌学思想,传承敦煌精神。

一、丛书内容

"敦煌文化·译丛"在传播内容上重视知识的可接受度,甄选了既有学术价值,又便于普及的敦煌学著作和敦煌文化读物进行翻译。所选书籍均为敦煌学著名专家所著,集学术性与科普性于一体,且呈现出一定的系统性,主题逐步涵盖敦煌文化完整版图,着力打造出相对全面的敦煌文化外宣丛书体系。本系列译丛采用中外语言对照的编纂方式,传播敦煌文化,交流敦煌学研究思想等。

"敦煌文化·译丛"以开放的模式分期分批编辑出版。第一辑包含《丝路明珠:敦煌》《艺苑瑰宝:莫高窟壁画与彩塑》《箫管霓裳:敦煌乐舞》及《遗响千年:敦煌的影响》四部作品的汉英对照读本。

《丝路明珠:敦煌》(郑炳林、李军著)以敦煌的历史、地位和周边名胜古迹为主题,分别讲述了从新石器时代、两汉、魏晋南北朝到西夏、元、明、清各个不同朝代历史背景下敦煌的发展和变迁;论述了丝绸之路开通后,敦煌作为中西交通线路上的重要枢纽、中西贸易的中转站和中央王朝经营西域的军事重镇的历史地位;介绍了包括莫高窟、榆林窟等佛教石窟,玉门关、阳关等城池关隘,及鸣沙山、月牙泉等自然景观在内的敦煌周边历史文化名胜和古迹。全书脉络清晰,语言生动,集资料性、故事性和知识性于一体,既突出了敦煌的地域文化特点,又展现了敦煌厚重的历史内涵,使这颗沉睡在茫茫大漠之中的璀璨明珠在世人面前焕发出夺目的光华。

《艺苑瑰宝:莫高窟壁画与彩塑》(赵声良著)概括介绍了敦煌彩塑和壁画的基本风貌,包括塑像、佛像画、飞天、故事画、经变画、山水画、装饰画等单元,并阐述了包含其中的文化价值、历史价值、艺术价值,展示出千年中国美术的脉络。这本书还对古代印度、中亚艺术与中国艺术的交流与融合作了分析,全书浸透着作者全方位学术研究的成果,以及自豪自信的文化情怀。文笔流畅,深入浅出,图文并茂,雅俗共赏,把博大精深的敦煌艺术成功地传达给了读者。

《箫管霓裳:敦煌乐舞》(王克芬、柴剑虹著)以敦煌莫高窟为主题,分别介绍了敦煌乐舞的人文背景及源流、经变画中的天宫乐舞、世俗画里的歌舞、特色鲜明的民族舞蹈、生动活泼的童子舞姿、敦煌乐舞的文化特征等内容。作者用凝练、简洁、流畅的笔触,以敦煌莫高窟壁画、彩塑为着眼点,文解图义,栩栩如生地展示了敦煌莫高窟壁画中丰富多彩的佛国乐舞形象。全书凝练紧凑,主题鲜明,语言流畅,专业性与普及性兼顾,为中外读者了解与欣赏敦煌乐舞打开了一扇大门。

《遗响千年:敦煌的影响》(刘进宝著)以敦煌文献的整理刊布与敦煌艺术探索和文艺创作为主题,分别介绍了敦煌学的产生背景、敦煌文献在各国的研究概况、中外文化艺术名人与敦煌的故事、敦煌艺术光辉照耀下的文学艺术创作成果、敦煌文物的保护及研究等内容。作者用通俗易懂、生动活泼的语言,将专业性与普及性融为一体,让读者与敦煌渐行渐近,相知相亲,向世人展现了敦煌文化在中国和世界所产生的深远影响。全书图文并茂、材料翔实、叙述生动,吸引中外读者走进敦煌辉煌灿烂的文化圣殿与艺术宝库。

这四部作品涵盖了敦煌文化中的重要板块,系统阐释了敦煌文化的历史发展、艺术价值与人文精神。一方面,从本体视角出发介绍敦煌的历史地理知识;另一方面,从认识视角出发展示敦煌文化艺术中最为人感知的两张名片——壁画雕塑与音乐舞蹈；最终，从价值视角出发凸显敦煌文化及敦煌学在全世界产生的影响。本系列译丛将促进敦煌艺术之美的国际化交流，补充与敦煌乐舞相关的深度双语语料，拓展敦煌历史地理相关的系统语言资料，为“敦煌在中国、敦煌学在世界”这一国际化命题提供了必要参考。

二、译介特点

“敦煌文化·译丛”以“传播敦煌文化，交流敦煌学思想”为主旨，采用“中英对照”的形式讲述敦煌故事、阐释敦煌精神。在译介方式上，运用多元的翻译策略和方法，进行文本对比与转换。在原文阐释上，一方面通过系统查阅历史文献、背景资料、中外敦煌学研究成果等，深刻理解原文语义；另一方面通过译者与原作者的对话与沟通，精准把握敦煌文化的精髓要义。在外文表达上，注重信息的有效表达，通过“中西合璧”的模式展开翻译，由中外译者通力合作，以“读者接受”为主导，运用适切的话语方式，综合的翻译方法，进行语言转换。译文尽可能贴近英语读者的表达习惯、思维模式、语言风格和理解能力，使所译作品不仅在文字上实现了“走出去”，同时使其文化内涵真正能够“走进去”，力图实现文化的深度传播。

“敦煌文化·译丛”的总体翻译原则：在充分理解和尊重原文的基础上，对于汉英语言文化中存在对应概念和表达的内容，尽量忠实于原文的内容和风格，力求准确再现原文的语言和文化信息。在遵循翻译基本原理的前提下，根据汉英两种语言和文化之间的差异，综合运用“归化”“异化”“融合化”等翻译策略，对原文部分内容进行适度的增减编改，灵活采用节译、概译、编译和解释性翻译等方法进行语言文本的转换。

“敦煌文化·译丛”的基本翻译方法：

1. 对于原文中文化概念和术语的翻译，一般采用我国官方出版物和官方网站中已有的外文表达。

2. 对于中国的历史朝代，在外文文本中补充了公元纪年法中的年份信息。但对于个别年代信息有争议的历史朝代，则不再标注年份。

3. 对于历史官衔名称，以“传播历史文化，兼顾读者理解”为目的，采用

“音译+名词”“音译+释义”等方法，一方面保留原有的文化特质，另一方面使读者易于接受；对于官衔、官职修饰词语过多的情况，则采用意译或概译的方法进行语义对应；对于官职官衔名在不同历史时期，虽名称未变，但语义内涵发生变化的，根据其语境中相应的含义进行转换。

4. 对于原文中出现的书籍名称，首先遵循“名从历史”“名从主人”的原则，沿用已有的译名。如果已有译名为汉语拼音，则在保留原有名称的基础上，增补英文译名；无英译文的书籍名称，则采用常规翻译方法进行文本对应。

5. 对于原文中的引文（如诗词、古籍文献），根据引文的作用进行有选择性的转换。若引文为核心论点，或用于描写相应的文化内容，且上下文未对引文内容进行解释或重述，则全文翻译；若引文仅用于衬托或强化相应的文化内容，且相关内容已在上下文说明或提及，则进行概译或省译。

6. 对于一些描写壁画形象的直白语言，为提升其艺术美感，采用“优化”的策略和“解释性翻译”的方法，进行语篇结构的扩充对应。

7. 对于宗教文化概念，首先采用已有的英文表达；对于有固定梵语表达的佛教概念，则采用“回译法”进行转换；没有约定俗成表达的宗教概念、中国本土宗教概念及其他宗教与中国文化相融合后产生的概念，则根据情况采用音译、直译或意译进行文本对应。

8. 对于需要补充文化背景信息的内容，一般采用“译者注”的方式进行补充说明，以便更有效地提高阅读理解力。包括但不限于下列情况：一是对于一些在历史演变过程中语义发生变化的文化名称，采用“译者注”的方式加以说明，如“刺史”这一官职名称，分别译为Inspector / Governor / Prefect，并通过“译者注”说明同一名称在不同历史时期因其职责发生变化采用不同译文的背景信息。二是对于一些特殊地名，为避免产生阅读障碍，在翻译的同时加“译者注”进行说明，如不以行政区划命名的大地区概念（中原、西域等），翻译的同时，通过“译者注”明确其内涵和范围；含有古代行政区划“州”“郡”“府”“县”“道”等的地名，在翻译行政区划词的同时适当增加“译者注”解释其含义；由于历史原因更改地名的，亦通过“译者注”加以阐明。三是当同音异义词音译后在译文中无法分辨时，也采用“译者注”的方式加以区分。

9. 本译丛遵循一致性原则，运用统一的翻译策略和方法，但同时也存在一些体现译者个体风格的差异化表达。

三、几点说明

1. 中文文本之外附加的内容，如附录等，经与中文作者沟通，不再收录。

2. 中文文本中个别问题需要进行勘误时，英译文转换正确的语义内容，同时增加必要的说明。

3. 本译丛在翻译过程中参考了大量国内外相关著作、辞典、图册、音像资料、网络资料及数据库等，具体参考目录将在每本书后单另列出。

最后需要说明的是，敦煌文化翻译是一项十分具有挑战性的工作，难点很多，难度很大。因此，作为"丝绸之路·敦煌文化翻译"工程的第一辑译丛，在翻译中难免存在许多不足之处，甚至可能有误译和错译之处。我们真诚期待广大读者、专家学者批评指正！

致 谢

"敦煌文化·译丛"在策划、翻译、出版过程中得到甘肃省委宣传部、中国外文局、兰州大学敦煌学研究所等单位的大力支持；在翻译过程中得到了著作者的翻译授权和学术指导；同时得到了甘肃省人民政府新闻办、兰州城市学院等单位的支持，在此一并感谢。

"敦煌文化·译丛"编委会

An Introduction to *Dunhuang Culture in Translation: A Series*

In recent years, Dunhuang culture—an emblem of the pride of Chinese civilization—has increasingly attracted the world's attention with its profound significance and unique charms. This has taken place against the backdrop of "Chinese culture going global," "telling China's story to the world," and the joint pursuit of the Belt and Road Initiative. Ever-increasing numbers of people both internationally and domestically want Dunhuang's veil of mystery to be lifted. Through reading this series, people can become more familiar with Dunhuang, paving the way to really "get into" Dunhuang. Thus, along the principles of "Dunhuang culture going forth into the world," as well as "telling Dunhuang's story," the *Dunhuang Culture in Translation* series has been compiled with the goal of communicating the concepts of Dunhuang culture, carrying on the spirit of Dunhuang, and promoting Dunhuang to an international audience.

Series Content

The *Dunhuang Culture in Translation: A Series* emphasizes appropriateness for its readers, selecting works in the field of Dunhuang studies which embody academic value and also can be made accessible to a general audience. All the books in this series were written by well-known experts in the field of Dunhuang studies, blending academic knowledge with popular science and presenting information in a systematic way, and using a compilation method in both Chinese and English. The topics cover the essential part of Dunhuang culture, resulting in a relatively comprehensive framework for disseminating this subject to the world. The translated volumes in this series use a Chinese-English format to promote Dunhuang culture and academic exchanges of Dunhuang studies.

Dunhuang Culture in Translation is a multi–volumed, inclusive series published in sets. The first set in the series includes four bilingual volumes: *Dunhuang: Pearl of the Silk Road*; *Art Treasures: Murals and Painted Sculptures in Mogao Caves*; *Raiment of Rainbows and Feathers: Music and Dance from the Dunhuang Murals*; and *Dunhuang: Its Everlasting Impact*.

Dunhuang: Pearl of the Silk Road (by Zheng Binglin and Li Jun) takes as its subject matter the history of Dunhuang as well as its surrounding attractions. It traces Dunhuang's development and changes against the historical background of different periods, from the Neolithic Age, the Han Dynasty, Wei, Jin, Northern and Southern dynasties to the Western Xia, Yuan, Ming, and Qing dynasties. This volume explores the opening of the Silk Road and Dunhuang's historical status as an important crossroads for Sino–Western exchanges, the part it played as an important hub for Sino–Western trade, and its role as a military center for the Central Plains' operations in the Western Regions. It introduces the Buddhist rock–cut cave temples of the Mogao Caves and the Yulin Caves, historical and cultural sites such as the Yangguan and Yumen passes, and surrounding natural scenic spots including the Mingsha Mountain and the Crescent Moon Spring. The whole book is presented with clear ideas and vivid language, integrating factual data, literary narrative, and scholarly expertise. It not only highlights the regional cultural characteristics of Dunhuang, but also reveals its profound historical connotations as well, making this bright pearl, sleeping in the vast desert, glow with its brilliance for the world to see.

Art Treasures: Murals and Painted Sculptures in Mogao Caves (by Zhao Shengliang) outlines the basic features of Dunhuang sculptures and murals, including polychromed statues, Buddhist iconography, apsaras, narrative paintings, sutra illustrations, landscape paintings, decorative motifs, and other elements, expounding their cultural, historical, and artistic value in addition to tracing the course of Chinese art for thousands of years. This volume, steeped in Dr. Zhao's comprehensive academic research and brimming with pride in Chinese culture, also analyzes the exchange and synthesis of visual arts from ancient India, Central Asia, and China. The writing is fluent and easy to understand, with copious illustrations accompanying the text. Sharing an appreciation of both the sophisticated and the popular, it successfully conveys Dunhuang's broad and profound art to its readers.

Raiment of Rainbows and Feathers: Music and Dance from the Dunhuang Murals (by Wang Kefen and Chai Jianhong) takes the Mogao Caves as its subject, introducing the cultural background and origins of Dunhuang music and dance, images of palace entertainment depicted in sutra illustrations, singing and dancing as found in secular paintings, distinctive ethnic dances, the lively lotus child dance, and more. The authors use concise and natural language to discuss the murals and the painted sculptures of the Mogao Caves, explaining the meaning of the images and vividly revealing the rich Buddhist and Chinese music and dance images found in Dunhuang wall paintings. Compact and concise, the book's themes are clear and the language is articulate, with an emphasis on balancing professional scholarship with accessibility to the public, opening the door for readers at home and abroad to understand and appreciate the performing arts of Dunhuang.

Dunhuang: Its Everlasting Impact (by Liu Jinbao) takes the compilation and classification of Dunhuang manuscripts, the exploration of Dunhuang art, and Dunhuang literary creation as its themes. It introduces the background of Dunhuang studies as a field, the research overview of Dunhuang manuscripts in various countries, the famous names behind Dunhuang studies both in China and around the world, and the literary and creative achievements in Dunhuang art, as well as the research, and conservation of Dunhuang relics. The author uses easy-to-understand, lively and dynamic language to integrate scholarship with mass-market appeal, allowing readers to "get closer" to Dunhuang, showing the profound influence of Dunhuang culture in China and internationally. The book's pictures and texts, informative materials, and vivid narrative style encourage both Chinese and English-speaking audiences to truly enter the brilliant cultural temples and treasure houses of Dunhuang.

The four works in this set form a system of their own, covering important areas of the Dunhuang cultural sphere, and systematically explaining the historical development, artistic value, and humanistic spirit of Dunhuang culture. On the one hand, the main objective of the books sets out to introduce the history and geography of Dunhuang, while on the other hand, it explores two of the most well-known aspects of Dunhuang arts: the visual arts and the performing arts. Finally, judging from its value, the set highlights the influence of Dunhuang culture and Dunhuang studies around the world. This collection of translations aims to promote international understanding of the aesthetics of Dunhuang art, supplement in-depth bilingual works related to Dunhuang music and dance, expand systematic language materials related to Dunhuang history and geography, and provide a must-have language reference for researchers of Dunhuang studies both in China and overseas.

Special Features of the Translation

Dunhuang Culture in Translation is organized around the themes of promoting Dunhuang culture and transmitting Dunhuang thought, telling the stories of Dunhuang, and expounding the spirit of Dunhuang in a Chinese-English format. In terms of translation methods, this series uses multiple strategies and methods to compare and translate texts. In terms of the interpretation of the original text, on the one hand, we can deeply understand the semantics of the original text through systematic review of historical documents, background materials, and research results in Dunhuang studies in China as well as internationally; on the other hand, we can accurately grasp the essence of Dunhuang culture through dialogue and communication between the translators and the original authors. In terms of foreign language expression, special attention has been paid to the effective expression of information. The translation has been done according to a Sino-Western model. The Chinese and English language translators have closely cooperated with one other, with reader accessibility as their primary consideration, using appropriate discourse modes and comprehensive translation methods to exchange languages. The translation is as close as possible to the idiomatic expression, modes of thought, language style, and reading comprehension of English-language readers, so that the translated text of the works not only achieves a "going out" in a literary sense, but simultaneously also allows the cultural connotations to truly "go in" and achieve a deep transmission into the readers' conceptualization.

The overarching translation principles of the *Dunhuang Culture in Translation: A Series* are as follows: on the basis of understanding and respecting the original text, for those expressions which have a corresponding concept and expression in English language and culture, the translation strives to accurately reproduce the original language and cultural information, faithful to the content and style of the original Chinese text. Moreover, on the premise of following standard principles of translation, according to differences between Chinese and English languages and cultures we have comprehensively employed translation strategies such as domestication, foreignization, and fusion to appropriately add, delete, edit, and modify the original content. We have adopted a flexible mixture of approaches such as abridged translation, generalized translation, compilation, and interpretative translation for language and text conversion.

The basic translation methods for the *Dunhuang Culture in Translation: A Series* are as follows:

1. For the translation of cultural concepts and terminology in the original text, foreign language expressions found in official publications and official websites of China have generally been used.

2. For historical dynasties, information for the dates using AD and BC has been added to the foreign language text. However, for historical dynasties with dates in dispute, the year is not noted.

3. For the translations of historical titles of official rank, our purpose is to enhance exchanges of history and culture, taking into account the readers' understanding. Thus, we have employed methods such as "*pinyin* transliteration + nouns," and "*pinyin* transliteration + gloss," on the one hand, retaining the original cultural characteristics of the titles, and, on the other hand, allowing readers to easily accept the title names. For official titles with multiple versions or modifiers, free translation or generalized translation methods have been used for semantic correspondence; for official titles from different historical periods, when the name has remained unchanged, but the semantic connotation has changed, the meaning has been conveyed according to the appropriate context.

4. For the titles of Chinese books, the principles of "using historical names" and "using names created by the original parties" have been followed. If an existing title is in *pinyin*, the English translation has been added on the basis of keeping the original name; if there is no English translation of the name of the classic text, conventional translation methods have been applied.

5. For citations or quotations in the original text (such as poems, classics), selective conversion has been carried out according to the function of the citation. If a quotation or citation functions as a core idea or is used to describe corresponding cultural content, and the context does not explain or restate the citation content, the full text is translated; if the quotation is only used to highlight or strengthen the corresponding cultural content, and the relevant content has been explained or mentioned in the context, general translation or deletion has been applied.

6. For certain basic, straightforward language describing mural imagery, in order to enhance their artistic beauty, "optimization" strategies and interpretative translation methods have been applied to expand the text.

7. For religious and cultural concepts, we have first adopted existing English terms and expressions where they exist; for Buddhist concepts with fixed, conventional Sanskrit names, we have used the back translation method to convert the terms from Chinese back into their original Sanskrit again. Religious concepts that are not expressed by conventional usage or fixed terms, native Chinese religious concepts, and concepts arising from the fusion of other religions and Chinese culture have been rendered by transliteration, literal translation or free translation based on the situation or context.

8. For the content that needs to be supplemented with cultural background information, we have generally used footnotes as supplementary explanations, in order to more effectively improve the readers' comprehension. This includes but is not limited to the following situations: First, for some cultural names whose semantics have changed in the course of historical evolution, we have used footnotes to explain them. For example, the official title of "*cishi*" is translated variously as Inspector, Governor, or Prefect, and a footnote is used to explain that the title for this post was modified over time due to changes in the position's responsibilities in

different historical periods. Second, for special place names, footnotes have been added to avoid confusion. For example, the concept of large geographical regions such as the Central Plains, the Western Regions, and so forth, was provided with footnotes to clarify their meaning and scope. Footnotes have been provided for place names with ancient administrative divisions such as "*zhou*" "*jun*" "*fu*" "*xian*" "*dao*" etc., where necessary or appropriate. Changes in place names due to historical reasons have also been clarified through the addition of footnotes. Third, when homophones cannot be distinguished in the translation after transliteration, footnotes or annotations have also been used to distinguish them.

9. This translation series follows the principle of consistency and uses unified translation strategies and methods, but some terms and expressions may vary and reflect the individual style of the translators.

Special Points for the Readers' Consideration

1. Appendices, indices, and glossaries in the original Chinese versions are not included in the volumes of this set, which is permitted by the original authors.

2. Where individual issues in the Chinese text have required correction, the information in the English translation has been presented in the corrected, revised form, and explanations have been added where necessary.

3. This translation series relies on a large number of Chinese and English language reference works, dictionaries, atlases, audiovisual materials, internet resources, and databases during the translation process. A specific bibliography is listed separately at the back of each volume.

One final thing to be said is that Dunhuang culture translation is a very demanding task, with many difficulties and great challenges. Therefore, as the first series in the Silk Road Dunhuang Culture Translation Project, there are inevitably many shortcomings in the translation, and there may even be mistranslations and errors. We sincerely encourage criticism and correction from readers, experts, and scholars in the field.

Acknowledgements

The *Dunhuang Culture in Translation : A Series* received strong support from the Publicity Department of the Gansu Provincial Party Committee, China Foreign Languages Publishing Administration, Institute of Dunhuang Studies of Lanzhou University, and other governmental offices in the planning, translation, and publication process of this series. Throughout the translation process, permission, authorization, and guidance were granted by the authors of each volume. The Information Office of the People's Government of Gansu Province, Lanzhou City University as well as other governmental offices and leaders all gave their encouragement and support to this project. We extend our heartfelt thanks and gratitude to them all.

Editorial Committee of *Dunhuang Culture in Translation: A Series*

目　录

Contents

目 录

Contents

莫高窟第 275 窟　交脚弥勒　北凉
Maitreya in Cross-Ankled Position, Mogao Cave 275　Northern Liang

序言一

1975年，中国与英国签订了教育交流协议，恢复了中断将近10年的留学生互换项目。我作为首批留学生之一，同14位同学到英国学习。与此同时，英国学生也到中国留学。很多年以后，我遇到其中一位当年曾经在北京大学留学的英国学者，那时她已经是大英图书馆的东亚部负责人。她告诉我正在做的一件事情就是和中国文物局合作，把大英图书馆收藏的来自敦煌的历史资料复制给中方，以此加深两国专家围绕敦煌学的研究活动。可见因为历史上的多种原因，大量敦煌资料流散在海外，这对中国是一种损失，但是也催化了国外对敦煌的关注。

然而，敦煌学不局限于仅仅流散在海外的史料研究，真正的研究中心永远在敦煌，永远在中国。比如石窟代表的敦煌文化就是搬不走的，敦煌背后的历史和哲学思想是搬不走的。近些年，中国学者对敦煌的研究成绩斐然，加之敦煌文化的博大精深，非常有必要通过翻译，把中国学者的研究成果，把敦煌文化的精华，大张旗鼓地传播出去。特别是"一带一路"倡议不仅强化了中国与沿线国家的经济活动，也拉近了文化上的联系。民心相通首先要以文明互鉴为依托，以文化传播为纽带，达到美美与共。敦煌文化重要，对外传播更为重要。然而，集历史、艺术、宗教为一体的敦煌学覆盖历史时段长，涉及艺术门类全，代表的宗教影响深，反映的社会发展广，要翻译成外文实在太难了。

令人欣喜的是，以甘肃文化翻译中心姜秋霞教授领衔的团队卧薪尝胆、呕心沥血达六年，终于把首批共四部中英文对照版的"敦煌文化·译丛"呈现给国内外的读者。这四部图书分别是《丝路明珠：敦煌》《艺苑瑰宝：莫高窟壁画与彩塑》《箫管霓裳：敦煌乐舞》和《遗响千年：敦煌的影响》。这套图书的出版标志着我国首次有计划、成规模地、系统地把敦煌文化最新的研究成果用英文对外介绍。四本书用当代的语言把一个中国故事的过去与现在讲述给国际受众。这个翻译出版项目成就有多大,其艰难历程就有多长。翻译难,中译外更难,敦煌文化的翻译难上加难。这六年来,姜教授的团队经历了多少艰辛,比如为寻找一个准确的词汇花费多少心血,为精准传达一个观点熬去多少时光,读者只需翻阅一下这四本书,就会一目了然。

既然难度这么大,为什么还要翻译?姜教授说:“翻译,不仅仅是语言的转换,更是对文化的阐释。翻译敦煌文化,不是简单的话码转换,也不是单纯的信息传递,更重要的是解释和阐释敦煌文化和历史遗存蕴含的哲学思想、人文精神、价值理念、道德规范;弘扬和传承蕴含其中的中华民族的文化精神、文化胸怀和文化自信。”通过她的话我感到,敦煌文化翻译反映了译者的一种家国情怀、对外传播的理想抱负和迎难而上的治学精神。没有坚定的信念、远大的抱负和刻苦的工作干劲,译者早已在翻译任务的困难面前望而却步。所以,在向译者团队表示祝贺的同时,我更想向他们表示崇高的敬意。

一套丛书有那么大的意义吗? 文明互鉴需要文化信息的交流,做好对外交流就是要拿出外国人读得懂、看得明白的作品来。展示文化自信,需要拿出难啃的硬骨头成果来。这套丛书就是文化自信的产物,敦煌文化对外传播的最新之作。

然而,“敦煌文化·译丛”的意义不仅仅在作品上。丛书的翻译还是翻译团队不断成熟的一个过程。“敦煌文化·译丛”是“丝绸之路·敦煌文化翻译工程”的第一期项目。启动后译者发现翻译的难度极大,文化概念的翻译难度尤其大。于是翻译团队又启动了“敦煌文化中英对照术语库”的编制工作,并在《敦煌文化关键词》完成后,再开始推进“敦煌文化·译丛”的工作。“敦煌文化·译丛”第一辑四部图书以及衍生作品的问世见证了一支年轻的翻译队伍从无到有、从小到大、从弱到强的发展壮大。而作为设在兰州城市学院的一个团队,译者们作为教师也在培育着更加年轻的译者。他们的精神和经验必然让他们带出一支对外传播的人才队伍。

“敦煌文化·译丛”的意义还在于填补了“一带一路”建设的一个空白。敦煌,曾经是古代丝绸之路的重镇,如今是“一带一路”建设的重要支点。丛书给敦煌乃至甘肃省的对外文化交流提供了精品之作，增添了灿烂的文化光彩。讲好中国故事，传播中国声音不是一句口号，需要一部部的作品来支撑和实现。“敦煌文化·译丛”不仅展示了一段辉煌的历史，更彰显了中国文化自信和文化繁荣在新时代的成果。四部作品宣扬的不仅仅是中国历史上的文化积累，它们所介绍的四个方面更是代表中国在文明互鉴过程中的四颗璀璨明星，反射中国文化发展的过去，照亮中国文化传承的当今，预示中国文化生生不息的未来。

也正因为如此，我们期待“丝绸之路·敦煌文化翻译工程”的下一个项目。

中国外文局原副局长
中国翻译协会常务副会长
黄友义

2020年10月

Foreword I

In 1975, China and the United Kingdom signed an educational exchange agreement, resuming the exchange program for foreign students which had been suspended for nearly 10 years. I went to the UK to study with 14 classmates as part of the first group of these students. At the same time, British students also came to study in China. Some years later, I ran into one of the British scholars who had studied at Peking University when I was studying in the UK. At the time we met, she was already head of the Department of Oriental at the British Library. She told me that she was working on a joint project with the State Bureau of Cultural Relics, replicating historical documents and materials from Dunhuang held in the British Library, in order to facilitate Dunhuang research by experts from our two nations. Due to various historical reasons, a large amount of Dunhuang materials were scattered in various places overseas. This may have been a loss for China, but it also catalyzed foreigners' attention on Dunhuang.

However, Dunhuang studies is not limited merely to the study of historical materials scattered around the world. The real center of research has always been in Dunhuang and in China. For example, Dunhuang culture, as represented by its cave temples, is irremovable. Likewise, the history and philosophical thought behind Dunhuang is also deeply rooted here. In recent years, Chinese scholars have made outstanding achievements in the study of Dunhuang, and, coupled with the profundity of Dunhuang culture, it has become truly necessary to make these research findings—along with the essence of Dunhuang culture—widely known through their translation. In particular, the Belt and Road Initiative has not only strengthened the economic activity between China and the countries along the route, but has also brought closer cultural ties between them. People-to-people exchange must first rely on cultural communication and mutual learning among civilizations so as to uphold the beauty and diversity of civilizations in the world. Dunhuang culture is important, but communication with the international community is even more significant. However, Dunhuang studies, which integrates history, art, and religion, covers a long historical period of time, involves a full range of arts, represents deep religious influences, and reflects a wide range of social developments. It is thus an extremely challenging task to translate the achievements of Dunhuang studies into another language.

It is now gratifying to see that the team led by Professor Jiang Qiuxia of the Gansu Cultural Translation and Interpreting Center has, after six years of hard work, completed the first four volumes of the Chinese-English bilingual *Dunhuang Culture in Translation* series, now being presented to readers at home and abroad. The titles of these four books are *Dunhuang: Pearl of the Silk Road*; *Art Treasures: Murals and Painted Sculptures in Mogao Caves*; *Raiment of Rainbows and Feathers: Music and Dance from Dunhuang Murals*; and *Dunhuang: Its Everlasting Impact*. The publication of this set of books marks the first time that China has introduced the latest Dunhuang culture research in English and Chinese at the same time, and on a planned, large-scale, and systematic basis. The four books use contemporary language to convey the past and present of a Chinese story to an international audience. This translation and publishing project has been a great achievement, and the process has been long and arduous. Translation in general is not an easy job and it is even more difficult to translate Chinese into another language; the difficulty in translating Dunhuang culture lies even beyond all this. For the past six years, Professor Jiang's team has gone through many hardships, for example, expending great effort researching and finding the exact vocabulary and terminology, and considerable time spent on accurately and faithfully conveying each author's point of view. Readers only need to browse through these four books and the difficulties they had to overcome will be made immediately evident.

Since it is so difficult, then why translate? As Professor Jiang said, "Translation is not merely the conversion of language, but also the interpretation of culture. Translating Dunhuang culture is not a simple code conversion, nor is it purely the transmission of information. More importantly, translation reveals and interprets the philosophical thought, humanistic spirit, and values contained in Dunhuang culture and historical relics, which is imbued with the cultural spirit, mind, and confidence of the Chinese nation." Her words convince me that Dunhuang culture translation reflects the translators' deep love for their country and their ideals and determination for communicating with the world at large, as well as their devoted academic scholarship in the face of challenges. Unless translators have firm beliefs, lofty commitment, and a strong work ethic, they may easily pull back from the difficulties of translation work. While congratulating the team of translators, I would also like to express my highest respect for them.

Why does a series of books hold that much significance? Mutual learning between civilizations requires the interchange of cultural information, and doing a good job in communication involves producing works that people from other countries can readily understand. Conveying cultural confidece requires extremely hard and sophisticated work. This book series, the latest achievement in the introduction of Dunhuang culture, is a product of that cultural confidece.

The significance of *Dunhuang Culture in Translation* however is not only in the finished works. The translation of the series also represents a process of continuous maturity of the translation team. *Dunhuang Culture in Translation* marks the first phase of a much larger program—the Silk Road Dunhuang Culture Translation Project. After its launch, the translators found that the work was extremely challenging, especially the translation of cultural concepts. Thus, the translation team began by compiling the Dunhuang Culture Chinese-English Terminology Database, and after the completion of the bilingual *Key Concepts in Dunhuang Culture*, it began to focus on the work of the *Dunhuang Culture in Translation* series. The publication of these four books and their related works of the first series of *Dunhuang Culture in Translation* witnessed the development and growth of a team of young translators starting from scratch, growing from small to large, and from weak to strong. Based at Lanzhou City University, members of this translation team are also teachers who are bringing up even younger translators. Their spirit and experience will inevitably guide them in fostering the next generation of talent for presenting information and culture to the international community.

What is significant is that the *Dunhuang Culture in Translation* series has filled a gap in the promotion of the Belt and Road Initiative. Dunhuang was once an important town on the ancient Silk Road and now holds an important position in promoting the Belt and Road Initiative. This book series provides excellent works for not only Dunhuang but also Gansu Province to conduct exchanges with the world, adding a superb new dimension in cultural communication. Telling China's story and getting China's voice heard is not just a slogan: it needs a series of solid works to help make it happen. *Dunhuang Culture in Translation* not only reveals a glorious history, but also demonstrates the achievements of Chinese cultural confidece and cultural prosperity in our present era. These four works make known not only the formation of culture in Chinese history, but the four facets they introduce also represent four bright stars of China in the process of mutual learning between civilizations. Reflecting the past of China's cultural development and illuminating the heritage of Chinese civilization, they herald the limitless future of Chinese culture.

It is precisely because of this that we now look forward to the next installment in the Silk Road Dunhuang Culture Translation Project.

Huang Youyi

Former Deputy Director-General of China Foreign Languages Publishing Administration

Vice President of Translators Association of China

October 2020

序言二

敦煌文化是丝绸之路文明的精髓,是中外文化交流背景之下形成的哲学思想、人文精神、价值理念、道德规范等,而丝绸之路是连接古代中国与中亚、南亚、东欧的经济文化的交通要道,因其贩运的商品主要是丝绸,所以称之为丝绸之路。同时还因其贩运的物品和使用的货币而被称作为玉石之路、白银之路、香药之路、茶马之路等。

丝绸之路还是一条中外文化交流的重要通道,西方的先进科学技术和文化都是通过这条通道传入中国的,同时中国的先进文化和科学技术也是通过这条国际通道传播到世界各国,中西文化经过这条道路互相碰撞、交融和接纳,促进了汉唐帝国和学术文化的发展。通过这条道路,印度的佛教、欧洲的景教、中亚的祆教和摩尼教进入中国,并在中国迅速传播开来,由于佛教寺院的建造和石窟的开凿,佛教造像的兴盛,犍陀罗佛教艺术流传中国,影响了中国佛教艺术及中国道教艺术的发展。

因景教艺术传入,中亚艺术风格传入中国,并影响了中古时期中国社会生活的方方面面。通过这条道路,产生于印度的天竺乐和中亚的康国乐、安国乐和新疆地区龟兹乐、疏勒乐、高昌乐等的音乐舞蹈相继传入并迅速传播开来,由外来音乐舞蹈和中国古代清乐融合而产生的西凉乐,成为中古中国乐舞的重要组成部分,推进了中国文化艺术的发展。

通过这条道路,中亚西域的物种、医技医籍、饮食、服饰、生活习惯等都进入中国,影响中国古代社会生活的各个方面。汉唐文化就是在对外来文化包容接纳的基础之上产生的。中国古代儒家典籍和道教以及先进的科学技术也是通过这条道路传播到中亚和东欧地区,推动了世界文化和科学技术的发展。古代中国通过这条道路了解世界,而世界也通过这条道路接纳中国。

敦煌文化形成之地的敦煌是丝绸之路东段和中段的交汇之地，也是丝绸之路的必经之地。敦煌最早见载于中国历史典籍《山海经》，《山海经》北山经记载敦薨之山出敦薨之水，敦薨之水西流注入泑泽，是为河源。

敦薨就是敦煌，是历史典籍对敦煌的最早记载。后来张骞出使西域，被匈奴扣押在河西及蒙古高原十余年，对这里的地理地貌非常熟悉，后来又到中亚从大月氏人那里收集到他们在敦煌一带生活的信息，敦煌一词很可能首先是从张骞开始使用，实际上就是敦薨的音译。

根据《汉书》的记载，实际上在汉朝设置敦煌郡之前的元鼎四年，敦煌一词已经开始使用。而敦煌地区的三危山就见载于《尚书·禹贡篇》，记载导黑水经过三危山流入南海，三危山就是敦煌的三危山，而黑水经我们根据《太平广记》和敦煌文书《瓜沙两郡史事编年并序》研究，就是流经敦煌的疏勒河，疏勒河在汉唐间曾称之为冥水，疏勒河上的沼泽湖泊也叫作乌泽，沿着疏勒河修建的军事屏障称之为昆仑障，都与黑有密切关系。

敦煌也是古代中国领导人行经之地，根据《穆天子传》的记载穆天子即位十五年，曾巡游至泑泽，即今天的罗布泊，前往罗布泊必须经过敦煌，因此周穆王十五年就曾来到敦煌。如果这个记载不误的话，公元前 962 年中国领导人已经来到了敦煌，到了新疆的罗布泊地区或者更远的哈密或者帕米尔高原一带。敦煌的龙勒山就因周时有龙马朝出咸阳，暮至寿昌，遗其衔勒，故名龙勒山。就是说周穆王时中原王朝已经同西域地区进行玉石贸易和马种交换。

汉武帝击败匈奴取得河西地区，置敦煌等河西四郡而拥有二关，玉门关、阳关是汉唐通西域的主要关隘，敦煌是汉唐中央政府经营西域的军事基地，同时也是来往商贾的都会城市。阳关是出敦煌到西域的和亲通使关隘，而与阳关对应的玉门关是出敦煌经营西域的军事关隘，俗称阴关或者凶关，与玉石贸易没有任何关系。

出敦煌西行分别有三条道路，南道至鄯善，中道到高昌，北道经伊吾，总汇敦煌。这三条道路都必须穿越戈壁沙漠地带，“上无飞鸟，下无走兽，复无水草”；“行旅负水担粮，履践沙石，往来困弊”；“西路险恶，人行迷误，沙河阻道，鬼魅热风，遇无免者”。这种情况说明没有充分的准备绝不敢贸然进入沙碛西行。

这样一来，经过沙碛考验的人们才能顺利来到敦煌，他们的精神和灵魂都经过严酷的自然环境的洗礼，有了一个质的升华。汉代李广利征大宛两次都是从敦煌出兵，两汉敦煌太守都参与经营西域，吐蕃占领敦煌之前的唐代，沙州刺史或者敦煌太守，经常参与经营西域的事务。

汉唐的敦煌是一个都会城市，国际化程度非常高。从两汉时期敦煌就居住着很多西域质子和西域商贾，特别是粟特人经常见载于出土文献和典籍中，到唐代更是这样，敦煌的胡人在唐朝中央军队中任职的很多，有的晋升为中央禁军的首领，像曹怀直，祖上帮助唐朝建功立业，被赐姓为曹，历代担任禁军要职。

特别是唐中宗神龙年间石城镇康艳典后裔部落随戍守播仙镇的凉州兵迁居敦煌，唐朝政府为安置这些粟特人在敦煌城周围专门设置了从化乡，从化乡最少有两个里四个村落，粟特人控制敦煌的市场贸易，出任市壁师并管理敦煌市场贸易。直到吐蕃时期敦煌粟特人康秀华仍然担任部落使，而安景旻出任敦煌都督。

张氏归义军时期，安景旻出任归义军节度使副使，而康秀华出任瓜州刺史左威卫将军，到张承奉时期，粟特人安怀恩出任押衙。914 年粟特人曹议金出任归义军节度使，敦煌成了粟特人领导下的归义军政权。除了粟特人，敦煌外来居民很多，有达怛人、回鹘人、突厥人、吐蕃人、波斯人、印度人、鄯善人、于阗人等，他们开店经营商品，经营酒店出卖食品，很多行市的头目都是这些胡人担任，特别是前往各地的商业贸易团体的头目都是由粟特胡人担任，胡商是敦煌市场贸易的主体，因此敦煌市场贸易的商人具有很高程度的国际性。

敦煌市场的商品也具有很高的国际性，敦煌地不产珍，献无奇玩，是一个贫乏的地方。由于敦煌地处交通要道，敦煌市场上商品非常丰富，有西域地区贩运而来的西州布、安西氎，有龟兹出产的胡粉，有中亚来的金青和水银，吐蕃地区的颜料石青、石绿和毛织品，波斯等地出产的胡锦和珠宝，伊州出产的铁器，于阗出产的玉石，东罗马的银器，西域印度的药材和香料，高丽出产的高丽锦，达怛和吐蕃出产的畜牧产品和兵器等，商品来自相邻各个地区或者中亚、南亚和东亚及中国内地各个地方。

作为交换的等价物是银币。金银器皿作为流通货币在晚唐五代的敦煌贸易市场比较常见,有罗马银盏、银盘子、金花银瓶子、银碗等;这些银器标明重量,用于支付物价,其性质显然是货币,不是作为一般意义上的器皿,表明银碗是作为货币流通于敦煌等地的贸易市场中; 在对外贸易中还使用丝绸支付物价;在对内或小宗贸易上多用实物特别是粮食支付物价,作为交换的等价物进行交换。因此货币也具有国际性。

敦煌是佛教最早进入的地区。敦煌文献是关于中国佛教最为详细和真实的记载。敦煌汉简中就已经记载了寺院,寺院内的一切均有助于重构中国寺院的面貌。敦煌文献中还保存有最早的汉文景教经典、摩尼教经典,虽然敦煌文献中没有祆教经典, 但是作为官府主办祆教祭祀仪式足以看出祆教的影响力。在敦煌佛教、道教、祆教、景教、摩尼教以及儒教之间的和谐共处超过相互排斥和争斗。特别是西域地区的胡腾舞、胡旋舞在敦煌地区非常流行, 敦煌人在重大节日都要踏苏幕遮, 出现于龟兹的舞蹈成为敦煌的流行舞。这种局面的基础就是敦煌多民族和平共处,互相包容,互相借鉴,共同发展。敦煌作为丝绸之路上的明珠,他的魅力就在于此。

丝绸之路也可称之为科技之路。西域地区的科学技术如医学、医方、天文历法等都是通过这条道路传入中国, 中国的科学技术也是通过这条道路传向西域地区。敦煌文献的记载就是很好的见证。我们要交代的是敦煌出产瓜得名称瓜州,传说狐狸吃瓜首尾俱入瓜中,表明敦煌出产的瓜很大。回鹘瓜和大食瓜,名见于敦煌文献中,回鹘瓜,又叫瓤桃,这些地方在晚唐五代时期属于回鹘统治地区,所谓伊州回鹘、西州回鹘,大概称之为回鹘瓜就是出产于回鹘地区。

大食瓜,就是出产在大食地区的瓜,这种瓜是什么瓜呢,我们认为是西瓜,西瓜原产地南非,后来传播到埃及,又从埃及传到中亚,金代陕西同州有个官员出使西域,从中亚引进并在中原地区大量传播开来,当时人对这种瓜没有统一的名称,所以按照以地命名的习惯,称之为西瓜,原意可能是西域的瓜、西方的瓜等。今天陕西大荔的瓜还是很有名的,个大皮厚瓤甜。

医学技术的交流通过丝绸之路也很明显, 汉唐时期虽然中医学很发达,但有些医术还没有西域波斯、印度先进,比如眼科中的白内障手术,就是从西域传入，唐史将其作为特殊案例记载。敦煌当地医学家的造诣是学兼中西。

敦煌是丝绸之路上的一颗明珠，敦煌文化是丝绸之路文明精髓所在，而丝绸之路是中西交通文化交流永恒的通途。第一，政治稳定是丝绸之路顺畅的基本要素，这包括历史上中央政权和丝绸之路沿线民族和国家的稳定。先秦时期，由于中原地区文化经济的发展，与周边地区形成很大的社会差异，这种差异导致一种稳定的向心力，加上周边民族对中原政府还不能构成威胁，中原政权虽然没有鼓励也并没阻止中外交往，中西交往属于一种原始状态进行，很多西域地区的特产通过丝绸之路流入中原地区，而中国的产品也经过这条通道进入西域。关于穆天子与西王母的会面，《山海经》关于河源和丝绸之路沿线的地理地貌的记载就是这一背景下的产物。

汉武帝凭借强大的军事实力打败匈奴，重新开启丝绸之路，开始了利用军事政治力量维系丝绸之路安全的时期，汉唐时期都是由国家经营沿线交通设施配置、道路维护和安全保障等，丝绸之路的兴衰几乎与国家政权稳定一致。宋代以后陆路衰落与海路有很大关系，但是沿线政治环境的变化因素起了极大的作用。

第二，经济利益的互惠是丝绸之路发展的基础，维系丝绸之路经久不衰的经济因素是利益的互惠。丝绸之路贸易有几个层面：首先是贡赐贸易，这是一种严重的不对等贸易，中央政府承受非常大的经济压力，贡赐之间的比例 1∶10 到 1∶40 左右，这种贸易是国家政治利益为主的贸易活动。其次是一般性贸易，基本上是由地方政府控制的经济贸易，由政府管理的贸易使团进行的贸易活动，这种贸易活动的利润都在 100%以上，使用等价物以金银丝绸为主，多数进行以物易物贸易，中国的丝绸外销和西域的香料宝物内售，有相当一部分的商人是西域胡人，在中国内地经营。胡商在中国进行的对外贸易和对内贸易，促进了汉唐社会经济繁荣发展，同时由于经济贸易的带动，沿线各地的经济也发展起来。特别是丝绸之路沿线物产并不丰富但地位十分重要的地区，财富经丝绸之路贸易在这些地区得到重新分配。经济上互惠是丝绸之路保持畅通的经济因素。

第三，丝绸之路文化研究是重新发展丝绸之路经济带的先决条件。今天我们研究丝绸之路经济带,更应当重视丝绸之路文化的研究。古代丝绸之路将古代沿线不同地区不同文化连接起来，这些文化通过文物文献等形式在丝绸之路沿线各个地区保存了下来，研究这些文物文献对揭示这一地区古代文明十分重要，研究该地区历史上对丝绸之路经营的经验和教训对今天有十分重要的借鉴作用,只有将其远古文明研究清楚,才有利于丝绸之路的发展。丝绸之路沿线的敦煌、高昌、哈密、库车、于阗等都是丝绸之路上的明珠,因此研究这些地区的历史文化就是丝绸之路的个案研究,是一项十分有意义的工作。

甘肃文化翻译中心组织翻译的"敦煌文化·译丛",就是响应习近平总书记敦煌讲话精神,弘扬传承敦煌文化,提高文化自信的一个有力举措。

兰州大学敦煌学研究所所长　郑炳林

2020 年 10 月

Foreword Ⅱ

Dunhuang Culture is the essence of Silk Road civilization, with philosophical ideas formed in the context of cultural exchange between China and the outside world. It also represents the spirit of humanism, the concept of values, and the code of ethics. The Silk Road was the major economic and cultural link connecting ancient China, the Central Asia, South Asia and Eastern Europe. The Silk Road is so–called because silk was the main commodity transported along the route. But the Silk Road was also known as the Jade Road, the Silver Road, the Spice Road, and the Tea and Horse Road, among others, because such goods and currencies were also transported and used along the route.

The Silk Road was also an important route for cultural exchange between China and the outside world. This international thoroughfare was the means by which the West's advanced science, technology, and culture reached China, and by which China's advanced culture, science, and technology spread to other nations of the world. Through the Silk Road, Chinese and Western cultures met, mingled, and accepted each other, bringing about developments of the Han and Tang empires as well as academic cultures that have influenced the world. It was via this route that India's Buddhism, Europe's Nestorianism, and Central Asia's Zoroastrianism and Manichaeism entered China and spread quickly. Buddhist temple construction and cave excavation, the rise of Buddhist iconography, and the spread of Gandharan Buddhist art into China all contributed to the proliferation of magnificent Chinese Buddhist art, facilitating the development of the Taoist art.

The presence of Nestorian art and Central Asian art styles in China influenced medieval Chinese society and lifestyles in a multitude of ways. The music and dance originated from Indian music, Central Asia music and music of Xinjiang region entered through the Silk Road and quickly spread. The mingling of foreign music and dance and ancient Chinese *Qingyue* music produced Xiliang music, which became an essential element of medieval Chinese music and dance, and furthered the development of Chinese culture and art.

Through the Silk Road, plant species, medical technology, diet, dress, and everyday habits all entered China, influencing the lifestyle of ancient Chinese society in various ways. The culture of the Han and Tang dynasties emerged on the basis of these outside influences. Ancient Chinese Confucian texts, Taoism and advanced science and technology also passed along the Silk Road on their way to Central Asia and Eastern Europe, promoting the development of culture, science, and technology throughout the world. Through the Silk Road, ancient China was able to understand the world, and the world was able to accept China.

Dunhuang, where Dunhuang culture emerged, is located at the crossroads of the eastern and central sections of the Silk Road; travelers had to pass through Dunhuang on their way. Among Chinese historical texts, Dunhuang was first mentioned in the *Classic of Mountains and Seas*, from which the *North Mountain Classic* records that the Dunhong river flowed down Dunhong Mountain, and then westward into Lop Nur, where it formed the source of the Yellow River.

Dunhong was thus the name for Dunhuang, and was the earliest reference to the site. Later, Zhang Qian had his mission to the Western Regions, but was detained by the Xiongnu for more than ten years in the west of the Hexi Corridor and on the Mongolian plateau, becoming very familiar with the geography and landforms of the area. Then he traveled to the Central Asia to gather information from the Greater Yuezhi people about their life in the Dunhuang area. It is very likely that the name Dunhuang originated with Zhang Qian; he actually transcribed "Dunhong" as Dunhuang.

According to the *Book of Han*, in the fourth year of the Yuanding Era, before the establishment of Dunhuang Prefecture in the Han dynasty, the name Dunhuang was in fact already in use. Moreover, the Sanwei Mountain, recorded in the *Book of Yugong*, through which the Heishui River flowed into the South China Sea was the one situated in Dunhuang, while according to our research into the *Extensive Records of the Taiping Era* and the Dunhuang document *Chronology and Preface of the History of Guazhou and Shazhou*, the Heishui River was the Shule River which flows through Dunhuang. In the Han and Tang dynasties, the Shule River was known as the Mingshui River ("Dark Water"). The marshy lakes on the Shule River were also called the Black Marsh. The military barriers built along the Shule River were called the Kunlun Barrier. All three have implications of "darkness" or "blackness."

In ancient China, Dunhuang was also a place which emperors and high-rank officials passed during their travel to the west. In his 15th year of regin, King Mu, once travelled to present-day Lop Nur according to the *Tale of King Mu*. To reach Lop Nur, one must pass through Dunhuang; that is to say, King Mu had been to Dunhuang. If this account is to be believed, then Chinese leaders had already been to Dunhuang by 962 BC, as well as to present-day Xinjiang's Lop Nur region, or even further to Hami or the Pamir Plateau. Dunhuang's Longle Mountain (*longle* meaning headstall of dragon horse) was so-named because during the Zhou Dynasty, a powerful steed known as "dragon horse" left its headstall there during its trip from Xianyang in the morning to Shouchang (part of Dunhuang) in the evening. That is to say, by the time of King Mu, the Kingdoms in the Central Plains had already exchanged jade and horse breeds with the Western Regions.

Emperor Wu of the Han Dynasty defeated the Xiongnu to gain control of the Hexi Corridor. He set up Dunhuang and three other prefectures on the western side with the Yumen Pass ("Jade Gate") and the Yangguan Pass, which were the main border controls in the western part of the Han and Tang dynasties. Dunhuang was a military base for the central governments of the Han and Tang dynasties, as well as a leading mercantile city. Yangguan Pass was for peace-making envoys from Dunhuang heading west, while Yumen Pass was a protected pass for merchants heading west. It was commonly known as the Yinguan Pass, and actually had nothing to do with the jade trade.

There were three routes heading west from Dunhuang: the southern road to

Shanshan; the central road to Gaochang; and the northern road going via Yiwu. These three routes all crossed the Gobi and desert. These western routes were treacherous: there were no birds above, no animals on the ground, and no succulent plants. Carrying water and grain, walking over sand and rocks, going to and fro, people got lost, and rivers of sand blocked the way while otherworldly hot winds inevitably blew. This indicated that travelers did not dare go to the western side of the moraine without adequate preparation.

Only people who knew the lay of the land were able to get to Dunhuang. Their spirits were baptized by the character-building harshness of such an environment. In the Han Dynasty, Li Guangli conquered Dayuan twice from his base in Dunhuang. The Dunhuang governors of the Eastern and Western Han dynasties were involved in the administration of the Western Regions; likewise, in the Tang dynasty before the occupation of Dunhuang by the Tubo, the Shazhou inspectors or governors were also often involved in running affairs in the Western Regions.

Dunhuang was a burgeoning international metropolis during the Han and Tang dynasties. From the time of the Eastern and Western Han dynasties, Dunhuang was home to descendants of hostages and merchants from the Western Regions. The Sogdians in particular are often mentioned in excavated documents and texts, even more so in those from the Tang Dynasty. Foreigners served in the Tang Imperial Army in large numbers. Some were even promoted to leadership roles, such as Cao Huaizhi, whose ancestors helped build the Tang Dynasty. They were granted the surname Cao, and successive generations of the family served important roles in the Imperial Army.

In particular, during the Shenlong Era of the Emperor Zhongzong in the Tang Dynasty, the descendants of Kang Yandian from the Shicheng Town moved to Dunhuang with the Liangzhou soldiers who guarded the Boxian town; the Tang government set up the Conghua township to house the Sogdians. Conghua was at least two *li* large and contained four villages. The Sogdians controlled and managed Dunhuang's market trade. When the Tubo took over Dunhuang, the Sogdian Kang Xiuhua served as a tribal commissioner, while An Jingmin was appointed governor.

During the *Guiyijun* period under the Zhang clan, An Jingmin served as deputy military commissioner of the *Guiyijun* Force, while Kang Xiuhua served as general of the prefect of Guazhou. In the Zhang Chengfeng period, the Sogdian An Huai'en was appointed to a position equal to the military commissioner. In 914, the Sogdian Cao Yijin was appointed as the *Guiyijun*'s military commissioner, and the Dunhuang *Guiyijun* Force came under Sogdian leadership. Apart from the Sogdians, there were considerable numbers of other foreign residents in Dunhuang, including Tartars, Uyghurs, Turkic people, Tubo people, Persians, Indians, Shanshan people and Khotanese. They set up shops and restaurants, with many business leaders of foreign origin. In particular, commercial and trade groups that traveled to various places were led by Sogdians. Foreign traders made up the majority of Dunhuang market traders. For this reason, Dunhuang's business community was strongly multinational.

The goods for sale in Dunhuang's markets also had a strongly international flavor. Dunhuang itself produced little, with no treasures or exotic goods to offer. But because of the city's location on a major transportation route, its markets offered a rich array of goods. There were textiles from the Western Regions, fine muslin from Anxi, *Hu* powder from Kucha (Qiuci), lapis lazuli and mercury from Central Asia, blue and green mineral pigments as well as woolen fabrics from Tubo, Persian brocade and jewelry, ironware from Yizhou, Khotanese jade, silverware from Byzantium, medicines and spices from western India, brocade from Korea, and livestock products and weapons from Tartary and Tubo. Merchandise arrived here from neighboring regions in Central, South, and East Asia as well as the interior of China.

Silver coins were the currency for trade. Gold and silverware were also used as common circulating currencies in the markets of Dunhuang in the Late Tang era. There were Roman silver chalices, silver plates, gold and silver bottles, silver bowls, and so on. The silverware with marked weight was used when paying for goods, so that its value was as a currency rather than as a functional utensil or vessel in the general sense, revealing that silverware was used as a currency in the markets of Dunhuang and other places. Silk was also used for payment in foreign trade, while in domestic or small-scale trade, goods—especially food or grain—were often paid in-kind. Goods were exchanged for equivalent value, so the currencies themselves were multinational.

Dunhuang was Buddhism's original point of entry into China. The Dunhuang manuscripts themselves offer the most detailed and accurate records of Chinese Buddhism and the monastery is mentioned in Han bamboo slips from Dunhuang. These records are helpful in reconstructing the architecture and appearance of ancient Chinese temples. Among the Dunhuang texts are also the earliest extant Nestorian and Manichaean scriptures in Chinese. Although the Dunhuang manuscripts do not include Zoroastrian classics, the influence of Zoroastrianism can be seen in the fact that Zoroastrian rituals enjoyed official sponsorship. In Dunhuang, the peaceful co-existence of Buddhism, Taoism, Zoroastrianism, Nestorianism, Manichaeism, and Confucianism overcame any mutual exclusion or contention. This is especially true of the *Huteng* dance from the Western Regions, which was extremely popular in Dunhuang. It was enjoyed on important festival days. This dance, which first appeared in Qiuci, became Dunhuang's favorite dance. The basis of this situation was the peaceful co-existence of the many ethnic groups in Dunhuang, as well as their mutual inclusiveness, mutual learning, and common development. Dunhuang was the pearl of the Silk Road, and therein lies its charm.

The Silk Road can also be called the Technology Road. Science and technology from the Western Regions, such as medicine, pharmacology, and the astronomical calendar, entered China via this route; Chinese science and technology, in turn, also flowed westward along the same route. The Dunhuang manuscripts provide historical evidence of this. Dunhuang produced so many melons that it was named Guazhou (land of melons). Legend had it that a fox could eat a Dunhuang melon with its head and tail in it, such was the size of the melons. Uyghur melons and Dashi melons are even mentioned in Dunhuang historical records, where Uyghur melons were also known as "*rangtao*." In the Late Tang period and Five Dynasties, the area was held by Uyghurs. Among the so-called Yizhou and Xizhou Uyghurs, Uyghur melons, as they were probably called, were those produced in Uyghur areas.

Dashi melons were those from Arabia. What type of melons were these? It is believed that they were watermelons, which were originally from South Africa, and later reached Egypt, and from there it was made into Central Asia. In the Jin Dynasty, an official from Tongzhou of Shaanxi travelled west as an envoy, and introduced watermelon, after which it became widespread. The people of the time did not have a uniform name for watermelons, so according to naming conventions, it became the *xigua*. This probably just meant "melon from the Western Regions" or "melon from the West." Today, the melons from the Dali county of Shaanxi are also very well-known, with a thick rind and sweet taste.

The exchange of medical technology along the Silk Road was evident. While traditional Chinese medicine was highly developed by the time of the Han and Tang dynasties, many medical skills were absent. Persia and India, however, was at the forefront in certain skills such as cataract surgery, and this was introduced via the West, with Tang dynasty historical records giving it a special mention. Dunhuang's local medical specialists were accomplished in both Chinese and Western methods.

Dunhuang was the Pearl of the Silk Road, the essence of Silk Road civilization, and an eternal thoroughfare for communication and cultural exchange between China and the West. First, political stability was a basic element for the smooth operation of the route. This included the stability of central political power throughout its history, as well as that of ethnic groups and nations along the route. In the pre-Qin period, owing to cultural and economic development of the Central Plains, great social differences took shape as compared with the surrounding areas. These differences led to a stable centripetal force, with the surrounding ethnic groups not having sufficient strength to threaten the government of the Central Plains. Although the Central Plains government did not encourage Chinese exchanges with foreigners, it is not known to have prevented them, either. Exchanges between China and the West were rudimentary. Many specialty goods from the Western Regions passed into the Central Plains via the Silk Road, and Chinese products also headed west via the same road. According to legend, King Mu and the Queen Mother of the West met in the area extending from the Shule River to Lop Nur; the *Classic of Mountains and Seas* which details the geography and landforms along the Yellow River and the Silk Road is a product of this background.

Emperor Wu of the Han Dynasty defeated the Xiongnu with his powerful military, opened up the Silk Road again, and started using the strength of his military government to sustain a period of peace along the Road. During the Han and Tang dynasties, the state operated transport facilities along the route, maintained roads, and guaranteed safety. The rise and fall of the Silk Road occurred almost in line with the stability of state power. After the Song Dynasty, the decline in overland routes was correlated to the rise of the maritime trade routes, but changes in the political environment along the Silk Road also played a major role.

Second, mutual economic benefit was the basis of development along the Silk Road. The reciprocity of benefits was the factor that sustained the Silk Road economically. There were several dimensions of trade on the Silk Road: foremost was tribute trade, which had serious disparities. The central government withstood enormous economic pressure, with the ratio between tributes roughly somewhere between 1 : 10 to 1 : 40. This kind of trade asserted national political interest above all else. This was followed by general trade, which was basically controlled by regional authorities with government–managed trade envoys conducting trade. Profits from this trading activity exceeded 100%. Gold, silver, and silk were the primary mediums of exchange used, with many traders also engaged in bartering. Quite a few of the merchants engaged in China's silk exports and the sale of the Western Regions' treasured spices within China were foreigners from the West. China's foreign–led exports and domestic trade boosted the economic fortunes of Han and Tang society. Driven by trade, places all along the Silk Road also received an economic boost. For Silk Road areas that were not very productive but were nonetheless in important locations, wealth was distributed thanks to trade along the route. Economic reciprocity was the key factor that kept the Silk Road running smoothly.

Third, research into Silk Road culture is a prerequisite for an economic revival along this route. Today, when we research the Silk Road economic belt, we should pay more attention to the culture that developed there. The ancient Silk Road brought together disparate regions and cultures along the route. These cultures have been preserved in forms of artifacts and other material in different regions along the Silk Road. Researching these artifacts is extremely important if we want to learn more of the ancient civilizations of this area. Researching the historical experiences and lessons from the Silk Road trade is a vital reference point for today. Only careful study of its ancient civilizations will benefit future Silk Road development. Places such as Dunhuang, Gaochang, Hami, Kucha, and Khotan are all "pearls of the Silk Road." For that reason, research into the historical culture of these regions amounts to a special case study. It is an immensely significant work.

The *Dunhuang Culture in Translation* series, organized by the Gansu Cultural Translation and Interpreting Center, is a powerful initiative with which to respond to the spirit of General Secretary Xi Jinping's Dunhuang speech, promoting Dunhuang culture and enhancing cultural confidece.

Zheng Binglin

Head of Institute of Dunhuang Studies of Lanzhou University

October 2020

序言三

翻译，让敦煌文化走向世界

敦煌文化是中华文明几千年不断融会贯通的典范，是中国文化精神的重要代表。曾经，敦煌文化经历“敦煌在中国，敦煌学在国外”的历史。诚然，自20世纪初，敦煌藏经洞的发现、敦煌部分文献流失海外，引发世界各国敦煌学者对敦煌文化的关注，在国外产生了众多敦煌学研究成果。但敦煌文化的“根”在中国，对敦煌文化的认识与理解，源于中国。敦煌学的国际化发展，则需要通过文化的传播与学术的交流形成共识、共知与共享。翻译，无疑是使敦煌文化走向世界、敦煌精神被全人类共享的重要途径。

一、翻译是敦煌文化对外传播的“言说者”

文化对外传播、交流与沟通的重要途径是翻译。翻译敦煌文化，就是对外“言说”敦煌文化，传播敦煌文化的各个方面、各种内容。敦煌文化是包括宗教、艺术、科技、文学、医药、农业、建筑、民俗等内容的综合文化体系。翻译敦煌文化，就是对外讲述敦煌开放交流的文明历史，展示敦煌在中西互学互鉴中形成的艺术，介绍敦煌的科技医药，以及讲述融合发展的宗教文化思想等。通过系统翻译，让世界认识敦煌文化，了解全面的敦煌文化、真正的敦煌文化。

翻译敦煌文化，就是言说和表达最具代表性的、最能体现敦煌文化之源流的优秀文化。就其文化内容而言，一方面转换语言为载体的文化内容，如敦煌文献、敦煌学研究成果、敦煌学术思想等；另一方面转换艺术为载体的文化信息。敦煌文化，就其文化载体而言，具有多元的符号形式。语言载体包含写经、变文、宝卷、简牍等文学与非文学形态；艺术载体包含石窟建筑、雕塑、壁画等。翻译敦煌文化，即对敦煌文化各种载体所蕴含的历史、宗教、文学、艺术等文化内容,及其文化思想和文化精神进行语言转换,精确表达。以翻译言说敦煌文化,既要用语言讲述语言文化,还要用语言讲述非语言文化。一般而言,翻译是语言文本的转换。但在敦煌文化翻译中,除了常规的语际翻译,还存在符际转换方式,即对艺术文化的翻译,运用语言进行“互文性”表达。通过语际与符际双重转换,构建敦煌文化对外传播的系统体系。作为敦煌文化对外传播言说者的翻译,需要注重“言说”的方式,构建有效的话语体系。翻译,在传播文化中,表达文化,沟通文化,协调不同语言之间的文化理解。话语方式、话语风格决定文化元素的显现方式,决定文化内容的接受度,从而决定文化传播的效果和效力,是实现文化传播与交流的基础。翻译敦煌文化,要协调“异化”“归化”转换策略,在尊重文化、名从历史的基础上,运用恰当适切的对外言说话语方式,针对文化内容、受众接受等用国际化语言表达方式,准确言说和表达敦煌文化,构建敦煌文化对外传播的完整叙事。

以翻译言说文化,不仅使敦煌文化充分“走出去”,更使敦煌精神深入“走进去”,有效实现敦煌文化的国际性传播与世界认同。

二、翻译是敦煌文化学术交流的“互动者”

翻译敦煌文化,就是搭建中外敦煌学术交流的互动平台,开展中外敦煌学研究的学术对话。20世纪初以来,国内外学者对敦煌文化的研究,产生了众多研究成果,建树颇丰。通过对中外敦煌学研究成果的互译,对话学术,交流思想,从而深化对敦煌文化的认识。诚然,博大精深的敦煌文化及其精神价值,依旧存在有待认识与研究的极大空间,但交流已有的学术思想,无疑对进一步研究敦煌文化、认识敦煌文化具有重要的意义。互译,为搭建互动机制、建构交互认知,提供必要的路径。

一是开展敦煌文献的互译,通过对各国拥有的敦煌文献进行翻译转换,补充因文献缺省造成的“认识差”,化解研究上的局限。敦煌莫高窟藏经洞发现的文献(包括写本、简牍),涉及佛教经典、道教经典、儒家典籍以及(敦煌)佛教文学、俗文学等文化内容,语言包含除汉文之外的藏文、回鹘文、于阗文、龟兹文、突厥文、粟特文和梵文等。敦煌文献是丝绸之路上中西文明交流的历史书写，是研究敦煌文化，以及其中蕴含的中国文化思想的重要文献资料。但敦煌文献因特殊的历史遭遇，一大部分遗书被劫掠至海外（如英国近万卷，法国五千余卷），有关同一文化内容的文献资料散藏于中、英、法、日、俄等不同的国家，造成各国对敦煌文化认识的支离破碎，导致敦煌学研究的片面性。通过文献资料的译入、译出，可以搭建国内、国外敦煌学的多维研究平台、系统认识平台，将历史片段缀合起来，将同一文化现象进行综合研究，从而形成世界范围内的“系统敦煌学”。

二是进行敦煌学研究成果的互译，通过互译，使学术思想产生碰撞、比较，从而打开各自封闭的敦煌学，经由“他者”的敦煌学术参照系，关照自身的研究，丰富自身的认识；在与“他者”的交流中、在思想碰撞中深化对敦煌文化的理解。

敦煌文化是在中西方文化交融中形成和发展的，具有综合的文化内容体系、多元的文化思想，以及多样的历史发展形态。它是一个内在结构相互作用的文化体系，存在各系统成分之间的内在关系，如敦煌艺术研究与宗教文化研究的互补，中西方文化交流与文化融合过程的历史关系，文化演变与朝代结构的互动等。对敦煌文化的认识，需要系统地研究，才能构成认识的互补体系；只有互为补充的认识，才能不断完善对敦煌文化认识体系的构建。不同国家、不同时代，基于各自专业领域的研究，难免存在“认识差”。通过中外敦煌学研究思想的双向翻译，进行学术交流与对话，在互动中学习，在交流中互鉴，不仅能够产生新思路和新成果，而且能够使各国学者更深刻地理解敦煌文化，一方面可以减少因文化差异造成的认识误差，减少误读与误解；另一方面通过不同时代、不同文化背景、不同信仰体系的学者对历史文明的学术对话，协调敦煌学研究中的审美心理和文化价值“差”，以便达成共识，形成对敦煌历史文化概念的共同解读，从而提升敦煌文化的交流深度，实现敦煌文化的高层次对话与互动传播。

三、翻译是敦煌文化精神的诠释者和世界传承者

翻译，不仅仅是语言的转换，更是对文化的阐释。翻译敦煌文化，不是简

单的语码转换，也不是单纯的信息传递，更重要的是揭示和阐释敦煌文化和历史遗存所蕴含的哲学思想、人文精神、价值理念、道德规范；弘扬和传承蕴含其中的中华民族的文化精神、文化胸怀和文化自信。敦煌文化是中西文化交流融合的典范，敦煌石窟建筑、壁画，以中原文化为基础，充分吸收了中亚、西亚佛教艺术思想内容，体现了多元文化交融互鉴的内在精神，是中华文明开放体系的重要代表。在综合、系统的翻译过程中，深刻阐释其文明历程、文化精髓，阐释敦煌文化文明交流融合的思想方法，诠释中华文明海纳百川、兼容并蓄、博采众长的文化精髓，挖掘世界文明共同的存在根源，以及人类共同的理想目标。

翻译是一种诠释，具有文化"阐释力"。翻译敦煌文化，就是在研究敦煌文化的前提下，诠释敦煌文化的深刻含义。翻译敦煌文化，是译者与敦煌文化思想、文化精神的交流和互动，是现代视域与历史精髓的互文。作为敦煌文化"诠释者"的翻译，是某种意义上的敦煌文化研究，是敦煌学的一种组成部分。但诠释不是自创性解读，正如孔子所言，文化的传承，要遵循"述而不作，信而好古"。真正的敦煌文化翻译，就是在精准理解与充分诠释的基础上向世界传播敦煌文化思想，传承敦煌文化精神。

敦煌文化是在中西文明的相遇、相识、相融中形成和发展的，是各种文明交流融汇的结晶，蕴含开放包容、互学互鉴的文化精神。翻译是文化的交流、思想的对话，其本身就是敦煌文化精神的"外显"形式。敦煌学研究成果的翻译，是学术思想的互学与互鉴，尤其建立在中外学者"中西合璧"方式上的合译，更是在互动的理解过程中实践敦煌精神，是传承与弘扬敦煌文化的又一种深化、物化、具象化的方式。敦煌文化翻译，以其特有的文化交流与对话方式，向世界讲述敦煌故事，传播敦煌思想，弘扬敦煌精神，让敦煌文化在交流中成为世界的文化，敦煌学研究成为"世界的敦煌学"，敦煌精神成为人类的思想精神。

兰州城市学院副校长　教授
甘肃文化翻译中心　主任　姜秋霞

2020 年 10 月

Foreword Ⅲ

Translation Connects Dunhuang Culture with the World

Dunhuang culture is a model of the continuous amalgamation of Chinese civilization over a span of thousands of years, and an important representation of the essence of Chinese culture. There was a time when Dunhuang culture experienced a historical reality of "Dunhuang itself is in China, yet Dunhuang studies is in the West." Of course, the discovery of the Dunhuang manuscripts at the beginning of the 20th century—with many of them taken overseas—brought the attention of scholars from all over the world to Dunhuang culture, and produced a large corpus of research from Dunhuang studies abroad. But Dunhuang culture is rooted in China, and the knowledge and understanding of Dunhuang culture originated in China. The international development of Dunhuang studies requires consensus, common knowledge, and sharing through cultural dissemination and academic exchange. Thus, translation is undoubtedly an important way to bring Dunhuang culture out to the world and for the spirit of Dunhuang to be shared by all humankind.

1. Translation is the voice of Dunhuang culture for the world community

Translation is an important method of cultural dissemination and communication. To translate Dunhuang culture is to introduce Dunhuang to the outside world, in other words, to share all aspects and content of Dunhuang culture. Dunhuang culture is a comprehensive cultural system that integrates religion, art, technology, literature, medicine, agriculture, architecture, and folk customs. Translating Dunhuang culture informs the public about the history of Dunhuang's civilization and its open exchanges, reveals the art of Dunhuang as a reflection of the mutual learning between China and the West, introduces Dunhuang's science, technology, and medicine, and explains the integration and development of its religious culture. Thus, systematic translation allows the world to not only know about Dunhuang, but also understand the true, comprehensive culture of Dunhuang.

Translating Dunhuang culture is to relate and express that which is most quintessential, reflecting the pinnacle of culture emanating from its source in Dunhuang itself. As far as cultural content is concerned, on the one hand, Dunhuang translation converts language—that of the Dunhuang manuscripts, Dunhuang studies, and Dunhuang academic theories—as a carrier of cultural content; on the other hand, it converts art as a carrier of cultural information. Dunhuang culture is embodied in multiple symbolic and semiotic forms. Language carriers include literary and non-literary forms such as scripture, *bianwen* (transformation texts), *baojuan* (prosimetric narratives), and bamboo slip archives; artistic carriers include rock-cut architecture, sculpture, and murals. Translating Dunhuang culture entails language conversion and the precise expression of its historical, religious, literary, artistic, and other cultural content contained in various carriers, as well as its cultural values and cultural spirit. The expression of Dunhuang culture through translation requires the use of both linguistic and non-linguistic conversion. Generally speaking, translation is the conversion of language text. However, in Dunhuang culture translation, in addition to the conventional interlingual translation, there is also an intersemiotic transformation method, which is to say that translation of art and culture uses language to express intertextuality. Through this interlingual and intersemiotic conversion, a systematic method for the communication of Dunhuang culture can be constructed. When we translate as the "voice" of Dunhuang culture, it is necessary to pay attention to the manner of "speaking," in order to construct an effective discourse system. Translation, in disseminating, expressing, and communicating culture, must coordinate cultural understanding between different languages. The style and mode of discourse—the foundation for achieving cultural dissemination and communication—determine how cultural elements appear, determine the acceptability of cultural content, and thus determine the effect as well as effectiveness of cultural transmission. When translating Dunhuang culture, it is necessary to closely coordinate both foreignization and domestication conversion strategies, and, on the basis of respecting culture and history, use appropriate foreign language expressions as well as international expressions for cultural content and audience acceptance. To accurately express Dunhuang culture, a complete narrative must be constructed for communicating Dunhuang culture to the world outside China.

Speaking through the language of translation not only enables Dunhuang culture to fully "go forth" into the world, but also enables the essence of Dunhuang to "go in" deeply as well, effectively realizing the international spread and world recognition of Dunhuang culture.

2. Translation is the liaison for Dunhuang cultural and academic exchange

Translating Dunhuang culture creates an interactive platform for academic exchange between China and the rest of the international community, facilitating academic dialogue between Chinese and overseas Dunhuang scholars. Since the beginning of the 20th century, academics both within China and abroad have produced much research on Dunhuang culture, making considerable achievements in the field. The understanding of Dunhuang culture can be deepened through the mutual translation of research findings in Dunhuang studies both within China and overseas, as well as through academic dialogue and the exchanging of ideas. It is true that there is still a great deal to be learned about Dunhuang with its extensive, profound culture and spiritual value, but the exchange of existing academic theories is undoubtedly of great significance for the further research and understanding of Dunhuang. Mutual translation provides a necessary pathway for constructing an interactive mechanism for the field and for the interchange of expertise.

The first task is to carry out the mutual translation of Dunhuang documents. The translation and conversion of Dunhuang documents owned by various countries can help supplement the deficiencies in understanding caused by dispersed and fragmented manuscripts, and thus resolving the limitations of research. The documents, manuscripts, and bamboo slip found in the Dunhuang Mogao Caves include Buddhist, Taoist, and Confucian classics, Buddhist scriptures unique to Dunhuang, popular literature, and other cultural content. In addition to Chinese, the languages include Tibetan, Uyghur, Khotanese, Kuchean, Turkic, Sogdian, Sanskrit, and more. The Dunhuang manuscripts constitute historical written records of the cultural exchanges between China and the West along the Silk Road. They are important documents for studying Dunhuang culture and the Chinese cultural thought contained therein. However, due to the special history of the Dunhuang documents, a large part of the manuscripts was unlawfully removed overseas, including nearly 10,000 manuscripts now located in the United Kingdom, and more than 5,000 in France. As a result, various countries have a fragmented interpretation of Dunhuang culture, leading to one–sidedness in research. Through the translation of documents and materials, a multi–dimensional research platform and a systematic understanding for Dunhuang studies at home and abroad can be developed, with historical manuscript fragments recombined to allow comprehensive research on the same cultural phenomena, thereby forming a worldwide system for Dunhuang studies.

The second task is to carry out the mutual translation of research findings in Dunhuang studies. Through mutual translation, academic theories can interact and undergo comparison, thereby broadening researchers' own closed–off Dunhuang research. Through "other" Dunhuang research and reference, scholars can reflect on their own research, enrich their own expertise, exchange ideas with the "other," and deepen the understanding of Dunhuang culture through the interaction of different theories.

Dunhuang culture was formed and developed as a fusion of Chinese and Western cultures. It comprises a comprehensive system of cultural content, ideology, and historical development. It is a cultural system with interactive structures, and there are internal relationships between the components of the system, as well. For example, Dunhuang art research and religious cultural studies complement one another; there has been a historical connection between the exchange of Chinese and Western cultures and the process of cultural diffusion; and there has been an interrelationship between cultural evolution and dynastic structures. The understanding of Dunhuang culture requires systematic research in order to form an interrelated branch of knowledge; only when mutual understanding is complementary, can the knowledge of Dunhuang culture be continuously improved. Differences in interpretation have been inevitable amongst different countries and throughout different eras, based on research in their respective professional fields. The Sino–Western translation of Chinese and international Dunhuang research findings and theories, academic exchange and dialogue, and interchange of ideas can not only generate new ideas and new results, but can also enable scholars from all over the world to have a deeper understanding of Dunhuang culture. On the one hand, this can reduce errors from misreading as well as misunderstandings caused by cultural differences. On the other hand, academic dialogue between scholars from different eras, cultural backgrounds, and religious viewpoints on historical civilizations can redress the gaps in Dunhuang research regarding its artistic and cultural value. This will better form a consensus and a common interpretation of Dunhuang historical and cultural concepts, thereby enhancing the depth of Dunhuang cultural exchange as well as enabling high–level dialogue and interactive communication on Dunhuang culture.

3. Translation is the interpreter and world inheritor of the spirit of Dunhuang culture.

Translation is not merely the conversion of language, but also the interpretation of culture. Translating Dunhuang culture is not simple code conversion, nor is it purely the transmission of information. More importantly, translation reveals and interprets the philosophical thought, humanistic spirit, and values contained in Dunhuang culture and historical relics, which is imbued with the cultural spirit, mind, and confidence of the Chinese nation. Dunhuang culture stands as a model of Chinese and Western cultural exchange and diffusion. Dunhuang cave temple architecture and murals are based on the Central Plains culture, which also absorbed the content of Central and Western Asian Buddhist art aesthetics and ideals, reflecting the inherent spirit of multicultural synthesis and mutual learning. Dunhuang is an important representation of the openness and inclusiveness of Chinese civilization. Comprehensive, systematic translation can profoundly explain Dunhuang's historical development and its cultural essence, reveal the thinking behind Dunhuang cultural exchange and integration, interpret the cultural essence of Chinese civilization, explore the common roots of world civilizations, and even tap into the common ideals of the human race.

Translation is a type of interpretation, with cultural interpretative power. Translating Dunhuang culture is to interpret the profound meaning of Dunhuang culture under the auspices of researching it. The translation of Dunhuang culture is the exchange and interaction between the translator and Dunhuang cultural ideology and spirit, as well as the intertextuality of modern vision and historical essence. To engage in translation as the "interpreter" of Dunhuang culture is indeed the study of Dunhuang culture in a certain sense, and is a component of Dunhuang studies in and of itself. However, interpretation is never self-generated. As Confucius said, the inheritance of culture must follow the principle of "transmitting but not innovating, loving antiquity and having faith in it." Dunhuang culture translation means sharing and inheriting the essence of Dunhuang culture on the basis of accurate understanding and full interpretation.

We can conclude that Dunhuang culture has formed and developed from the encounter, acquaintance, and fusion of Chinese and Western civilizations. It is the crystallization of the exchange and synthesis of various civilizations, and contains a cultural spirit of openness, inclusiveness, and mutual learning. Translation is cultural exchange, a dialogue of ideas, and itself is the "external" form of Dunhuang's cultural essence. The translation of Dunhuang studies involves the interchange and mutual appraisal of academic ideas. In particular, co-translations based on the Sino-Western cooperation by Chinese and foreign scholars put the spirit of Dunhuang culture into action. Through the process of interactive understanding, the inheritance and promotion of Dunhuang culture is further deepened and substantiated. Dunhuang culture translation brings the story of Dunhuang to the world, shares Dunhuang thought, and promotes the essence of Dunhuang via its unique cultural exchange and methods of communication. Thus Dunhuang culture becomes the world's culture in the exchange, Dunhuang studies becomes the world's Dunhuang studies, and the spirit of Dunhuang culture becomes humankind's ideological spirit.

Jiang Qiuxia
Professor and Vice President of Lanzhou City University
Head of Gansu Cultural Translation and Interpreting Center
October 2020

莫高窟第 238 窟　胁侍菩萨　北魏

Attendant Bodhisattva, Mogao Cave 238　Northern Wei

敦煌历史沧桑

History of Dunhuang

敦煌，位于河西走廊最西端，是甘肃、新疆、青海、内蒙古等省区交界之地。同时，它也是古代中原进入西域的门户。古代敦煌的地域范围，要比今天敦煌市的范围大，还包括党河流域和疏勒河流域的广大地区。这里是连接东西方文化的陆上丝绸之路的必经之处，在中国历史的舞台上扮演过重要角色。其历史更是源远流长，从新石器时代的刀耕火种到两汉时期的设置郡县；从魏晋南北朝时期各个民族政权的激烈争夺到隋唐时期的繁荣昌盛；从吐蕃时期佛教的迅速发展到归义军时期的苦心经营；从西夏政权的统治到元、明、清时期的日渐衰落，可以说各个时代的敦煌历史在一定程度上折射出了中国各个历史时期的风貌。

Dunhuang, located at the western end of the Hexi Corridor, lies at the junction of Gansu, Xinjiang, Qinghai, and Inner Mongolia. It also served as a gateway to the Western Regions from the Central Plains of China. Ancient Dunhuang, covering the areas of the Danghe River Basin and the Shule River Basin, was larger in size than the present-day Dunhuang City. It was a crucial point along the Silk Road which connected Eastern and Western cultures and played an important role in Chinese history. Dunhuang witnessed great changes throughout Chinese history: from the slash-and-burn cultivation in the Neolithic Age to the establishment of prefectures and counties in the Han Dynasty （206 BC –AD 220）; from the struggle for power amongst various ethnic groups in the Period of the Wei, Jin, and Northern and Southern dynasties (220–589) to the reunion and prosperity in the Sui （581–618） and Tang (618–907) dynasties; from the rapid development of Buddhism in the Tubo to the painstaking governance in Dunhuang during the *Guiyijun* Period （a local regime ruling Dunhuang from 851 to 1036）; and from the rule of the Western Xia (1038–1227) to its decline in the Yuan (1206–1368) , Ming (1368–1644) , and Qing (1616–1911) dynasties. It is safe to say that the history of Dunhuang, to some extent, mirrors the history of China.

两汉以前的敦煌

Dunhuang Before the Han Dynasty

关于"敦煌"一名的含义,古人曾有解释。唐代颜师古在为班固所著的《汉书·地理志》作注时,曾引用东汉应劭的说法,认为"敦"是"大"的意思,"煌"即"盛"的意思,合起来就是形容敦煌是一个地广繁盛之地。唐朝宰相李吉甫在《元和郡县图志》中也解释说:"敦,大也,以其广开西域,故以盛名。"从字面意思上看,上述两种解释大同小异。按照这种解释,则"敦煌"一名应当是汉武帝设郡时的汉语命名。但据《史记》及《汉书》的记载,"敦煌"一名的出现远比汉武帝于河西地区设置郡县的时间要早。而在上

In ancient times, "Dunhuang" embodied different meanings. The historian Yan Shigu, a scholar from the Tang Dynasty, when annotating the *Book of Han*: *Treatise on Geography*, cited the Eastern Han historian Ying Shao as writing that the word "*dun*" meant "being large in size" and "*huang*" meant "being prosperous;" so when put together, "Dunhuang" referred to a vast piece of prosperous land. Li Jifu, a Grand Councilor during the reign of Emperor Xianzong of the Tang Dynasty, explained in the *Yuanhe Maps of Prefectures and Counties* that "*dun*" meant "large" and that the area enjoyed a reputation for being the route to the Western Regions[①]. The two definitions above have much in common literally. Therefore, "Dunhuang" was the Chinese name given to this place when it was made a prefecture during the reign of Emperor Wu of the Western Han Dynasty. However, according to the *Records of the Grand Historian* and the *Book of Han*, the emergence of the name "Dunhuang" was actually far earlier than that. In these two books, "Dunhuang" was always recorded together with the word "Qilian" which originated from the Xiongnu

---

① The Western Regions (*Xiyu* in Chinese pinyin) was a historical name used by China to refer to area west of the Yumen Pass. Although the specific area changed over time, it primarily referred to Central Asia, but could also include the Tarim Basin in present-day Xinjiang, as well as other regions to the west of China, including India. The Western Regions were an important part of the Silk Road and also played an important role in the transmission of Buddhism into China.

述诸书的记载中，敦煌多与“祁连”同时出现。“祁连”一词来源于匈奴语，“祁连”，也即“天山”。既然“敦煌”与“祁连”连用，这也就证明“敦煌”并非敦煌郡或敦煌县，而应与“祁连”一样，都是当地土著居民称呼的汉语音译。《史记》和《汉书》中与敦煌相关的记载，多是由张骞于元朔三年（前126年）从西域返回长安后所带回来的信息转化而来，所以敦煌汉名的发明者很可能就是张骞。至于“敦煌”一词的原意，早在东汉时就无法考证了。所以，应劭便从汉语的字面意思上给予解释。虽然学者对“敦煌”一词的来源还存在不同看法，如有月氏语音译、匈奴语音译、吐火罗语音译、羌语音译、氐人命名等多种说法，甚至还有学者认为“敦煌”一词既不是汉语语词，也不是少数民族语词，而可能与希腊人有关，但现在绝大多数学者已经认同了“敦煌”为少数民族语词音译的观点。

早在上古时期，敦煌地区就已经有人类活动。我国考古

language (“Qilian” was also called “Tianshan” in Xiongnu language). Thus, instead of being a name for a prefecture or a county, “Dunhuang” was the transliteration from the local dialect into Chinese. Actually, the records about Dunhuang in the two books were mostly based on the information brought back by Zhang Qian after his return to Chang'an (present-day Xi'an) from the Western Regions in the 3rd year of Yuanshuo Era (126 BC). In this sense it was probably Zhang Qian who created the name “Dunhuang” in Chinese characters. But the original meaning of “Dunhuang” could not be verified as early as the Eastern Han Dynasty, and as a result Ying Shao offered an explanation on its literal meaning. In spite of various opinions on the origin of the name “Dunhuang,” such as transliteration from such languages of ethnic tribes as Yuezhi, Xiongnu, Tokharoi, Qiang and Di, and even the opinion that it is neither a Chinese word nor one from ethnic minority languages but it came from the Greek language, most scholars today share the view that Dunhuang is a name transliterated from an ethnic minority language.

There is evidence to suggest that people began settling in the Dunhuang area before the Xia Dynasty (around 2070 BC–1600 BC). Chinese archaeologists have found dozens of ruins in the Hexi Corridor (the area west of the Yellow River) where Dunhuang is located, dating from the Neolithic Age. In 1976, archaeologists found a site of cultural ruins at

工作者在河西走廊发现了几十处新石器时代遗址，敦煌正处于这些古文化分布区内。1976年，考古工作者在今疏勒河的玉门市火烧沟发现了一个古文化遗址。它所处的年代为公元前1600多年左右，大致相当于中原地区的夏朝。遗址中的文物十分丰富，除陶器、石器、铜器、金银器外，还有马、牛、羊、猪等动物的骨骼，尤其以羊骨最为普遍。火烧沟遗址的这一特征，与史书中所记载的羌人、西戎牧羊的记载相吻合。考古发掘表明，火烧沟人的文明程度并不比中原地区落后。从他们已经使用石锄、石磨盘、铜铲、陶器等器物的种类看，他们已经有了分工较细的手工业。而遗址中还有玛瑙珠、海贝和蚌饰，这些

Huoshaogou in Yumen City near the Shule River, which dated back to about 1600 BC (equivalent to the Xia Dynasty in the Central Plains①). A rich variety of cultural relics were unearthed including pottery, stoneware, bronzeware, goldware, and silverware as well as bones of horses, cattle, sheep, and pigs. In particular, the large number of sheep bones found there bears proof to historical records about the practice of raising sheep of Qiang and peoples in the Western Regions. Archaeological excavations show that local civilization did not lag behind the development in China's Central Plains. Judging from the types of tools ancient people at Huoshaogou used, such as stone hoes, millstones, copper shovels and pottery, it can be seen they had already had a fine division of skilled labor. The excavation of agate beads, seashells, and clam ornaments which were non-locally produced indicates that they had exchanges with the outside world. In their society, sheep raising was given priority in addition to agriculture and skilled trades, and transactions with the outside world began to develop. As far as the level of social development is concerned, sacrificial objects unearthed from tombs show apparent division between the rich and the poor as well as a social hierarchy. Some tombs contained only a small

---

① The Central Plains (*Zhongyuan* in Chinese) refers to both a geographical area of China as well as the historical center of political power and culture. The area in present-day Henan Province was originally China's cradle of civilization, particularly the regions in the Yellow River Valley. Later the term "Central Plains" was used to signify this area, and also included parts of the nearby provinces of Shandong, Shanxi, Hebei and Shaanxi. Generally speaking, it can be interpreted as "interior China" or "inland China" and the imperial dynasties located there.

均非当地出产，说明他们和外界已有交换关系。他们的社会生活以牧羊业为主，兼营农业、手工业，与外界也有了一定的交换关系。在社会发展阶段上，火烧沟墓葬贫富分化和等级差别非常明显。有的墓葬的随葬品仅有少量的陶器，而有的不仅有数量较多的陶器，往往还伴随着铜器以及金、银、玉器和绿松石珠、玛瑙珠、贝、蚌等。有的墓葬里不仅用大量的牲畜随葬，甚至还出现了人殉。以上证据都显示火烧沟文化和中原地区同时或稍后就已经进入了早期奴隶社会。

继火烧沟文化而起的是玉门市骟马类型文化。1957年，甘肃的考古工作者曾在骟马城发掘出一个新石器时代遗址，出土了一批夹沙的红褐色或灰色平底陶器，说明那时当地的生产力已经达到较高的水平。但是，就目前的研究状况来看，我们对战国以前敦煌先民的了解还很不充分，有待今后的考古发现做进一步的补充。

敦煌有可靠文字记载的历史最早可以上溯到春秋战国时期。当时，河西走廊的主体民族是月氏人，他们的游牧区域东达河西走廊东部和陇右地区，西至塔里木盆地

amount of pottery, while others included not only a large number of pottery, but also rich objects made from copper, gold, silver, jade, urquoise beads, agate beads, shells and clams, and so forth. Some were buried with livestock and even sacrificial humans. It was evident that people in Huoshaogou had already entered the early stage of slave society simultaneously with, or a bit later than the people in the Central Plains.

Shanma culture in Yumen City grew out of Huoshaogou culture. In 1957, at a ruin site of the Neolithic Age in Shanma City, some archaeologists found a large amount of sandy brown or grey pottery with flat bottoms. The discovery indicates that productivity at the time had reached a high level. However, the existing researches do not provide us with enough information on the early settlers in Dunhuang before the Warring States Period (475 BC–221 BC). Thus, it is necessary to carry out further studies.

The earliest reliable written records of Dunhuang can be traced back to the Spring and Autumn Period (770 BC–476 BC) and the Warring States Period. At the time, the main ethnic group in the Hexi Corridor was the Yuezhi, whose territory extended from the eastern part of the Tarim Basin and the eastern area of the Tianshan Mountains to the east of

东部和天山东部地区。而当时的敦煌地区则主要是乌孙人放牧和繁衍生息之所。此外,敦煌地区还有塞种胡。

秦朝时期,居住在河西走廊东部地区的月氏不仅是当地最强大的民族,而且在当时整个北方地区也是最强盛的民族之一。此时生活在北方的匈奴人面临着东有东胡,西有月氏的两难局面。为了取得月氏人的信任,匈奴的头曼单于将太子冒顿送到月氏充当人质。此后,头曼欲废冒顿而立其少子,于是就进攻月氏,希望借月氏人之手除掉冒顿。冒顿盗得月氏好马,才得以逃归匈奴,并最终杀头曼而自立。秦朝末年,月氏击败了同在河西走廊游牧的乌孙人,乌孙王难兜靡战死,普通民众则大量投奔匈奴。难兜靡之子昆莫逃到匈奴后,被冒顿收养,敦煌遂被月氏占据。而在秦汉之际,匈奴在冒顿的率领下日益强

the Hexi Corridor and Longyou area[①]. Dunhuang during this period was the home of the nomadic Wusun people, where they lived and grazed their livestock. In addition, the Saka also inhabited there.

During the Qin Dynasty (221 BC–206 BC), the Yuezhi living in the eastern area of the Hexi Corridor became the most powerful group not only in the local area but of the entire northern China. Thus, the Xiongnu living in the north found themselves in a dilemma, being jammed between the Eastern Hu people in the east and the Yuezhi in the west. In order to win the trust of the Yuezhi, Touman Chanyu (chieftain of the Xiongnu) sent his eldest son, crown prince Modu, to the Yuezhi as a hostage. Later, intending to abandon Modu as the future leader of his people and to support his younger son, Touman launched an attack on the Yuezhi in the hope that Modu would be killed by the Yuezhi people. However, Modu stole a fine horse and escaped. Returning to the Xiongnu, he killed his father, Touman, and proclaimed himself chieftain of the Xiongnu. In the late Qin Dynasty, the Yuezhi defeated the Wusun who also roamed the pastureland in the Hexi Corridor, and killed their chief, Nandoumi. As a result, the Wusun had to seek shelter with the Xiongnu, where Kunmo, son of Nandoumi, was adopted by Modu. Dunhuang then fell under the

① Longyou area refers to the area west of the Longshan Mountain, the present-day Liupan Mountain.

大起来，先是打败东胡，又趁中原战乱之机夺取了河套以南的鄂尔多斯地区，接着在汉文帝前元四年（前176年）左右派右贤王大破月氏。两年后，冒顿死，其子继位，是为老上单于。这以后，匈奴对月氏的攻势更加猛烈，月氏王被杀，他的头骨被老上单于制作成饮器。大部分月氏人怀着对匈奴的深仇大恨离开故土，向西逃到伊犁河流域；小部分留下来的就退避到祁连山中。后来，西去的那一部分月氏人就被称为大月氏，留下的称为小月氏。约在汉文帝后元三年（前161年），已经长大成人的难兜靡之子昆莫在匈奴支持下，率领所统之部，远袭伊犁河流域。大月氏抵挡不住，除少量人留居原处外，大部人又继续西迁，经大宛（今乌兹别克斯坦费尔干纳盆地一带），来到妫水（今阿姆河）之畔，在北岸建立王庭，迫使南岸的大夏臣服。妫水流域土地肥饶，环境相对安宁，大月氏人便在这里定居下来，生活方式也逐渐由游牧过渡到农耕。河西走廊从此归入匈奴治下，包括敦煌

entire control of the Yuezhi. At the turn of the Qin and Han dynasties, the Xiongnu grew increasingly strong under the leadership of Modu. They first defeated the Eastern Hu people, and later occupied Erdos south of the Hetao area by taking advantage of the wars in the Central Plains. In the 4th year of Qianyuan Era of Emperor Wen (176 BC), Xiongnu troops under the command of *Youxian* Prince inflicted a decisive defeat on the Yuezhi. Two years later, Modu died and his son succeeded to the throne under the name of Laoshang Chanyu. After that, the Xiongnu launched more attacks on the Yuezhi. Finally, the Yuezhi chief was killed, and his skull was made into a drinking vessel. The majority of Yuezhi people with a deep hatred to the Xiongnu fled westward to the basin of the Ili River, where they settled and later became known as the Greater Yuezhi. The others withdrew into the Qilian Mountains, and were known as the Lesser Yuezhi. In the 3rd year of Houyuan Era of Emperor Wen (161 BC), Kunmo, already an adult and backed by the Xiongnu, attacked the Greater Yuezhi. As a result, most people of the Greater Yuezhi had to migrate further westward through Dayuan (present-day Fergana in Uzbekistan) to the Guishui River (present-day Amu Darya), where they established their state on the northern bank and compelled the Bactrians (*Daxia* in Chinese) on the southern bank to accept their rule. Gradually, their lifestyle shifted

在内的河西走廊西部由匈奴浑邪王统治,东部则由休屠王驻守。此后,匈奴又控制了西域,就连新立的汉王朝也屡次受其侵扰。匈奴占据河西走廊和西域之后,除了在占领区征收赋税之外,还严重地破坏和阻碍着中西交通,并与羌人联结,严重威胁着汉朝的安全。

from nomadism to farming as a result of the fertile land and peaceful environment in the Guishui River area. After that, the Hexi Corridor was under the rule of the Xiongnu, with Prince Hunye being in charge of the western part including Dunhuang, and Prince Xiuchu in charge of the eastern part. Hereafter, the Xiongnu conquered the Western Regions and even harassed the newly-established Han Dynasty many times. The Xiongnu not only levied taxes in their occupied areas, but also disrupted and cut off transportation between the Central Plains and the Western Regions. Furthermore, they also formed an alliance with the Qiang people, posing a severe threat to the security of the Han Dynasty.

两汉时期的敦煌

Dunhuang During the Han Dynasty

西汉初年，久经战乱的汉王朝社会经济极端残破，统治阶级内部也矛盾重重，根本无力对匈奴的侵扰进行有力的反击，所以只好用和亲、赠送财物等方式缓和与匈奴的关系，换取了短暂的和平。但西汉王朝的和亲政策并不能满足匈奴贵族的贪欲。匈奴经常侵扰汉朝的边郡，杀掠人民。对此，西汉桓宽所著的《盐铁论》记载，"汉兴以来，修好，结和亲，所聘遗单于者甚厚；然不以重质厚赂之故改节，而暴害滋甚"，"匈奴数和亲，而常先犯约……反复无信，百约百叛"。

经过70多年的休养生息，汉王朝日渐富强。公元前140年，汉武帝即位。这时的西汉国力充实，而且中央集权也大大加强，汉武帝开始筹划反击匈奴。此时，归降汉朝的匈奴人将匈奴击破月氏并以月氏王之头作为饮酒器具之事汇报给汉朝。汉武帝有攻灭匈奴的雄图

Suffering from a severe economic depression and political chaos during years of war, the Western Han Dynasty in its early years was forced to marry its princess to chieftain of the Xiongnu (*chanyu* in Chinese) in an effort to stop the border raids. Along with marriage alliances (*heqin* policy in Chinese), the Han government sent gifts to bribe the Xiongnu aiming to avoid the attacks. A temporary peace settlement was eventually reached between the parties. Such policies, however, could not placate the rulers of the Xiongnu, who frequently invaded the borders and killed or robbed the local people there. As recorded by Huan Kuan in his *Discourses on Salt and Iron*, "Since the founding of the Han Dynasty, emperors married the princesses to Chanyu of the Xiongnu with abundant 'betrothal gifts' to form marriage alliances; however, the Xiongnu did not abide by the peace treaties and broke them many times."

After over 70 years of recovery, the Han Dynasty grew more and more powerful and prosperous. In 140 BC, Emperor Wu of the Han Dynasty succeeded to the throne and began to make preparations for a military confrontation against the Xiongnu, as the Han empire was now consolidated politically, militarily, and economically. On hearing the

大志，听到这个消息，就希望能与月氏取得联系，以便共同夹击匈奴。于是，汉武帝便下诏招募能出使月氏的使者。正在西汉政府出任低级官吏的张骞应募出使。

汉武帝建元年间（前140～前135年），月氏还生活在伊犁河、楚河流域，而匈奴在将月氏逐出河西后，不仅控制了祁连山以北直至天山、阿尔泰山东端的大片土地，而且还控制了包括准噶尔盆地在内的阿尔泰山南麓，以及原来可能役属于月氏的塔里木盆地绿洲周围的国家。所以，张骞要出使月氏必须要穿过匈奴的控制区。而张骞与堂邑氏胡奴甘夫等人出陇西，途经匈奴领地的过程中，被匈奴俘虏并送至单于王廷。对于汉朝希望联合月氏攻击匈奴的意图，匈奴当然不能接受。单于便质问张骞：“月氏在我们匈奴的北方，汉朝怎么能向他们派遣使节？假设我们想经过汉地出使南越，汉朝能允许我们这么做吗？”于是，匈奴就

news that the Xiongnu ruler had killed the chief of the Yuezhi and had made a drinking vessel out of his skull, Emperor Wu hoped to form an alliance with the Yuezhi so as to combat the Xiongnu. Then Zhang Qian, a junior official, was appointed as the envoy to the Yuezhi.

During the Jianyuan Era of Emperor Wu (140 BC–135 BC), the Yuezhi people lived around the Ili River and the Chuhe River. After the Xiongnu expelled the Yuezhi out of the Hexi Corridor, they took control of a large area stretching from the north of the Qilian Mountains to the east of the Tianshan Mountains and the Altai Mountains, the area of the Junggar Basin, as well as some areas around the Tarim Basin which had once been under the rule of the Yuezhi. Consequently, to get to the territory of the Yuezhi, Zhang Qian and his guide Ganfu, a Xiongnu who had been captured in war, had to pass through lands under control of the Xiongnu. Unfortunately, they were captured and sent to Chanyu's palace, where Chanyu questioned them: "How dare your Han government dispatch a diplomatic envoy to the Yuezhi, which is located to the north of our territory? If I wanted to dispatch an envoy to the State of Nanyue and cross through the lands of the Han Dynasty, would you permit me to do that?" Hence, the Xiongnu forced Zhang Qian to stay and made him marry a Xiongnu woman. More than a decade passed, during which Zhang raised a family with the woman but never forgot his mission. He still kept his staff which indicated his identity as an envoy from the Han government. As his stay

将张骞等人扣留下来，并将匈奴的女子嫁给张骞。经过10余年的时间，虽然张骞与胡妻已经有子，但他不忘自己的使命，仍然保留着代表汉朝使者身份的节杖。由于留居匈奴的时间渐长，匈奴也就对张骞失去了戒心。张骞趁游牧到匈奴西界之机，率领部属逃离匈奴而继续向月氏进发。经过数十天的艰苦跋涉，张骞到达西域的大宛国。大宛早就听说汉朝的富饶，但苦于匈奴的阻隔而不能和汉朝取得联系。所以，当大宛王见到张骞后喜出望外，便询问他想去什么地方。张骞回答说："我代表汉朝出使月氏，但是被匈奴所阻隔。现在我从匈奴逃出来，希望大王能派人送我到月氏。如果真的能到达月氏，等我返回汉朝后，汉朝廷一定会送给大王很多财物，以表示感谢。"大宛王于是为张骞等人配备了翻译人员，送张骞等人到达康居后，再由康居派人将他们送到大月氏。

张骞在大月氏逗留了一年多时间。此时，大月氏已在妫水流域定居。此地土地肥沃，且极少受到外族的入侵，所以已没有报复匈奴的意愿。无奈之下，张骞决定返回汉朝。此时匈奴仍占据着河西走廊

lengthened, the Xiongnu loosened their watch on him. One day, while grazing animals on the western border of the Xiongnu territory, Zhang Qian led his followers on a westward escape to the Yuezhi. After trekking for dozens of days, they reached Dayuan where they were warmly welcomed because the King of Dayuan admired the affluence of the Han and was eager to establish contact with the Han Dynasty. When the King of Dayuan asked Zhang Qian where they wanted to go, Zhang replied, "I am an imperial envoy to the Yuezhi on behalf of the Han Dynasty, but unfortunately, my mission was interrupted by the Xiongnu. Since having escaped from the Xiongnu, I hope you can help me get to the Yuezhi. If I can arrive there and then return successfully to the Han Dynasty, the emperor of the Han will present you with abundant gifts as a token of his appreciation." The King of Dayuan provided Zhang Qian with translators and ordered his soldiers to escort them to the State of Kangju and then on to the Greater Yuezhi.

Zhang Qian spent a year in the Greater Yuezhi, aiming to build an alliance with them against the Xiongnu. The Yuezhi, however, were too settled to start a war because of their peaceful life in the fertile land near the Guishui River. On learning this, Zhang Qian lost hope and decided to return to the Central Plains. Unfortunately,

地区，张骞想沿着祁连山进入羌中地区以归汉，但在途中再次被匈奴截获。一年之后，匈奴单于死，国内大乱，张骞与胡妻及甘夫一同逃亡归汉。张骞为人宽厚，深得西域胡人爱戴。而张骞所带的甘夫为胡人，射箭的技艺高超，在逃亡途中食品匮乏的时候，就射禽兽作为食物。最初，张骞出使时，使团有 100 余人。经过 13 年的岁月，唯有张骞和甘夫两个人得以返回汉朝。虽然张骞此次出使并没有达到联合月氏夹击匈奴的目的，却给汉王朝带回了有关匈奴及西域的丰富情报(图 1)。

汉武帝元光二年（前 133 年)的马邑之谋，是西汉王朝与匈奴由“和亲”到战争的转折点，揭开了抗击匈奴的序幕。在元朔二年(前 127 年)的河南之战中，汉王朝收复了“河南地”。元狩二年(前 121 年)春，将军霍去病率军越过祁连山，进击河

on his return trip by which he wanted to travel along the Qilian Mountains and enter the area of the Qiang people, he was again captured by the Xiongnu who still occupied the Hexi Corridor. One year later, Chanyu of the Xiongnu died. In the midst of the chaos and infighting among the Xiongnu, Zhang Qian, Ganfu, as well as Zhang's wife and son all escaped. On his journey home, Zhang Qian was helped by the local Xiongnu, and assisted by Ganfu who was skilled at archery, hunting game when they were short of food. Finally, only Zhang Qian and Ganfu returned to the Han territory alive. By that time, 13 years had passed since Zhang Qian set off from the Han court with more than one hundred men. Although he did not achieve his aim of creating an alliance with the Yuezhi against the Xiongnu, Zhang brought back considerable detailed information on the Xiongnu and the Western Regions (Fig.1).

The Battle in Mayi in the 2nd year of Yuanguang Era of Emperor Wu (133 BC) was the turning point of the relationship between the Han Dynasty and the Xiongnu based on the marriage alliance, marking the beginning of war against the Xiongnu. In the 2nd year of Yuanshuo Era (127 BC), the Han Dynasty regained the lost territory of Henandi① after the Battle in Henan. In the 2nd year of Yuanshou Era (121 BC), under the leadership of General Huo Qubing, the Han troops crossed the Qilian Mountains to attack the Xiongnu in the Hexi Corridor. In the summer of the same year, General Huo entered the Hexi

① Henandi refers to the area in the south of the bend of the Yellow River in the Han Dynasty.

图1　莫高窟第323窟　张骞出使西域图　初唐

Fig.1　Envoy Zhang Qian's Mission to the Western Regions, Mogao Cave 323　Early Tang

西走廊的匈奴。同年夏，霍去病再次进入河西，重创匈奴。就连休屠王的祭天金人也被汉军所获，并作为战利品带回长安。河西之战的胜利，使匈奴失去了水草丰盛、宜于牧畜的祁连山和焉支山，匈奴受到重创。他们哀叹道："亡我祁连山，使我六畜不蕃息；失我焉支山，使我嫁妇无颜色。"河西的匈奴在一年之内连遭两次重创，已不堪支持，而浑邪王

Corridor again and inflicted heavy damage on the Xiongnu, even carrying back to the capital city Chang'an the golden statue used by the Prince Xiuchu as an artifact for holy rituals. After the Battle in the Hexi Corridor, the Han Dynasty resumed its reign in the Qilian Mountains and the Yanzhi Mountain which were ideal pastureland for grazing. Defeated by Huo Qubing, the Xiongnu sighed in despair, "Having lost our Qilian Mountains, our cattle have no place to breed; Having lost our Yanzhi Mountain, our women marry without splendor."[①] Huo Qubing's two victories dealt heavy blows to the tribes of Xiongnu princes

① It is quoted from *Eighteen Lectures on Dunhuang* translated by Imre Galambos.

和休屠王恐单于怪罪，就派人与在黄河沿岸修筑边塞的汉朝将军李息联系，希望归附汉朝。李息马上把这个消息上奏给汉武帝。汉武帝开始担心匈奴诈降，随即派霍去病前往迎降。而此时休屠王反悔，所以浑邪王就杀掉休屠王，并收编了他的部众。霍去病当机立断，率军驰入浑邪王营中，"斩其欲亡者八千人"，率领其部众渡黄河东进。此次匈奴降汉者共4万余众。浑邪王被护送至长安，受到汉武帝的隆重接待，并封浑邪王及亲信数人为侯，将匈奴部众安置于原陇西、北地、上郡、朔方、云中5郡故塞之外。

汉武帝对匈奴的用兵，经过元狩二年（前121年）的河西之战，取得了很大的胜利，出现了金城、河西以西及南山至盐泽地区"空无匈奴"的局面。据《史记·大宛列传》的记载，张骞曾向武帝献策说："现在匈奴刚刚被汉击败，而原来浑邪王所控制的河西地区无人居

Hunye and Xiuchu who were both stationed at the Hexi Corridor. Afraid of being punished by Chanyu, the two princes contacted General Li Xi of the Han Dynasty, who was then building a frontier fortress along the Yellow River, to negotiate their surrender. After the news was reported to Emperor Wu, suspecting that the Xiongnu were merely pretending to surrender, he ordered General Huo Qubing to deal with this issue. It turned out that Prince Xiuchu changed his mind and was killed by Prince Hunye who then took over the troops of Xiuchu. On seeing this, Huo Qubing led his troops into the camp of Hunye, and continued to march eastward after across the Yellow River, killing 8,000 Xiongnu men who refused to surrender. At last, nearly 40,000 Xiongnu soldiers surrendered to the Han Dynasty. Prince Hunye was escorted to Chang'an, where he was warmly received. Prince Hunye and his trusted followers were given the titles of marquess by Emperor Wu and his Xiongnu soldiers were then stationed in the frontier areas of Longxi, Beidi, Shangjun, Shuofang, and Yunzhong.

Emperor Wu won a great victory when he fought against the Xiongnu in the Battle in the Hexi Corridor. Consequently, no more harassment from the Xiongnu would be seen in Jincheng Prefecture, the area west of the Hexi Corridor, and the area from the Nanshan Mountain to the Lop Nor. According to the *Records of the Grand Historian*: *Dayuan*, Zhang Qian once suggested to Emperor Wu, "No people live in the area which was occupied by Prince Hunye after the defeat of the Xiongnu. People in the Western Regions have always admired the prosperity of the Han Dynasty,

住。西域的蛮夷通常都爱慕大汉的财物,如果现在用财货贿赂乌孙,招徕他们向东发展,占据浑邪王的故地,与汉朝结为兄弟,他们势必要听从大汉的号令,如此则切断了匈奴的右臂。"武帝采纳了张骞的建议,派遣他出使乌孙,可见当时汉王朝还没有向河西徙民屯田的意图。但张骞的计策并未得到乌孙的认同,汉王朝这才于元狩四年(前119年)以后,派官吏和士卒5万多人渡过黄河,在朔方郡以西至令居(甘肃永登)之间开凿渠道并设置屯田,开始为经营河西走廊准备条件。酒泉、张掖地处匈奴与西羌两大族之间,地理位置十分重要。而西羌之反叛与匈奴之勾连有极大的关系。汉武帝为了隔绝西羌和匈奴之间的联系,以制止匈奴势力的卷土重来,于元鼎六年(前111年)平定西羌后,同年随即派遣数万人渡过黄河修筑令居城,并设置张掖、酒泉郡。此外,还在上郡、朔方、西河设置开田官,派遣士卒60万人防戍屯田,以进一步开发河西。

so if we can make good use of our wealth to attract the Wusun people to ally with us so that they can move eastward into the area that was once controlled by Hunye, that would be a great loss to the Xiongnu." Emperor Wu took Zhang's advice and dispatched him to the State of Wusun, indicating that at that time the Han Dynasty had no intention of sending people and opening up wasteland in the Hexi Corridor. Zhang Qian's plan was, however, not accepted by the ruler of the Wusun. Under these circumstances, in the 4th year of Yuanshou Era (119 BC), the Han Dynasty dispatched over 50,000 officials and troops across the Yellow River to dig canals and open up the wasteland in the area from west of Shuofang Prefecture to Lingju County (present-day Yongdeng County in Gansu), paving the way for the administration of the Hexi Corridor. Located in the area between the Xiongnu and the Western Qiang, Jiuquan and Zhangye played an important geographical role. In order to cut off the link between these two tribes so as to prevent further invasions from the Xiongnu, in the 6th year of Yuanding Era (111 BC), Emperor Wu sent tens of thousands of people to develop Lingju County and established Zhangye and Jiuquan prefectures after defeating the Western Qiang. In addition, the Han government dispatched agricultural officials directing 600,000 soldiers to cultivate the wasteland in Shangjun, Shuofang, and Xihe and to strengthen the garrisons of the frontier, further boosting the

西汉王朝除希望通过河西走廊西通大夏外，还曾一度欲打通由昆明抵大夏之路。但汉武帝所派遣的柏始昌、吕越人等使团，都在昆明被少数民族所杀，携带的财物也被抢走。虽然汉武帝曾派遣将军郭昌、卫广等，率领长安附近三辅之地的有罪之人及巴蜀将士数万人前往昆明，以讨伐阻拦汉朝使者的少数民族，并获得胜利。但此后所派遣的使团，仍然无法顺利通过昆明。而汉王朝正是在由昆明通大夏的计划失败后，才下决心经营由河西走廊通西域诸国道路的。

元封二年（前 109 年），汉武帝遣使经酒泉抵达大夏。元封三年（前 108 年），又派遣赵破奴讨伐西域的姑师国。汉军想要讨伐姑师，就必须首先经过楼兰。赵破奴率轻骑700 余人先攻陷了楼兰王城，俘虏楼兰王，“遂破姑师”。同年，武都氐人叛乱，被迁徙酒泉郡。元封四年（前 107 年），王恢以佐赵

development of the Hexi area.

In fact, the Western Han Dynasty had hoped to connect with Bactria not only by way of the Hexi Corridor, but also through a southern route via Kunming. Unfortunately, the diplomatic corps led by Bai Shichang and Lü Yueren were killed and their belongings were robbed by the local ethnic tribes in Kunming. Although Generals Guo Chang and Wei Guang who were then sent out by Emperor Wu succeeded in leading several tens of thousands of ex-convicts and soldiers to fight against the tribes who had intercepted the Han diplomatic corps sent to Kunming, the corps that followed still could not pass through Kunming. Due to the failure of reaching Bactria by way of Kunming, the Han Dynasty determined to open the route to states or kingdoms in the Western Regions via the Hexi Corridor.

In the 2nd year of Yuanfeng Era (109 BC), Emperor Wu dispatched envoys to Bactria via Jiuquan. A year later, he sent General Zhao Ponu to conquer the State of Gushi by way of Loulan①. To achieve this, with 700 light cavalrymen, Zhao Ponu first broke into the capital of Loulan, capturing the King of Loulan, and then conquered Gushi. In the same year, the Di people inhabiting Wudu rebelled and then were forced to move to

① Loulan is an ancient kingdom along the Silk Road on the northwestern edge of the Lop Nor and was renamed Shanshan in 77 BC.

破奴击楼兰有功，封为晧侯。同年，西汉王朝修筑了自酒泉至玉门的障塞，设置了玉门都尉，完成了整个河西走廊的军事防御设施。而为了配合李广利讨伐大宛的战争，汉朝在元封五年(前106年)至六年(前105年)，分出酒泉郡一部分设置敦煌郡，分出武威郡一部分设置张掖郡，这就是历史上著名的“河西四郡”。

根据《汉书·地理志》的记载，汉代敦煌郡有6个属县，即敦煌、冥安、效谷、渊泉、广至与龙勒(图2)。敦煌县主要位于党河东西两岸的绿洲。对于敦煌郡属县的范围，吴礽骧、余尧进行了系统的研究。其中，敦煌县的西境自大方盘城向东南至今南湖店附近。敦煌县北境为疏勒河，汉朝的行政管辖范围在沿疏勒河南岸所修筑的塞墙以内。东境的界线与今敦煌与瓜州县的分界基本一致。南境在今土尔根达坂山，包括今肃北蒙古族自治县的西部。冥安县主要位于冥水支流的下游绿洲，其四境东至冥水，南至大雪山，西接广

Jiuquan Prefecture. In 107 BC, Wang Hui was conferred the title of a marquess for his assistance in General Zhao's conquest of Loulan. Meanwhile, fortresses from Jiuquan to Yumen were built and a Commandant of Yumen was appointed, indicating that military fortifications in the Hexi Corridor were established. From 106 BC to 105 BC, to assist General Li Guangli's conquest over Dayuan, the Han Dynasty set up Dunhuang Prefecture separately from Jiuquan Prefecture, and Zhangye Prefecture separately from Wuwei Prefecture as well. They were collectively known as the Four Prefectures in the Hexi Area in history.

According to the *Book of Han*: *Treatise on Geography*, there were six counties in Dunhuang Prefecture in the Han Dynasty: Dunhuang, Ming'an, Xiaogu, Yuanquan, Guangzhi and Longle (Fig.2). As for the coverage of counties in Dunhuang Prefecture, scholars Wu Rengxiang and Yu Yao researched it comprehensively. Dunhuang County was situated on the oasis along the banks of the Danghe River, with its western border stretching from the Big Fangpan Warehouse southeast to present-day Nanhudian; the northern end of it was near the Shule River (The area within the southern bank of the Shule River was under the administration of the Han Dynasty); the eastern end was similar to the border which separated present-day Dunhuang and Guazhou County; in the south it bordered on Tu'ergendaban Mountain, covering

至县境，北至乱山子。效谷县主要分布于今敦煌甜水井北，在西水沟、东水沟和芦草沟下游形成的绿洲上。据《汉书·地理志》颜师古的注文，汉武帝元封六年（前105年），济南人崔不意在出任渔泽尉期间，身体力行，劝导民众耕作田地，“以勤效得谷”，使粮食获得丰收。所以，汉政府将此县命名为效谷县。

the western part of present-day Subei Mongol Autonomous County. Ming'an County was located on an oasis around the lower reaches of the branch of the Mingshui River, bordering the area of the Mingshui River in the east, the Daxue Mountains in the south, Guangzhi County in the west and Luanshanzi in the north. Xiaogu County was mainly located on an oasis (north of present-day Tianshuijing of Dunhuang) surrounded by the lower reaches of three rivers of West Shuigou, East Shuigou, and Lucaogou. It bordered the frontier wall of the Han Dynasty to the north, the Sanwei Mountain to the south and the watchtowers in Yihe to the west; the eastern border was unknown. Based on notes from Yan Shigu for the *Book of Han*: *Treatise*

图2 汉代敦煌古城遗址

Fig.2 Ruins of Dunhuang from the Han Dynasty

由于人为开发的不合理，加之洪水冲刷和风蚀等原因，这片绿洲今已沦为红柳、沙窝地。其北至汉塞墙，南至三危山，西至宜禾临介燧，东境不明。渊泉县因地多泉水而得名，主要分布于冥泽以西的诸泉之间的绿洲上。东至冥泽，北至塞墙，西境无考，南境与冥安县相接。广至县，即唐朝的常乐县，主要分布于榆林河下游绿洲（图 3）。

on Geography, in the 6th year of Yuanfeng Era (105 BC), Cui Buyi from Jinan was appointed the Commandant in charge of Fishery, who personally led the local people to cultivate the land. As a result, people reaped the fruits of their hard work, with a harvest of grain. Hence, the county was named Xiaogu County by the government. But because of soil exhaustion resulting from over-worked land, as well as floods and wind erosion, such an oasis has turned into a desert populated with tamarisk shrubs. Yuanquan County, given the name for its abundant springs, was located on an oasis west of Mingze Lake, bordering Mingze Lake to the east, the fortification walls to the north, and Ming'an County to the south. There

图 3　汉广至城南垣(邵如林　摄)

Fig.3　South Wall of Guangzhi County from the Han Dynasty (Photo by Shao Rulin)

其东接冥安县，西与效谷县接壤，南抵大雪山，北至汉塞墙。龙勒县主要分布于今南湖绿洲，包括今敦煌县西部和阿克塞哈萨克族自治县北部。其东境在南湖店一带，北境为疏勒河，西境在玉门都尉所属的障塞亭燧之分布区域，这个区域北部在库穆塔克沙漠的东缘，即今哈拉齐以东，南部在今大红山一带(图 4)。

西汉在敦煌进入西域的必经之道上设置玉门关

is no confirmed record concerning its western end. Guangzhi County （also known as Changle County during the Tang Dynasty）was located on an oasis around the lower reaches of the Yulin River（Fig. 3）. It bordered Ming'an County to the east and Xiaogu County to the west, stretching as far as the Daxue Mountains to the south and the Han fortification walls to the north. Longle County was situated on the Nanhu oasis which covered the western part of present-day Dunhuang and the northern part of present-day Aksai Kazakh Autonomous County. Its eastern border was near Nanhudian, the northern border was the Shule River, and the western border was in the area with scattered fortifications and watchtowers, which was in the jurisdiction of the Commandant of Yumen. Its northern part bordered the eastern edge of the

图 4　西汉龙勒县遗址

Fig.4　Ruins of Longle County from the Western Han Dynasty

和阳关，此外还修筑了城障烽燧、塞墙、天田等严密的军事防御设施和观察、通信系统。除了沿疏勒河南岸的塞墙外，在塞墙终点以西，还有沿南、北方向设置的邮驿亭燧（图 5）。同时，大致按地方行政区划，设置了玉门、阳关、中部、宜禾等四部都尉，都尉下置候官、候长、燧长等官属。此外，还驻有屯田士卒。正是由于设置了这一整套完整周密的军事防御体系，才保证了中西交通的畅通和河西四郡的开发，进而为魏晋南北朝、隋唐时期河西经济、文化的繁荣奠定了基础。

为了巩固这一军事要地，汉王朝一方面迁徙内地的贫民、罪犯来此定居，另一方面征发大批兵士到此戍守。向河西移民的对象，据《汉书·地理志》载：“其民或以关东下贫，或以报怨过当，或以悖逆亡道，家属徙焉。”也

Kumtag Desert (the eastern area of the present-day Halaqi) and the southern part was in the area near the presnt-day Dahong Mountain (Fig.4).

The Western Han government established the Yumen Pass and the Yangguan Pass along the road from Dunhuang to the Western Regions. Rigorous military defense systems and observation and communication systems were equipped, such as watchtowers, fortification walls along the southern bank of the Shule River and reconnoitering facilities. In addition, postal stations and beacon towers were also established (Fig.5). Furthermore, based on the administrative division, the government appointed four Commandants with junior military officers as their subordinates to manage Yumen, Yangguan, Zhongbu and Yihe. Assigned garrison troops were stationed there to open up wasteland. Such a complete and thorough military defense system guaranteed the further development of the Four Prefectures in the Hexi Area and the smooth communication between China and the West, which laid a solid foundation for the cultural and economic prosperity of the Hexi Corridor in the Wei, Jin, Northern and Southern dynasties as well as the Sui and Tang dynasties.

In order to consolidate this important military fortress, on the one hand, the Han government moved a larger number of paupers and prisoners from the Central Plains to the Hexi area; on the other hand, large amounts of soldiers were conscripted to garrison there. The record from the *Book of Han*: *Treatise on Geography* showed that people who migrated to the Hexi area included poor farmers, prisoners, and political offenders. What is more,

图5 汉代当谷燧遗址(邵如林 摄)

Fig.5 Beacon Tower Ruins from the Han Dynasty (Photo by Shao Rulin)

就是说这些人主要是生活没有着落的农民、刑事犯罪者和犯有叛逆罪的政治犯。此外,还有一些是自愿迁徙到河西的,也有的是屯田戍卒在服役期满后自愿留下,也有被强制迁徙到河西的少数民族。中原人士的迁入,改变了河西地区的民族结构,带来了中原地区较为先进的生产技术,促进了敦煌地区农业的发展。

为了解决众多移民和

some people volunteered to settle in the Hexi area, some soldiers who ended their military service of garrisoning the frontier chose to stay, and some ethnic minorties were expelled to move there forcefully. Such a migration from the Central Plains changed the population's composition in the Hexi area. Meanwhile, advanced production technologies were introduced, which promoted agricultural development in Dunhuang.

In order to meet the food supply demands of soldiers and migrants in the Hexi Corridor, the Han government carried out the *tuntian* policy[①] in which soldiers were assigned to defend the territory and farm the land simultaneously. It was

① *Tuntian* policy is the one implemented by the government to send garrison troops to reclaim wasteland to arable land. It was instituted as early as the Western Han Dynasty, during the reign of Emperor Wu, when soldiers on distant expeditions were set to work converting and farming the conquered land, both to provide food for the army and to convert the land into agricultural land.

军士的粮食问题，汉王朝在河西走廊地区大力推行屯田政策。屯田是且守且耕，亦农亦兵，军事活动与农业生产相结合的一种措施。戍边是汉代农民的徭役之一，因此汉政府以戍边名义，征发大批的农民到边疆和新占领区去戍守或田耕。在屯田的名义下，他们一方面守边，一方面从事农业生产。汉代边郡的屯田规模很大，为了便于管理，还设置了专门的管理机构和组织系统。屯田的收获，不仅解决了边防的给养，供应往来丝绸之路的使者和商人，还可以在市场上出售，以资调节。当内地发生灾害时，还能调拨屯田积谷用以赈灾。河西的屯田，使封建的生产方式得以在当地推行，而且达到了预期的效果。边郡粮库充足，戍边力量加强，遏制了匈奴骑兵的掠夺。

汉宣帝神爵二年（前60年），西汉政府在西域正式设置了第一个代表西汉王朝的统治机构——西域都护府，管辖阳关、玉门关以西，包括

a combination of military activity and agricultural production. During the Han Dynasty, one type of corvée labor for farmers was to garrison the frontiers. Therefore, the Han government moved substantial numbers of farmers to the frontiers and newly-occupied lands where such people would garrison the areas and farm the land. The government also arranged a special organization to facilitate management of the land. The crops from the harvest not only were provided as food for the army, emissaries, and merchants, but also could be sold in the markets. When any natural disaster happened in the Central Plains, the crops could also be allocated for disaster relief. Generally, the feudal production mode was implemented in Dunhuang via the *tuntian* policy with the desired effects that the grain reserves for the army were sufficient and the strength of the garrison was enhanced. All these measures were beneficial in effectively preventing assaults by the Xiongnu.

In the 2nd year of Shenjue Era of Emperor Xuan（60 BC）, the first official administrative organization—Protectorate of the Western Regions—was established to govern the vast area west of the Yangguan Pass and the Yumen Pass, including present-day Xinjiang and the lands in the eastern part of the Balkhash Lake, marking the official control of the vast Western Regions by the Han government. This was the culmination of more than 50 years of administration of Western Regions based in Dunhuang, after the defeat of the Xiongnu by

今我国新疆和巴尔喀什湖以东的广大地区。西域都护府的建立,是广大西域地区正式归属西汉政府的标志,是西汉打败匈奴,以敦煌为基础,经营西域半个多世纪的结果。这对丝绸之路的畅通和繁荣、东西方文化交流的加强有着重大意义。

西汉末年,中原战乱,河西地区却相对稳定,许多中原大族为躲避战乱而西迁此地。公元1世纪初,就有不少三辅(京兆府、左冯翊、右扶风)地区的人前往河西。《后汉书·孔奋列传》就记载孔奋因天下扰乱,想找一个安定富庶的地方侍奉老母,遂选中河西。而据《后汉书·窦融列传》记载,窦融出身于扶风平陵的世家大族。其高祖父曾出任张掖

the Western Han Dynasty. This development was a key factor in the prosperity of the Silk Road and the communication between the East and the West.

In the late Western Han Dynasty, compared with the turmoil caused by wars in the Central Plains, the Hexi area remained relatively peaceful, causing numerous large clans with wealth and power to move westward. In the early years of the 1st century, many people living in the jurisdictional area of the Three Guardians① who administered the capital city moved into the Hexi area. Records from the *Book of the Later Han*②: *Biography of Kong Fen* showed that Kong Fen considered the Hexi area as a stable and rich location where he could support his aged mother peacefully. Another record from the *Book of the Later Han*: *Biography of Dou Rong* recorded that Dou Rong was born of an aristocratic family in Pingling County, Fufeng Prefecture near the capital. His great-great-grandfather had been appointed as the Governor of Zhangye Prefecture, and his granduncle was once the Commandant of the Qiang Tribe, so Dou Rong was familiar with the customs of the Hexi area. When the Central Plains were involved in wars, Dou Rong regarded the Hexi area as a politically, economically and militarily secure place where he could protect his

---

① Three Guardians were called *sanfu* in Chinese, referring to the Metropolitan Governor, the Guardian of the Left and the Guardian of the Right.

② The Western Han Dynasty was also known as the Early Han Dynasty, and the Eastern Han Dynasty was likewise also known as the Later Han Dynasty.

太守，从祖父曾出任护羌都尉，因此窦融熟悉河西地区的风俗。在中原大乱、人人自危的形势下，窦融从政治、经济、军事上考虑，将河西看作可以据地自守、保全家族之地，自请为张掖属国都尉。到河西后，他结交和善待当地大族豪杰，取得了地方势力的支持。当时，由于天下大乱，人民没有依靠，而河西经常面临羌胡的进攻，地方豪强大族急需有一个能保护他们利益的政权。所以，他们就推举世代在河西担任官吏的窦融为河西五郡大将军，组建起统一的河西地方政权，抗击来犯的匈奴、羌胡，使河西出现了安定的局面，史称“时天下扰乱，唯河西独安”“兵马强盛，仓库有畜，民庶殷富”。大族的到来，不仅为河西带来了大量的生产力和先进的生产技术，更重要的是带来了中原的文化。

东汉建立以后，光武帝刘秀对据有“河西完富，地接陇蜀”的窦融也很重视，特“赐融玺书”，并“授融为凉州

large family. He then recommended himself to be appointed the Commandant of Zhangye. After being dispatched to the Hexi area, he made friends with local powerful families and thus gained support from them. Because of the turmoil in the Central Plains and aggression from the Xiongnu and the Qiang in the Hexi area, such large clans were in urgent need of an authority to protect them. Considering that Dou Rong's ancestors had been officials in the Hexi area, they recommended Dou Rong as the General-in-Chief of Five Prefectures in the Hexi Area who then organized the local authority, so as to resist the invasion from the Xiongnu and the Qiang tribes. Under such circumstances, the Hexi area remained continually at peace. It was recorded in history books that "Only the Hexi area remained peaceful at that time, while the rest of the world was in chaos. With strong military forces, abundant crops and cattle, people were living a happy and rich life there." All in all, the clans from the Central Plains brought with them advanced technology and abundant labor, as well as a new culture.

After the Eastern Han Dynasty was established, Liu Xiu, Emperor Guangwu, attached great importance to Dou Rong who managed prosperous Hexi area, and bestowed upon him the governorship of Liangzhou in an imperial edict. During the Eastern Han Dynasty, the eastern part of the Hexi area was frequently invaded by the Qiang, while the western part was relatively safe. Later, the Northern Xiongnu once

牧”。东汉时期,河西东部地区常常受到羌人的侵扰,西部相对平安。与此同时,北匈奴日益崛起，而东汉王朝却日益衰落。匈奴重新控制西域，汉朝在西域的统治逐渐崩溃。代替西域都护主管西域事务的护西域副校尉长驻敦煌，敦煌太守则成为东汉王朝在西域地区采取军事行动的实际负责人，敦煌成为当时汉王朝控制西域的军政中心(图 6)。

东汉后期，由于政治黑

again grew into the power and gradually took back control of the Western Regions, while the Han Dynasty lost the control over this place. The Vice Colonel of the Western Regions, who replaced the post of Protector-General of the Western Regions, was stationed in Dunhuang for a long time, while the Governor of Dunhuang Prefecture effectively became the de facto leader of military activity in the Western Regions. Dunhuang thus became the military and political center in charge of the Western Regions under the Han Dynasty (Fig.6).

In the late Eastern Han Dynasty, the Yellow Turban Rebellion broke out. The separatist forces in different regions developed rapidly and were involved in the upheaval by

图 6　东汉时期的五铢钱

Fig.6　Ancient Coins from the Eastern Han Dynasty

暗，爆发了黄巾大起义。在镇压农民起义的过程中，各地割据势力急剧扩张，全国出现了军阀大混战的局面。在中原大乱、社会生产力遭受严重破坏的时候，河西地区相对安定，但汉末以来的大动乱或多或少也波及了河西，特别是河西的东部地区。河西豪强大族趁军阀割据之际，纷纷发展自己的势力。金城边章、韩遂在河西地区是有名的大族，被北宫伯玉、李文侯领导的羌胡起义军劫持为首领。后来，韩遂将这支队伍转变成自己的私人武装，割据金城、关陇地区，给东汉政府带来了很大的威胁。在韩遂和边章的影响下，金城和酒泉地区都发生了动乱。在这种情况下，河西地区的地方官员纷纷上书，请求政府设置新的机构以加强管理。兴平元年(194年)，东汉政府分别在凉州和河西四郡设置雍州，任命陈留人邯郸商为雍州刺史。这时，武威太守空缺，东汉政

warlords all over the nation, resulting in great damage to the social productive forces in the Central Plains. By contrast, the Hexi area was relatively stable. However, the turmoil somewhat impacted the eastern part of the Hexi Corridor. Many rich and powerful families were developing their own forces there. For example, Bian Zhang and Han Sui from Jincheng Prefecture, representatives of powerful clans in the Hexi area, were kidnapped and then made leaders by the insurrectionary army of the Qiang and the Xiongnu led by Beigong Boyu and Li Wenhou. Later, Han Sui reorganized the troops to be his private force and occupied the region of Jincheng Prefecture and Guanlong① area, which threatened the Eastern Han Dynasty greatly. Influenced by Han Sui and Bian Zhang, rebellions broke out in Jincheng and Jiuquan prefectures one after the other. On this occasion, the local officials submitted their request to the central government for new institutions to strengthen administration of the Hexi area. In the 1st year of Xingping Era (194), the Eastern Han government set up Yongzhou (an administrative region) in Liangzhou and in the Four Prefectures in the Hexi Area respectively. Handan Shang from Chenliu Prefecture was appointed the Regional

① Guanlong refers to the area including the central part of Shaanxi and eastern part of Gansu.

府任命敦煌人张奂的儿子张猛出任,企图以此稳定河西。但邯郸商和张猛本来就有矛盾，他们到任后，又明争暗斗。建安十四年(209年),张猛杀害了邯郸商。建安十五年(210年),韩遂讨伐张猛,张猛畏罪自焚。但是,这次动乱时间较短，对社会生产的破坏不大，而对敦煌基本上没有产生什么影响。

Governor of Yongzhou①. At the same time, the Han government sent Zhang Meng, the son of Zhang Huan from Dunhuang, as the Governor of Wuwei Prefecture in an attempt to stabilize the Hexi area. So many conflicts, however, existed between the two men that Zhang Meng killed Handan Shang in the 14th year of Jian'an Era (209). In 210, Han Sui attacked Zhang Meng, who then committed suicide. Fortunately, the unrest was not long lived, bringing minimal destruction to production and almost exerting no effect on Dunhuang.

---

① Regional Inspector / Regional Governor / Prefect (*cishi* in Chinese): Originated from 106 BC (the 5th year of Yuanfeng Era of Emperor Wu during the Western Han Dynasty), it was a regular supervisory post intended to provide disciplinary surveillance over personnel in all units of territorial administration in a geographically prefixed Region (*bu* or *zhou*). The whole country was divided into thirteen *zhou* at the time. From the Eastern Han Dynasty, the Regional Inspector gradually became locally powerful governor who was able to deal with the administrative and military affairs. In 188, *cishi* was replaced by *zhoumu*. During the period of Three Kingdoms, *cishi* was rebuilt again. The Tang Dynasty added *dao* (circuit) on top, maintaining a three-tier system (*dao-zhou-xian*, circuit-prefecture-county) and renaming the previous *jun* (prefecture) as *zhou*. *Cishi* then was still established as a governor of a *zhou*. The Song adopted the same system as the Tang. During the Ming and Qing dynasties, *cishi* was another name of *zhizhou*.

魏晋南北朝时期的敦煌

Dunhuang During the Wei, Jin, and Northern and Southern Dynasties

东汉灭亡之后，中原在经过了军阀割据混战之后，最后形成了魏、蜀、吴三国鼎立的局面。敦煌地区在曹魏的统治之下，生产有了进一步的发展。西晋虽经历了短期的统一，但八王之乱、永嘉之乱很快就将西晋推入了灭亡。之后，晋室南迁，北方少数民族入主中原，大批中原人士西迁。在此后的十六国时期（304—439年），敦煌先后归属于前凉、前秦、后凉、西凉、北凉5个政权。

建安末年，曹操开始消灭甘肃东部的割据势力。此时，武威的颜俊、张掖的和鸾、酒泉的黄华等人都举郡反叛东汉。他们自号将军，互相攻击，比较安定的河西地区也变成了当地割据

After the fall of the Eastern Han Dynasty, a tripartite division of China among the kingdoms of Wei, Shu, and Wu, known as the Three Kingdoms (220–280), came into being as a result of internecine warlord fights in the Central Plains. Dunhuang underwent further production development under the rule of the Kingdom of Wei. The Western Jin (265–317) then enjoyed a short-lived national unity, which was subsequently destroyed by the War of the Eight Princes from 291 to 306 and the Yongjia Uprising in 311. The royal families of the Western Jin were forced to move southward, the tribes from the north moved into the Central Plains, and a large number of people from the Central Plains migrated westward. Thereafter, China entered the period of the Sixteen Kingdoms (304–439), and Dunhuang was under control by the Former Liang, the Former Qin, the Later Liang, the Western Liang, and the Northern Liang successively.

In 220, Cao Cao, the Chancellor of the Eastern Han Dynasty, prepared to attack the separatist forces in eastern Gansu. At the same time, Yan Jun in Wuwei, He Luan in Zhangye, and Huang Hua in Jiuquan led rebels against the Eastern Han government. They claimed themselves generals and attacked each other, causing the relatively stable Hexi area to be an arena for local separatist forces.

者角逐的战场。颜俊感到自己力量不足，于是就表面上归顺曹操，并把自己的母亲和儿子送到曹操那里做人质，企图借助曹操的力量消灭其他对手。但是,此时曹操正考虑攻伐占据四川的刘备,没有余力顾及河西的事情,于是就听取张既的意见，不理睬颜俊，以坐收其毙。结果,河西各割据势力在混战了一年多后,和鸾杀死了颜俊,武威的王秘又杀死了和鸾。河西各地的割据者在相互争斗中不断削弱着自己的力量。但是,这次混战并未能波及敦煌,敦煌豪族也没有主动介入斗争。

当张掖、武威、酒泉的割据势力在河西东部争斗不休时，敦煌仍然比较平静。直到这场混战的后期，敦煌张恭才卷入了战争。最初，敦煌太守马艾卒于任上，但河西东部地区战乱不断，隔断了敦煌与中央的联系。由于无法得到中央的任命，而敦煌郡的

Feeling weak by himself, Yan Jun pretended fealty to Cao Cao and allowed the latter to take his own mother and son as hostages in an attempt to defeat other competitors by means of Cao Cao's force. However, Cao Cao paid no attention to the Hexi area, as he was planning an attack on Liu Bei who was in Sichuan, so that in the end he did not accept Yan Jun's allegiance. Thus after more than one year of the melee among the various separatist forces in the Hexi area, He Luan killed Yan Jun, but was then killed in turn by Wang Mi from Wuwei. Separatist forces constantly undermined their own power during the infighting. However, Dunhuang was not affected, and the gentry in Dunhuang were not actively involved in the ongoing clashes.

Peace remained in Dunhuang while the separatist forces in Zhangye, Wuwei, and Jiuquan were fighting hard in the eastern part of the Hexi area. It was not until the later phase of the conflicts that Zhang Gong in Dunhuang was involved in the war. Initially, Ma Ai, the Governor of Dunhuang, died while in office, but the central government was unable to appoint a new one as the contact between Dunhuang and the imperial court was cut off due to the constant infighting in the eastern part of the Hexi area. As a result, Zhang Gong, the Officer of Personnel Evaluation Section in Dunhuang, was elected the Chief Official by the locals to manage Dunhuang on the basis of his knowledge and prudent behavior. During the Han Dynasty, the Officer of

功曹张恭的学识和品行素来为人所景仰，所以就被当地人推举为长史以管理敦煌。汉朝的时候，功曹为郡守的总务官，除掌管人事外，还得以参与一郡的政务。张恭为敦煌大族，其出任功曹，本身就已经说明敦煌豪族的强大。马艾死后，郡人又推张恭行长史事，意味着敦煌豪族掌握了敦煌郡的军政大权。

张恭上任后，派遣其子张就东去觐见曹操，以请求中央政府派遣敦煌太守赴任。这时，黄华和张进各自占据了酒泉和张掖郡，希望张恭能与他们进行联合。所以，黄华在张就到达酒泉的时候，将其扣留，并威胁其说服张恭。而张就始终没有屈服，并偷偷地写信给张恭，希望父亲不要考虑自己的安危，迅速出兵进攻黄华等人。张恭得到书信后，马上派兵进攻酒泉沙头、乾齐二县。随后，张恭亲自率军为先头部队提供后援。此外，

Personnel Evaluation Section was the governor's assistant, who was not only in charge of personnel, but also involved in governmental affairs of the prefecture. That Zhang Gong, from one of the local large families, got such a position indicated how powerful and influential the landlords were at that time and that these prominent families in Dunhuang then had mastery over local military and political power.

After Zhang Gong took office, he sent his son Zhang Jiu to visit Cao Cao, requesting that the imperial court appoint a governor. At the time, Huang Hua and Zhang Jin respectively occupying Jiuquan Prefecture and Zhangye Prefecture hoped that Zhang Gong could join them. They even detained Zhang Jiu and threatened him in order to influence Zhang Gong. Zhang Jiu refused to give in and secretly advised his father in a letter to grasp this opportunity to launch a surprise attack against Huang Hua regardless of his own security. Accepting his son's advice, Zhang Gong sent troops to attack Shatou and Qianqi counties in Jiuquan. Zhang then personally led his army to provide backup for the vanguard. In addition, he also sent two hundred cavalrymen to travel along the northern frontier fortresses in Jiuquan and then across the northern river at Zhangye to meet Yin Feng, the Governor of Dunhuang Prefecture appointed by the imperial government. In Zhangye, Zhang Jin had to ask for help from Huang Hua, but the latter hesitated to give a hand because he was afraid of rear counterattacks by Zhang Gong. Consequently, Huang Hua

张恭还派遣铁骑200,沿着酒泉北部边塞,出张掖北河,以迎接中央政府派遣的敦煌太守尹奉。占据张掖的张进连忙向黄华求救。黄华虽然想出兵救援,但又生怕张恭袭击其后方,只能降附于金城太守苏则,而张就最终也得以平安返回敦煌。

曹魏政权建立后,对河西的战略地位十分重视,因而对河西地区官员的任命也分外慎重。魏明帝时,任命曾为长安令时"清约有方,吏民畏而爱之"的仓慈为敦煌太守。仓慈到任后,大刀阔斧地采取了一系列的改革措施,取得了开发敦煌地区的显著效益。首先,针对东汉末年以来敦煌地区大姓雄张、地方机构瘫痪的现象,仓慈采取了"抑制豪强,抚恤贫寡"的政策,以削弱当地豪强大族的势力。为了保证这一政策能够付诸实施,仓慈在敦煌境内推行根据人口多少来计算赋税的办法,这样就废除了当地豪强所加在百姓身上的

surrendered to Su Ze, the Governor of Jincheng Prefecture. Eventually Zhang Jiu returned to Dunhuang safely.

After the establishment of the Wei regime (220–265), the strategic position of the Hexi area was realized and great attention was paid to the appointment of officials for the region. Emperor Ming of Wei appointed Cang Ci as the Governor of Dunhuang Prefecture, for he had a reputation for honesty and was respected by the local people when he served as the Magistrate of Chang'an County. After he was in office, Cang Ci put in place a series of drastic reforms, which brought significant benefits to the development of Dunhuang. Faced with two major problems—paralysis of the local government and the rise of powerful landlords in Dunhuang since the Eastern Han Dynasty—he adopted a policy of "suppressing the landlords and supporting the poor" to clamp down on the power of the local big families. To ensure the implementation of this policy, Cang Ci carried out a new taxation system based on a per capita calculation. In this way he abolished miscellaneous taxes inflicted on the common people by local landlords and lessened the burden on the populace. This measure guaranteed social stability and enhanced the governance of the Wei regime over Dunhuang. It was also helpful in changing the situation whereby local landlords owned the majority of fields while common people were virtually deprived of arable land.

Before Cang Ci took office, many traders

杂税，减轻了人民的负担。这一措施，使社会呈现安定局面，加强了曹魏政权对敦煌地区的统治能力，改变了此前当地豪强田地有余、小民无立锥之地的状况。

在仓慈上任之前，虽然有很多西域商人前来敦煌地区从事贸易活动，但是，由于敦煌长期没有地方长官进行管理，地方政府不能有效地保护外地商人的正常活动。而当地的豪强经常通过欺诈及不公平贸易等方式阻挠西域商人的正常经营活动，引起了西域诸国商人的不满，前来经商者锐减。针对此项弊端，仓慈立即采取措施，以确保西域商人的利益。如果西域等外地商人要在内地经商的话，敦煌地方政府便给他们发放称为“过所”的通行证；如果他们愿意在敦煌本地进行交易，敦煌郡政府以郡库所藏物品，与其进行公平合理的贸易。为了保证西域商人的人身安全，只要他们一进入敦煌境内，都能得到由当地政府委派吏民护送

from the Western Regions came and engaged in commercial activity in Dunhuang, but lacked protection by the local government because of the absence of a governor. Moreover, the local powerful landlords often obstructed these traders from normal business activities by fraud and unfair trade. Complaints arose and the number of traders from the Western Regions dropped sharply. Noticing this, Cang Ci took immediate measures against these practices to ensure the interests of these merchants. If the Western traders intended to travel to the Central Plains for business via Dunhuang, they would be granted an official pass named *guosuo* by the Dunhuang government. If they were willing to do business in Dunhuang, the local government would trade what was stored in the prefectural depot with them at a fair and reasonable price. In order to ensure their personal safety, the traders were escorted by official soldiers as long as they stayed in Dunhuang. Obviously, these measures ensured western traders their personal security and commercial interests, which consequently contributed to the active exchanges between the Western Regions and the Central Plains, and to the smooth flow of the Silk Road and prosperity of Dunhuang. With Cang Ci's tireless efforts, the trade and traffic between the Central Plains and the Western Regions returned to normal, creating an economic boom in Dunhuang. According to the *Records of the Three Kingdoms: Book of Wei, Annals of*

的待遇。显而易见,这些措施的实施,使外籍商人在河西或内地的经营活动获得了安全和利益的保障。这对于活跃中西交流、保证丝绸之路的畅通、繁荣敦煌地区的社会经济,都具有重要意义。经过仓慈的不懈努力,终于使东西贸易和交通恢复正常,使敦煌出现了繁荣兴旺的景象。根据《三国志·魏志·文帝本纪》记载,曹魏初期,曾有焉耆、于阗、鄯善、龟兹等西域国家向朝廷进贡,文帝甚至还得到了西域某国奉献的“径寸大珠”。

仓慈开发敦煌地区的政策被当地各族居民及西域商人所接受,收到了良好的效果。仓慈本人也由此深受各族人民的爱戴,史称“民夷翕然称其德惠”。当仓慈逝世的消息传来后,敦煌境内的人悲痛欲绝。西域商人得知这一噩耗后,聚集在戊己校尉及西域长史机构所在地举行哀悼仪式,有很多人以西域胡人的风俗以刀割耳、划面,以示悲痛。此外,西域胡商还为仓慈设立了专门的祭祀场所。各族人民对仓慈的感情感人肺腑,从一个侧面说明其对敦煌开发的成就之卓

Emperor Wen, during the early Wei, states in the Western Regions such as Yanqi, Khotan, Shanshan, and Qiuci (also known as Kucha) paid tribute to the imperial court, with Emperor Wen even receiving a large round precious stone presented by a state in the Western Regions.

The policies for the development of Dunhuang carried out by Cang Ci were supported by local residents of all ethnic groups and merchants from the Western Regions, which brought about positive results, and thus Cang Ci himself enjoyed tremendous popularity among the people. At the news of his death, people were so grief-stricken that some traders from the Western Regions gathered in the headquarters of *Wuji* Colonel and the Chief Official of the Western Regions, and held a mourning ceremony according to the custom of the nomadic groups such as scratching their ears or faces with knives. In addition, these traders created a shrine in his memory. People of all ethnic groups showed their love and respect for Cang Ci, illustrating the brilliant achievements he made for the development of Dunhuang and the benefits its people had enjoyed.

After Cang Ci passed away, Wang Qian from Tianshui and Zhao Ji from Jincheng were successively appointed as the Governor of Dunhuang Prefecture, but attained more limited achievements during

著和各族人民所得到的实惠。

仓慈死后，天水人王迁继任敦煌太守。王迁虽然竭力效法仓慈，但是，治绩不如仓慈。后来，金城人赵基接任敦煌太守，但是其作为还不如王迁。曹魏齐王嘉平（249—254年）年间，皇甫隆走马上任敦煌太守。皇甫隆到敦煌后，致力于发展当地农业生产，并积极改变当地的落后风俗，为开发河西做出了贡献。

虽然耧耕法早在汉武帝时就由赵过发明，并且已广泛应用于农业生产中，但当皇甫隆到敦煌前，当地百姓仍在沿用最原始的耕种方式，严重影响了农业生产。皇甫隆亲自为当地农民示范，以推广先进的耧耕法。耧耕法在敦煌施行后，节省了过半的劳力，而所收获的粮食却增加了五成，收到了事半功倍的效果。此外，敦煌地区

their tenure. During the Jiaping Era of the Kingdom of Wei (249–254), Huangfu Long served as the Governor of Dunhuang Prefecture, making contributions to the development of local agricultural production and bringing positive changes in backward local customs.

Firstly, he personally demonstrated *lougeng*① to local farmers after he noticed local people were still following the most primitive farming methods, which seriously hindered agricultural production. With that, more than half of the labor was saved, and the grain harvest increased by fifty percent. Secondly, after a careful investigation of the fields, he introduced the drip irrigation method (*yan* irrigation). He found that the land in Dunhuang was abundant in alkali and when farmers irrigated this type of land with melting snow from the Qilian Mountains, they would "accumulate enough water, moisten the land, and then do the farming." However, the side effect of this primitive irrigation was land compaction, which consequently was very labor intensive for both humans and animals, and seriously affected food production as well. Thus, by the new drip irrigation method, the production conditions in Dunhuang significantly improved. Finally, Huangfu Long

① *Lougeng* refers to the animal-drawn ploughing, an advanced method of tillage invented by Zhao Guo as early as the Western Han Dynasty.

土地砂碱成分大，当农民利用祁连山雪水灌溉时，往往“灌溉滀水，使极濡洽，然后乃耕”。这种原始的浇灌方式，产生的副作用是地块容易板结，这不但增大了人畜的劳动强度，而且严重影响了粮食产量。皇甫隆通过实地考察后，认识到了这里土地含砂碱成分较大的特点，因地制宜，一改过去蓄水灌溉的传统方法，推广薄水漫浇法（即“衍溉”）。这样，敦煌地区的生产条件得到了明显改善。皇甫隆还发现敦煌当地有一些陈规陋习，需要立即革除之。如妇女在做裙子时，“挛缩如羊肠，用布一匹”。用一整匹布来做条裙子，只能如同羊肠一样盘结在身上，这既不美观，又十分浪费，而且活动起来也极不方便。于是，皇甫隆以郡太守的名义下令当地妇女禁止穿这种羊肠裙，改穿在中原地区流行的简易裙。皇甫隆在敦煌地区所实施的举措，对河西尤其对敦煌地区的开发起到了不可低估的作用，缩小了敦煌地区与中原的差距。

曹魏咸熙二年(265 年)，司马炎代魏称帝，建立晋朝，史称西晋。西晋在河西设置凉州刺史部，敦煌属凉州刺史所管。西晋初年，东吴降将吾彦被任命为敦煌太守。在吾彦

found certain outdated local customs needed abolishing immediately, such as women's dresses which looked like a sheep's gut wrapping all over the body. Since a whole piece of cloth was needed in making such a dress, and the dress was neither attractive nor economical and caused much difficulty for women, Huangfu Long ordered the local women to wear the simply-cut skirt which was popular in the Central Plains. These initiatives implemented in Dunhuang greatly contributed to the development of the Hexi area, helping to narrow the gap between Dunhuang and the Central Plains.

In the 2nd year of Xianxi Era (265), Sima Yan established the Western Jin. Then Command of the Regional Governor of Liangzhou was set up in the Hexi area; Dunhuang was under its jurisdiction. In the early years of the Western Jin, Wu Yan was appointed the Governor of Dunhuang Prefecture. He laid emphasis on agricultural production and led local farmers to farm the land, which further developed the rural economy so that people were living a sufficient and rich life. Meanwhile, the society was relatively stable. Thus Wu Yan won trust and respect from the local people. His achievements and virtues were

担任敦煌太守期间，他亲自带领当地百姓从事农业生产，使得敦煌一带的农业经济进一步发展，出现了“家给人足，晏然富庶”的局面。同时，社会秩序也比较安定，百姓对吾彦非常信赖和爱戴，所以《晋书》中就称赞他“镇抚数年，恩威并著”。

晋惠帝永宁元年（301年），西晋朝廷任命安定乌氏（今甘肃平凉西北）人张轨出任护羌校尉、凉州刺史。张轨年少时就好学，并且很有胆识。他到任后，一方面积极发展农业，另一方面也重视加强当地的军事建设，以保护凉州等地的安全。由于张轨对凉州的辛勤治理，使得凉州成为富庶、安定之所。而在西晋元康年间，司马氏集团内部发生了诸王争权夺利的“八王之乱”。八王之乱持续了16年的时间，极大地动摇了西晋的统治基础，各地方势力及北方诸民族纷纷起来反晋。一时间，中原地区烽烟四起。为了躲避战乱，关中和

recorded in the *Book of Jin*.

In the 1st year of Yongning Era of Emperor Hui (301), the Western Jin court appointed Zhang Gui from Wushi (the northwest area of present-day Pingliang in Gansu) as the Colonel of the Qiang Tribe and Regional Governor of Liangzhou. Since childhood, Zhang Gui had been studious in learning and courageous in action. After his arrival, he was actively involved in the development of agriculture while he simultaneously attached great importance to strengthening local military construction to guarantee the safety of Liangzhou, making Liangzhou prosperous and stable. Meanwhile, during the Yuankang Era (291–299), a power struggle among feudal princes from the Sima clan led to the War of Eight Princes in the Central Plains that lasted for 16 years and greatly undermined the rule of the Western Jin. Forces in various regions and from northern ethnic groups rebelled against the imperial court. For a time, revolts were pervasive in the Central Plains and large numbers of aristocratic families and common people were forced to move westward to Liangzhou and other places in the Hexi area so as to avoid the upheaval caused by war. In the 2nd year of Jianxing Era (314), Zhang Gui died in Liangzhou. His son Zhang Shi succeeded him as the Regional Governor of Liangzhou, establishing the regime of the Former Liang with Dunhuang under its jurisdiction.

Although Liangzhou was the ruling center

中原的世家大族及普通民众纷纷西迁到凉州等地以避乱。建兴二年(314 年),张轨卒于凉州,其子张寔继任凉州刺史,正式建立前凉政权,而敦煌正在前凉的管辖范围之内。

前凉张氏的统治中心虽在凉州,但敦煌仍是当时西北地区的重镇。张轨时期就曾大量依靠敦煌人士如宋配、阴充、阴澹、氾瑗等人充当谋士。由于这些人的辅佐,河西生产有了较大发展,人口有所增加,使张轨能"威著西州,化行河右"。西晋建兴十二年(324 年),张骏执掌前凉政权后,不仅提拔宋配、氾瑗等人为谋士,还在敦煌兴办教育,促进了当地文化事业和经济的发展。建兴三十三年(345 年),张骏将敦煌、晋昌、高昌三郡和西域都护、戊己校尉、玉门大护军三营合并成为沙州,任命胡校尉杨宣为刺史,治所就在敦煌。据唐朝所修撰的《沙州都督府图经》记载,杨宣任内,曾组织民众兴修水利,建五石斗门,堰水溉田,建成长 15 里的"阳开渠";他还曾用自家的万斛粮食买石头修理城北北

of the Former Liang, Dunhuang still maintained its strategic importance in the western area at that time. During Zhang Gui's administration, he relied heavily on advisers from Dunhuang such as Song Pei, Yin Chong, Yin Dan, and Fan Yuan. Assisted by these men, Zhang Gui had "prestige and popularity west of the Yellow River" for agricultural production greatly progressed and the population increased. In the 12th year of Jianxing Era of Western Jin Dynasty (324), Zhang Jun came to power over the Former Liang. He not only promoted Song Pei, Fan Yuan, and others to be his consultants, but also set up schools in Dunhuang, which facilitated local education, culture and economy. In the 33rd year of Jianxing Era (345), Zhang Jun merged prefectures of Dunhuang, Jinchang and Gaochang with military jurisdictions under the command of the Protector-General of the Western Regions, the *Wuji* Colonel, and the Grand Commandant of Yumen, renaming it Shazhou. Yang Xuan was appointed the Regional Governor of Shazhou, working in Dunhuang. According to the *Pictorial Records of Superior Prefecture of Shazhou* compiled during the Tang Dynasty, Yang Xuan actively promoted water conservation construction in Dunhuang. He organized the local population to develop irrigation infrastructure, and build sluices (*doumen*

府渠上的平河斗门。斗门由垒石做成，长40步，宽3丈，高3丈，到唐朝时仍在正常使用，可见其坚固程度。此外，沙州太守阴澹也曾于任内在城西南修7里长渠，可将州城西南的水引至西北的水渠，灌溉城西的大片土地，使这一地区的百姓受益不少，安居乐业，故此渠被称为“阴安渠”。

前凉到了张天锡时，关中的前秦苻坚政权灭掉了前燕，为全面征伐前凉解除了后顾之忧。前秦建元十二年(376年)，在前秦大军压境的情况下，张天锡战败投降，包括敦煌在内的河西地区归入前秦治下。前秦灭前凉后，苻坚派遣梁熙为持节、西中郎将、凉州刺史，领护西羌校尉，镇守凉州等地。梁熙向西域各国派遣使节，以宣

in Chinese) used for water irrigation, and 15-*li*-long "Yangkai Canal;" he also traded his own grain for stones to repair the Pinghe Sluice over Beifu Canal. *Doumen*, built on a stone base, was forty *bu* long, three *zhang*① wide, and three *zhang* high; they were still being used in the Tang Dynasty. In addition, Yin Dan, the Governor of Shazhou, organized people to build a seven-*li*-long canal in the southwest of the town, known as the "Yin'an Canal," through which the water southwest of the prefecture flowed to the northwest, irrigating large tracts of land, and benefiting the local populace considerably.

During the period of Zhang Tianxi's rule of the Former Liang, the Former Qin in Guanzhong② under the control of Fu Jian exterminated the Former Yan, which wiped out the barriers to the complete conquest of the Former Liang. Zhang Tianxi, confronted with massive troops from the Former Qin, surrendered in the 12th year of Jianyuan Era of the Former Qin (376), and the Hexi area, including Dunhuang, was annexed by the Former Qin. Fu Jian then appointed Liang Xi as an official commissioned with special authority, the West Commandant, Regional Governor of Liangzhou, and Concurrent Colonel of the West Qiang Tribe to guard Liangzhou and its adjacent areas. Liang Xi sent envoys to other states in the

---

① *Li*, *bu* and *zhang* are Chinese length units. One *li* equals to 500 meters, one *bu* equals to approx. 1.7 meters, and one *zhang* equals to approx. 3.3 meters.

② Guanzhong is a historical region of China corresponding to the lower valley of the Weihe River. It refers to the central part of present-day Shannxi.

扬苻坚的威德，并以绢帛等财物分赐给各国国王。不久,西域就有10多个国家前往长安进贡，其中车师前部王、鄯善王亲自前往长安朝贡。鄯善王休密驮等人看到前秦的宫宇壮丽、仪卫严整，敬服异常。因此,他们就建言苻坚，认为虽然此时大宛诸国也向前秦进贡，但并非真心归附，希望前秦能够延续汉朝在西域设置都护的惯例,并承诺如果前秦出兵,他们将承担引导的任务。于是建元十八年(382年),苻坚派遣骁骑将军吕光为持节，都督西讨诸军事，与陵江将军姜飞、轻骑将军彭晃等率军7万余人,出征西域。为巩固经营西域的基地，苻坚迁江汉百姓1万户、中原百姓7000余户到敦煌。这是继汉武帝之后，对敦煌又一次大规模的移民。大批中原士族和百姓的到来，又一次促进了敦煌地区的开发。

383年，苻坚在淝水之战中战败，前秦帝国也随之土崩瓦解。前秦所属各族将

Western Regions with the aim of promoting Fu Jian as a benevolent ruler, and of bestowing gifts including silk on rulers. Soon, more than ten states paid tribute to the Former Qin, among whom the Ruler of the Nearer Jushi and the King of Shanshan went to the capital of Chang'an in person. They were so impressed with the magnificent palaces and ceremonial guards in Chang'an that they advised Fu Jian to conquer other states and continue the practice of setting Protectorate in the Western Regions, because although these states such as Dayuan were friendly and paid tribute to the Former Qin, they did not hold true allegiance. They even promised their services as guides if the Former Qin dispatched troops. Then, in the 18th year of Jianyuan Era (382), Fu Jian sent Lü Guang as an official commissioned with special authority, the Commander-in-Chief of Armies Attacking the Western Regions, together with Jiang Fei, the *Lingjiang* General, and Peng Huang, the *Qingqi* General, to lead an army of about 70,000 infantry soldiers and cavalry soldiers to the Western Regions. He also ordered 10,000 households of commoners from the Jianghan region in the South of China and over 7,000 from the Central Plains to migrate to Dunhuang. The influx of large numbers of intellectuals and common people advanced production technologies so as to promote the development of Dunhuang. This was the second large-scale migration after that during the reign of Emperor Wu in the Western

领纷纷拥兵割据，先是鲜卑慕容垂在河北地区脱离前秦，接着羌族首领姚苌出奔渭北，匈奴刘卫辰率众割据河朔之地。河西鲜卑乞伏国仁听到苻坚战败，也召集部众10余万人，控制了陇西。短短的一两年时间内，北方各地先后出现了后燕、西燕、后秦、西秦及夏等几个少数民族政权。中原的大动乱，也对河西地区产生了影响。前秦凉州刺史梁熙，这时杀掉了前秦宗室、流放在西海郡的行唐公苻洛，准备以河西之地割据自保。而张天锡的儿子张大豫在淝水之战后，得到长水校尉王穆的帮助，暗地里潜回河西，投奔了鲜卑秃发部，继而藏匿于武威附近的魏安，准备起兵河西，以恢复前凉张氏的统治。而此时，苻坚所遣征伐西域的吕光的军队也正在东归的路上，河西地区的形势一时间极度复杂。

Han Dynasty.

Fu Jian was defeated in the Battle near the Feishui River in 383, which symbolized a complete collapse of the Former Qin. Afterwards, the leaders of ethnic groups subjected to the Former Qin began to set up their own separate powers. At first, Murong Chui from the Xianbei minority north of the Yellow River broke away from the Former Qin, followed by Yao Chang, leader of the Qiang people, and Liu Weichen, chieftain of the Xiongnu, who all declared rebellions. Hearing the news that Fu Jian was defeated, Qifu Guoren from the Xianbei in the Hexi area assembled more than 100,000 followers, establishing an independent state and putting Longxi (an area west of the Longshan Mountain) under his control. Within the next year or two, there appeared many ethnic states such as the Later Yan, the Western Yan, the Later Qin, the Western Qin and the Xia throughout the northern part of China. The upheaval in the Central Plains had an impact on the Hexi area. Liang Xi, the Regional Governor of Liangzhou from the Former Qin, prepared to protect himself in the Hexi area by killing Fu Luo, the Duke of Xingtang from the Former Qin, who was exiled in Xihai Prefecture. Meanwhile, with the help from Wang Mu, the Colonel of Changshui, Zhang Dayu, the son of the Former Liang's last prince Zhang Tianxi, secretly arrived in the Hexi area where he sought shelter with the Tufa troops of the Xianbei. He then made secret preparations in Wei'an near Wuwei Prefecture for a revolt to resume the rule of the

吕光从长安出发西征，经过河西走廊，出玉门关，经鄯善和车师而到达焉耆，焉耆王泥流请降。随后，吕光引兵包围了西域大国龟兹国都，龟兹王以财宝为诱饵，请得周围小国数十万人前来营救，但也为吕光所败。至前秦建元二十年（384 年）九月，吕光攻克龟兹，塔里木盆地周边诸国大为震动，纷纷前来请降，“王侯降者三十余国”。吕光出征西域，是为了扩大前秦声威，实现恢复汉朝设置西域都护的传统，同时也是为了确保前秦后方秦陇的安全。而在吕光攻破龟兹后，曾有意留在西域称王，但其部下多来自中原，不肯留在西域，加以苻坚引军南下攻晋，不知胜败，部下将领都劝说吕光返回中原。于是，吕光先是扶立原龟兹王之弟为王，并为诸国改换了汉朝所赐的旌节

Former Liang. At the same time, the troops led by Lü Guang were on their way returning eastward from the Western Regions. Thus, the situation in the Hexi area was extremely complex.

Lü Guang and his troops left Chang'an on a military expedition through the Hexi Corridor, the Yumen Pass, and the Kingdoms of Shanshan and Jushi; they finally reached the state of Yanqi (Karasahr), where Ni Liu, the ruler of Yanqi, begged for surrender. Subsequently, Lü Guang's troops surrounded the capital city of Qiuci, which forced the King of Qiuci to ask for help from its adjacent states by luring them with treasure, but they were all defeated. By September① of the 20th year of Jianyuan Era of the Former Qin (384), Lü Guang conquered Qiuci, shocking the other states along the rim of the Tarim Basin so much that they came to surrender in succession. The original purpose of Lü Guang's military expedition was to expand the prestige and ensure the safety of the Former Qin by re-establishing the Protectorate of the Western Regions which began in the Han Dynasty. After conquering Qiuci, Lü Guang changed his mind and intended to become the ruler of the Western Regions himself. His followers, however, refused to settle there since most of them came from the Central Plains and were homesick. In the meantime, Fu Jian led his

① The month and date before 1912 expressed in the book are set in the lunar calendar.

后，于385年初，押运着两万驼财宝和万匹骏马东返。当吕光行至高昌时，太守杨翰开城迎降，在这里吕光得到了苻坚战败的消息。吕光听从部将杜进的建议，利用“赴难”的旗号急速东进。一路上，敦煌太守姚静、晋昌太守李纯都以郡降附吕光。至此年九月，吕光大军进军到酒泉，在这里遭到了梁熙军队的抵抗。吕光在政治上有堂而皇之的理由，而更为重要的是其手下还有7.5万多名久经沙场的劲旅，所以很快就击败了梁熙的军队。此后，武威太守彭济擒获梁熙，投降吕光。吕光顺利进入凉州，自称凉州刺史、护羌都尉，开始了在河西的统治。

吕光虽然占领了河西地区，但同时还有多种势力并存于河西。原来逃匿在魏安的张大豫、王穆，这时在焦松、张济等人的拥护下，

army southward to attack the Jin Dynasty, but no news came whether he succeeded or not; his subordinate generals then persuaded Lü Guang to return to the Central Plains. On such an occasion, Lü Guang first supported the brother of the former King of Qiuci as the new king and also changed the *jingjie*① granted in the Han Dynasty. Lü Guang started to head back eastward in early 385, with abundant spoils and about 10,000 horses acquired in the Western Regions. When arriving in Gaochang, Lü Guang was met with a welcome surrender from Yang Han, the Governor of Gaochang Prefecture; he also received the news that Fu Jian was defeated. In response to the proposal offered by Du Jin, his subordinate general, Lü Guang moved swiftly eastward under the pretext of "rescuing Fu Jian." Along the way, Yao Jing, the Governor of Dunhuang Prefecture, and Li Chun, the Governor of Jinchang Prefecture, surrendered. By September of 385, Lü Guang's army reached Jiuquan where they were confronted with Liang Xi's troops. However, Lü Guang soon defeated Liang Xi, because he was skilled in military strategy, high-sounding in political reason and more importantly, because his troops of more than 75,000 were battle-hardened. Thereafter, Peng Ji, the Governor of Wuwei Prefecture, captured Liang

① *Jingjie* refers to a ceremonial gift bestowed on administrative governors by the national government. It represented that the holder had right to fulfill the political and military power.

起兵攻陷昌松郡(今武威东南),进逼凉州。不久,祁连都尉(今武威、张掖之间)严纯、建康太守(治所在今甘肃高台县骆驼城)李隰起兵响应。后来张大豫战败被杀,王穆奔逃建康。387年,王穆占领酒泉,敦煌大姓索嘏、名士郭瑀起兵响应,运粮支援酒泉。同年,西平太守(治所在今青海西宁)康宁自称匈奴王。而原吕光麾下大将彭晃,也发动叛乱,东结康宁、西通王穆。吕光凭借军事力量的强大,东征西讨,历时3年,终于镇压了各地的反抗,占有了整个河西地区。389年,吕光自称"三河王",设置自丞、郎之下的百官,在境内发布大赦命令,改年号为"麟嘉",正式建立起割据政权。麟嘉七年(395年),凉州内乱,凉州及张掖以东,有数千户西奔敦煌、晋昌,为敦煌又一次输入了大量的人力。至396年,吕

Xi and surrendered so that Lü Guang easily occupied Liangzhou, claiming the titles of the Regional Governor of Liangzhou and Commandant of the Qiang Tribe, and establishing his reign in the Hexi area.

In fact, many other forces still co-existed in the Hexi area. With the backing of Jiao Song, Zhang Ji, and others, Zhang Dayu and Wang Mu, who had been hiding in Wei'an, revolted and occupied Changsong Prefecture (southeast of present-day Wuwei) to advance on Liangzhou. Soon, Yan Chun, the Commandant of Qilian (Qilian refers to the area between present-day Wuwei and Zhangye), and Li Xi, the Governor of Jiankang Prefecture (the seat being in present-day Camel City in Gaotai County of Gansu) responded decisively to the revolt. Later, Zhang Dayu was defeated and killed. Wang Mu fled to Jiankang and then occupied Jiuquan in 387 where he received the support from Suo Jia and Guo Yu who had revolted in response in Dunhuang. In the same year, Kang Ning, the Governor of Xiping Prefecture (his office being in present-day Xining, Qinghai) claimed Attila, Head of the Xiongnu. Meanwhile, Peng Huang, the former general under the command of Lü Guang, also rebelled by allying with Kang Ning in the east and Wang Mu in the west. Faced with such a complex situation in the Hexi area, Lü Guang spent three years suppressing revolts and occupying the entire Hexi area by his powerful military force. In 389, Lü Guang claimed himself the Prince of Sanhe, organized system of civil

光又自称天王，改元龙飞，建国号为大凉，史称后凉。

397年，吕光亲率大军进击西秦乞伏乾归，其弟吕岩兵败被杀，吕光被迫引兵退还凉州。而早已占据河湟地区的鲜卑秃发乌孤趁机进兵广武郡，进而占领金城郡，自称大都督、大单于、西平王，从东面形成了对后凉政权的威胁。吕光派兵讨伐，反为所败。接着，吕光在凉州城内杀死了匈奴卢水胡人首领沮渠罗仇兄弟。罗仇之侄沮渠蒙逊率参加罗仇兄弟葬礼的卢水胡万余人，于临松结盟起兵，蒙逊之兄男成在晋昌起兵响应。男成推举建康太守段业为大都督、龙骧大将军、凉州牧，据有建康。不久，段业建国号为凉，史称北凉，并改年号为神玺。蒙逊起兵受挫后，率众归附段业，成为后凉西面的劲敌。398年，后

service officials lower than Counselor-in-Chief and court attendant, announced an amnesty order in the territory, and began the Lingjia Era. A separatist regime was formally established. In the 7th year of Linjia Era (395), Liangzhou witnessed civil strife which caused several thousand households to flee from Liangzhou and the area east of Zhangye to Dunhuang and Jinchang, providing Dunhuang with more manpower again. In 396, Lü Guang claimed himself Heavenly Prince, signifying a claim to the imperial title. He changed the era name to Longfei and founded the Da Liang, known as the Later Liang in history.

In 397, Lü Guang launched a major attack against Qifu Qiangui, the prince of the Western Qin. In the war, Lü Yan, Lü Guang's younger brother, was killed, and Lü Guang had to retreat to Liangzhou. Tufa Wugu, prince of the Xianbei, who had occupied the Hehuang area①, captured prefectures of Guangwu and Jincheng, where he claimed himself the Grand Commander-in-Chief, Grand Chanyu and *Xiping* Prince, threatening the Later Liang to the east. Lü Guang sent his troops to attack but failed. Subsequently, Lü Guang executed Juqu Luochou and his brother, the leaders of the Lushui Hu people, a branch of the Xiongnu, in Liangzhou. This provided the pretext for Juqu Mengxun, the nephew of the

① Hehuang area refers to a large area located between the upstream of the Yellow River and its tributaries Huangshui River and Datong River.

凉敦煌太守孟敏、晋昌太守王德举郡投降段业。此时，吕光所控制的疆域只剩下武威一郡。399年，吕光病死。在面对强大外患的情况下，吕氏兄弟内部又为争夺天王王位互相争斗不已，最终，吕光的侄子吕隆掌握了政权。但经过多次政治动乱，吕氏后凉政权的实力更为削弱。401年，后秦姚兴派遣陇西公姚硕德领兵伐凉。七月，后秦军至凉州，后凉大败，巴西公吕陀率2.5万多人降于后秦。到九月的时候，在凉州城内的关中人多有与后秦里应外合之心。吕隆外有强敌，内有叛臣，统治已无法继续维持，于是遣使请降于后秦。虽然吕隆投降后秦，但只是派遣50家文武旧臣及子弟入长安充当人质，而吕隆本人还居住在凉州。到了403年，因沮渠

Juqu brothers, to lead more than ten thousand Lushui Hu people to rebel in Linsong Prefecture. Juqu Nancheng, Juqu Mengxun's brother, joined in the rebellion in Jinchang Prefecture and recommended Duan Ye, the Governor of Jiankang Prefecture, to be the Grand Commander-in-Chief, *Longxiang* General-in-Chief and Regional Governor of Liangzhou①. Soon Duan Ye changed the era name to Shenxi, signifying a declaration of independence and the establishment of the Northern Liang. The new regime was then strengthened after Juqu Mengxun surrendered to Duan Ye with his troops, and formed a huge threat to the Later Liang in the west. In 398, Meng Min, the Governor of Dunhuang Prefecture, and Wang De, the Governor of Jinchang Prefecture from the Later Liang, surrendered, too. Until then, a large portion of territory in Lü Guang's control was taken over by the Northern Liang except for Wuwei Prefecture. Lü Guang died of illness in 399, causing the brothers from Lü's clan to begin a pitched struggle for the title of Heavenly Prince in spite of strong aggressors pressing in from all sides. Ultimately, Lü Long, the

① Regional Governor of Liangzhou (Liangzhou *mu*): *Zhoumu*, abbr. *mu*. During the reign of Emperor Wu of Han Dynasty, the whole country was divided into thirteen regions / provinces (*zhou* in Chinese), with an Regional Inspector (*cishi*) to supervise the officials in each of regions. *Zhoumu* or *mu* was originated in 7 BC, superseding less prestigious Regional Inspector (*cishi*). Thereafter, the two titles alternated irregularly and evolved into the post for the governor of a region. By the end of the Northern and Southern Dynasties, the title was displaced by *cishi* again.

蒙逊等势力频繁攻击凉州，而城内又出现了乏粮困境，吕隆只好在这年的七月率僚属入居长安，后凉灭亡。

在获得敦煌和晋昌后，段业于敦煌、晋昌以西设立沙州，并以孟敏为沙州刺史。孟敏则以敦煌大族李暠为敦煌郡所属效谷县的县令。孟敏出任刺史后，曾在敦煌城西南18里修建了长20里的水渠，引甘泉水灌溉农田，人称“孟授渠”。孟敏的德政促进了当地农业的发展，使百姓受惠良多，所以在神玺二年（398年）孟敏死后，当地百姓为其立庙致祭，称为“孟庙”。此后，敦煌护军冯翊人郭谦、沙州治中敦煌人索仙等人，推举李暠为宁朔将军、敦煌太守。

在李暠出任敦煌太守期间，段业自称凉王。由于段业和沮渠蒙逊不信任李暠及敦煌大族，所以段业曾派遣索嗣代替李暠出任敦煌太守。为此，敦煌大族

nephew of Lü Guang, seized power. But constant political turmoil weakened the Later Liang's regime. In 401, Yao Xing from the Later Qin sent Yao Shuode, the Duke of Longxi, to launch an attack to the Later Liang. In July of the same year, the army of the Later Qin arrived in Liangzhou and the Later Liang suffered a crushing defeat with more than 25,000 soldiers under the command of Lü Tuo, the Duke of Baxi, surrendering to the Later Qin. In September, people from Guanzhong living in Liangzhou intended to collaborate with the Later Qin. Confronted with powerful attackers outside and traitors inside, Lü Long had to request submission to the Later Qin by sending emissaries to Chang'an as hostages, including approximately 50 officials and their younger generation, while Lü Long was still in Liangzhou. By July of 403, due to frequent attacks from Juqu Mengxun's forces and the extreme shortage of food supplies, Lü Long and the rest of his followers were forced to retreat to Chang'an, marking the end of the Later Liang.

After occupying Dunhuang and Jinchang, Duan Ye established Shazhou to the west of Dunhuang and Jinchang. He appointed Meng Min as the Regional Governor of Shazhou, who then appointed Li Hao from a big clan in Dunhuang as the Magistrate of Xiaogu County under the administration of Dunhuang Prefecture. Meng Min made great achievements in promoting the development of local agriculture. He was in charge of the construction

联合起来进行抵制。当索嗣到达敦煌后，被李暠打得大败，迫使段业不得不杀索嗣以拉拢李暠，并任命他为持节、"都督凉兴已西诸军事、镇西将军，领护西夷校尉"。这样，以李暠为代表的敦煌汉人大族就正式取得对当地的统治权。紧接着，在天玺二年(400 年)十一月，晋昌太守唐瑶又移檄凉州各郡，推举李暠为大都督、大将军、凉公领秦凉二州牧，护羌校尉。于是，李暠在境内进行大赦，建年庚子，建立了独立于北凉政权的割据政权——西凉。敦煌在历史上第一次成为一个独立政权的都城。

西凉立国之前，河西走廊以汉民为最多。后凉发生动乱时，河西走廊东部的汉人又有很多避乱西迁到敦煌。这样敦煌一带又成了河西走廊地区汉民集中的地区，这就为西凉立国奠定了基础。后凉崩溃时，河西走廊中部已被

of a 20-*li*-long canal in the southwest of Dunhuang for farmland irrigation, which was called Mengshou Canal, granted by Mr. Meng. Local people benefited from Meng Min's benevolent measures so greatly that they built a memorial temple in his honor named Temple of Meng after his death in the 2nd year of Shenxi Era (398). Later, Li Hao was recommended to be the *Ningshuo* General and Governor of Dunhuang Prefecture by Guo Qian, the Military Protector of Dunhuang, and Suo Xian, the Assistant Governor of Shazhou.

When Li Hao was served as the Governor of Dunhuang Prefecture, Duan Ye claimed himself the Prince of Liang. Since Duan Ye and Juqu Mengxun mistrusted Li Hao and the gentries in Dunhuang, Suo Si was sent to replace Li Hao as the Governor of Dunhuang Prefecture. However, he met with resistance and was defeated by Li Hao. Duan Ye was then forced to kill Suo Si to forge an alliance with Li Hao, who was then appointed as an official commissioned with special authority, *Zhenxi* General, and Concurrent Colonel of the Western Tribes to manage military affairs in Dunhuang. As a result, Li Hao, as the representative of Han people, gained the official right to administrate Dunhuang. In November of the 2nd year of Tianxi Era (400), Li Hao was elected the Grand Commander-in-Chief, General-in-Chief, Duke of Liang, Concurrent Regional Governor of Qinzhou and Liangzhou, and Colonel of the Qiang Tribe by Tang Yao, the Governor of Jinchang Prefecture, and some

卢水胡所占领，敦煌汉族人民为抵制卢水胡势力的西来，于是就迅速支持李暠，建立起了西凉政权。正是因为西凉政权是在汉族大族和民众支持下建立起来的，所以政权建立之后，在名义上始终接受东晋的统治。李暠曾先后两次派人上表东晋朝廷，表示要奉东晋的正朔。

因为西凉主要是由河西汉族建立起来的政权，所以立国后非常重视农业生产和传统的儒家文化。西凉政权统治时期，建立了县、乡、里三级行政管理机构，实行严密的编户制度，并鼓励生产，敦煌地区出现了五谷丰收、百姓乐业的景象。李暠在立国之初，即派兵屯守阳关、玉门关，并在附近实行屯田，以作为新政权的第一项重要措施。在李暠称凉公之初，他在敦煌的南门外新建靖恭堂，作为听政、阅武之所。堂内悬挂历代圣帝名王、忠臣孝子、烈士贞女的画像，李暠亲自为画像作序。此外，还“立泮宫，增高门学生五百

administrators in other prefectures. Li Hao accepted the rulership, declared an amnesty in his territory, initiated the Gengzi Era, and thus established the Western Liang, a new separatist regime independent from the Northern Liang. It was the first time in Chinese history that Dunhuang had become a capital city of an independent regime.

Before the founding of the Western Liang, the majority of residents along the Hexi Corridor were Han people. Some people of Han ethnicity from the eastern Hexi Corridor came to Dunhuang to seek shelter when there was unrest in the Later Liang. Dunhuang naturally became a place where Han people gathered, which laid the foundation for the establishment of the Western Liang. However, the central part of the Hexi Corridor was occupied by the Lushui Hu people when the Later Liang disintegrated. In order to prevent the Lushui Hu people from migrating westward, the ethnic Han in Dunhuang gave Li Hao their support. It was precisely because of the Western Liang being established through the support of the Han people that the Western Liang nominally accepted the rule of the Eastern Jin. Li Hao sent messengers twice to express his obedience to central government.

After its establishment, the Western Liang attached great importance to agricultural production and traditional Confucian values. Three-tiered administrative bodies of county, town, and village with a strict household

人”。不仅如此，在西凉政权中，还重用当时的著名的儒士，如刘昞，在酒泉隐居时，有受业弟子500余人，著有《略记》《凉书》《敦煌实录》等书；再如宋繇，前凉末年在酒泉时，“闭塞诵书，昼夜不倦，博通经史，诸子群言，靡不余览”。他是李暠最亲近的大臣，李暠临终前就以他为顾命大臣。

西凉政权在李暠统治时期，重农兴儒，团结内部以对抗外敌，境内出现了一派兴旺安定的景象。于阗、鄯善等西域王国也来此朝贡，敦煌俨然有都城之派。但毕竟敦煌地狭人稀，人力、物力有限，所以卢水胡沮渠蒙逊取代段业，控制北凉政权之后（401—439年），北凉对西凉构成很大威胁，使得李暠不得不于建初元年（405年）迁都酒泉。此次迁都，西凉政权从敦煌带走的人户有2.3万之多，严重削弱了敦煌的实力。再加上西凉将注意力转向东方，敦煌失去了经营西域的

registration system were set up. Dunhuang prospered and people were happy to work. As the first important measure on agriculture since the founding of the Western Liang, soldiers were dispatched to garrison the Yangguan and the Yumen passes and to reclaim the vast wasteland in the vicinity. As for education and culture, Li Hao built Jing Gong Hall outside the south gate of Dunhuang as early as proclaiming himself the Duke of Liang, where he discussed political affairs and reviewed military activities. Portraits of wise emperors, saints, loyal and dutiful persons, and virgin martyrs were hung on the walls inside the hall. Li Hao personally wrote inscriptions to these portraits. In addition, he set up *pangong*, a school of higher education, with an enrollment of 500 advanced students. Moreover, he installed renowned scholars in important positions, such as Liu Bing who taught more than 500 disciples and wrote such books as *Brief Records*, *Book of the Former Liang*, and *Historical Records of the Hexi Area* when living in seclusion in Jiuquan. Another example of a learned man was Song Yao who had never been tired of reading books day and night and thoroughly understood the classics, historical books and opinions from previous scholars. He was the closest minister to Li Hao , and was trusted and appointed to help manage state affairs when Li Hao was dying.

During Li Hao's reign, the Western Liang was thriving and prosperous, based on his attention to agriculture and education as well as

基地作用。因此,当417年李暠去世之后,敦煌也随之衰败。嘉兴四年(420年),北凉灭西凉,沮渠蒙逊派遣以前被段业所杀的敦煌大族索嗣之子索元绪为敦煌太守。但索元绪不得人心,很快就被敦煌当地人赶走,而拥戴李暠第六子李恂据敦煌继续抵抗。421年,北凉王沮渠蒙逊亲率大军讨伐敦煌。城破之后,蒙逊对敦煌进行大规模的屠城。莫窟第275窟保留了多幅与摧残肉体相关的图画,正是这个惨痛事件对西凉遗民心理带来重大影响的外在表现(图7)。

西凉灭亡后,李暠夫人尹氏、少子李翻以及李翻之子李宝,都被沮渠蒙逊迁到凉州。不久,李宝与舅父唐契向北逃亡到伊吾,臣服于柔然;尹夫人则由凉州向西逃亡,最终通过河西走廊到达伊吾。西凉的遗民听到李宝滞留在伊吾的消息,前往

internal unity against outside enemies, which enticed Khotan, Shanshan and other states in the Western Regions into paying tribute. All these contributed to turning Dunhuang into a capital city. However, due to the narrow geographical area, a sparse population, and limited material resources, and more importantly because of the threat posed by the Northern Liang that was controlled by Juqu Mengxun then, Li Hao was forced to move his capital from Dunhuang to Jiuquan in the 1st year of Jianchu Era (405). The relocation of the capital weakened Dunhuang, because approximately 23,000 households moved from Dunhuang to Jiuquan. Besides, the Western Liang shifted its focus eastward, which deprived Dunhuang of an important base for administrating the Western Regions. Therefore, Dunhuang began to decline after Li Hao's death in 417. In the 4th year of Jiaxing Era (420), the Northern Liang exterminated the Western Liang and Juqu Mengxun sent Suo Yuanxu, the son of Suo Si, to be the Governor of Dunhuang Prefecture. Suo Yuanxu was so unpopular with the local people that he was forced to leave, while Li Xun, the sixth son of Li Hao, was supported by the locals to stay in Dunhuang and continue the resistance against the Northern Liang. In 421, Juqu Mengxun carried out a punitive expedition against Dunhuang. Finally, Dunhuang was occupied, where Mengxun went on a massacre. The mural in Mogao Cave 275 shows the scene of the slaughter which illustrates the tragic event that psychologically scarred the rest of the people of the Western Liang (Fig.7).

图 7　莫高窟第 275 窟　毗楞竭梨王本生　北凉

Fig.7　Jataka Tale of King Bhilanjili, Mogao Cave 275　Northern Liang

归附者有2000多户，在伊吾形成了一支西凉政权的残余势力。

北魏太延五年(439年)，拓跋焘攻占凉州，凉王沮渠牧犍投降，北凉灭亡。但由于北魏此时尚未深入河西西部，所以牧犍之弟无讳就组织力量在敦煌据守。随着北魏军队的推进，442年，无讳放弃敦煌，率大批民众西撤，占据鄯善，后入高昌，仍号“河西王”。北凉王族的这次撤退，带走了大批的敦煌户口，其中包括为躲避兵祸而逃亡到敦煌的河西文化精英。在北凉灭西凉和北魏灭北凉的两次兵祸之中，敦煌的民众或被屠杀，或被迫西迁，使得敦煌在经济和文化各方面都遭到了前所未有的破坏。

北魏太平真君三年(442年)，李宝趁沮渠无讳撤离之机，占据敦煌，并派李怀达入魏归降。虽然北魏封李宝为沙州牧、敦煌公，但对其并不信任。所以

After the demise of the Western Liang, Lady Yin, Li Hao's wife, Li Fan, Li Hao's youngest son, and Li Bao, Li Hao's grandson, were brought to Liangzhou by Juqu Mengxun. Before long, Li Bao and his maternal uncle Tang Qi fled northward to Yiwu and surrendered to Rouran Khaganate, a state established by proto-Mongols. Lady Yin fled westward along the Hexi Corridor, also eventually reaching Yiwu. When hearing the news that Li Bao was in Yiwu, the Western Liang's loyalists of more than 2,000 households went to show their allegiance to him, thus forming the remnants of the Western Liang regime.

In the 5th year of Taiyan Era (439), Tuoba Tao, the third emperor of the Northern Wei, conquered Liangzhou. Juqu Mujian, the emperor of the Northern Liang at the time, surrendered, showing the Northern Liang's perishment. Juqu Wuhui, Juqu Mujian's younger brother, still guarded Dunhuang with his forces. With the Northern Wei's army advancing, in 442, Juqu Wuhui had to abandon Dunhuang. He withdrew westward with a large number of people, occupied Shanshan and then went to Gaochang with the title of Prince of Hexi. A large number of people left Dunhuang during this withdrawal, including the cultural elites who had fled to Dunhuang earlier in the war. During these two disasters, that is, the Western Liang being destroyed by the Northern Liang and the Northern Liang vanquished by the Northern Wei, the residents in Dunhuang were either

到 444 年，李宝就被征召到北魏的首都平城，北魏直接控制了敦煌。为经营西域和抗击北方的柔然，北魏于此建敦煌镇。当时的敦煌镇辖有晋昌戍、酒泉军、乐涫戍、张掖军等，大致相当于西汉时期敦煌和酒泉两郡之地。镇守敦煌的官吏不仅有大将、镇将的名号，还有敦煌镇大将的名号，可见当时敦煌的重要地位。北魏太平真君六年(445 年),太武帝派成国公万度归率大军,出敦煌,西击鄯善,后更破焉耆和龟兹。此战使西域大部分都为北魏所控制,丝绸之路再次打通，西域商人纷纷前来贸易。但好景不长，北方的柔然控制了敦煌以西的西域地区,并直接控制了吐鲁番盆地。延兴二年至四年(472—474 年)，敦煌军民在镇将尉多侯、乐洛生的率领下，数次击败强大的柔然骑兵,保住了敦煌。但在严峻的形势面前，北魏上层对

slaughtered or forced to move westward, which made Dunhuang suffer unprecedented damage both economically and culturally.

Li Bao occupied Dunhuang in the 3rd year of Taiping Zhenjun Era (442) by taking advantage of Juqu Wuhui's withdrawal, sending Li Huaida as an envoy to display his intention of surrender to the Northern Wei. Although Li Bao was appointed as the Regional Governor of Shazhou and Duke of Dunhuang, he could not be completely trusted. In 444, he was summoned to Pingcheng, the capital city of the Northern Wei, leaving Dunhuang falling under the direct control of the imperial court of the Northern Wei. In order to develop the Western Regions and fight against Rouran Khaganate in the north, Dunhuang Garrison was built with jurisdiction over Jinchang Garrison Troops, Jiuquan Army, Leguan Garrison Troops, and Zhangye Army, roughly equivalent to the area of two prefectures of Dunhuang and Jiuquan in the Western Han Dynasty. The officials guarding Dunhuang were titled General-in-Chief, Garrison Commander, and Garrison Commander-in-Chief of Dunhuang, which showed how militarily significant Dunhuang was at the time. In 445, Tuba Tao ordered Wan Dugui, the Duke of Cheng, to conquer Shanshan and then states of Yanqi and Qiuci. Most parts of the Western Regions fell under the control of the Northern Wei after this subjugation. The Silk Road was reopened, and traders from the Western Regions returned to do business. However, the situation did not last for

是否要继续保有敦煌发生了分歧，不少人建议后撤凉州，放弃敦煌。给事中韩秀则认为，如果放弃敦煌，不仅凉州不保，关中也无宁日。孝文帝支持韩秀的意见，为加强敦煌的守备，升敦煌镇将为都大将。太和九年（485年），穆亮任敦煌镇都大将，其为政宽简，并赈恤穷乏，敦煌经济得到恢复。经济的复苏，激发了民众从事宗教文化活动的热情，莫高窟第238窟就是北魏时期所开凿的洞窟（图8）。

由于受到北方六镇起义的影响，北魏正光五年（524年），孝明帝颁布诏书，命令天下诸州镇的军户，只要不是因为犯罪而发配的，一律免为平民。此外，镇改名为州。敦煌因盛产美瓜而被命名为"瓜州"，下辖敦煌等5郡。为了巩固在河西的统治，孝昌元年（525年），北魏皇室元荣被任命为

long, because Rouran had part of the Western Regions to the west of Dunhuang under its control, and took the direct control of the Turfan Basin. From the 2nd to the 4th year of Yanxing Era (472–474), soldiers and civilians in Dunhuang led by Wei Duohou and Le Luosheng, garrison commanders of Dunhuang, fought hard against the powerful cavalries from Rouran and defended Dunhuang. In the face of this grim situation, officials with high rank at the court of the Northern Wei had diverging views concerning Dunhuang. A number of them suggested retreating to Liangzhou, which would mean abandoning Dunhuang. Han Xiu, the Supervising Secretary, cautioned that if they gave up Dunhuang, Liangzhou's security could not be guaranteed and neither could it be peaceful in the Guanzhong region. Emperor Xiaowen accepted Han Xiu's advice and promoted the Garrison Commander of Dunhuang to be the Garrison Commander-in-Chief of Dunhuang in an attempt to strengthen its defensive power. In the 9th year of Taihe Era (485), Mu Liang was appointed the Garrison Commander-in-Chief of Dunhuang, who relaxed administrative control and offered relief to those in need. This contributed to the economic recovery of Dunhuang. Because of this, people were enthusiastically engaged in religious and cultural activities, which can be proved by Mogao Cave 238 constructed during the Northern Wei Dynasty (Fig.8).

Affected by the Revolt in the Six Garrisons along the northern border, Emperor Xiaoming of the Northern Wei issued an edict in the 5th year of

图 8　莫高窟第 238 窟　胁侍菩萨　北魏

Fig.8　Attendant Bodhisattva，Mogao Cave 238　Northern Wei

瓜州刺史，并于4年之后受封为东阳王。由于敦煌地处西陲，所以并没有受到北魏末年政治动乱的波及。即使是在北魏分裂为东魏和西魏的形势下，元荣仍在敦煌维持了较为安定的统治。元荣本人笃信佛教，不仅出资抄写佛经，还大力开凿洞窟。元荣作为西魏的瓜州刺史，其统治延续到了西魏大统十年(544年)。元荣崇信佛教的做法，对普通官员和民众起到了强烈的示范作用，他们在莫高窟开凿了很多大型洞窟(图9、图10)。

557年，宇文觉废西魏恭帝拓跋廓，建立北周，与此前取代东魏的北齐形成对峙局面。据《周书》记载，韦真、李贤和于义曾先后出任瓜州刺史。李贤和于义都曾在莫高窟开窟造像。尤其是被封为建平公的于义，在莫高窟营建史上，

Zhengguang Era (524) that all military families in the prefectures or garrisons were free to be civilians as long as they had not been exiled due to criminal offenses. The garrison (*zhen* in Chinese) was then renamed *zhou*. Dunhuang was renamed Guazhou for the reason that it was rich in melons (*gua* in Chinese), and was given jurisdiction over five prefectures including Dunhuang. In order to consolidate rule in the Hexi area, in the 1st year of Xiaochang Era (525), Yuan Rong from the imperial clans of the Northern Wei was appointed the Regional Governor of Guazhou; four years later he was conferred the title *Dongyang* Prince, whose rule was extended to the year 544. Thanks to its peripheral location, Dunhuang was relatively stable and free from political turmoil during the end of the Northern Wei, even as the Northern Wei split into the Eastern Wei and the Western Wei. As a strong believer in Buddhism, Yuan Rong not only financed the copying of sutras, but also actively patronized the construction of temple caves. Influenced by Yuan Rong, many officials and ordinary civilians also built large caves in Mogao (Fig.9 and 10).

In 557, Tuoba Kuo, Emperor Gong of the Western Wei, was forced to yield the throne to Yuwen Jue. The Western Wei ended and the Northern Zhou was established. Thus a confrontational situation came into being between the Northern Zhou and the Northern Qi which had previously replaced the Eastern Wei. According to the *Book of Zhou*, Wei Zhen, Li Xian, and Yu Yi served successively as the Regional Governor of Guazhou. Li Xian and Yu Yi mobilized the local

图 9　莫高窟第 285 窟　五百强盗成佛图　西魏
Fig.9　Karma Tale of the Five Hundred Robbers, Mogao Cave 285　Western Wei

图 10 莫高窟第 249 窟 野猪图 西魏
Fig.10 Painting of Wild Boar, Mogao Cave 249 Western Wei

更是具有重要的地位。建德三年（574 年），北周武帝灭佛，但瓜州的佛教似乎只是开窟造像的短暂停歇，而并未受到太大的影响（图 11）。

西魏末到北周初，西域突厥部族兴起。柔然在突厥和中原政权的打击下，势力衰弱，这就解除了西域交通的障碍，中原地区与西域各国的交往迅速发展。一时间，鄯善、于阗、龟兹等国纷纷派出使者向北周通好，并进

people to construct caves and sculpt statues in Mogao. Yu Yi, the Duke of Jianping, in particular contributed greatly to the construction of the Mogao Caves. In the 3rd year of Jiande Era (574), Emperor Wu of the Northern Zhou decreed the persecution of Buddhism, but it had minimal impact on Buddhism in Dunhuang, despite a brief hiatus in creating statues in the Mogao Caves (Fig.11).

Turkic tribes (*tujue* in Chinese) began to rise up in the Western Regions during the period from the end of the Western Wei to the beginning of the Northern Zhou. Rouran Khaganate was weakened from attacks by the Turkic tribes and the Central Plains regime, thus the barriers in traffic to the Western Regions were eliminated, bringing the rapid development of contact between the imperial government in the Central Plains and the states in the Western Regions. For a time, Shanshan, Khotan, Qiuci and others sent envoys to the

献名马和当地特产，这对提升宇文泰的军事实力很有帮助。所以，北周与西域各国保持了较为密切的联系。大象元年（579 年），北周静帝宇文衍将赵王宇文招的女儿宇文芳封为千金公主，嫁给突厥沙钵略可汗，以和亲的手段维持了与西北地区少数民族的正常关系。

Northern Zhou and offered fine horses and local specialities, which were helpful in enhancing the Northern Zhou's military strength. Therefore, the Northern Zhou always maintained relatively close contact with the states in the Western Regions. In the 1st year of Daxiang Era (579), Emperor Jing married the Princess Qianjin, Yuwen Zhao's daughter, to Shabolue Khan, the Turk's chieftain, in an effort to maintain peaceful relations with the tribes in northwestern China.

图 11　莫高窟第 301 窟　供养人与牛车　北周末隋初

Fig.11　Donors and Oxcart, Mogao Cave 301　Late Northern Zhou to Early Sui

隋至唐前期的敦煌

Dunhuang from the Sui Dynasty to the Early Tang

581年，北周末代皇帝的外祖父杨坚取代北周建立隋朝，又在8年后一举消灭了偏安江南一隅的陈朝。自西晋末年以来形成的分裂割据局面终于结束，而出现了一个大一统的中央王朝。隋朝建立后，主要的军事压力来自于西北地区的突厥和吐谷浑，其中突厥的危害尤大。为了减少突厥对中国北方的侵扰，北齐和北周曾争相向其馈赠大量金银财物。对此，突厥的可汗十分得意地夸耀道："既然在我们南面的两个儿子如此孝顺，我怎么会担心财用贫乏呢！" 隋文帝开皇二年（582年），突厥对西北地区进行了大规模的劫掠，造成了武威、天水、金城、上郡、弘化、延安等地"六畜咸尽"的严重局面，极大地威胁着隋朝在西北地区的

In 581, Yang Jian, grandfather of the last emperor of the Northern Zhou, seized the throne by force, establishing the Sui Dynasty. Eight years later, he defeated the Chen Dynasty located near the Yangtze River, which marked the reunification of China and the formation of a unified central authority under his reign, after centuries of division since the fall of the Western Jin. At the beginning of its establishment, the Sui Dynasty faced threats from the Turks and the Tuyuhun in the northwest, especially from the Turks. In order to prevent invasion by the Turks against northern China, the Northern Qi and the Northern Zhou had presented a large amount of gold and silver to them. The Khan of the Turks had said proudly, "Now that we have two filial sons in the south, how can we worry about a shortage of money?" In the 2nd year of Kaihuang Era of Emperor Wen (582) of the Sui Dynasty, the Turks pillaged and looted the northwestern region, which plunged the people of Wuwei, Tianshui, Jincheng, Shangjun, Honghua, and Yan'an into misery and suffering, even any animal not being seen over these regions, which threatened the rule of the Sui Dynasty over that area. To counterattack the Turks, the Sui government adopted a tactic of military attack combined with sowing discord within the Turks.

统治。为了反击突厥并解除统一南朝时的后顾之忧，隋朝对突厥采取了军事进攻和反间相结合的策略，并成功地实施了由长孙晟提出的“远交而近攻，离强而合弱”的具体部署，终于使突厥内部发生分裂。在经过一系列的内讧事件后，突厥的势力遭到了严重的削弱，不再对隋朝构成严重威胁。随着突厥威胁的解除，隋朝又全力对付吐谷浑，并最终将其制服，从而使隋朝西北边境得以安宁。

随着西北安定环境的出现，隋王朝加强了对河西地区的控制，在河西设置敦煌、张掖、武威等郡，并派遣军队前往戍守。由于在河西地区驻军较多，而河西远离内地，军事供给困难。为了解决这个问题，隋文帝在河西地区实行了农牧并重的措施，缓解了军粮供应的不足。

开皇初年，隋文帝曾“罢天下诸郡”，改州、郡、县三级制为州、县两级制，敦煌曾一度被废郡为县。仁寿元年(601 年)，隋文帝令天下各州起塔供养舍利，瓜州莫高窟的崇教寺也在

The Sui successfully carried out the strategy proposed by Zhangsun Sheng to “actively establish diplomatic ties with distant neighbors and attack close enemies; avoid direct conflict with powerful forces and make alliances with weak ones.” Finally, it created internal dissension within the Turks, making them unable to unite against the Sui. With the elimination of the threat from the Turks, the Sui government then tackled the problem of the Tuyuhun with all its strength successfully. The northwestern border of the Sui Dynasty could then enjoy peace and tranquility.

With stability in the northwest secured, the central government began to take a series of measures strengthening its control over the Hexi area, such as establishing prefectures including Dunhuang, Zhangye, and Wuwei, as well as stationing troops there. Yet the increasing number of troops and their distant location from the Central Plains caused a problem with military supplies. In order to solve it, Emperor Wen implemented the measure of paying equal attention to farming and animal husbandry there, thus easing the pressure on military provisions in the Hexi area.

In the 1st year of Kaihuang Era (581), Emperor Wen abolished the three-tiered administrative system—region (*zhou* in Chinese), prefecture (*jun*), and county (*xian*)—and established two levels instead:

其列。此时的敦煌由于魏晋南北朝时期的衰败，虽经东阳、建平时期的恢复，仍不能与河西其他诸州比肩，故隋代经营西域的基地在张掖。但隋代在莫高窟开凿了大批的石窟，敦煌地区甚至还出土了一些隋皇室成员的写经，可见隋王朝对敦煌的重视(图 12)。

经过 10 余年的发展，到隋炀帝继位时，敦煌已呈现出“户口滋盛，中外仓库，无不盈积”的局面。隋炀帝

region and county. As a result, Dunhuang was set up as a county instead of a prefecture. In the 1st year of Renshou Era (601), he issued an order that Buddhist stupas would be constructed to enshrine Buddhist relics in every region of China, including the Chongjiao Temple at the Mogao Caves in Guazhou. Because of its decline during the Wei, Jin, and Northern and Southern dynasties, Dunhuang lagged behind other places in the Hexi area; Zhangye thus became the center for the Sui government in managing the Western Regions. A large amount of caves in Mogao were still built, however. Copied Buddhist scriptures belonging to the Sui nobility have been unearthed in the Dunhuang area, indicating that the Sui still attached significance

图 12　莫高窟第 303 窟　供养人、车马及山林　隋

Fig.12　Scenes of Donors, Horses and Carriages, and Forest, Mogao Cave 303　Sui Dynasty

时期随着对北方民族的军事征服,隋朝的疆域进一步拓展。与此相适应,屯垦这种特殊的生产方式也以河西走廊为基地向北拓展。所以,在隋炀帝时期,河西地区屯垦达到了隋朝的全盛期。隋炀帝时期的重臣裴矩就明确指出,丝绸之路“总凑敦煌,是其咽喉之地”,形象地将敦煌比喻为丝绸之路的咽喉,表明隋代对敦煌及河西的认识,在汉代的基础上又有了新的突破,是对敦煌及河西地位认识的一次飞跃(图 13)。

隋炀帝是一个好大喜功的皇帝,为了扩大隋王朝在西域的政治影响,隋炀帝即位后采取了多种措施,由中央政府在河西地区直接控制隋王朝与西域诸国及西北少数民族的商品贸易,促进了张掖、武威、敦煌等国际性大都市的形成。而在河西地区主持这项事务的官员,也就是上文中所提及的裴矩。裴矩(548—627年),字弘大,河东闻喜人。

to Dunhuang (Fig.12).

After over ten years of development, when Emperor Yang of the Sui acceded to the throne, Dunhuang had evolved into an area with a large population and abundant products. The Sui Dynasty further expanded its territory with Emperor Yang's conquest of the northern tribes. Accordingly, the established production mode of stationing troops and reclaiming wasteland expanded northward along the Hexi Corridor and reached its golden age. Pei Ju (548–627), an important official in Emperor Yang's reign, pointed out explicitly that Dunhuang was the strategic passage along the Silk Road, showing that the Sui achieved a new realization of the importance of Dunhuang and the Hexi area based on their roles during the Han Dynasty. This notion also could be regarded as a major leap for the recognition of the status of these areas (Fig.13).

Emperor Yang was an ambitious ruler, and he thereby attempted a series of measures to enhance political influence over the Western Regions after his enthronement. For instance, he decided that the central government would directly control trade with the states in the Western Regions and the northwestern ethnic minorities, which helped Zhangye, Wuwei, and Dunhuang to gradually become urban areas engaged in international trade. During this period, Pei Ju was the official in charge of the trade issue in the Hexi area. From Wenxi County in Hedong area, Pei's family had had

图 13　莫高窟第 305 窟　飞天　隋

Fig.13　Flying Apsaras, Mogao Cave 305　Sui Dynasty

其家族世代以文学见长，“五举秀才，再举孝廉”，为人广为称赞。裴矩幼年丧父，但他勤奋好学，智略过人，并留心时事，志向高远。杨坚建立隋朝后，裴矩在内史省担任了给事郎的低级

high reputation for their literary art for generations and was widely praised for being recommended as *xiucai*① five times and then *xiaolian*②. Though his father died when Pei Ju was young, he was diligent and intelligent; moreover, he kept up with current affairs and had lofty aspirations. When Emperor Wen (Yang Jian) established the Sui Dynasty, Pei Ju became the Supervising Secretary in the Department of Secretariats. He was in charge of

---

① *Xiucai* was originally a standard of recommending or nominating talented persons by local officials. *Xiu* means being excellent and *cai* refers to a talented person.

② *Xiaolian* was the standard of nominating civil officers started by Emperor Wu of the Han Dynasty in 134 BC. *Xiao* means being filial for one's parents and ancestors and *lian* means being incorrupt and righteous. It lasted until its replacement by the imperial examination system during the Sui Dynasty.

文官。在隋朝灭亡南陈的战役中，裴矩担任了杨广元帅府记事，负责接收陈朝的图籍。后来，在平定岭南王仲宣、周师举叛乱的过程中，得到隋文帝杨坚的赏识，从此青云直上。他先后担任民部侍郎和内史侍郎，成为隋朝政府中的重要官员。而在隋初，随着突厥对隋朝西北威胁的解除，丝绸之路再度畅通，西域各国前来河西地区经商者络绎不绝，武威和张掖遂成为两个国际性贸易都市。大业三年(607 年)，隋炀帝派遣时任吏部侍郎的裴矩前往张掖，由他主持这里的互市。

裴矩到达张掖后，充分利用此处多西域胡商的有利条件，通过与他们接触，充分了解了西域诸国的自然地理、风土人情等情况。同时，他还翻阅了大量的图书典籍，积累了丰富的文字和第一手的访问

receiving the territory figures and household registers of the Chen Dynasty when serving as a secretary to the Supreme Commander Yang Guang during the overall Sui campaign to conquer the Chen Dynasty and reunite China. Later, in the war of pacifying rebellions by Wang Zhongxuan and Zhou Shiju in the Lingnan ① area, Pei Ju won recognition from Emperor Wen and received rapid promotions, going to Vice Minister of the Ministry of Revenue and Vice Director of the Secretariat successively. During the early years of the Sui Dynasty, the threat from the Turks to its northwestern part gradually subsided. The Silk Road was unblocked once again and a continuous stream of merchants from the states in the Western Regions came to the Hexi area, turning Wuwei and Zhangye into international trading cities. In the 3rd year of Daye Era (607), Emperor Yang sent Pei Ju, the Vice Minister of the Ministry of Personnel, to Zhangye and put him in charge of the frontier trade there.

Pei Ju learned from a substantial number of merchants from the Western Regions, gaining an understanding of geography and customs in different states. Meanwhile, he read profusely from ancient books and records, and accumulated manuscripts and first-hand interview materials, which formed the basis for his three-volume work titled *Maps of and Notes on the Western Regions*, relating to history and geography of the Western Regions. When Pei Ju went to Zhangye for a

① Lingnan refers to a large area south of the five ranges in south China.

资料。在此基础上，他写成了记载西域历史地理的《西域图记》，并献给隋炀帝。当裴矩第二次主持张掖互市时，还派人前往高昌、伊吾等地，邀请各国国王、使节及商人入朝。同时，裴矩还注意以张掖为中转站，进而为长安、洛阳等地招引诸国使臣及商人，而他们在入隋的路途中，各地政府都会提供食宿。在裴矩的努力下，西域各国经河西前往长安、洛阳者络绎不绝。

大业五年（609 年）六月，隋炀帝亲临张掖，并登焉支山。高昌王麹伯雅、伊吾吐屯设及西域 27 国使者在道旁觐见。这是我国封建社会唯一的一次中原王朝皇帝西巡张掖的活动。为了显示隋王朝的富庶，隋炀帝命令武威、张掖一带的百姓身着节日盛装，前来夹道欢迎。隋炀帝还陈设了可以拆卸组装的活

second time, he sent people to states of Gaochang and Yiwu to invite the kings, diplomatic envoys, and merchants to the Central Plains. He also established Zhangye as a transfer point for leading envoys and merchants from the Western Regions to Chang'an and Luoyang①; the local governments along the road provided room and board for visitors. Numerous people from the Western Regions streamed into Chang'an and Luoyang as a result of Pei's efforts.

In June of 609, Emperor Yang personally visited Zhangye, where he climbed the Yanzhi Mountain. Emissaries from 27 states in the Western Regions, headed by Qu Boya, the King of Gaochang, paid homage to the Emperor along the roadside. This was the only time that an emperor from the Central Plains toured Zhangye. To show the wealth and prestige of the Sui Dynasty, Emperor Yang ordered that the people in Wuwei and Zhangye should be dressed in their holiday finest and line the streets to give him a warm welcome. He also brought along a detachable and assembled palace—Guanfeng Palace—where he had a banquet with kings from the Western Regions and enjoyed performances of nine pieces of ethnic music, such as "Qiuci" and "Liangzhou." It can be said that this trade mission was unprecedented in history for its scale, number of participants, and

① During the Sui Dynasty, the capital was Chang'an (which was renamed Daxing during 581–605), and later Luoyang.

动宫殿——观风行殿，与麹伯雅等人开怀畅饮，并观赏了具有民族特色的《龟兹》、《凉州》等九部乐。这次盛会规模之大、规格之高、人数之多、耗资之巨，都可谓史无前例。通过隋王朝主持的互市活动，有力地促进了河西地区的发展，刺激了河西地区经济的繁荣，使得张掖、武威、敦煌等地成为西北经济的重心，也促使它们进入了当时国际性贸易大都市的行列(图 14)。

隋大业十三年(617年)，武威鹰扬府司马李轨趁中原大乱之际，自称河西大凉王，在武威举兵自立。在部下曹珍、安修仁等人的策划下，很快就攻陷了张掖、敦煌、西平等地，控制了整个河西走廊。并于第二年，也就是李渊建立唐朝的同时，僭称帝号，并改元安乐。为了消除后顾之忧，刚刚平定中原地区的李渊想通过招抚的方式收复河西，于是派遣使者前往凉州通好，为李轨所拒绝。此后，李

expenditure. The trade policies under the Sui Dynasty effectively accelerated development of the Hexi area and stimulated an economic boom, turning Zhangye, Wuwei, and Dunhuang into commercial centers in northwestern China and international trade cities at that time (Fig.14).

In 617, Li Gui, the Commander of Yingyang Garrison in Wuwei, proclaimed himself the Prince of Daliang in the Hexi Area while the Central Plains were in political turmoil. Assisted by his subordinates, Cao Zhen and An Xiuren, he captured Zhangye, Dunhuang, and Xiping, quickly gaining control over the entire Hexi Corridor. In the following year, when Li Yuan established the Tang Dynasty in the Central Plains, Li Gui proclaimed himself the emperor in the Hexi area, and changed the title of his reign to Anle. In order to eliminate threats to his new regime, Li Yuan, who had just pacified the Central Plains, wanted to retake the Hexi area by offering amnesty and military enlistment to its rebels. He sent envoys to Liangzhou, attempting to establish good terms with Li Gui, but was rejected. After this rebuff, Li Yuan sent An Xinggui, the older brother of An Xiuren, as an envoy to the Hexi area again. The An clan were Sogdian merchants originally, and possessed great power after being long-term residents in the Hexi area. When Li Gui rejected the Tang government for a second time, An Xinggui conneted with the local people to raise an army,

图 14　莫高窟第 402 窟　供养菩萨　隋

Fig.14　Bodhisattva Making Offerings, Mogao Cave 402　Sui Dynasty

渊再次派遣使者前往招抚，这次的使者就是安修仁的哥哥安兴贵。凉州的安氏家族本是长期居住在河西的粟特商人，在凉州当地有强大的势力。在李轨再次拒绝唐朝的招降后，安兴贵联络凉州当地的胡人起兵，包围了凉州城。李轨战败投降，被押解到长安处死。

唐朝在夺得河西地区之后，依照在全国改郡为州的通例，将敦煌郡更名为瓜州，任命贺拔行威为瓜州刺史。由于当时唐朝刚刚建立，对全国的统治并不巩固，所以在唐高祖武德三年（620年），贺拔行威举兵反唐。直到武德五年（622年）五月，瓜州土豪王干才将贺拔行威斩首，并重新归降唐朝。此后，唐将瓜州分为瓜州和西沙州两个州，新的瓜州统辖晋昌和常乐两个县，治所设在晋昌。西沙州领敦煌、寿昌二县，治所在敦煌，所管辖的范围大为缩小。而从称其为“西沙州”看，可知此时唐政府将其作为大唐疆域的最西端。

唐武德六年（623年）六月，敦煌当地人张护、李通又发动叛乱，拥立沙州别驾窦伏明为城主，被

and besieged Liangzhou. Finally, Li Gui was defeated and sent to Chang'an, where he was executed.

After regaining the Hexi area, following the policy of turning prefecture into *zhou*, the Tang Dynasty renamed Dunhuang Prefecture as Guazhou and then appointed Heba Xingwei as the Prefect of Guazhou. However, as the Tang Dynasty was newly established and its rule over the country was not consolidated, Heba Xingwei was able to raise an army to rebel against the imperial government in the 3rd year of Wude Era of Emperor Gaozu (620). Two years later, Heba Xingwei was beheaded by Wang Gancai, a powerful member of the local gentry, who then surrendered himself to the Tang Dynasty. From then on, the central government divided Guazhou into two parts—Guazhou and Xishazhou (*xi* meaning west). The newly-established Guazhou governed two counties—Jinchang and Changle—with the seat in Jinchang. Xishazhou governed Dunhuang and Shouchang counties together with the local government in Dunhuang, where jurisdiction was greatly narrowed. As one can see from the name of Xishazhou, the Tang Dynasty regarded this area as the westernmost end of its territory.

In June of 623, Zhang Hu and Li Tong, two local residents of Dunhuang, instigated another uprising. They installed

瓜州长史赵孝伦击败。此年九月，窦伏明归降，但敦煌还面临着突厥汗国和吐谷浑等外患侵扰的威胁。所以在唐朝初年，唐朝关闭了西北关津，不许百姓于此出境。正是这样的原因，唐玄奘西行求法之际，才不得不采取偷渡出关的方式。但随着唐朝国力的提升，包括敦煌在内的全国各地的形势日趋稳定。政治上的安定，极大地促进了敦煌当地经济、文化的发展，人们从事宗教活动的热情重新被燃起（图 15）。

唐太宗贞观四年（630 年）八月，据守高昌东境的东突厥欲谷设部降唐。与之相伴随，此年九月，占据伊吾 7 城的石万年亦率众来降。从石万年的姓氏上来看，他应该是中亚粟特诸国中的石国人。唐朝因置其地为西伊州。这是唐政府在碛外地区所创置的第一个州郡，标志着唐朝在西域地区经略的开端，具有划时代的意义。到贞观六年（632 年），

Dou Fuming, the Administrative Aide of Prefect of Shazhou, as the governor, who was then defeated by Zhao Xiaolun, the Chief Official of Guazhou. In September, Dou Fuming surrendered himself to the Tang Dynasty, but Dunhuang still faced threats from the Turks and the Tuyuhun. As a consequence, in the early years of the Tang Dynasty, the government closed the western passes and ferries; the local people were prohibited to leave the country from these locations. Hence, when Xuanzang was starting his pilgrimage to India, he had to leave secretly from this area. As the power of the Tang Dynasty increased, the situation across the country gradually stabilized, including Dunhuang. The local economy and culture flourished under a stable political environment, which resulted in renewed participation in religious activities (Fig.15).

In August of the 4th year of Zhenguan Era of Emperor Taizong (630), the Yugushe tribe of the Eastern Turks occupying the eastern part of Gaochang surrendered to the Tang government. In September, Shi Wannian, who had occupied the seven towns of Yiwu, also led his people to surrender to the Tang. His family name, Shi, indicated a person from Chaj, a Sogdian state in Central Asia. Territory under Shi Wannian's control was established as Xiyizhou, the first prefecture established out of the desert, symbolizing the beginning of the Tang Dynasty's management of the Western Regions, which was of an epoch-making

图 15　莫高窟第 57 窟　说法图　初唐

Fig.15　Dharma-Preaching Scene, Mogao Cave 57　Early Tang

唐政府将西伊州改为伊州，表明了唐政府有继续西进的意图。而唐政府既然在敦煌以西已经设置州郡，那么再将敦煌称为“西沙州”也就没有实际意义了。所以，贞观七年（633 年），唐朝去掉西沙州的“西”字，敦煌正式更名为沙州。

significance. In 632, the imperial government renamed Xiyizhou as Yizhou, indicating that the government intended a continuous westward expansion. Now that the government established *zhou* or prefectures to the west of Dunhuang, it was meaningless to call Dunhuang "Xishazhou." In 633, the government

由于占据今青海一带的吐谷浑频繁侵扰唐朝的陇右地区，威胁着丝绸之路的安全，所以贞观八年(634年)十一月，唐朝在与吐蕃秘密结成共同讨伐吐谷浑的军事联盟之后，唐军以李靖为西海道行军大总管，统帅大军兵分5路，进击吐谷浑。5路大军的分工十分明确，其中侯君集主攻河源，李道宗主攻鄯善，李大亮主攻且末，李道彦主攻赤水，高甑生主攻盐泽。此外，还调遣铁勒酋长契苾何力所统帅的铁勒精骑助战。次年三月，诸路大军会师于鄯州。李靖、侯君集、李道宗等人连兵并进，先后在牛心堆、赤水源等地取得大捷。吐谷浑可汗伏允无奈之下，被迫逃往于阗；在唐军的不断追击下，最终被部下所杀。从此，吐谷浑对河西走廊的威胁被消除。

贞观十三年(639年)十二月，唐太宗又以陈国公、

removed "*xi*" (west) from its name and Dunhuang was officially renamed Shazhou.

In November of 634, the Tang government formed a secret military alliance with the Tubo[1] to suppress the Tuyuhun who frequently invaded and harassed the Longyou area, threatening the security of the Silk Road. The Tang government appointed Li Jing as the Regional Commander-in-Chief of the Xihai Circuit to advance against the Tuyuhun, branching the army out into five columns. The division of labour in the army was clear—Hou Junji attacked Heyuan, Li Daozong attacked Shanshan, Li Daliang attacked Qiemo, Li Daoyan attacked Chishui and Gao Zengsheng attacked Yanze. In addition, the central government dispatched Qibi Heli, the chieftain of the Tiele tribe living in the north of China, to assist the fighting with his experienced riders. In March of 635, all branches converged in Shanzhou, and then Li Jing, Hou Junji, and Li Daozong made a concerted push, winning military victories in Niuxindui and Chishuiyuan. Fu Yun, the Khan of the Tuyuhun, was forced to flee to Khotan, being routed by the Tang army, and was finally killed by his subordinates. After this, the threat from the Tuyuhun to the Hexi Corridor was removed.

In December of the 13th year of Zhenguan Era (639), Emperor Taizong appointed Hou

① Tubo was a local regime located on Qinghai-Tibet Plateau.

吏部尚书侯君集为交河道行军大总管，率军讨伐被西突厥控制的高昌。高昌乃流沙以西唯一的汉族移民政权，其历代国君皆奉行效忠中原王朝的传统政策。但就在贞观十三年，长期分裂的西突厥重新统一，成为西域的霸主。为了抵制唐朝影响在西域诸国中的扩散，西突厥支持高昌与唐朝为敌。在西突厥的指使下，高昌写信给当时漠北势力强大的薛延陀汗国，声称“既自为可汗，与汉天子敌也，何须拜谒其使”，希望离间薛延陀与唐朝的关系。而当薛延陀将此事上奏给唐朝之后，李世民从经营西域的角度出发，决定出师西征高昌。贞观十四年(640年)九月，在侯君集的率领下，唐军攻克了高昌的都城，随后在高昌设置了西州，并将高昌王麴智盛押送至长

Junji, the Duke of Cheng and Minister of the Ministry of Personnel, as the Regional Commander-in-Chief of the Jiaohe Circuit to suppress Gaochang, which was occupied by the Western Turks. Gaochang was the only regime governed by ethnic Han immigrants west of the desert, and its kings pursued a traditional policy of pledging loyalty to the Central Plains governments in ages past. Yet the long-disunited Western Turks reunified in 639, becoming the hegemonic force in the Western Regions. In order to resist the expansion of the Tang's influence on the states in the Western Regions, the Western Turks supported Gaochang in resisting the Tang government. Acting on the Western Turks' instigation, the King of Gaochang wrote a letter to the Khan of the Syr-Tardush Khanate which was then the most powerful Khanate north of the Gobi Desert. It stated, "We are the Khans of our own Khanates, which means we are antagonistic to the Emperor in the Central Plains, so there is no need for us to pay a formal visit to his envoys," hoping to drive a wedge between the Syr-Tardush Khanate and the Tang Dynasty. However, the Khan of the Syr-Tardush Khanate reported this information to the Tang government. Considering the management strategy of the Western Regions, Emperor Taizong decided to conquer Gaochang. In September of 640, the army under the command of Hou Junji captured the capital city of Gaochang, set up Xizhou there, and finally sent Qu Zhisheng, the King of Gaochang, to Chang'an under armed guard. From that point on, Gaochang was in the

安。由此，高昌故地被正式纳入唐朝版图。

贞观十八年（644年），唐朝派遣郭孝恪为西州道行军总管，以栗婆准等人为向导，率军出银山道，以讨伐为西突厥所控制的焉耆。贞观二十二年（648年），唐朝又攻取了龟兹。唐高宗显庆三年（658年）五月，唐朝将安西都护府由西州迁至龟兹，并设置了龟兹、于阗、焉耆、疏勒4镇，即“安西四镇”。但自龙朔二年（662年）开始，吐蕃王国就与西突厥余部联合，与唐朝争夺西域。安西四镇曾在唐朝和吐蕃之间几经易手。武周长寿元年（692年），王孝杰收复4镇，吐蕃遭受重创，唐朝对西域的控制得以加强。此后的近百年间，唐朝一直控制着西域，安西四镇建制也比较稳定。在唐朝争夺西域和经营西域的过程中，有很多沙州兵奔赴前线。沙州和西州两地

territory of the Tang Dynasty.

In 644, the Tang government appointed Guo Xiaoke as the Regional Commander-in-Chief of the Xizhou Circuit and Li Pozhun as his guide so as to conquer Yanqi which was still under occupation by the Western Turks. The Tang captured Qiuci in 648. Then in May of the 3rd year of Xianqing Era of Emperor Gaozong (658), the Tang Dynasty moved the Protectorate of Anxi from Xizhou to Qiuci and established the “Four Garrisons in Anxi,” including Qiuci, Yutian (Khotan), Yanqi, and Shule. However, the Tubo had been keeping an alliance since 662 with the remnants of the Western Turks, vying with the Tang for control to the Western Regions. The ownership of these four garrisons shifted between the Tang and the Tubo several times. In the 1st year of Changshou Era of Empress Wu Zetian (692), General Wang Xiaojie recaptured the Four Garrisons in Anxi, striking a heavy blow to the Tubo and enhancing the Tang’s control over the Western Regions. For the following one hundred years, the Tang occupied the Western Regions and the organization system of the Four Garrisons in Anxi remained stable. During the process of contention for the ownership to the Four Garrisons in Anxi, many soldiers from Shazhou rushed to the frontlines. Moreover, the transfer of officials between Shazhou and Xizhou was quite frequent, records of which can be found in documents on Dunhuang and Turfan. In the reign of Empress Wu Zetian, the central government set up the Doulu Army in Shazhou.

官员迁转也十分频繁，敦煌吐鲁番文献中多次出现沙州人任职西州和西州人任官敦煌的相关记载。武周时，中央政府在沙州设置了豆卢军。为了进一步提升河西地区的军事防御能力，唐睿宗景云二年(711年)，唐朝设置河西节度使，治所在凉州，统有赤水、大斗、建康、宁寇、玉门、墨离、豆卢、新泉8军，此外，还辖有白亭等守捉。此后，河西军政日益发展，成为唐王朝兵强马壮的军事重地。而据史书的记载，此时设在沙州城内的豆卢军，有官兵4300人，是河西节度使麾下的一支举足轻重的武装力量(图16)。

唐王朝通过县、乡、里各级基层政权组织和完备的户籍制度，对敦煌地区实行有效的管理和严密的控制。沙州下辖敦煌、寿昌二县，共13乡。唐朝的各种制度有效地在敦煌实施，敦煌的生产稳步发展，而榆林窟第15窟所保留下来的技法精妙的伎乐天，正是此时敦煌生产力高度发达的侧面反映(图17)。唐代地方官吏比较重视水利建设，劳动人民在戈壁

To further upgrade its defense capabilities in the Hexi area, in the 2nd year of Jingyun Era of Emperor Ruizong (711), the Tang Dynasty set up the Military Commissioner of the Hexi Area, headquartered in Liangzhou. Eight armies were under its command, including the Chishui, Dadou, Jiankang, Ningkou, Yumen, Moli, Doulu and Xinquan armies; the Military Commissioner also administered several defense detachments. From then on, the military and political powers in the Hexi area gradually gained strength, and Hexi became an important place for military affairs with its powerful army. According to historical records, there were a total of 4,300 soldiers and officials in the Doulu Army stationed in Shazhou, who played a decisive role under the management of the Military Commissioner of the Hexi Area (Fig.16).

The Tang government implemented effective management and tight control in Dunhuang through grass-roots organizations at different levels—county, township and village—and a comprehensive household registration system. In Shazhou, there were two counties—Dunhuang and Shouchang—with thirteen townships. Various effective policies were carried out in Dunhuang, making production increase steadily. The mural depicting celestial musicians and dancers in Yulin Cave 15 reveals the fact that production force in Dunhuang was

图 16　莫高窟第 431 窟　马夫与马　初唐
Fig.16　Groom and Horses, Mogao Cave 431　Early Tang

滩上扩大了耕地面积。从敦煌文献的记载看，敦煌当时的灌溉渠道很多，水渠灌溉系统得到完善。敦煌城四周就有5条水系、84条水渠构成的水利网，主渠“三丈渠”就因渠宽三丈而得名。此外，还配之以严密的官府配水制度，设置专职官员和管理人员对水资源进行管理。敦煌

highly developed at the time (Fig.17). The local officials in the Tang Dynasty attached great importance to water conservation projects, helping the local populace to expand the Gobi Desert's agricultural acreage. According to Dunhuang documents, there were numerous irrigation canals at the time; the irrigation system had been improved with 5 hydrographic nets and 84 canals around the city, which constituted a complete water conservation net. The main canal—Sanzhang Canal—got its name for being three *zhang* wide. In addition, the government also established an official water distribution system and appointed full-time

图 17 榆林窟第 15 窟 伎乐天 唐

Fig.17 Celestial Musician and Dancer, Mogao Cave 15 Tang Dynasty

莫高窟唐代的经变中画有曲辕犁，表明当时最先进的农业生产工具已在敦煌使用(图 18)。

关于河西的屯田，《旧唐书·郭元振传》载："大足元年，迁凉州都督、陇右诸军大使。先是，凉州封界南北不过四百余里，既逼突厥、吐蕃，二寇频岁奄至城下，百姓苦之。元振始于南境硖口置和戎城，北界碛中置白亭军，控其要路，乃拓州境一千五百里，自是寇虏不复更至城下。元振又令甘州刺史李

officers and staff to allocate water resources. The Quyuan plough in the illustration paintings of the Mogao Caves in the Tang Dynasty reveals that the most advanced agricultural technology was implemented in Dunhuang (Fig.18).

In regard to the *tuntian* policy of sending garrison troops to reclaim wasteland in the Hexi area, the *Old Book of Tang: Biography of Guo Yuanzhen* states that "Guo Yuanzhen was made the Commander-in-Chief of Liangzhou and Commissioner-in-Chief of Armies in the Longyou Area in the 1st year of Dazu Era (701). At that time, the length of

图 18　莫高窟第 23 窟　雨中耕作　盛唐
Fig.18　Ploughing in the Rain, Mogao Cave 23　High Tang

汉通开置屯田，尽水陆之利。旧凉州粟麦斛至数千，及汉通收率之后，数年丰稔，乃至一匹绢籴数十斛，积军粮支数十年。”唐代从高宗、武后至玄宗时期，一直都在河陇地区大兴屯田，使敦煌农业得到了长足的发展。唐王朝还十分重视河西的畜牧业，并以一套严密的组织机构进行管理。盛唐时期敦煌的商品经济繁荣，这里的市场上，有来自中原的丝绸、瓷器，也有来自西域的玉石、珍宝；有北方的驼马、毛织品，也有本地出产的手工业品。敦煌的人口在玄宗天宝年间达到了 3 万余人，是前秦以来的又一个高峰（图 19）。“是时中国盛强，自安远门西尽唐境万二千里，闾阎相望，桑麻翳野，天下富庶者无如陇右”，正是这一时期的真实写照。这里的陇右也包括敦煌在内。唐政府对西域的管理政策和措施超

Liangzhou's coverage from the south to the north was less than 400 *li*. The Turks and the Tubo forces were known to pillage the city frequently, causing people suffering a lot. Guo established Herong town in Xiakou to the south, and the Baiting Army in the desert to the north, serving as warning posts and counterattack points as well. Thereafter, the coverage of Liangzhou extended to 1,500 *li* long, the raids from the Turks and the Tubo decreased, and the local people were able to enjoy peace. He also ordered his subordinate Li Hantong, the Prefect of Ganzhou, to develop irrigation system and promote reclamation of wasteland. Such measures allowed the region, which previously suffered food shortages, to have a sufficient supply of food, and allowed the military to be supported as well." During the Tang Dynasty, from Emperor Gaozong and Empress Wu Zetian to Emperor Xuanzong's reign[①], the government had garrison troops and farmers continuously reclaim large amounts of wasteland in the Hexi and Longyou areas, helping Dunhuang make rapid progress in agriculture. The Tang also paid great attention to animal husbandry and managed it rigorously. During the High Tang period, Dunhuang was basking in an economic boom.

① During the Tang Dynasty, two emperors' temple names are Xuanzong in Chinese Pinyin. Emperor Xuanzong of Tang, also commonly known as Emperor Ming of Tang, reigned from 712 to 756, while Emperor Xuanzong Ⅱ of Tang was on the throne from 847 to 859.

图 19　莫高窟第 320 窟　未生怨故事画　盛唐
Fig.19　Enemy While Still Unborn，Mogao Cave 320　High Tang

过了历代王朝。特别是安西都护府的设立，对敦煌乃至整个西部边疆的和平，都起到了巨大的作用。由于边疆安宁，当时的敦煌佛法进入鼎盛时期(图 20)。

“渔阳鼙鼓动地来，惊破霓裳羽衣曲”，天宝十四年(755年)，安禄山以奉密诏诛杨国忠为名，自范阳起兵发动叛乱。由于唐朝承平日久，百姓多不习兵戈，所以叛军长驱直入，很快就占领河北广大地区，进而占领唐朝的东都洛阳，并继续挥兵西进。此时唐玄宗听信监军太监的谗言，诛杀大将高仙芝、封长清，可谓自毁长城。尔后起用的哥舒翰由于病重不能视

In the markets, there were silk and ceramics from the Central Plains, jade and jewelry from the Western Regions, camels, horses, and woolen products from the north, and handicrafts from local areas. Dunhuang had a population of about 30,000 in the Tianbao Era of Emperor Xuanzong, a peak not seen since the Former Qin (Fig.19). It is recorded that "at that time, China in the Tang Dynasty was powerful and prosperous, and there were 12,000 *li* from the Anyuan Gate of Chang'an to the border in the west. People lived in stability and products were abundant. No other place in the empire was as affluent and populous as Longyou area." Here Dunhuang was included. The Tang's management policy and measures taken to the Western Regions exceeded that of all the previous dynasties. The establishment of the Protectorate of Anxi particularly played an important role in guaranteeing the security of Dunhuang as well as the whole of the western borderland. Owing to the peace and safety there, the practice of Buddhism in Dunhuang prevailed and reached its zenith at that time (Fig.20).

"But rebels beat their war drums, making the earth quake / And 'Song of Rainbow Skirt and Coat of Feathers' break."① The above poem relates the beginning of the An Lushan Rebellion in the Tang Dynasty. An Lushan instigated a revolt in Fanyang in the 14th year of Tianbao Era (755) under the pretext of receiving a secret imperial edict to kill Yang Guozhong. As people lacked military training and

① These two lines are quoted from the poem "The Everlasting Regret" by Bai Juyi. It is translated by Xu Yuanchong.

图 20　莫高窟第 194 窟　菩萨　盛唐
Fig.20　Bodhisattva，Mogao Cave 194　High Tang

事，而将领互不统属，再加上临阵轻敌，最终导致潼关失守，玄宗仓皇逃窜。在玄宗出逃途中，下诏命令河西、陇右等地，除留少数士卒驻守外，其余精兵都要勤王平叛。在当时唐王朝统治岌岌可危的情况下，调兵平叛自然无何厚非，但这一道命令也直接导致了河西、陇右地区防戍力量的空虚，为吐蕃占领这些地区埋下了伏笔。

“安史之乱”平定后，由于唐中央安抚政策不当，引起了平叛将领仆固怀恩的不满，于是联合回鹘、吐蕃进攻唐朝，危及京师长安。为了解京师之危，河西节度使杨志烈派监军柏文达率河西锐卒 5000 人，袭击仆固怀恩的后方基地灵州，迫使怀恩回援。仆固怀恩派吐蕃、吐谷浑等精兵 2000 余骑夜袭柏文达，结果柏文达大败，所率士卒死者过半。而当柏文达率幸存者返回凉州时，杨志烈居然声称这次

practice owing to the long-term peace, the rebel army drove straight in, quickly occupying the vast area in Hebei, and then the eastern capital—Luoyang—before going on the attack westwards. Meanwhile, deluded by slander from a eunuch, Emperor Xuanzong killed the senior generals Gao Xianzhi and Feng Changqing, which brought about his own destruction. The succeeding General Geshu Han could not deal with military affairs as he was suffering from a serious illness, which caused the military officers to turn against each other. This, coupled with an underestimation of the enemy, finally led to the fall of the Tongguan Pass. Emperor Xuanzong was forced to flee from Chang'an and ordered all the designated troops in the Hexi and Longyou areas to resist and suppress the rebellion, except for some soldiers remaining in the garrisons. There was little choice considering the critical situation for the Tang Dynasty, but this order led directly to the weak defense of the Hexi and Longyou areas, leaving a hidden risk for occupation by the Tubo.

After the pacification of the rebellion, General Pugu Huai'en allied with the Uyghurs and the Tubo to attack the Tang, as he was not satisfied with the conciliatory policy of the central government. To rescue the capital city from the siege, Yang Zhilie, the Military Commissioner of the Hexi Area, ordered Bai Wenda, the Army Supervisor, to assault the rebels' rear base—Lingzhou—with 5,000 crack troops in Hexi, forcing Huai'en to provide reinforcements. Pugu Huai'en then sent approximately 2,000 soldiers

行动有安定京室之功，而士卒死伤并不是什么了不起的事，结果造成士卒的极大不满。所以在广德二年（764年）吐蕃围攻凉州时，士卒没有尽力抵抗，吐蕃很快就攻陷凉州。此时，吐蕃已经占领了陇右地区的秦、成、渭等州，东归的道路被切断。无奈之下，杨志烈自凉州突围后，率众西奔甘州，最终为沙陀所杀。

此后，吐蕃先后占领了甘、肃、瓜等州。河西节度使杨休明及周鼎等人率众节节西逃，退到沙州时，已无路可退。由于此时吐蕃已经切断唐中央政府与敦煌的联系，所以敦煌已经成为一片孤岛。而沙州刺史周鼎不顾个人安危，率众固守。为了夺得敦煌这个河西西端的军事重镇，吐蕃赞普不仅派遣宰相尚绮心儿率吐蕃军队攻城，甚至亲自前往

of the Tubo and Tuyuhun on horseback to attack Bai Wenda late at night, inflicting a crushing defeat on Bai with half of Bai's soldiers died. When Bai Wenda took the survivors back to Liangzhou, to their surprise, Yang Zhilie maintained it was their duty to defend the capital city, so their meritorious service was not worthy of recognition in his eyes. His comments hurt soldiers deeply and were a great blow to soldiers' morale, and consequently, when the Tubo besieged Liangzhou in the 2nd year of Guangde Era (764), the soldiers did not make an all-out effort to resist the aggression; the prefecture was quickly captured by the Tubo. Meanwhile, the Tubo had occupied Qinzhou, Chengzhou, and Weizhou in Longyou area, cutting off Yang Zhilie's route of withdrawing eastward. Reluctantly, he broke through Liangzhou, and then led his army westward to Ganzhou, where he was finally killed by the Shatuo, a tribe of the Turk.

From then on, the Tubo occupied Ganzhou, Suzhou, and Guazhou in succession. Yang Xiuming, the Military Commissioner of the Hexi Area, and Zhou Ding, the Prefect of Shazhou, led the army to retreat westwards. They suffered one defeat after another until there was no way back in Shazhou. Being cut off from contact with the central government by the Tubo, Dunhuang was left isolated, but Zhou Ding, with no regard to his personal safety, led the army to fight against the invaders. To capture Dunhuang, the important military post on the western end of the Hexi area, btsan-po (the ruler) of the Tubo not only sent Shangqi Xin'er, the Grand Councilor, to lay siege

南山督战。为了抵御吐蕃的猛烈进攻，周鼎派人前往回鹘求救，但经过一年多的时间，回鹘也没有派来援兵。无奈之下，周鼎计划焚毁沙州城，带领军民经漠北回鹘道返回中原。由于路途遥远险恶，周鼎的建议并没有得到多数人的支持。周鼎手下的都知兵马使阎朝利用大家的不满情绪，缢杀了周鼎，自领州事。在阎朝带领沙州军民抵抗了 8 年时间后，由于缺乏军粮，阎朝命令沙州地方政府以绫一端换取百姓麦一斗。结果，响应阎朝命令的民众很多。对此，阎朝高兴地说："人民还有粮食，我们还可以死守。"又过了两年多的时间，沙州城内的粮食都吃完了，守城的器械也消耗殆尽，阎朝在与吐蕃达成"毋徙它境"的协议后，率众投降吐蕃。至此，沙州军民已坚守孤城 11 年矣！

to the city, but also headed for the Nanshan Mountain to command the fight personally. In order to defend the attack from the Tubo, Zhou Ding sent an emissary to seek help from the Uyghurs, but one year later, no any reinforcement was dispatched. Reluctantly, Zhou Ding decided to implement a scorched earth policy in Shazhou, and led the army and civilians back to the Central Plains via Uyghurs' territory. But few supported him, considering the distant and dangerous journey. Taking advantage of the dissatisfaction with Zhou, Yan Chao, a subordinate of Zhou Ding, assassinated Zhou, appointed himself to govern the prefecture and continued the resistance against the Tubo for another eight years. As supplies ran short for the army, Yan Chao adopted another measure in which the local government bartered a bolt of damask silk in exchange for three kilograms of grain, which helped them to temporarily solve the problem. Yan gained confidence from that and thought they could defend the city as long as civilians had grain in their hands. However, two years later both grain and ammunition in Shazhou were completely exhausted. Yan Chao had to reach an agreement with the Tubo on the condition that they surrender to the Tubo without relocating. Until that moment, the soldiers and citizens in Shazhou had been holding onto the isolated city for 11 years.

吐蕃统治时期的敦煌

Dunhuang Under the Reign of the Tubo

吐蕃是今天我国藏族的前身。关于吐蕃的起源,汉文史料中主要有发羌说和秃发说两种说法。发羌说认为吐蕃源自中国古代的发羌,而秃发说则认为吐蕃是南凉秃发氏南徙帕米尔高原之后形成的。在松赞干布担任吐蕃赞普时期(617—650 年),吐蕃迅速强大起来,建立了统一而强大的奴隶制国家。为了共同的利益,唐朝贞观八年(634 年)讨伐吐谷浑时,曾与位于吐谷浑之南的吐蕃结盟。按照唐、蕃之间的密约,此次讨伐吐谷浑应当由唐军从东方、吐蕃自西方夹击。但松赞干布却趁李靖等率军与吐谷浑大战之机,坐收渔翁之利,将吐谷浑的南部并入吐蕃。对此,敦煌本《吐蕃大事纪年》记载,贞观九年(635 年),"赞普亲自出巡,在北道,既未发一兵抵御,亦未发一兵进攻,迫使唐人及吐谷浑人岁输贡赋。由此,首次将

The people of the Tubo were the early predecessors of the Tibetan minority in China. According to the records, there are two schools of thought concerning the origin of the Tubo tribe: the Faqiang theory and the Tufa theory. According to the Faqiang theory, the Tubo originated from the Faqiang people of ancient China, while the Tufa theory holds that the Tubo formed when the Tufa clan of the Southern Liang moved southward to the Pamirs. During the reign of btsan-po Songtsen Gampo (617–650), the founder and ruler of the Tubo kingdom, the Tubo quickly rose to power and established a unified slave-holding state. For mutual interests, the Tang Dynasty allied with the Tubo in the 8th year of Zhenguan Era (634) to attack the Tuyuhun. According to a secret pact between the Tang and the Tubo, the Tang forces would have attacked the Tuyuhun from the east and the Tubo forces from the west simultaneously. However, Songtsen Gampo profited from the war between the Tang and the Tuyuhun and as a result he annexed the southern part of Tuyuhun into his territory. It was recorded in the *Annals of the Tubo* in Dunhuang manuscripts that in the 9th year of Zhenguan Era (635) Songtsen Gampo went on a

吐谷浑人收归治下。”虽然唐朝向吐蕃“岁输贡赋”的记载未免为夸张之词，但此时吐蕃已吞并吐谷浑大片领土则确是事实。此后，吐谷浑名义上是一个独立的国家，但实际上领土已经被一分为二，北部属唐，南部则属吐蕃。

吐谷浑被瓜分之后，唐与吐蕃的结盟基础也就不复存在。为了建立与吐蕃之间的缓冲地带，唐朝册封了前吐谷浑可汗慕容顺为王，继续统治吐谷浑部族。由于吐谷浑国内局势不稳，慕容顺很快就被国人杀害。随后，唐朝又册立了慕容顺之子诺曷钵为王，并派大军护送其回国继位。贞观十年(636 年)，唐朝将弘化公主嫁给诺曷钵。看到这种情形，松赞干布也频繁遣使到唐朝，请求与唐朝通

campaign to the north and forced the Tang and the Tuyuhun to send tribute to him in the form of grain and military taxes annually, in lieu of war. It was the first time that the Tubo had occupied and governed the Tuyuhun. Though it was somewhat of an exaggeration to say that the Tang government "paid tribute in the form of grain and military taxes annually" to the Tubo, it was a fact that the Tubo had already annexed vast areas of territory belonging to the Tuyuhun. From then on, the Tuyuhun Khanate was a nominally independent state, with its territory divided into two parts, the northern part belonging to the Tang and the southern part to the Tubo.

After the Tuyuhun's lands were partitioned, the basis for an alliance between the Tang government and the Tubo ceased to exist. In order to establish a buffer zone with the Tubo, the Tang Dynasty conferred the title of prince on Murong Shun, the former Khan of the Tuyuhun, and allowed him to govern the tribes again. However, due to political instability, Murong Shun was assassinated by his own people. The Tang government then allowed his son Murong Nuohebo to succeed the throne and be escorted back to the Tuyuhun by Tang's army. In 636, the Tang married Princess Honghua to Nuohebo. In light of this situation, Songtsen Gampo frequently dispatched envoys to the Tang government, hoping to create the marriage alliance between the Tubo and the central government. Rebuffed by the Tang Dynasty, the Tubo carried out reprisals on the Tuyuhun, forming alliances with other states and attacking the Tuyuhun and the Tang-controlled Songzhou numerous times. After the

婚。被唐朝拒绝之后，吐蕃迁怒于吐谷浑，于是联合羊同等国多次进攻吐谷浑，并进攻唐朝的松州。在经过松州之战后，唐蕃双方达成了谅解，唐太宗接受了松赞干布通婚的请求。贞观十五年(641 年)，文成公主入蕃和亲，成为唐蕃之间和平的使者。在此后的一段时间里，唐蕃之间的关系在很大程度上得到改善。但随着唐太宗和松赞干布的相继去世，唐蕃之间的和亲关系名存实亡。

在 7 世纪后半叶，唐朝和吐蕃之间为了争夺安西四镇，曾经进行过长时间的战争。而在唐玄宗开元年间，唐蕃双方更是进行了长达 12 年的武装对抗。进入天宝年间，由于与唐朝的战争多次战败，吐蕃方面损失惨重，民怨沸腾，而赞普的威信丧失殆尽。在天宝十三年(754 年)年底，吐蕃大族发动宫廷政变，吐蕃赞普弃隶缩赞被刺身亡，这使得吐蕃元气大伤。之后不久，唐朝就爆发了“安史之乱”，国势一落千丈。吐蕃趁机攻占了唐朝的河陇广大地区(图 21)。

Battle in Songzhou, the Tang reached an understanding with the Tubo and complied with their request to intermarry with the Tang. In 641, to establish peace between the two parties, Princess Wencheng married Songtsen Gampo. A harmonious relationship between the Tang and the Tubo lasted for some years. After Emperor Taizong and Songtsen Gampo passed away, however, the relationship between two parties deteriorated rapidly, existing in name only.

In the latter half of the 7th century, the Tang Dynasty had been fighting against the Tubo over control of the Four Garrisons in Anxi for many years. During the Kaiyuan Era (713–741) of Emperor Xuanzong, the armed confrontations between the two parties went on for twelve years. In the Tianbao Era (742–756) of Emperor Xuanzong, Tubo people were boiling with resentment after suffering so many defeats in conflicts with the Tang, and the btsan-po of the Tubo lost people's support as a result. At the end of 754, the wealthy and powerful families of the Tubo staged a palace coup and the btsan-po Qili Suozan was assassinated, which greatly sapped the vitality and power of the Tubo. Before long, however, the An Lushan Rebellion broke out in the Tang Dynasty, causing the imperial government's power to suffer a disastrous decline. The Tubo seized upon this chance to occupy the vast Hexi Corridor and Longyou area (Fig.21).

图 21　莫高窟第 112 窟　反弹琵琶图　吐蕃占领敦煌时期

Fig.21　Reverse *Pipa*–Playing，Mogao Cave 112　Period of Tubo's Occupation of Dunhuang

吐蕃占领河、陇地区之后，首先面临的一个问题就是如何处理广大新占领区的民族关系。当时,吐蕃人、孙波人属于嫡系部队；吐谷浑人和党项人已被吐蕃收编，但仍有相当多较为独立的杂牌军;此外,还有被征服的河西地区的汉人。从当时的实际情况看，汉人是河西地区的主要经济支柱。吐蕃刚开始进入河西，在军事进攻的同时,横加劫掠,到处抢夺,子女玉帛,悉归帐下。当地百姓没有任何政治上的保障，从而造成了当时社会动荡不安。在能够有效地控制新占领区之后，吐蕃统治者以强硬的措施消除社会上的不安定因素,镇压反抗势力,推行蕃化政策,清查户口,重新造籍。瓜沙大族虽然在当地依然影响很大，但汉人的社会地位低于吐蕃人，甚至低于一些同样被吐蕃征服的少数民族。由于吐蕃统治者笃信佛教，敦煌地区的佛教活动并没有因此受到太大的影响(图 22)。

After taking over the Hexi and Longyou areas, the first problem the Tubo faced was how to deal with the complex interethnic and socioeconomic relationships in this vast area. At the time, people of the Tubo and the Sumpa (*Sunbo* in Chinese) were under Tubo's direct control. The Tuyuhun and the Tanguts had already been incorporated into the Tubo's own troops, and there were also quite a number of independent miscellaneous troops; in addition, the ethnic Han also lived in the occupied Hexi area. In reality, the Han people were the economic pillar in the Hexi area. When the Tubo occupied this area, they immediately plundered and pillaged on a widespread basis. The lack of political stability for the local civilians caused social turbulence and unrest. After the Tubo were able to effectively control the newly-occupied area, the governor put down the unrest through a series of measures: suppressing the rebels, implementing a Tibetanization policy, checking registered permanent residents and enacting a new household registration system. Although the great clans in Guazhou and Shazhou remained influential among the local people, the Han people were still lower in social status than the Tubo people, even lower than the other ethnic minorities conquered by the Tubo. Fortunately, on account of the Tubo ruler's devout Buddhist beliefs, Dunhuang's Buddhist activities and projects were not affected by Tubo's attitudes toward the ethnic Han (Fig.22).

图 22　藏经洞出土的普贤菩萨图
吐蕃占领敦煌时期
(8 世纪末—9 世纪初)
Fig.22　Image of Samantabhadra
Found in the Library Cave
Period of Tubo's Occupation of Dunhuang
(ca. late 8th Century to early 9th Century)

敦煌虽然在贞元二年(786年)陷蕃,但沙州人民从来没有真正屈服，反抗斗争此起彼伏。贞元十一年(795年),沙州玉关驿户氾国忠等人逃往瀚海沙漠，不幸为吐蕃擒获,被流放到酒泉。次年七月十一日，氾国忠等人从吐蕃手中抢得马匹和兵器后从酒泉脱逃,潜回敦煌。由于其行踪比较隐秘，而吐蕃官吏又疏于防范，氾国忠等人趁夜深人静之机攻入沙州城内,杀掉了吐蕃监使等官吏。由于当时正处在秋收农忙之际，沙州城内的百姓多在郊外农田过夜，沙州当地官吏难以组织力量抵抗，所以汉人地方长官只能躲避在沙州城内著名的龙兴寺内。事后，其向吐蕃政府报告此事时，只能以前往龙兴寺是为了保护身在寺内的高僧摩诃衍而搪塞了事。天快亮的时候,此位官员召集百姓10余人前往营救吐蕃节儿。当他们到达子城南门附近节儿住宅时，节儿已经纵火烧舍,“伏剑自裁，投身火中，化为灰

Although Dunhuang was captured by the Tubo in the 2nd year of Zhenyuan Era(786), the people in Shazhou never yielded and their resistance never ceased. In the 11th year of Zhenyuan Era (795), Fan Guozhong and a band of followers fled Dunhuang into the vast desert, but unfortunately they were captured by the Tubo forces and subsequently exiled to Jiuquan. On July 11, 796, Fan Guozhong and his followers seized horses and weapons from the Tubo, planning a stealth attack on Dunhuang. Taking advantage of the lax defenses, Fan and others crept into Dunhuang in the depth of night, where they killed the Commissioner of the Tubo and other officials. Since this was during the harvest season and people were busy in the fields, most of the civilians were not in the city at the time, making it impossible for the local government to organize an effective resistance. A Han official was forced to hide out in the Longxing Temple. When reporting the event back to the Tubo governor, he made the excuse that he went to the temple to protect a distinguished monk named Moheyan. At dawn, this Han official called upon a dozen of local men to rescue the Head of the City, but when they approached his residence at the south gate of the walled town, they found that he had burned down his own house and committed suicide. Fan Guozhong and his men achieved a considerable victory through this anti-oppression with the aim of killing

烬”。氾国忠等人的这次起义，主要的目标就是所谓的“蕃官”即吐蕃官吏,带有浓郁的反民族压迫色彩，而在进攻沙州的过程中，确实也取得了不小的战果。所以沙州当地的官吏在向吐蕃统治者汇报时，哀叹“今蕃军将等，或在或亡，不知实数”。而吐蕃派驻沙州的最高统治者节儿,也被迫伏剑自裁,引火自焚。但由于氾国忠等人寡不敌众,最终被擒获。其在吐蕃统治者审讯时，明确承认“谋杀蕃官是实”,反映了吐蕃占领河西初期，蕃汉之间的民族矛盾是相当尖锐的。

吐蕃统治者为了维护其统治的长久，不得不改变统治方式，争取新占领区的百姓，积极与当地世家大族合作，采取较为缓和的统治政策。如率领敦煌军民坚守10年的阎朝就被任命为部落使。在吐蕃统治时期的敦煌文书中,他被称为“大蕃部落使河西节度太原阎公”。“部落使”是吐蕃授予他的官职，

officials of the Tubo. When local officials reported the event to their Tubo governors, they wailed, “we cannot account for the exact number of the Tubo officials involved in the event, and do not know whether they are even alive or dead.” At the same time, Fan Guozhong and his followers were outnumbered, and when they were eventually caught by the Tubo and interrogated, they confessed that they had murdered the Tubo officials. This event reveals that the conflicts and ethnic tensions between the Han and the Tubo were extremely fierce during the initial period of Tubo’s reign in the Hexi area.

In order to maintain a stable reign, the Tubo realized that they had to change political tactics. They began with negotiating with people in the occupied areas, cooperating with local influential clans and carrying out more moderate policies. For example, Yan Chao, who had led the soldiers and common people in guarding Dunhuang for more than ten years, was appointed as the Commissioner of a Tribe. It was recorded in Dunhuang documents that he was given the titles of the Military Comissioner of the Hexi Area as well as the Commissioner of a Tribe, of which the former was his title before he surrendered to the Tubo, and the latter was the one conferred by the Tubo, showing his dual roles during the reign of the Tubo. Yan Chao was later suspected of plotting a rebellion against the Tubo and was murdered by poison placed in his shoes. At the time, the local

"河西节度使"是他投降吐蕃前担任的职务,表明他具有双重的身份。但此后吐蕃怀疑阎朝有反蕃的举动,所以暗地里将毒药放入阎朝的靴子内,使阎朝中毒身亡。而吐蕃统治者所依靠汉人的中坚力量,主要是敦煌当地张、阴、索、李等大族势力。此外,吐蕃统治者还从生活习惯和文化传统上推行蕃化政策,企图借此来消除民族隔阂,进而消除人民的反蕃情绪。吐蕃占领敦煌初期,尚乞心儿便让沙州人民改易穿着、学说蕃语、赭面文身。《张淮深碑》载:"河洛沸腾……并南蕃之化……抚纳降和,远通盟誓,析离财产,自定桑田。赐部落之名,占行军之额。由是行遵辫发,体美织皮,左衽束身,垂肱跪膝。"《阴处士修功德记》中也有"熊罴爱子,拆襁褓以文身;鸳鸯夫妻,解鬟钿而辫发"的记载。由此可见,吐蕃统治者在敦煌地区迫使汉人说蕃语、左衽而服、辫发、文身,甚至从婴儿就开始做起。其目的是想从语言、风俗、传统等民族间的明

wealthy and powerful families of the Han ethnic group were the dominant sociopolitical force, on which the Tubo depended in governing the area, including the Zhang, the Yin, the Suo, and the Li clans. Additionally, the Tubo rulers also attempted to eliminate ethnic tensions and hostile resistance against them by carrying out a Tibetanization policy aimed at changing the social and cultural traditions of the Han people. During the initial period of the Tubo's reign, Shangqi Xin'er ordered the local people in Dunhuang to change their style of dress, paint red ochre on the faces, tattoo their bodies, and learn to speak the Tibetan language. On the Zhang Huaishen Stele and in the *Merits and Virtues of Yin Jiazheng*, it was recorded that the Tubo rulers re-distributed Han people's belongings and farmlands, and forced them to be enrolled in tribes and armies, speak Tibetan, wear Tibetan-style clothing, braid their hair, and tattoo their bodies, even the infants and young children were no exception. They aimed to bridge the gap between the two ethnic groups by eliminating significant differences in language, customs, and traditions, thereby to achieve long-term peace and stability in Dunhuang. The Tibetanization policy was carried out not only in Dunhuang, but also in the whole Hexi Corridor, but these policies did not ameliorate the subjugated Han people's bitter hatred to the Tubo and yearning for their native land.

显差别上消除隔阂，达到长治久安的效果。吐蕃的蕃化政策不限于敦煌一地，而是在整个河西地区推行。但这些政策并没有消除汉族人民对吐蕃统治者的痛恨和对大唐的怀念。

长庆二年(822 年),唐朝政府派刘元鼎前往吐蕃结盟。河西等地的汉人见到唐朝使者的麾盖,纷纷跪拜迎接。到龙支城时，有耄耋千余人跪拜并向刘元鼎泣诉:“我们以前被吐蕃军队俘虏至此，到现在子孙都不敢忘记自己是大唐的子民。对我们这些人，朝廷是否还放在心上？收复河西的军队什么时候才能来到？”言语之际,已是呜咽不止。刘元鼎暗地里询问,才得知他们原来是丰州人氏。虽然汉人不忍心放弃唐服,但这是吐蕃统治者所严令禁止的,只是在每年祭祀的时候,汉人才被允许穿上唐装。每到这个时候,吐蕃统治区的汉人“被衣中国之服,号恸而藏之”。

为了巩固统治,吐蕃在河陇

In the 2nd year of Changqing Era (822), the Tang government sent Liu Yuanding to form an alliance with the Tubo. When the Han people in the Hexi area saw the envoys from the central government, they fell to their knees. When Liu Yuanding and his men arrived at Longzhi Town, over one thousand elderly people knelt before Liu, crying, “We were captured and brought here by the Tubo army. All this time, we’ve never forgotten that we are people of the Tang Dynasty. Does the government still remember us? When will the Tang army come to recapture the Hexi area?” Liu Yuanding secretly inquired about their situation, knowing that they came from Fengzhou. The local Han people were unwilling to abandon their Tang-style clothing, but wearing it was strictly prohibited by the Tubo governors. Only when carrying out sacrificial or annual ancestor worship rituals were the ethnic Han allowed to wear their native apparel, and during these times the Han people would “wear their Tang clothing and weep bitterly in secret.”

To consolidate their rule, the Tubo set up five *tongjia*① ten-thousand-household tribes and one larger region under the

① *Tongjia*, *delun*, *agusa*, *xidongsa*, and *qingsan* in Chinese are transliterations of “mtong khyab,” “bde blon,” “rgod sar”, “stong sar”, and “phyug mtshams” respectively in the Tubo language.

地区设5个通颊万户部落和一个德论进行管辖，并设立一系列军镇用以镇守。吐蕃占领敦煌后，首先设置了由节度使—乞利本—节儿—都督、监军—部落使—判官等官员构成的职官系统，以便统治。由于敦煌地区的居民以汉人为主，吐蕃为了进行有效的统治，在任用吐蕃官员的同时，还任用汉人为辅助官员。吐蕃统治者正是用这种双轨制的职官体系，才得以在河西地区维持近百年的统治。敦煌从军镇体制上属瓜州，其城主称为“节儿”。吐蕃占领敦煌之后，对敦煌进行了许多变革。790年，吐蕃按其本身的制度，将沙州百姓按职业分成若干个部

control of *delun* in the Hexi and Longyou areas; meanwhile, they established many military towns to garrison the frontier. After the occupation of Dunhuang, the Tubo set up a political system for ruling this area, including Military Commissioner, *qiliben* (a chief governor), *jie'er* (the head of a city), Army Supervisor, Commissioner of a Tribe, and assistant tribal chieftains. Since the Han people constituted the majority of the residents in Dunhuang, each time the Tubo government appointed a Tubo official, they would also give an ethnic Han citizen a post of assistant official. Through this double-tiered official system, the Tubo was able to maintain its rule in the Hexi area for a hundred years. According to the military town system, Dunhuang was subordinated under the jurisdiction of Guazhou and its head was *jie'er*. The Tubo also carried out reforms in Dunhuang. In 790, the Tubo divided the people of Shazhou into several tribes according to their occupations, such as the tribe for farming, sericulture, and production, the tribe for military defense, the tribe of the Sangha (Buddhist clergy), and the tribe of the Taoist priests and their family members or relatives①. The size of each tribe was equal to a town in the Tang Dynasty and its internal organization was similar to the original tribe of the

① The tribe for farming, sericulture, and production (*simian* in Chinese), the tribe for military defense (*xingren*), the tribe of the Sangha (*sengni*) and the tribe of the Taoist priests and their family members or relatives (*daomen biaoqin*) are translated versions by Chinese scholars according to these tribes' functions and composition of residents.

落，如“丝绵部落”“行人部落”“僧尼部落”“道门亲表部落”。一个部落大致辖原来的一个乡，其内部的组织情况与吐蕃本部的部落制相似。部落有部落使，下设将，将有将头。其最基本的单位是千户（部落），千户之下是小千户（即500户组织），设小千户长一人。小千户之下为百户（将），百户长称“勒曲堪”。最后是10户组织，10户长称“勒堪”。820年前后，增置军事系统的阿骨萨、悉董萨部落。824年，又增置通颊军事部落。吐蕃改变了敦煌的军政管辖体制，虽然是为了加强统治，具有重要的军事因素，但从内部组织上看，其经济因素也很重要，即为了征收“突税差科”。因此，“部落—将”制，并非单纯的军事组织机构，乃是集政治、军事、经济三位一体的组织系统，即官府户籍制度。吐蕃统治时期的户口登记是十分详细的，家庭成员的出生、死亡、出家、嫁娶都有详细的记载。

吐蕃统治时期，改变了唐代前期实行的均田制，实行突田制。突作为土地的计量单位，1突等于10亩。计口授田，大体上是每人1突，即10亩（图23）。土地税被称

Tubo. Each tribe had its Commissioner of a Tribe, assisted by head commander and commanders. The basic demographic unit of a tribe was the *qianhu* (an administrative division of tribes of one thousand households). The sub-unit of the *qianhu* was the half *qianhu* (five hundred households), and below that was the *baihu* (one hundred households). The smallest unit of organization was the *shihu* (ten households). Each organizational unit also had a leader, subordinate to the Commissioner of a Tribe. From 820 to 824, the Tubo government also added three military tribes, such as *agusa* tribe, *xidongsa* tribe and *tongjia* military tribe to their social organization system. Although the change in the political and military governance system was based on martial law with the aim of reinforcement of political rule, economic factors were also crucial for the Tubo, namely to collect taxes and impose harsh levies. Thus the tribal system was not only a military organization, but also a kind of feudal household registration system, integrating the politics, the military, and the economy into one. During the reign of the Tubo, household registration records were so detailed that the family's births, deaths, marriages, and even becoming a monastic were all recorded.

Tubo's reign saw changes in the

图 23　莫高窟第 285 窟　耕获图　吐蕃占领敦煌时期

Fig.23　Plowing and Harvesting Scene, Mogao Cave 285　Period of Tubo's Occupation of Dunhuang

为“突田”。交纳“突田”被称为“纳突”。吐蕃在河西所实行的赋税制度，除保留旧有的奴隶制成分外，主要吸收唐及所占领地区的赋税制度，并设有“税务官”“税吏”来执行任务。交纳的物品有小麦、青麦、布、油等，按户交纳。突田制下的百姓除了纳突之外，还有差科，即服官府的徭役，包括身役、知更、远使等。但吐蕃时期的社会经济发展缓慢，虽然继续计口授田，但部落编制不利于组织生产。僧尼的大量增加，减少了劳动人口。地子税和突税的征收，使百姓的负担大增。吐蕃统治者为了防止汉族百姓的反

juntian system[①] implemented in the Tang Dynasty, and the *tutian* policy was carried out instead. Here *tu* was a unit of land measurement; one *tu* was equal to ten *mu*[②]. Farmlands were allocated based on population, with each person being assigned one *tu* (Fig.23). *Tutian* referred to the land tax by the Tubo, so that paying *tutian* was called *natu* (*na* in Chinese meaning paying), that is, paying the land tax. With respect to the taxation system in the Hexi area, besides retaining the established slavery system, the Tubo assimilated the taxation system of the Tang Dynasty and of their occupied areas, and also appointed tax officers and tax collectors to fulfill the task. Households paid the tax per family unit with wheat, barley, cloth, edible oil, and other commodities. Under the *tutian* system, people not only paid land tax, but were also forced to labor for the local government including labor service, night watch, and service as an envoy abroad. Social and economic development under the Tubo's reign was slow and the organization of production was hindered by the imposed tribal system, although the amount of land allocated by the government was based on the number of people in a family. Furthermore, the increasing number of monks caused the available labor pool to decrease and the imposed land taxes

---

① *Juntian* system, also called equal-field system, was a historical system of land ownership and distribution in China. It was introduced into practice by Emperor Xiaowen of the Northern Wei and continued through the Sui and Tang dynasties. The system worked on the basis that all land was owned by the government, which would then allocate it to individual families. Every individual was entitled to a certain amount of land, depending on their ability to supply labor.

② *Mu* is a Chinese area unit, equal to 0.667 hectares or 1.6 acres.

抗，将民间铁器全部收缴，严重影响了农业生产。唐朝的货币被废除，交易退回到了以物易物。

吐蕃占领敦煌时期，也正处于吐蕃王朝的佛教前弘期，而敦煌又恰是当时的一个佛教中心，因此这里的佛教得到了保护(图 24)。此外，

and *tutian* taxes inflicted ever greater burdens on people. In order to prevent the local ethnic Han from starting an uprising, the Tubo rulers confiscated all the iron tools from the residents, strongly hindering the development of agricultural production. In addition, the currency of the Tang Dynasty was abolished so that transactions reverted to a barter system.

The Tubo occupied Dunhuang in the early stage of Buddhist transmission in China,

图 24　莫高窟第 159 窟　吐蕃赞普礼佛图　吐蕃占领敦煌时期

Fig.24　Tubo's Btsan-po Venerating the Buddha, Mogao Cave 159
Period of Tubo's Occupation of Dunhuang

不少不愿与吐蕃统治者合作的落蕃官员和世家大族中的人物，也投入空门寻求解脱。因此，这时的沙州佛教空前繁荣，寺院从吐蕃统治前期的13所增加到末期的17所，僧尼从300余人猛增到1000人以上。在吐蕃统治者的扶持之下，寺院经济空前繁荣，敦煌的寺院和内地一样，有寺户和土地，不受官府管辖，享有种种特权。吐蕃在敦煌的统治一直持续到宣宗大中二年（848年）。由于处于吐蕃的统治之下，所以敦煌免受唐武宗灭佛的影响，使得敦煌佛教持续发展（图25）。

when Dunhuang was the center of the Buddhist world and thus received both patronage and protection from the Tubo (Fig.24). Moreover, many high-ranking officials and members of the local Han gentry, not wanting to cooperate with the Tubo government, engaged in a sort of passive resistance by entering monastic life as Buddhist monks. Consequently, Dunhuang witnessed the prosperity of Buddhism: the number of temples increased from 13 in the initial period of the Tubo's reign to 17 at the end of its reign; the population of monks tripled from an initial number of approximately 300 to over 1,000. Under the patronage and support from the Tubo government, the temple economy flourished as never before, so that the temples in Dunhuang, as in the Central Plains, had their own legal residence status, owned their own land, and enjoyed various privileges and independence from the local government. The Tubo reigned over Dunhuang until the 2nd year of Dazhong Era (848). It was under the Tubo's rule that Dunhuang escaped the anti-Buddhist religious persecution by Emperor Wuzong of the Tang Dynasty, thus allowing the continuous development of Buddhism in this area (Fig.25).

图 25　莫高窟第 158 窟　涅槃变中的各国王子　吐蕃占领敦煌时期
Fig.25　Princes in *Nirvana Sutra* Illustration Painting，Mogao Cave 158
Period of Tubo's Occupation of Dunhuang

归义军时期的敦煌

Dunhuang During the Period of the *Guiyijun* Regime

唐宣宗大中二年(848年),沙州人张议潮率众起义,驱逐吐蕃,在敦煌建立了以汉人为主的政权。大中五年(851年),唐王朝于敦煌置归义军政权,任命张议潮为归义军节度使。从此,直至宋仁宗景祐三年(1036年)西夏攻占敦煌为止,除张承奉一度建立的西汉金山国和敦煌国之外,归义军政权在张、曹两大世家的统治下,共历180余年。

张氏家族自魏晋以来就是敦煌当地的世家大族,具有相当强的势力。张议潮之父张谦逸在吐蕃统治敦煌时期曾出任都督一职。张议潮出生在吐蕃占领敦煌时期,他亲身经历了吐蕃统治者的残暴,因此在青年时代就忧国忧民。唐宪宗元和十年(815年),17岁的张议潮抄下一

In the 2nd year of Dazhong Era of Emperor Xuanzong Ⅱ of the Tang Dynasty (848), Zhang Yichao from Shazhou led an uprising to expulse the Tubo and established a regional regime based on the Han ethnic group in Dunhuang. In 851, the Tang Dynasty set up a new government in Dunhuang, appointing Zhang Yichao as the Military Commissioner of the *Guiyijun* Force. The *Guiyijun* regime (851–1036) lasted for more than 180 years under the rule of the two aristocratic clans of the Cao and Zhang families, until Dunhuang fell to the Western Xia in the 3rd year of Jingyou Era of Emperpor Renzong of the Song Dynasty (1036). These two clans governed Dunhuang continuously during this period, except for a brief interruption when Zhang Chengfeng established the State of Jinshan and the State of Dunhuang.

The Zhang clan had been an influential aristocratic family in Dunhuang since the Wei and Jin dynasties. Zhang Yichao was born in the period of the Tubo regime, and his father Zhang Qianyi served as the Commander-in-Chief of Dunhuang during that time. Suffering the tyranny of the Tubo rulers by himself, Zhang Yichao had a deep concern for the fate of his country and people since his youth. When he was 17 years old in the 10th year of Yuanhe Era

首《无名歌》来表达对广大受苦受难民众的同情。成年后，张议潮私下里结交敦煌的豪杰及名门望族、释门教首及僧徒等各方面力量，秘密积蓄力量，准备起义归唐。

唐宪宗会昌二年(842年)，吐蕃赞普朗达玛由于灭佛，被佛教徒刺杀，吐蕃本部的奴隶平民也发生起义，吐蕃国内陷入一片混乱的境地。吐蕃原洛门川讨击使论恐热和鄯州节度使尚婢婢之间为争权夺利，展开混战，殃及河西及陇右地区。唐朝趁此机会，决心收复河陇。唐武宗会昌四年(844年)三月，唐政府“以回鹘衰落，吐蕃内乱，议复河湟四镇十八州”。唐宣宗大中元年(847年)五月，河东节度使王宰率军于盐

of Emperor Xianzong (815), he copied and circulated a poem “An Unnamed Song” to express his sympathy for the suffering people. After he grew into an adult, Zhang Yichao began secretly planning an uprising to return Dunhuang to the Tang's rule, involving army personnel, prominent citizens, Buddhist monastics, and other influential people.

In the 2nd year of Huichang Era (842), btsan-po Langdarma of the Tubo was assassinated by the Buddhists for his policies of persecuting Buddhism. Slaves and civilians also had an rebellion of their own, leaving the Tubo in chaos. In the meantime, Lun Kongre, the former Commander of the Luomen River, and Shang Bibi, the Military Commissioner of Shanzhou, fought each other for power, which devastated the Hexi and the Longyou areas. Taking advantage of this opportunity, the Tang government determined to regain the Helong area①. In March of the 4th year of Huichang Era of Emperor Wuzong (844), the Tang government declared, “The Uyghurs have declined and the Tubo are going through a civil strife, so it is high time to propose regaining the four garrisons and eighteen prefectures in the Hehuang area.” Wang Zai, the Military Commissioner of Hedong, defeated Lun Kongre in Yanzhou in May of the 1st year of Dazhong Era of Emperor Xuanzong II (847). In the following December, Cui Gong, the Military Commissioner of Fengxiang, also defeated the Tubo and recovered the Qingshui area. Due to the collapse of the Tubo

① Helong area refers to the Hexi area and the Longyou area.

州大败论恐热。次年十二月，凤翔节度使崔珙也击败吐蕃，收复了清水地区。大中三年(849年)，占领唐朝秦州、原州和安乐州3州及萧关等7关地区的吐蕃守将，由于看到吐蕃王国崩溃、归国无望的现实，所以纷纷归附唐朝。对此，唐政府喜出望外，马上命令西北边境的凤翔、邠宁、朔方等节度使派兵进驻上述地区，并随即派遣官员前往管理。

由于驻守于河陇东部的吐蕃守将的归附，所以唐政府收复3州7关并没有花费太多的周折。几乎与此同时，河西西部的敦煌地区也发生了翻天覆地的变化。大中二年(848年)，张议潮趁吐蕃内乱之际，联合当地的汉人及包括粟特人在内的多个少数民族把吐蕃统治者赶出了沙州。随后，张议潮又收复了瓜州。收复沙州和瓜州后，张议潮派遣押衙高进达等10道专使入京献捷，以取得与唐政府的联系。当时河西重镇肃州、甘州、凉州等地仍为吐蕃所有，尚未收复。因此，沙州使者只能绕道漠北而行，到达了唐朝的天德军。在天德军使李丕的帮助下，使者于大中五

regime, the Tubo generals who had controlled three prefectures such as Qinzhou, Yuanzhou, and Anlezhou, and seven passes pledged their allegiance to the central government in 849. The Tang government then ordered the Military Commissioners in Fengxiang, Binning, and Shuofang along the northwestern border to station troops in those areas, and sent officials to supervise them.

After the surrender of Tubo generals stationing east of the Helong area, the Tang government had little difficulty in recovering its three prefectures and seven passes. At the same time, the situation in Dunhuang had also changed dramatically. In 848, seizing an opportunity in the midst of the Tubo's civil strife, Zhang Yichao expelled the Tubo from Shazhou, allying himself with the local Han and other ethnic minorities including the Sogdians. He next recovered Guazhou. After that, Zhang sent ten special envoys successively to Chang'an to report his victories with the aim of establishing contact with the central government. However, certain strategically important places such as Suzhou, Ganzhou, and Liangzhou were still under the control of the Tubo, forcing the envoys from Shazhou to make a detour via the desert to the Tiande Army of the Tang. With the help of Li Pi, a military officer of the Tiande Army, the envoys arrived in Chang'an in

年(851年)年初辗转到达京师长安。当唐宣宗看到张议潮的进表时,感叹道:“俗话说关西出名将,果然名不虚传!”大臣们也纷纷拍手称快,欢呼万岁,以示祝贺。在得知张议潮自沙州起事的消息后,唐政府在大加赞叹的同时,很快就授予张议潮沙州防御使之职,可见唐政府对张议潮起事的欢迎和支持。而张议潮在大中二年(848年)收复沙、瓜二州后,并没有停止进军的步伐。大中二年(848年)至大中四年(850年)间,张议潮“缮甲兵,耕且战,悉复余州”,相继收复肃州、甘州及伊州等地,并很快派出了以其兄张议潭为首的第二批使团。大中五年(851年)八月份,张议潭使团到达唐都长安。唐政府在得知张议潮“悉复余州”的消息后,于十一月设立归义军,授张议潮为归义军节度使,命其统领沙、瓜、甘、肃、鄯、伊、西、河、兰、岷、廓等11州(图26)。

由于晚唐政府政治腐败、

851. Upon reading the report from Zhang Yichao about the uprising in Shazhou, Emperor Xuanzong Ⅱ exclaimed, “the reputations of the great generals from the Guanxi[1] area are certainly well-deserved.” Soon, Zhang Yichao was conferred the title of the Defense Commissioner of Shazhou, which demonstrated the approval and support for the uprising from the central government. Meanwhile, Zhang continued his military campaigns after these victories. From 848 to 850, Zhang Yichao stockpiled weapons and trained soldiers, cultivated the land, and simulataneously fought against the Tubo, eventually recovering Suzhou, Ganzhou, and Yizhou. He dispatched a second group of envoys with the leader Zhang Yitan, his older brother, to Chang’an, who reported the good news to the Tang government in August of 851. In November, the Tang government established the *Guiyijun* Force and made Zhang Yichao its Military Commissioner in charge of 11 prefectures including Shazhou, Guazhou, Ganzhou, Suzhou, Shanzhou, Yizhou, Xizhou, Hezhou, Lanzhou, Minzhou, and Kuozhou (Fig.26).

Due to rampant political corruption, separatist warlords, and peasant rebellions in the Late Tang, the Tang empire lost its ability to effectively manage the Hexi area. Under such circumstances, Zhang Yichao emerged

---

① Guanxi refers to the area west of the Hangu Pass.

图 26　藏经洞出土的天王图　唐 (9 世纪)

Fig.26　Image of Heavenly King Found in the Library Cave　Tang Dynasty (in the 9th Century)

国力衰微，又面临着藩镇割据、农民起义等严峻的局面，所以已经失去经营河西的能力。在这种情况下，经营河陇地区的任务就自然而然地落在张议潮身上。张议潮收复河西后，在努力发展经济的同时，也在大力加强守备，以稳定河西局势。而此时虽然名义上归义军收复了整个河西地区，但吐蕃残余及回鹘势力的存在仍然威胁着归义军政权的安全。大中十年（856年）左右，吐谷浑王纠集吐蕃等族前往侵扰沙州。这个消息被归义军侦查得知，张议潮随即调兵遣将，主动出击。当他率军进至沙州西南时，与吐谷浑的军队遭遇。吐谷浑王看到张议潮早有准备，不敢交战，只得狼狈逃窜。张议潮挥师追击1000多里，一直深入到吐谷浑境内，活捉其宰相三人，当场斩首以儆效尤。此外，还俘虏300多人，夺得驼马2000多匹。

在沙州以北约1000里左右的伊州城西，有纳职县，这里聚集着回鹘及吐蕃残部，频繁劫掠伊州，俘虏人民，抢夺牲畜，闹得民心不安。为了解除这

as the most suitable leader for governing the Helong area, who not only made great efforts to boost the economy, but also vigorously strengthened military defenses so as to stabilize the situation in the Hexi Corridor. However, although it seemed that the *Guiyijun* regime had recovered the entire Hexi area, the remnants of the Tubo and the Uyghurs forces still remained a threat. Sometime around the 10th year of Dazhong Era (856), the chieftain of the Tuyuhun mustered the Tubo and other forces to invade Shazhou. On hearing the news, Zhang Yichao deployed his troops and officers in counter-offense, engaging the Tuyuhun forces in the southwest of Shazhou. The Tuyuhun immediately fled in panic after discovering that Zhang had made sound preparations for battle. Zhang Yichao led his troops to rout the Tuyuhun forces more than 1,000 *li* until they crossed into Tuyuhun's territory, where three chancellors of the Tuyuhun were executed, more than 300 soldiers were taken prisoners, and 2,000 camels and horses were confiscated by Zhang's troops.

To the west of Yizhou, 1,000 *li* north of Shazhou, was Nazhi County where the remnants of the Uyghurs and the Tubo gathered and frequently raided livestock and harassed the local people. In order to relieve the threat there, in June of 856, Zhang Yichao led his troops into battle to strike

一威胁，大中十年(856年)六月，张议潮又亲率甲兵，进击纳职的回鹘部族。由于回鹘没有料到张议潮突然率兵至此，一时大惊失色，措手不及。张议潮遂指挥大军四面围攻，奋勇冲杀，“不过五十里之间，杀戮横尸遍野”。回鹘大败，“各自苍黄抛弃鞍马，走投入纳职城，把牢而守”。这场战役，张议潮大获全胜，收夺驼马一万余头。

虽然在大中五年(851年)获得唐政府承认之前，张议潮已经收复了沙、瓜、甘、肃、伊等5州，但河西地区最重要的军镇——凉州却仍在吐蕃的控制之下。在打败吐谷浑及回鹘后，大中十二年(858年)，张议潮又亲自率蕃、汉精兵7000余人，踏上了收复凉州的征程。在经过三年的艰苦战斗后，咸通二年(861年)，张议潮顺利收复凉州，并开始采取实际的措施予以管理。据敦煌写本《张淮深碑》的记载，此时归义军“西尽伊吾，东接灵武，得地四千余里，户口百万之家，六郡山河，宛然而旧”，

back against the Uyghurs in Nazhi County. Zhang's attack caught the Uyghurs unprepared, who were then besieged by brave soldiers, causing many enemy casualties. "The dead bodies were scattered within 50 *li*, and the Uyghurs discarded their horses and weapons and then flew pell-mell to Nazhi town." Zhang claimed total victory, taking more than 10,000 camels and horses.

Although Zhang Yichao had regained control over Shazhou, Guazhou, Ganzhou, Suzhou, and Yizhou before he was recognized by the Tang government in the 5th year of Dazhong Era (851), Liangzhou, a key strategic military town, remained under the control of the Tubo. Therefore, in the 12th year of Dazhong Era (858), after defeating the Tuyuhun and the Uyghurs, Zhang launched a campaign to regain Liangzhou. Commanding more than 7,000 soldiers from Han and other ethnic groups, he succeeded in recapturing Liangzhou in the 2nd year of Xiantong Era (861) after three years of bitter struggle. As a governor, Zhang carried out many effective and practical measures in administrating Liangzhou. According to the "Zhang Huaishen Stele" in Dunhuang manuscripts, at the time, "the *Guiyijun* regime controlled a vast area covering Yiwu to the west and Lingwu to the east with a breadth of 4,000 *li* from east to west and a population of more than 1,000,000." It showed that the *Guiyijun*

控制区域空前扩大，归义军进入鼎盛时期(图 27)。

早在归义军建立初期，张议潮为了避免唐政府的猜忌，曾于大中七年(853 年)派兄长张议潭入京充当人质。但归义军对凉州的收复和管理，触动了唐政府已十分脆弱的神经。鉴于藩镇纷纷割据的局面，唐政府唯恐归义军过于强大，也会走上尾大不掉的老路，从而威胁到唐中央的安全，所以，咸通八

regime had reached its zenith (Fig.27).

As soon as the *Guiyijun* regime was established, Zhang Yichao sent his older brother Zhang Yitan to Chang'an in the 7th year of Dazhong Era (853) as a hostage so as to avoid mistrust from the central government. But the recovery and administration of Liangzhou nevertheless touched a nerve with the Tang, which was facing the worrisome situation in which some military governors had set up their own separatist regimes by force. As

图 27　莫高窟第 156 窟　张议潮出行图(部分)　晚唐

Fig.27　Section of *Procession of Zhang Yichao*, Mogao Cave 156　Late Tang

年(867年),唐政府趁先前入质的张议潭病故之际，将张议潮召入京师长安。张议潮入京之后,唐政府对其优待有加,在授予他检校司徒的崇高荣誉之余,还任命他为右神武统军;同时还在长安左街宣阳坊赐宅给张议潮。天子所赐粮料,可支持其9年之用度。此外,还在义谷川赐予庄院田地，价值高达百千万贯。唐政府之所以给张议潮这么高的优待，是为了把张议潮长期羁绊在长安，以达到继续控制归义军的目的。

张议潮在入朝之前，由于自己的儿子年纪尚小，所以他把归义军的大权交给了侄子张淮深掌管,此即“太保咸通八年归阙之日，河西军务，封章陈款,总委侄男淮深,令守藩垣”。张淮深为张议潮兄长张议潭之子。张议潭在入质之前,曾担任沙州刺史。张议潭入京之后,刺史一职由其子张淮深继任,这时张淮深刚刚21岁。他接任沙州刺史之后，一方面沿袭了父亲在位时所制定的政策，另一方面又有所创新，史称:“初日桃蹊,三端继政,琴台旧曲,一

a result, the Tang government summoned Zhang Yichao to Chang'an when Zhang Yitan died in the 8th year of Xiantong Era (867) for fear that the *Guiyijun* Force would become too powerful to be easily controlled. After Zhang's arrival, the Tang government conferred preferential treatment upon him by promoting him to prestigious positions such as honorable Acting Minister of Civil Administration and Commander-General of Right Shenwu Army, and granting him a huge mansion with an abundant food supply, which could sustain him for nine years. In addition, he was given an estate and lands along the Yigu valley. It seemed that Zhang Yichao was treated highly, but the real intention of the Tang government was to detain him in Chang'an so as to control the *Guiyijun* regime indirectly.

Before Zhang Yichao departed for Chang'an, he commissioned his nephew Zhang Huaishen to manage the *Guiyijun* regime because his own son was too young to assume such responsibilities. Zhang Huaishen was the son of Zhang Yitan, who had been the Prefect of Shazhou before he was sent to Chang'an as a hostage. Zhang Huaishen then succeeded his father's post at the age of 21. On the one hand, he followed his father's policies; on the other hand, he made some innovations. As the Hexi area with many ethnic minorities had been in the control of the *Guiyijun* regime

调新声。”由于河西地区是刚刚收复,境内有很多的少数民族,民族问题异常复杂。在归义军向中央报告河西情况的上表中,提到“河西诸州,蕃、浑、嗢末、羌、龙狡杂,极难调服”。如果民族问题处理不好,很可能会引发新的民族冲突。张淮深制定了正确的民族政策,使得归义军境内的少数民族接受归义军政权的教化,“羌龙嗢末,雷威慑伏,训以华风,咸会驯良,轨俗一变”。

张淮深在接替张议潮掌管归义军之初,其统治并不是十分稳固,甚至有人直接向他的权威发起挑战。例如押衙马通达自恃是张议潮的亲信,在上给张淮深的状文中口气十分无礼,还提出种种无理要求。面对不利的形势,张淮深沉着应对,在压制、打击反对派的同时,制定和实施各项政策以巩固自己的统治和权威。在人事任命方面,他任用当时敦煌地区的名士张景球、苏翚、张大庆等人为自己的僚

for a short time, the social relations could be complex, which was revealed in Zhang Huaishen's document to the emperor that "it was quite difficult to deal with the relations among ethnic minortities in the Hexi area, such as the Tubo, the Tuyuhun, the Wamo, the Qiang, and the Long." If ethnic tensions could not be managed well, they were likely to trigger new conflicts. In this respect, Zhang Huaishen carried out sound ethnic policies, causing the ethnic groups' acceptance of the *Guiyijun* regime. It was recorded that "the tribes such as the Qiang, the Long and the Wamo had been uncultivated and fierce. After they were cultivated by the Han's culture, they became docile and benevolent."

In fact, Zhang Huaishen's rule was not stable when he first took over the command of the *Guiyijun* regime. He was frequently challenged by other officers. For example, Ma Tongda, who was once a trusted follower of Zhang Yichao, was insolent toward Zhang Huaishen and put forward many unreasonable demands. In the face of this unfavorable situation, Zhang Huaishen suppressed and pushed back against the opposing factions on the one hand, and implemented policies to consolidate his rule and authority on the other hand. As for the appointment of personnel, he appointed prominent citizens in Dunhuang such as Zhang Jingqiu, Su Hui, and Zhang Daqing as his advisers and assigned many of his own trusted followers, including Suo Xun, to

属，同时他在归义军政权内部大量安插索勋等亲信。在经济方面，他继续执行张议潮时期制定的政策，允许百姓根据自愿和互利的原则互换土地，称为"博地"，政府给予登记造册；同时还允许百姓耕种那些绝户地和不愿承担差科赋役的人家的土地，称为"请射"。张淮深还大兴屯田，进行水利疏通，使敦煌地区的农业生产有了显著的进步。在其统治下，河西地区成为"荷插如云，万亿京坻""黎人不失寒耕""岁有丰于年稔""军食丰泰，不忧寇敌"的富庶之地。

此外，张淮深还积极地利用佛教维护其统治的稳定。唐初，河西的佛教十分兴盛，"安史之乱"后，河西地区虽为吐蕃所占，但由于吐蕃统治者也笃信佛教，所以崇佛的风气并没有减退。归义军统治时期，历任归义军统治者都非常注意借助佛教来维护统治，张淮深也不例外。他采取了一系列尊崇佛教的做法，以拉近同僧团和普通

positions within the regime of *Guiyijun*. In economy, he continued the policies made by Zhang Yichao such as *bodi* and *qingshe*. *Bodi* was a system whereby people were allowed to voluntarily exchange their land with others for mutual benefit; this transaction would be registered by the local government. *Qingshe* meant that people could be allowed to cultivate the land on behalf of owners who were childless or were unwilling to pay taxes and provide corvée labor. In the meantime, Zhang Huaishen carried out *tuntian*-style land cultivation as well as canal and river dredging projects, which greatly promoted the development of agriculture in Dunhuang. Under his rule, the Hexi area became a prosperous and stable place where the food supply for the army and civilians was sufficient and there were no concerns about invasions from enemies. The cultivated lands were as wide as clouds and the harvested crops piled up as big as mountains.

Zhang Huaishen also actively took advantage of Buddhism to maintain his rule. In the early Tang period, Buddhism in the Hexi area was flourishing. After the An Lushan Rebellion, the Hexi area was occupied by the Tubo whose rulers were also devout believers in Buddhism; the practice of Buddhism in Dunhuang remained thriving. During the period of the *Guiyijun* regime, successive governors paid attention to Buddhism with the aim of maintaining their rule. Zhang Huaishen was no exception. He adopted a series of measures to

僧侣、信众之间的距离。首先，他注意搞好同僧界尤其是与僧界上层的关系，以期利用他们的影响力及号召力为自己服务。张淮深为了宣扬自己的政绩，曾请归义军当时第一手笔都僧统唐悟真为其撰写德政碑。镌碑完毕之后，张淮深在与索勋、李明振等政界高层欢聚之余，对悟真等僧界头面人物也没有丝毫的懈怠，除了在作为归义军节度使使衙的西衙招待他们外，还给予他们"鞍马缣细"的赏赐。另外，在张淮深统治时期，敦煌还多次设置方等道场，广度僧尼。所以，当地僧尼数量得到快速增长。这也是在此时期佛教发展的最直接的表现。张淮深统治末期，沙州的僧尼数量维持在1000人左右。而在张淮深统治最为鼎盛的乾符年间，僧尼的数量更为庞大。僧尼数量的大量增加，一方面表明张淮深对佛教的支持，

improve the relationship with monastic leadership, ordinary monks, and lay followers. First of all, he cautiously cultivated his relationship with monks, especially with senior leaders, so as to make use of their influence among the local residents in serving him. To propagandize his own achievements, Zhang Huaishen invited Tang Wuzhen, the chief Buddhist controller and well-known writer, to commemorate his benevolent rule on a stele. When celebrating the completion of the stele with high-ranked officials such as Suo Xun and Li Mingzhen, he also hosted prominent figures from the monastic community at his official residence and granted them horses and bolts of expensive fabric as rewards. Also, during his rule, Zhang established various bodhimaṇḍas[①], which was of great help in rapidly increasing the number of monks. At the end of his rule, the number of monks in Shazhou numbered approximately 1,000. And during the Qianfu Era, at Zhang's height of his power, the number of clergy would be higher. The increasing number of monks was a reflection both of Zhang's support to Buddhism as well as the economic development in Dunhuang. As a result of all these measures, Zhang Huaishen strengthened his rule in the *Guiyijun* regime. In spite of

① Bodhimaṇḍa is a position for believers' awakening, or a place used as a seat, where the essence of enlightenment is present.

另一方面，也表明张淮深统治时期敦煌的社会经济发展到了一个新的高度。然而，虽然张淮深通过打击反对派、安插心腹、发展社会经济、崇信佛教等方式，巩固了自己在归义军的地位，但最终确定其统治地位的是他随后不久获得的一连串重大的军事胜利。

840年，生活在漠北草原的回鹘汗国被其他部族击败，一部分部众随回鹘乌介可汗南下，一部分部众则随庞特勤西迁，而西迁的回鹘部众陆续进入河西走廊和天山东部地区。咸通末年到乾符初年，一支回鹘在河西的甘州地区强大起来，建立了自己的小政权。这股回鹘屡次向唐政府上表，请求唐中央政府予以承认。乾符元年(874年)冬，唐政府派出使团前去对其册封。当使团到达河西地区时，恰逢回鹘被凉州地区的嗢末和吐谷浑击破，所以唐政府的这次册封活动最后不了了之。河西回鹘被击破后，向西逃窜，进入归义军统治区域的腹地。这些回鹘在逃亡的过程中分成了两支：其主力在回鹘王子的带领下生活在瓜州和肃州间的地区；另一支则以向归义军投降献款为名，骗得了归义军的瓜州城。

above effective measures, it was the following successive victories in battle that secured his dominant position in Dunhuang.

In 840, the Uyghurs living in the prairies north of the Gobi Desert were defeated by other tribes, resulting in the collapse of the Uyghur Khanate. Some of the troops and people followed Wujie Khan southward, while others followed another leader Pang Teqin westward, entering into the Hexi Corridor and the eastern area of the Tianshan Mountains. In the last year of Xiantong Era or the 1st year of Qianfu Era(874), a branch of the Uyghurs in Ganzhou became stronger and established their own regime. They then submitted the request for admission to the Tang Dynasty repeatedly. In the winter of 874, the central government sent a diplomatic corps to confer titles upon them but in vain, because the Uyghurs were defeated by the Wamo and the Tuyuhun in Liangzhou before the diplomatic corps arrived. After being defeated, the Uyghurs escaped westward and entered the heartland of the *Guiyijun*'s domain. As they fled, they split into two: the main force was led by the Uyghurs' prince to live in the area between Guazhou and Suzhou; and the other feigned surrender to the *Guiyijun* regime and occupied Guazhou. Realizing

由于瓜州对于保障归义军的安全极为重要，所以张淮深亲自率军出征，一举将这些回鹘驱逐出瓜州。当唐政府得知张淮深收复瓜州的消息后，很快就给予其大量的赏赐。

但回鹘被驱逐出瓜州后，并没有离开归义军的辖区，所以张淮深对其进行了持续的打击，抓获千余名的俘虏。张淮深抓获俘虏后，一方面让负责判理行狱、维持治安的都虞侯对他们进行严加看管，另一方面让属下起草奏表上书给唐政府，以汇报战绩。得到消息后，唐政府马上派散骑常侍李众甫等人，前往沙州犒赏张淮深。据敦煌文献记载，赏赐给张淮深的物品包括“金银器皿，锦绣琼珍”。这些物品被陈列在举行重大活动的马球场上，归义军军民争相观看，一时间可谓万人空巷。此外，唐政府还授予张淮深检校散骑常侍之职，以示殊崇。归义军的官员和民众纷纷对张淮深表示祝贺。

但是在唐朝使节返回后不久，活动在肃州和瓜州之间

the key position of Guazhou for safeguarding the *Guiyijun* regime, Zhang Huaishen led his troops personally to dislodge the invaders completely. The Tang government soon rewarded him handsomely when learning of his victory.

Although the Uyghurs had been expelled from Guazhou, they did not actually leave the *Guiyijun*'s administration district. Zhang Huaishen continued pursuing and attacking them, capturing approximately 1,000 enemy soldiers. Zhang ordered an Inspector-in-Chief who was responsible for sentence and penalty and public security to guard the prisoners. He then asked his subordinates to send a report of his military victories to the central government. After receiving the information, the imperial government dispatched a delegation headed by Li Zhongfu, the Cavalier Attendant-in-Ordinary, to Guazhou in order to reward Zhang Huaishen. According to Dunhuang documents, the rewards included gold and silver vessels, silk, jade, and other rare treasures, which were exhibited in a ceremony for all to see, with the whole town turning out to celebrate the event. In addition, the central government conferred the title of Acting Cavalier Attendant-in-Ordinary on Zhang as a special distinction. The officials and common people extended their hearty congratulations to him.

But no sooner had the envoys returned to the capital than the remaining forces of the

的回鹘主力在回鹘王子的率领下再次来犯，一直进逼到距离沙州很近的西桐海地区，准备偷袭沙州城。回鹘的动向被归义军负责侦察敌情的游奕使白通吉探知，并很快通报给节度使张淮深。张淮深得知消息后，召集将领和精兵，准备与回鹘决战。但是，参谋张大庆却认为“金风初动，兵不可妄动。季秋西行，兵家所忌”，企图阻挠张淮深出兵。但这并没有影响张淮深的决心。在经过一番布置之后，张淮深率军“凿凶门而出”，即从沙州城的北门出城，以示“有死无回之决心”。这场战役的场面十分宏大，《张淮深变文》对此有详细的记载：“先锋远探，后骑相催，铁骑千队，战马云飞。分兵十道，齐突穹庐，鼙鼓大振，白刃交麾，匈奴(代指回鹘)丧胆，獐窜周诸。头随剑落，路满僵尸。”变文还对张淮深称

Uyghurs, maneuvering between Suzhou and Guazhou, invaded the *Guiyijun*'s domain once again under the leadership of their prince. The troops advanced on the Xitonghai area close to Shazhou, ready for a stealthy attack. Their movements were detected by Bai Tongji, a spy who was responsible for observing the enemy and providing intelligence. He quickly reported it back to Zhang Huaishen. Learning this news, Zhang summoned together his generals and soldiers, ready to fight against the Uyghurs. But his counselor, Zhang Daqing, maintained, "At the beginning of autumn, troops should not take rash actions, because it is a taboo to march westward in the autumn." He used this superstition as a subterfuge to prevent Zhang Huaishen from dispatching the army, but Zhang Huaishen's determination was not dampened. After mustering his troops, Zhang led them out of the city from the so-called ominous gate, north gate of Shazhou, showing their determination of fighting to death in battle. The battle scene was recorded in the *Narrative Literature of Zhang Huaishen* that "the vanguards pried into the information, and the following troops urged themselves forward. The powerful troops branched out ten columns and poured onto the battlefield with beating drums; the fight against the enemies was harsh and brutal. The Uyghurs fled in terror from the brave soldiers, their corpses strewn all over the battle field." This narrative also praised Zhang Huaishen: "After returning in triumph, he was authorized by the Tang government to govern the five prefectures in

赞有加："自从司徒归阙后，有我尚书独进奏。持节河西理五州，德化恩沾及飞走。天生神将□英谋，南扫西戎北扫胡。万里能令烽烟灭，百城黔首贺来苏。"这几场针对回鹘的战役都发生在唐朝的乾符年间，维系了归义军政权。而且，这也是张淮深引以为豪的功绩，史称"乾符之政"。

由于张淮深政绩突出，所以在很短时间内唐政府就多次对其进行封赏。人称："恩被三朝，官迁五级。""三朝"指唐宣宗、唐懿宗、唐僖宗三朝，证明张淮深在上述三个皇帝在位期间一直备受恩宠。又称"才拜貂蝉之秩，续加曳履之荣。五稔三迁，增封万户"，意即张淮深刚被唐政府授予散骑常侍的勋衔，马上又晋升为检校户部尚书之衔，在短短5年之内就连升了三级。

张淮深为了庆祝其所获得的封赏，再加上这一段时间敦煌地区"时因景泰，五稼丰登"，所以，其亲自主持对莫高窟北大像的改建和莫高

the Hexi area. His bravery and wisdom benefited all the people there. He defeated the ethnic tribes in the north and the south, and chiefs from hundreds of towns came to extend their congratulations to him." These battles against the Uyghurs helped Zhang Huaishen maintain his rule of the *Guiyijun* regime. His merits and achievements were known in history as the "Rule of the Qianfu Era" for they occurred during the Qianfu Era (874–879) of Emperor Xizong of the Tang Dynasty.

For his outstanding military and political achievements, Zhang Huaishen was rewarded repeatedly by the Tang Dynasty over a short period of time. According to the historical records, "Zhang Huaishen enjoyed the rewards and promotions bestowed by three emperors in the Tang Dynasty including Xuanzong Ⅱ, Yizong, and Xizong. In particular, he was promoted three levels within five years." That is, soon after he was conferred the title of Cavalier Attendant-in-Ordinary, he was promoted to the position of Acting Minister of the Ministry of Revenue.

In order to celebrate his promotions as well as the grain harvest in Dunhuang, Zhang Huaishen personally directed the reconstruction of the Northern Great Buddha Statue in Mogao, as well as the construction of Cave 94. The Northern Great Buddha Statue is now Mogao Cave 96, commonly known as the Nine-Storey Tower. It was first constructed in the 2nd year of Yanzai Era of Empress Wu Zetian (695)

窟第94窟的营建。北大像即今莫高窟第96窟，俗称九层楼。北大像最初建于武周延载二年(695年)。窟前建有4层楼阁，到张淮深执政期间，楼阁经历了近200年的风雨，已栋梁摧毁、破败不堪。张淮深为了庆祝自己的“乾符之政”，决定对其进行重修。《张淮深碑》中对修建的过程有详细的描述：“于是杍匠治材而朴斵，郢人兴役以施功。先竖四墙，后随缔构……旧阁乃重飞四级，靡称金身；新增而横敞五层，高低得所。”张淮深把北大像外的楼阁由原来的4层扩建为5层。新修之5层佛殿，“玉豪扬采，与旭日而连晖；结脊双鸱，对危峰而争耸”，十分壮观。改建过的五层楼气势恢宏，被称为“五阁仙层”。此外，张淮深还在北大像附近凿窟一所，即今天的莫高窟第94窟。《张淮深碑》对第94窟开凿的过程也进行了详细的记载：“更欲镌龛一所，踌躇瞻眺，余所竟无，唯此一岑，嵯峨可劈。匪限耗广，务取工成。情专穿石之殷，志切移山之重。

with a four-storey tower for protecting the colossal Buddha inside the cave. When Zhang Huaishen assumed command of Dunhuang, the building had suffered exposure to the elements for nearly 200 years, falling into disrepair and decay. He decided to rebuild it as part of the celebrations for his “Rule of the Qianfu Era.” The detailed description about the reconstruction can be found on the Zhang Huaishen Stele that “the carpenters collected timbers to carve into different pieces, and the Buddhist followers came to help. Four walls were built up and then the main structure... the old four-storey tower was plated with gold and another new storey was built.” Zhang directed that an additional story be added as part of the renovations. The newly-built cave temple with five storeys was grand and impressive, known as the “Five-Storey Immortal Palace.” In addition, he directed another cave to be built near the Northern Great Buddha Statue, later known as Mogao Cave 94. The process of building the new cave was recorded at great length. “A new cave was designed to be built. However, no other suitable places could be found except the place near the Five-Storey Immortal Palace. No matter how many materials would be expended, the cave must be erected. People's anticipation and determination were so ardent and firm that the stone would be penetrated and the mountain would be

于是稽天神于上，激地祇于下。……是用宏开虚洞，三载功充，廓落精华，正当显敞。”窟内除了塑有释迦主尊、侍从一铺外，还绘有规模宏大的壁画，四壁绘有各种经变画16铺，其中有药师经变和报恩经变等。在94窟完工之时，张淮深还举行了大规模的庆祝活动，“庆窟设斋，数千人供”，从“榆杨庆设，斋会无遮”等描写看，招待的对象中有很多僧侣。

张淮深重修寺院之事，《张淮深碑》也有记载：“爰因搜练之暇，善业遍修，处处施功，笔书难尽……又见龙兴大寺，(下残)”。从上下文的关系看，下文应该是介绍张淮深重修龙兴寺的具体情况，可惜文书残缺。张淮深所重修的龙兴寺是唐中宗即位后诏令天下修建的寺院，位于沙州城的东北隅。由于此寺由唐中宗诏建，而且以“龙兴”为名，而张氏一直以渥洼龙种自誉。所以，张淮深重修寺院的真正目的应该是为了向世人宣布自己的正统地位，是在宗教行为掩盖之下的政治行动。同时张淮深重修佛像、开凿石

removed. People worshipped the heaven and the earth for completion of the cave... Three years later, the exquisite and spacious cave was finished successfully.” Inside the cave, the statues of the Buddha and his attendants were erected, and it also included large-scale murals and 16 splendid sutra illustration paintings on the walls. When the project was completed, Zhang Huaishen held a lavish celebration, with many monks as invited guests. The event was recorded in the Zhang Huaishen Stele.

According to the Zhang Huaishen Stele, Zhang also rebuilt the Longxing Temple in northeastern Shazhou. “In addition to training troops, Zhang extended his philanthropic acts and projects in many places... the Longxing Temple was rebuilt. (The following part is unclear).” It can be inferred what followed should be the records of how the temple was reconstructed. This temple had originally been built by Emperor Zhongzong in the Tang Dynasty after his enthronement. It was built according to his decree and was named Longxing. “*Long*” in Chinese culture symbolizes the Son of Heaven, or Emperor, while “*xing*” means flourishing. Zhang Huaishen had always been flaunting himself as the descendant of the Chinese dragon in Wowa pool, so his real intention to rebuild the temple and construct the new cave and sculptures was to bolster his legitimacy. It can be said that his actions

窟等活动，真正目的更多的也是为了政治上的目的和利益。尽管如此，但这些深层次的实用性目的在表面上必须通过崇敬佛法的功德形式出现，这就不可避免地推动了敦煌地区的崇佛风气和民众的开窟、修寺的积极性。

此时，张淮深在表面上虽然风光无限，但他一直有一个心病，那就是节度使的旌节问题。旌节制度由来已久，史称“旌节之制，命大将帅及遣使于四方，则请而佩之。旌以专赏，节以专杀”。唐高宗永徽年间之后，驻守地方的都督，如果带“使持节”的名号，那他就是节度使，不带节者就不是节度使。所以，旌节是地方节度使的权力象征。只有获得由中央政府授予的旌节，才表示获得了中央政府的认可，他的统治才具有合法性。虽然唐末藩镇割据，但是这些平时骄横的地方将领也得千方百计地求取旌节，否则其统治就会隐藏很大的危机。而张淮深现在面临的就是这个问题。张

were ultimately political in the guise of religion. Although pragmatic politics were most likely part of the underlying motive of this exhibition of Buddhist piety, it cannot be denied that such activities resulted in the propagation and development of Buddhism in Dunhuang.

Zhang Huaishen was now riding on the crest of success. However, the issue of *jingjie* had long been a prize that Zhang coveted. The *jingjie* system was long-standing, historically an ancient type of banner hoisted on a feather-bedecked mast, symbolizing that the holder was officially authorized to command generals and envoys. The holder of the banner had the right to reward or punish other officials. After the Yonghui Era (650–655) of Emperor Gaozong of the Tang Dynasty, the local Commander-in-Chief would be regarded as the real Military Commissioner if he held the title of official commissioned with special authority (banner-holder). The banner was thus the symbol of authority for the local military governor, indicating that only when he obtained the banner conferred by the central government, could his command be considered legitimate. As a result, although the military governors set up separatist regimes by force during the late Tang period, these ambitious military generals did everything in their power to obtain an authorized banner, or their rule would face an underlying potential for future crisis. Now, Zhang Huaishen faced this

淮深在叔父张议潮入朝后，开始代掌归义军。很快他就开始请求唐政府承认他的统治，授予他节度使的旌节。但当时张议潮仍在世，唐政府希望通过他牵制归义军，所以虽然对张淮深优宠有加，但在求节问题上却迟迟未予答复。咸通十三年(872年）张议潮病逝之后，唐政府依然因循以前的政策，对张淮深的请节一味拖延。张淮深屡请旌节而不获，使得归义军内反对派的势力再一次抬头，严重威胁着张淮深的统治。虽然张淮深在执政之初通过任用亲信、打击反对势力、发展生产等措施，基本稳定了统治，继而通过对外作战，确立了自己在归义军的权威，但堂弟张淮鼎始终是他心底的一个隐患。张淮鼎是张议潮的亲子，张议潮早就有心把他培养成为归义军的接班人，只是由于张议潮入朝时，其年龄太小，

problem as well. He had been head of the *Guiyijun* regime ever since his uncle Zhang Yichao went to Chang'an as a hostage. Zhang Huaishen at the time had requested approval for his rulership through the official banner of the Military Commissioner. Zhang Yichao, however, was still alive and well, situated in Chang'an, and the government wanted to continue controlling the *Guiyijun* regime through him. Therefore, the government simply conferred numerous honorary titles as well as rewards on Zhang Huaishen regardless of his request for the banner. In the 13th year of Xiantong Era (872), Zhang Yichao died of illness, but the central government still followed their previous policy, delaying Zhang Huaishen's request. The result was the rise of an opposition faction within the *Guiyijun* regime that greatly threatened Zhang's rule. Although Zhang Huaishen had firmly established his position early on by appointing his trusted followers, smashing the opposition's power, and gaining victories in battlefield, his cousin Zhang Huaiding was still a worry lurking in his mind. Zhang Huaiding was the son of Zhang Yichao, and his father had intended to cultivate him as the successor of the *Guiyijun* regime. But Zhang Huaiding was quite young when his father went to the royal court so that it was necessary to temporarily hand over the authority to Zhang Huaishen. As time went on, Zhang Huaiding grew up while Zhang Huaishen could not receive strong backing from the central government; numerous factions that had been discontent with Zhang Huaishen gathered and

才不得不将大权暂时交给张淮深。随着时间的推移，张淮鼎逐渐长大成人，而张淮深又得不到唐政府强有力的支持，对他心存不满的人就趁机积聚在张淮鼎的周围，伺机夺取归义军大权。甚至就连深受张淮深信任的连襟张文彻，也对张淮深的请节活动横加干涉，表明张淮深已身处险境，归义军政权也已处在分裂的边缘。

文德元年(888 年)，唐僖宗去世，唐昭宗继位。唐昭宗继位之后，实行新政，希望改变唐后期所面临的严峻形势，而授予张淮深节度使旌节则是这次新政的内容之一。文德元年十月十五日，负责押送旌节的专使和副使共 20 余人的庞大使团到达沙州，正式授予张淮深节度使之位。唐政府迟来的承认并没有消除张淮深所面临的危机，而家族内部的权力争夺更是加速了悲剧的到来。大顺元年(890 年)，张议潮之子张淮鼎发动政变，杀死张淮深，成为归义军的统治者。但张淮鼎在位时间并不长，不久就因病去世。因子承奉年幼，淮鼎死前托孤于索勋，索勋遂代承

sought the chance to overthrow his authority over the *Guiyijun* regime. Even Zhang Huaishen's trusted brother-in-law, Zhang Wenche, constantly undermined his request for the banner, indicating his rule was in jeopardy of split and the power of the *Guiyijun* regime was waning.

In the 1st year of Wende Era (888), Emperor Xizong passed away and Emperor Zhaozong succeeded to the throne. Emperor Zhaozong began to implement new policies to solve problems arising during the late Tang. One of the new policies was to confer the banner of military commissioner on Zhang Huaishen. On October 15th, 888, a mission of about 20 people led by a special envoy arrived in Shazhou and conferred the title of Military Commissioner on Zhang Huaishen. But approval from the central government came too late to help him solve his own political crisis. The internal power struggles within the Zhang clan accelerated into impending tragedy. In the 1st year of Dashun Era (890), his cousin Zhang Huaiding staged a coup and killed Zhang Huaishen, and then became the governor of the *Guiyijun* regime. He was not in place for long before he died of illness. Before his death, Zhang Huaiding entrusted his son Zhang Chengfeng to Suo Xun, the son-in-law of Zhang Yichao, to help manage the *Guiyijun* regime. In September of the 1st year of Jingfu Era (892), the

奉自立，执掌归义军。景福元年(892 年)九月，唐政府遣使前往沙州，正式授予索勋节度使之职。这就引起了以李氏在内的敦煌诸多大族的不满。景福二年(893 年)九、十月间，张议潮嫁给李明振的第十四女率领诸子诛杀了索勋，立张承奉为节度使，但实权却操纵于李氏手中。李氏三子分别担任了沙州、瓜州和甘州刺史，张承奉只能处于傀儡的位置。李氏总揽大权，必然引起张氏家族及其支持者的不满，896 年初，沙州发生了倒李扶张政变，李氏家族被迫下台，张承奉开始真正掌握政权。光化三年(900 年)，唐政府承认了张承奉的统治，授予其归义军节度使和沙瓜伊西等州观察使，将归义军的势力范围限定于河西西部及西域东部地区。经过 10 年的政治动

central government sent imperial envoys to Shazhou to confer the title of Military Commissioner on Suo Xun, provoking dissension among the great families in Dunhuang, including the Li clan. The next year, Zhang Yichao's 14th daughter, who was married to Li Mingzhen, assassinated Suo Xun with the aid of the Li family. Zhang Chengfeng was then elected as the Military Commissioner, but the real power was held by the Li clan. Three men from the Li clan took the crucial positions of Prefects of Shazhou, Guazhou, and Ganzhou, with Zhang Chengfeng relegated to mere puppet status. Such a situation in turn caused resentment among the Zhang family and their supporters. In early 896, the Li family was forced to step down because of a coup and Zhang Chengfeng eventually took back political power. In the 3rd year of Guanghua Era (900), the Tang government confirmed Zhang Chengfeng's rule and conferred the positions of the Military Commissioner of the *Guiyijun* Force and Surveillance Commissioner of the Prefectures of Shazhou, Guazhou, Yizhou and Xizhou in the Hexi Corridor on him, which limited the *Guiyijun*'s sphere of influence within the western part of the Hexi Corridor and the eastern area of the Western Regions. After experiencing upheaval for ten years, the *Guiyijun* regime had declined so greatly that it was impossible to revive its past glory.

In the process of internecine power struggles among the *Guiyijun* leaders, the Uyghurs in Ganzhou were gaining strength again and received official support from the central government in the 1st year of Guanghua Era (898). Meanwhile, the

乱，归义军的实力受到了极大的消耗，再也无力重振归义军当年的雄风。

正在归义军上层忙于争权夺利之际，甘州地区的回鹘悄然再度强盛起来，并于光化初年(898 年)得到了唐政府的册封。唐政府不仅册封了甘州回鹘的可汗，还同意将公主嫁给甘州回鹘可汗。为了对此表示感谢，在昭宗被朱温围困于凤翔期间，甘州回鹘曾通过朔方节度使向唐政府上表，希望领兵前往凤翔救援。只是由于昭宗君臣害怕回鹘势力过于强大而不可遏制，所以没有同意回鹘的请求。此后，甘州回鹘积极向西发展，力图扩大自己的领土(图 28)。

907 年，唐朝灭亡，代之而起的是五代十国，各地藩镇纷纷独立。而在910 年左右，敦煌得到了唐朝灭亡的消息，于是，张承奉就在沙瓜二州范围内建立起了自己的小王国——西汉金山国，进而自称圣文神武白帝，也称金山白帝。金山国建立后，张承奉积极向外扩展，力图恢复张议潮时期掌控河西全境

Khan of the Uyghurs in Ganzhou was allowed to marry a princess from the Tang Dynasty. In order to express their gratitude, the Uyghurs showed their request through the Military Commissioner of Shuofang to save Emperor Zhaozong who was kidnapped in Fengxiang. But their offer was declined, as the Emperor and his ministers were afraid that the Uyghurs would become too powerful to be controlled. Thereafter, the Uyghurs in Ganzhou actively expanded their territory westward (Fig.28).

In 907, the Tang Dynasty finally collapsed and the Five Dynasties and Ten Kingdoms period (907–960) began. The country fell into a period of regional warlordism. Around 910, when the news of the fall of the Tang Dynasty reached Dunhuang, Zhang Chengfeng established the State of Jinshan in the prefectures of Shazhou and Guazhou and later entitled himself Emperor Bai. Zhang Chengfeng actively expanded his territory to control the entire Hexi area as what his grandfather Zhang Yichao had done. Severe conflicts inevitably arose between the State of Jinshan and the Ganzhou Uyghurs. The Uyghurs frequently attacked the State of Jinshan in the name of their political allegiance to the central government and of suppressing rebellion of Zhang. The forces from the State of Jinshan, though, defeated them several times, its power remained weak. In July of

的局面。这样就与甘州回鹘的利益发生了严重的冲突。而甘州回鹘一向以效忠中原王朝作为自己的政治口号,所以他们就利用张承奉僭制称帝为借口,在张承奉立国之后不久,频繁派兵进攻金山国。虽然金山国曾数次击退甘州回鹘的进攻,但毕竟实力不济。所以,在 911 年 7 月,甘州回鹘军队在可汗之子狄银的率领下,打到了沙州城下。金山国在派遣罗通达前往吐蕃搬兵未果的情况下,被迫与回鹘签订了城下之盟,与甘州回鹘建立父子之国的关系。张承奉被迫取消“西汉金山国”国号和“圣文神武白帝”的帝号。

914 年,归义军前任节度使索勋的女婿曹议金取代张承奉。曹议金吸取了张承奉失败的教训,主动放弃金山国号,仍称归义军节度使。掌握归义军政权之后,曹议金努力改善与周边民族的关系,不仅通好甘州,而且还娶回鹘可汗女为妻,与回鹘确定和亲关系。这在一定程度上缓和了与甘州的关系(图 29)。后梁贞明四年(918 年),归义军所派遣的使者顺利到达后梁的首都洛阳,受到后梁王朝的热情款待和册封。为了庆贺中央王朝对归

911, the Ganzhou Uyghurs' troops attacked Shazhou under the leadership of Di Yin, the Khan's son, which forced Zhang Chengfeng to seek help from the Tubo. Finally, without any military support from the Tubo, the State of Jinshan was forced to establish an alliance treaty with the Uyghurs, in which the Uyghurs and the State of Jinshan formed a father-son relationship and Zhang Chengfeng abolished the titles of the State of Jinshan and Emperor Bai.

In 914, Cao Yijin, the son-in-law of Suo Xun who was the former Military Commissioner of the *Guiyijun* Force, replaced Zhang Chengfeng. Having learned from Zhang Chengfeng's failure, Cao Yijin didn't adopt the title of the State of Jinshan but still retained the title of the Military Commissioner of the *Guiyijun* Force. He made great efforts to improve relations with neighboring ethnic groups, getting along well with the Ganzhou Uyghurs. He also married the Khan's daughter from the Uyghurs, easing tensions to a certain extent (Fig. 29). In the 4th year of Zhenming Era of the Later Liang (918), messengers sent by the *Guiyijun* regime successfully reached Luoyang, the capital city of the Later Liang, where they enjoyed the hospitality and were granted with

义军的册封，曹议金在莫高窟开凿了今天的第98窟。后唐同光三年（925年），甘州回鹘可汗病死，新继位的可汗由于年幼不能服众。曹议金趁此机会，亲自率兵征讨甘州回鹘，改变了金山国时期建立的父子之国的关系。新立的回鹘可汗娶曹议金与回鹘公主之女为妻，成为

honorific titles by the imperial court. To celebrate and commemorate this event, Cao Yijin constructed Mogao Cave 98. In the 3rd year of Tongguang Era of the Later Tang (925), the Khan of the Ganzhou Uyghurs died. The new Khan in the line of accession was too young to assume leadership. Taking this opportunity, Cao Yijin led an expedition

图28　莫高窟第100窟　回鹘公主出行图　五代

Fig.28　Procession of the Uyghur Princess, Mogao Cave 100　Five Dynasties

曹议金的子婿。由于曹议金较为妥善地处理了归义军的内政外交关系，使归义军发展成为西北地区较为强大的地方势力。曹议金不仅与甘州回鹘联姻，清泰元年(934年)，曹议金又嫁女于于阗国王李圣天。在莫高窟第98窟中，就画

against the Uyghurs in Ganzhou, thus altering the relationship between them. The young Khan of the Uyghurs subsequently married Cao Yijin's daughter, becoming Cao's son-in-law. As Cao Yijin was skilfull in handling both domestic and foreign affairs, the *Guiyijun* Force became more powerful in northwestern China. Cao not only managed to form marriage alliance with the Uyghurs, but

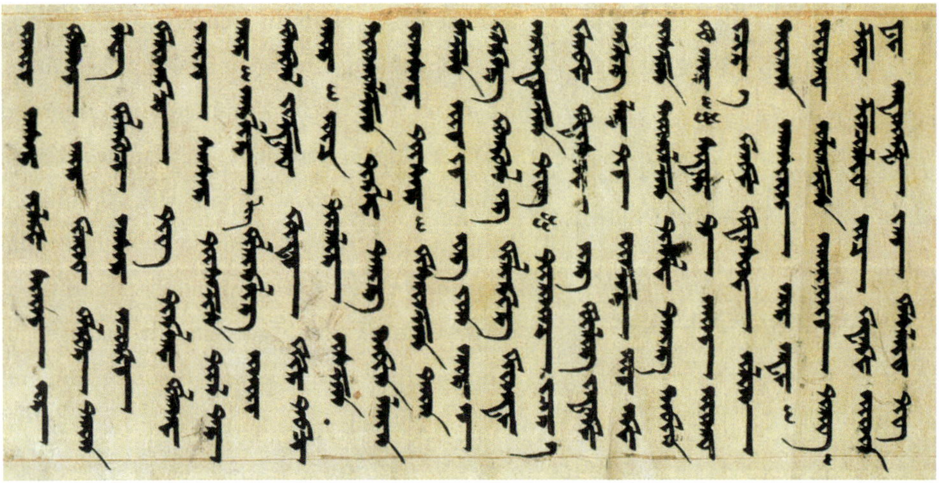

图 29　藏经洞出土的回鹘文写本

Fig.29　Uyghur Language Manuscripts from the Library Cave

有李圣天与曹议金之女的画像（图 30）。

清泰二年(935 年)，曹议金病卒。之后，其子曹元德、元深、元忠相继担任归义军节度使。在曹元忠之侄曹延禄担任节度使期间，于阗国王又将李圣天之女嫁于曹延禄。根据少数民族的风俗，李圣天的女儿被称为天公主。在莫高窟第 61 窟中，此位天公主被记作“大朝大于阗国天册皇帝第三女天公主李氏”(图 31)。在曹元德至曹元忠时期，归义军的统治一直比较稳定，以农业为代表的社会经济持续发展。对此，莫高窟第 61 窟的壁画中有一定程度

also married his daughter to Li Shengtian, the King of Khotan, in the 1st year of Qingtai Era (934). The portraits of Li Shengtian and his wife, Cao Yijin's daughter, can be seen in Mogao Cave 98 (Fig.30).

In the 2nd year of Qingtai Era (935), Cao Yijin passed away. The position of the Military Commissioner of the *Guiyijun* Force was then transferred successively to three of his sons: Cao Yuande, Cao Yuanshen, and Cao Yuanzhong. During the period when Cao Yanlu, Cao Yuanzhong's nephew, was the Military Commissioner, Li Shengtian, the King of Khotan, married one of his daughters to Cao. According to their ethnic customs, she was called the Princess of Heaven. In Mogao Cave 61, she was referred to as "Lady Li, Princess of Heaven and the third daughter of the King of Khotan" (Fig.31).

图 30　莫高窟第 98 窟　于阗国王李圣天、王后供养像　五代

Fig.30　Donor Painting of the Khotan King and Queen, Mogao Cave 98　Five Dynasties

的反映(图 32)。宋真宗咸平五年(1002 年)，曹延禄族子曹宗寿发动政变。在内外交困的情况下，曹延禄与弟瓜州防御使延瑞被迫自尽。随后，曹宗寿自称敦煌王，开始代理归义军的军政事务，并于咸平五年(1002 年)八月获得北宋政权的正式册封。为了对中央表示感谢，曹宗寿曾数次遣使北宋，以贡献西北地区所特产的美玉和名马。大中祥符七年(1014 年)，曹宗寿卒，其子衙内都指挥使贤顺继位。1036

The *Guiyijun* Force was relatively stable during the rule of Cao Yuande, Cao Yuanshen and Cao Yuanzhong. Attention was paid to agriculture, and socioeconomic conditions continued to improve, which was illustrated in the murals of Cave 61 (Fig.32). In the 5th year of Xianping Era of Emperor Zhenzong of the Song Dynasty (1002), Cao Zongshou, the nephew of Cao Yanlu, led an uprising. Beset by external and internal troubles, Cao Yanlu and his brother Cao Yanrui, the Defense Commissioner of Guazhou, were forced to commit suicide. Later, Cao Zongshou declared himself Prince of Dunhuang and put himself in charge of political and military affairs of the *Guiyijun* regime. His authority was confirmed

图 31 莫高窟第 61 窟 女供养人 五代、宋

Fig.31 Painting of Female Donors, Mogao Cave 61 Five Dynasties and Song Dynasty

图 32　莫高窟第 61 窟　弥勒经变(部分)　五代
Fig.32 Section of *Maitreya Triple Sutra* Illustration, Mogao Cave 61　Five Dynasties

年，西夏占领沙州，归义军政权基本结束(图 33)。就在归义军政权末期，在回鹘的压力下，归义军政权出现了回鹘化的趋势。这个时期又被称为沙州回鹘时期。

归义军政权时期的内政，主要是恢复或改变旧制。归义军政权建立后，即取消了吐蕃时期的部落、将制，恢复重建唐前期的州、县、乡、里制。开始时恢复的是 10 个乡，另外新出现一个赤心乡，共 11 个乡，即敦煌乡、莫高乡、神沙乡、平康乡、龙勒乡、

by the Northern Song in August of 1002. In order to express his gratitude, Cao Zongshou sent delegations to present the Northern Song with unique jades and fine horses from the northwest. In the 7th year of Dazhong Xiangfu Era (1014), Cao Zongshou died, and his son Cao Xianshun succeeded as ruler. In 1036, the Western Xia occupied Shazhou, and the *Guiyijun* regime basically ended (Fig.33). As the *Guiyijun* regime was disintegrating, they encountered pressure from the Uyghurs and were influenced greatly by the Uyghurs as well. Therefore, this period was also known as Shazhou-Uyghurs period.

During period of the *Guiyijun* regime, the rulers internally focused on the restoration or modification of the old system. They abolished

图 33 藏经洞出土的引路菩萨图 五代

Fig.33 Painting of Bodhisattva Guiding the Deceased Five Dynasties

玉关乡、洪池乡、洪闰乡、效谷乡、赤心乡、慈惠乡。这只是归义军前期敦煌诸乡的基本情况，实际上这一时期敦煌县、乡的建制要更为复杂。此后，还出现了通颊乡和退浑乡。在土地制度方面，归义军政权建立之初，就开始调查人口、土地，分配无主荒地，尽可能地恢复唐制。唐中叶以后，土地私有制迅速发展。归义军时期的私有土地包括官僚地主占地、寺田和小自耕农的民田。私有土地的发展主要是通过请射和买卖两个途径实现的。此外，这时的土地所有者之间可以任意对换土地。在赋税制度方面，归义军政权在重新登记人口和调整土地的基础上，还制定了新的赋税制度，即据地出税的制度，主要包括地子、官布和柴草三项。这些对内的统治政策既体现着当时唐宋时期的共同特征，也具有归义军政权的自身特点。

the tribal systems and political systems as practiced during the Tubo period, and reestablished the administrative division of prefecture, county, township and village that had existed in the Early Tang period. At the beginning 10 townships were resumed, and a new township named Chixin was set up. In total, there were 11 townships, including Dunhuang, Mogao, Shensha, Pingkang, Longle, Yuguan, Hongchi, Hongrun, Xiaogu, Chixin and Cihui. This was the general situation of townships around Dunhuang during the early period of *Guiyijun* regime. Later, the townships of Tongjia and Tuihun were added. As for the land system, a survey of the population and the land began from the beginning of the *Guiyijun* regime, and wasteland was allocated so as to have the Tang system restored as much as possible. After the Mid-Tang, there was a rapid development of private ownership of land. Private land in the period of the *Guiyijun* regime consisted of land owned by bureaucrat landlords, land for temples and land for smallholders. The development of private land mainly depended on *qingshe* and trading. Furthermore, landowners at that time had the right to exchange land at their own will. As for the taxation system, a new tax system was developed based on the new population registration system and the adjustment of land, and tax could be paid with grain, official cloth, and crops. These policies for internal affairs not only had similarities with those of the Tang and Song dynasties, but possessed their own unique characteristics of the *Guiyijun* regime.

西夏元明清时期的敦煌

Dunhuang During the Western Xia, the Yuan, Ming and Qing Dynasties

1031 年，在我国西北地区建立起了一个以党项族为主体的少数民族政权——西夏。至 1227 年，西夏为蒙古所灭，其建国历史长达 196 年。1036 年，西夏攻陷瓜、沙二州，成为敦煌新的统治者。

北宋初年，已经崛起并日益强大的西夏开始挺进河西，与甘州回鹘的冲突日渐频繁。1008 年和 1010 年，西夏曾两次进攻甘州回鹘，但均为回鹘所败。当时西夏的首领为李德明，其子李元昊，骁勇善战，谋略过人。1028 年，李元昊率军进攻回鹘，一举攻下了甘州城，并因此被李德明立为太子。1032 年，李元昊又领兵攻破由吐蕃六谷蕃部据守的凉州城，将河西东部控制在自己手中。1036 年，元昊再次领兵西进，一举攻陷了瓜、沙、肃三州。自此，西夏控制了整个河西走廊地区（图 34）。

李元昊称帝之初，加紧

The Western Xia was a state established in 1031 by the Tanguts (*Dangxiang* in Chinese), an ethnic minority in the northwest of China. The Tanguts' rule had lasted for 196 years until it was destroyed by the Mongolians in 1227. In 1036, after conquering Guazhou and Shazhou, the Tanguts became the new ruler of Dunhuang.

In the early years of the Northern Song Dynasty, the increasingly powerful Tanguts began to move to the Hexi area, which resulted in frequent conflicts with the Uyghurs in Ganzhou. In 1008 and 1010, the Tanguts attacked the Uyghurs in Ganzhou twice, but failed. Li Yuanhao, son of the Tangut leader Li Deming, was a brave and skillful commander and tactician. He was then made crown prince after he conquered Uyghur-controlled Ganzhou in 1028. In 1032, Li Yuanhao occupied Liangzhou which had been held by the Liugu tribe of the Tubo, and the eastern part of the Hexi Corridor then fell under his control. In 1036, Li advanced westward further and conquered Guazhou, Shazhou, and Suzhou. The Tanguts then controlled the entire Hexi Corridor (Fig.34).

After the establishment of the Western Xia, Li Yuanhao turned his attention to consolidating his political power and expanding his forces, hoping to ally with the State of Liao in an attack

图 34　榆林窟第 3 窟　普贤变　西夏

Fig.34　Samantabhadra Illustration Painting, Yulin Cave 3　Western Xia

自己的政权建设，扩充实力，并希望联合辽国共同进攻宋朝。宋朝为了防御西夏的进攻，派遣资政殿学士陈执中为陕西都部署兼经略安抚沿边招讨等使，任命秦州知州曹琮为秦凤副都部署。北宋庆历元年(1041 年)，曹琮正在谋划联合包括原占据凉州和甘州等地的吐蕃和回鹘共同抗击西夏。恰恰在此之际，沙州镇国王子写信给曹琮，声称："我本唐甥，天子实吾舅也。自党项破甘、凉，遂与汉绝，今愿帅首领为朝廷击贼。"沙州镇国王子主动表示要率众与宋王朝合击西夏，正好与曹琮等人的计划不谋而合。于是，曹琮随即将此计划上奏于朝廷，得到了宋仁宗的赞许。从沙州镇国王子自称唐朝外甥，并称中央皇帝为舅的记载看，其应是回鹘首领(图 35)。此时已是西夏占领敦煌 5 年之后，敦煌的回鹘首领仍然可以上书宋朝，以表达希望与中原王朝联合以赶走西夏统治者的信息。在庆历六年(1046 年)，即

against the Song Dynasty (960–1279). To avoid attack from the Western Xia, the Song government appointed Chen Zhizhong, Academician of the Hall for Aid in Governance, as the Administrator of Shaanxi, Military Commissioner, Pacification Commissioner, and Bandit-suppression Commissioner, and Cao Cong, the Prefect of Qinzhou, as the Vice Administrator of Qinfeng. In the 1st year of Qingli Era of Emperor Renzong of the Northern Song Dynasty (1041), when Cao Cong was planning to resist the Western Xia with the Tubo and the Uyghurs who once occupied Liangzhou and Ganzhou, he received a letter from the Uyghur leader *Zhenguo* Prince in Shazhou, who stated that "I was originally the nephew of the Tang's Emperor, but was blockaded from the government since the Tanguts' occupation of Ganzhou and Liangzhou; hence I am willing to lead the troops in attacking the Western Xia." The proposal from *Zhenguo* Prince in Shazhou coincided with Cao Cong's resistance against the Western Xia. He submitted the letter to Emperor Renzong and received permission for his plan (Fig.35). This event occurred 5 years after the Western Xia's occupation of Dunhuang, which meant the leader of the Uyghurs could still submit a written statement to the imperial court expressing his intention to drive out the Tanguts via cooperation with the central government. In the 6th year of Qingli Era (1046), ten years after Dunhuang was conquered by the Western Xia, an epigraph bearing the era name of the

图 35 榆林窟第 21 窟 水月观音 沙州回鹘时期

Fig.35 Image of Water-Moon Avalokitesvara, Yulin Cave 21

Period of Uyghur Occupation of Shazhou

西夏占领敦煌 10 年之后，敦煌莫高窟第 444 号洞窟里还出现了北宋的年号题记(图 36)。而据《宋会要》瓜沙二州条记载，被西夏占领以后敦煌地区仍多次入宋朝贡，最晚一次已迟至皇祐四年(1052 年)十月。这些记载表明在西夏占领敦煌后的一段时间里，其对敦煌的统治

Northern Song could be seen in Mogao Cave 444 (Fig.36). According to records on Guazhou and Shazhou in the *Institutional History of the Song Dynasty*, the last tribute presented by Dunhuang to the Song imperial court occurred in October of the 4th year of Huangyou Era (1052). These records reveal that the power of the Western Xia in Dunhuang at the time was no more powerful than that of the Cao clan or the Uyghurs who

还比较薄弱，原来控制敦煌政权的曹家和回鹘势力仍比较强大，随时准备寻找合适的时机，与中原王朝一起推翻西夏的统治(图 37)。

但在 1052 年之后，敦煌与北宋的联系中断，敦煌当地的石窟中也不再沿用北宋的年号。同样在第 444 窟，出现了西夏“天赐礼盛国庆二年(1070 年)”的题记，这是敦煌莫高窟和榆林窟出现最早有明确西夏纪年的题记。而自第

had once ruled Dunhuang, both of which were looking for an opportunity together with the central government to overthrow the rule of the Western Xia (Fig.37).

But after 1052, the relation between Dunhuang and the central government gradually broke off; the era names of the Northern Song Dynasty were no longer used in the Buddhist cave temples in Dunhuang. By contrast, "the 2nd year of the Tianci Lisheng Guoqing Era of the Western Xia (1070)" could be found in an inscription in Mogao Cave 444, marking the first record of a definite era name of the Western Xia. Later, such era names of the Western Xia as Da'an, Zhenguan,

图 36　莫高窟第 444 窟　窟檐外景　北宋

Fig.36　Exterior Eaves of Mogao Cave 444　Northern Song Dynasty

图 37　莫高窟第 409 窟　回鹘王供养像　五代、宋初
Fig.37　Donor Painting of the Uyghur King, Mogao Cave 409　Five Dynasties and Early Song

一个西夏年号题记出现以后，西夏的大安、贞观、雍宁、正德、乾祐、光定等年号陆续在莫高窟及榆林窟中出现。这就证明，在国庆年间之后，西夏对敦煌的控制逐渐加强，原居住在这里的汉族和回鹘等族人民与中央王朝的联系也被彻底切断。

由于党项是一个崇奉佛教的民族，在立国之前就信仰佛教。立国之后，在最高统治者的亲自倡导和示范宣扬下，佛教在西夏境内普遍流行。所以，在占领敦煌之后，西夏人在早已成为佛教圣地的莫高窟和榆林窟频繁进行佛事活动(图 38、图 39)。如莫高窟第 130 窟是唐开元年间僧人处谚和乡人马思忠等人开凿的一个大型洞窟，中唐时，曾有人重新涂抹窟壁并装绘了甬道。而西夏占领敦煌之后，则重新装绘了甬道全部壁画和窟内的绝大部分壁画，同时还在窟前修建了殿堂，增塑了四大天王像。其殿堂宽五间(21. 6 米)，进深四间(16. 3 米)，地面全用砖铺盖，其纹饰为西夏时期流行的八瓣莲花、四角云头纹。其规模是莫高窟所发现的所有窟前建筑

Yongning, Zhengde, Qianyou, and Guangding appeared in the Mogao and Yulin caves. It demonstrates that since 1069, the Western Xia's rule in Dunhuang became increasingly powerful, which resulted in the complete breakdown of relations between the Han people as well as the Uyghurs in Dunhuang and the central government.

Buddhism, the religion followed by the Tanguts, gained further popularity under the Western Xia through official patronage and governmental support. Buddhist activities and ceremonies were frequently held in the Mogao and Yulin caves, the sacred sites for Buddhism, after Dunhuang was occupied by the Tanguts (Fig.38, 39). For example, Mogao Cave 130 was originally cut by a monk named Chuyan and other villagers during the Kaiyuan Era of the Tang Dynasty. In the Mid-Tang, the walls and corridors of the cave were repainted. Under the Western Xia regime, all the murals in the corridors and chambers of Cave 130 were painted over, and the cave was remodeled with a hall housing four statues of the Heavenly Kings. The hall was 21.6 meters wide and 16.3 meters long, with the ground paved with bricks decorated in the popular eight-petal lotus and arabesque cloud pattern at the time. This is the largest and most magnificent architectural structure among the ruins in front of the caves in

图 38　榆林窟第 29 窟　女供养人　西夏
Fig.38　Painting of Female Donors, Yulin Cave 29　Western Xia

遗址中，最大、最宏伟壮观的窟前建筑。榆林窟第 19 窟有一则西夏画师所题的汉文题记，该窟壁画具有浓郁的西夏民族特色，是西夏艺术宝贵的代表作品。从壁画的艺术水平看，此位西夏画师当是西夏本族画师中的佼佼者。兴建和重修洞窟是离不开物质基础支持的。从西夏在敦煌等地宣扬佛教的规模，及莫高窟和榆林窟壁画中所反映的西夏统治敦煌时期当地农业、手工业的形象资料看，敦煌地区的手工业、农牧业、商业都得到了较大的发展。但为了和北宋进行战争，西夏政府曾

Mogao Caves. In Yulin Cave 19, there is a Chinese inscription written by a painter from the Western Xia; as the murals in this cave are characterized by Western Xia artwork, the painter is likely a prominent local artist. Financial and material supports were no doubt indispensable for building and remodeling the caves. Therefore, based on the magnitude of Buddhist dissemination as well as scenes depicted in the Mogao and Yulin caves, it can be seen that skilled trades, animal husbandry, and commerce in Dunhuang achieved greater development during that period. However, the Western Xia government urged local residents to migrate eastward in order to fight against

图 39　莫高窟第 237 窟　水月观音　西夏

Fig.39　Image of Water-Moon Avalokitesvara, Mogao Cave 237　Western Xia

向东迁徙敦煌民众,使敦煌受到很大的削弱。1109年,瓜、沙、肃三州发生饥荒,百姓流亡他乡。此后,随着海上交通的发展及陆上丝路的衰落,敦煌失去了丝路贸易中转站的地位。

蒙古兴起后,出征西夏。曾于1205年侵扰瓜、沙地区。1224年,蒙古骑兵围攻沙州长达半年时间,使敦煌受到了严重的破坏。1227年3月,蒙古汗国终于占领敦煌。同年6月,西夏被蒙古灭亡。敦煌被蒙古占领后,被划入了八都大王的封地。蒙古民族创业之初期,以和林为中心的蒙古高原,是当时东方世界的政治中心。和林时代的东西联结陆路交通的主要干线,是天山南路或北路,沿此路线东行直接可达和林。因此,敦煌的地位进一步衰落。

元世祖至元八年(1271年),马可·波罗和父亲尼古拉·波罗和叔父玛窦·波罗从西方开始他们的第一次东方之行。来到蒙古后,忽必烈接见了波罗兄弟,并任命波罗兄

the Song Dynasty, which weakened Dunhuang greatly. In 1109, Guazhou, Shazhou, and Suzhou suffered a serious famine, causing an exodus of people leaving their native land. From that point on, with the development of maritime transportation and the decline of the overland trade routes between the East and the West, Dunhuang lost its status as a major international trading hub and trade transfer point along the Silk Road.

The Mongols were the next to rise to power. They launched an expedition against the Western Xia, invading Guazhou and Shazhou in 1205. Then in 1224, the Mongolian cavalry laid siege to Shazhou for six months, causing severe destruction to Dunhuang. In March of 1227, the Mongols finally occupied Dunhuang, and in June, they vanquished the Western Xia. After its occupation, Dunhuang was assigned to the Prince of Badu's fiefdom. At the early stage of the Mongolian Empire's rise, Karakorum (*helin* in Chinese) on the Mongolian Plateau was the political center of the East. During the Karakorum period, the main routes connecting the East and the West ran either north or south of the Tianshan Mountains, by which people could go directly eastward to Karakorum. As a result, Dunhuang declined even further.

In the 8th year of Zhiyuan of Emperor Shizu of the Yuan Dynaty (1271), Marco Polo, his father Niccolò and his uncle Maffeo went on their first trip together to the East. When they arrived in Mongolia, Kublai Khan, the ruler of Mongolia and the first emperor of the Yuan

弟为大汗的使臣，他们以使节的身份被派遣去西方。忽必烈委托他们带给教皇一封亲笔信，请求派遣教士百人来蒙古。同时又命令他们返回东方时，去耶路撒冷带回圣墓的灯油。波罗兄弟回到威尼斯的当时，原来的教皇已逝世，新教皇还没有选举出来，而且，教皇的选举工作进行得很不顺利，一时难以决定。因此，忽必烈要求派遣百人教士的事情没能如愿。于是，马可·波罗一行等携带着圣墓的灯油返回东方。

波罗兄弟的第一次东方之行没有记录，但根据马可·波罗《东方见闻录》推测，在忽必烈汗即位不久，他们从君士坦丁堡出发，渡过伏尔加河，经由布喀刺、邪米思干大城、别石把、黑水城，再经天德至上都。这条路线是通过天山山脉南麓，沿西夏领土北边东行的。马可·波罗第二次旅行路线，是从威尼斯

Dynasty, met them and then dispatched them back to the West as ambassadors. Kublai Khan entrusted them with a letter to the Pope, requesting one hundred priests to be sent to Mongolia. At the same time, he hoped they could bring back consecrated oil from the Holy Sepulchre in Jerusalem. But when they arrived back in Venice, the Pope had died and a new one had not yet been elected. Therefore, Kublai Khan's first request was not fulfilled, and they were only able to return to Mongolia with the holy oil.

There are no records verifying Niccolò and Maffeo Polo's first trip to the East. However, according to *The Travels of Marco Polo*, soon after Kublai Khan ascended the throne, the Polos started their journey from Constantinople, across the Volga River, through Bukaci, Samarkand, Beshbalik, Khara-Khoto, Tiande City, and finally to Shangdu. This route was through the southern foot of the Tianshan Mountains and along the northern part of territory of the Western Xia. For the second trip, Marco Polo started from Venice to Jerusalem, then through Armenia, Chorasmia, Balkh, Kashgar, Woduan, Lop Nor, Shazhou, Suzhou, Ganzhou, Eliheya (present-day Ningxia), Tiande City, and then to Shangdu. This route went along the southern edge of the Tarim Basin, through some of the cities in the Hexi Corridor, such as Dunhuang and Anxi, finally reaching the capital. It was recorded by Marco Polo that most people in Dunhuang believed in Buddhism except for Nestorians and Arabs (Fig.40). According to historical records, during the Yuan Dynasty, if people from the Central

先到耶路撒冷，通过亚美尼亚去花剌子模，从此到巴里黑、喀什噶尔、斡端、罗布泊，再经沙州、肃州、甘州、额哩合牙（宁夏），最后经天德至上都。这是一条通过塔里木盆地南边，经由敦煌、安西等河西走廊各城市，之后走向大都的交通路线。而据马可·波罗的记载，虽然此时敦煌有少部分的大食人和景教徒，但绝大多数居民仍然是佛教徒（图 40）。而据史书记载，元代时从中原前往于阗的八答山采宝玉，仍然要经过敦煌，并沿塔里木盆地南缘西去。

1277 年，元朝重设沙州，隶属于肃州，归元朝中央政府管辖。元政府授予当地百姓田种、农具，以发展经济。1280 年，沙州升格为路，设总管府，统瓜、沙二州，直接肃属于甘肃行中书省。《元史·地理志》载："沙州路……元太祖二十二年，破其城，以隶八都大王。至元十四

Plains mined gems or jade from the Bada Mountain in Khotan, they must travel through Dunhuang and then walk westward along the southern edge of the Tarim Basin.

In 1277, the Yuan government reestablished Shazhou, annexing it as part of Suzhou and administered by the central government. The imperial court provided the locals with seeds and tools so as to develop agriculture. In 1280, Shazhou's status was upgraded into Route① with a Route Command, attaching to Branch Secretariat of Gansu and administrating both itself and Guazhou. This was recorded in the *History of the Yuan Dynasty*: *Treatise on Geography* that "... The town was conquered in the 22nd year of Emperor Taizu of the Yuan Dynasty and was put under the fiefdom of Prince of Badu. In the 14th year of Zhiyuan Era, it was reestablished as a prefecture, and then upgraded to be Route Command of Shazhou three years later, having jurisdiction over Guazhou." Its notes explained that "Shazhou, in which lived

① In the Yuan Dynasty, the Route (*lu* in Chinese) was a stable governmental region governed by one of the Route Commands, which in routine have communicated with the Secretariat and its Six Ministries in Beijing, either directly or indirectly through an appropriate Branch Secretariat. Below Route Commands in the hierarchy of territorial administrative were prefectural-level units of three kinds: Superior Prefectures, ordinary Prefecrures and Military Prefectures. Below the prefectures in hierarchy, at the lowest level of the formal governmental structure, were counties, each headed by a Magistrate.

图 40　莫高窟第 3 窟　北壁　吉祥天　元

Fig.40　Image of Lakshmi，North Wall of Mogao Cave 3　Yuan Dynasty

年复立州，十七年升为沙州路总管府，瓜州隶焉。"其注释曰："沙州去肃州千五百里，内附贫民，欲乞粮沙州，必须白之肃州，然后给予，朝廷以其不便，故升沙州为路。"元成宗时，为开发河西，曾在敦煌等地实行屯田。大德七年(1303年)，御史台臣言："瓜、沙二州，自昔为边镇重地，今大军屯驻甘州，使官民反居边外，非宜。乞以蒙古军万人分镇险隘，立屯田以供军实为便。"此外，敦煌还成为元朝与西北藩王斗争的重要基地。虽然敦煌在地理位置上失去了以往的优势，但人们在莫高窟从事各种宗教活动的热情并没有消退(图41)。

明朝建立以后，虽然冯胜曾在1372年击败河西地区的元军，但在此后的一段时间里，敦煌仍为元朝残部据守。洪武五年(1372年)，明政府以肃州的嘉峪关作为西部的边关，敦煌被弃置关外。洪武二十四年(1391年)，明朝进军哈密，沙州蒙

impoverished residents, was far away from Suzhou, so that if people in Shazhou needed to apply for emergency relief grain, they had to report to Suzhou and it was then distributed. Therefore, the central government upgraded Shazhou to avoid such inconvenience." During the reign of Chengzong of the Yuan Dynasty, in order to develop the Hexi area, the government carried out the *tuntian* policy. In the 7th year of Dade Era (1303), an official from the Censorate reported, "Guazhou and Shazhou had been important frontier prefectures. Now troops quartered in Ganzhou, which forced officials and people to live out at the frontier. Such a situation was not beneficial. The better way was to dispatch troops to guard these two garrison posts and to carry out the *tuntian* policy to supply food to the soldiers." Ultimately, Dunhuang deteriorated into a staging ground for the conflicts between the landholders in the northwest and the central government. Although Dunhuang had lost its prestige geographically, people's devotion for the religious activity remained strong (Fig.41).

After the establishment of the Ming Dynasty, General Feng Sheng defeated the Yuan troops in the Hexi area in the 5th year of Hongwu Era of Emperor Taizu of the Ming Dynasty (1372), but Dunhuang was still in the charge of remnants of the Yuan troops. In the same year, the Ming government established the Jiayu Pass in Suzhou as a border pass in the west, which meant Dunhuang was deserted out of the frontier. In the 24th year of Hongwu Era (1391), Ming troops attacked Kumul, where the Mongolian Prince of

图 41　莫高窟第 332 窟　男供养人　元
Fig.41　Painting of Male Donors, Mogao Cave 332　Yuan Dynasty

古王子归顺明朝。永乐年间，明政府在嘉峪关外设置了 7 个少数民族机构，史称“关西七卫”，以作为明帝国西陲的“屏藩”，而沙州（敦煌）正是“关西七卫”之一。据史书记载，永乐二年（1404 年），蒙古部落后裔酋长困即来、买住等人率其部众归附。于是，明政府就在敦煌设置沙州卫，以此二人为指挥使，赐给他们冠带和袭衣。沙州卫就

Shazhou surrendered. During the Yongle period (1403–1424), the Ming government set up seven ethnic minority organizations out of the Jiayu Pass as defensive barriers in the western area, known as Seven Guards West of the Jiayu Pass. Shazhou (Dunhuang) was one of them. It was recorded that in the 2nd year of Yongle Era (1404), Kunjilai and Maizhu, two Mongolian chiefs, surrendered, whereupon the Ming government set up the Shazhou Guard and appointed them as local military commanders granted with the ceremonial attire of imperial officials. After that, Shazhou Guard became the first local government combining military and

成了明初在敦煌所设的第一个军政合一的地方政府机构。但明政府并没有进行具体的行政管理，既不派官员前去督察其内部事务，也没有派遣军队驻扎，只是替蒙古部族设置了一些水利、农耕设备，并帮助他们在困难时期渡过难关。如在宣德元年(1426年)，困即来因为敦煌当地发生灾荒，派人向明政府求救，明政府随即派遣宦官张福前往赈济；宣德七年(1432年)，又因敦煌发生旱灾，明朝皇帝命令肃州向敦煌运送救济粮五百石。经过洪武及永乐年间的经营，敦煌出现了户口繁衍、畜牧富饶的景象。但后来由于明政府对七卫的管理放任自流，处于七卫最西端的敦煌和其他六卫一样，成为边疆部落任意争夺之地。尤其是在明朝中后期，政府对关西七卫之间的相互争夺和攻伐采取了不干预政策，使得当时的敦煌长期处于哈密和

political power together in Dunhuang during the early Ming. But the Ming government neither dispatched administrative officials to supervise and manage affairs nor stationed any troops in Shazhou Guard, except helping them out in times of need with water conservation projects, farming, or food relief. For instance, the Ming government distributed food aid twice when Dunhuang suffered a famine in the 1st year of Xuande Era (1426) and a drought in the 7th year of Xuande Era (1432). During the Hongwu and Yongle periods (1368–1398; 1403–1424), Dunhuang enjoyed a brief period of prosperity with an increased population and abundant livestock. But later, due to the government's loose supervision on the management of the Seven Guards, Dunhuang, like the other six guards, was involved in the battles among the frontier tribes. In particular, during the mid and late Ming, the central government adopted a non-intervention policy regarding the conflicts among the Seven Guards, which left Dunhuang involved in the fight between the Kumul Khanate and tribes in Turfan for a long time.

In the 10th year of Xuande Era (1435), because of invasion from the Kumul Khanate as well as fears of attack from the Wala tribe of the Mongols, Kunjilai led approximately 200 of his troops to migrate into Kuyu (45 kilometers south of present-day Guazhou). In the 9th year of Zhengtong Era of Emperor Yingzong (1444), Kunjilai died. His two sons fought over inheriting the post, with one of them intending to surrender to the Wala tribe. On seeing this, Ren Li, the Garrison Commander of Gansu, sent out troops to

吐鲁番的争夺之下。

宣德十年(1435年),沙州被哈密侵扰,困即来又害怕蒙古部落的瓦剌部的逐步进逼,于是便率领部众200余人迁到今瓜州东南部45公里处的苦峪地。英宗正统九年(1444年),困即来死,他的两个儿子争夺继承权,其中一个儿子密谋投奔瓦剌。于是,明朝的甘肃镇将任礼就派兵将困即来的部众200余户、1200余人迁到甘州,敦煌遂空。关西七卫之一的罕东卫指挥使思结趁机占领敦煌。到思结的孙子只克时,吐鲁番强大,频频侵扰哈密。只克为了与吐鲁番相抗衡,于成化十五年(1479年)请求在敦煌“立卫赐印”,以抵御吐鲁番。于是,明政府将敦煌划归罕东左卫,任命只克为指挥使,并命令其在敦煌筑城以增强敦煌的防御能力。正德十一年(1516年),吐鲁番占据哈密,敦煌成为对抗吐鲁番的最前线。由于只克之子乞台力无力抵御,只能率众迁移到肃州境内。他的部下帖木哥、土巴二人占据了敦煌并降服于吐鲁番。由于吐鲁番势

relocate about 1,200 followers in 200 households of Kunjilai to Ganzhou, leaving Dunhuang a vacant city. At the time, Sijie, the Commander of Handong Guard, seized the chance to occupy Dunhuang. While under the control of Sijie's grandson Zhike, Kumul was frequently invaded by the powerful Turfan tribe. In order to fight against the Turfan, Zhike requested the central government to establish Dunhuang Guard in the 15th year of Chenghua Era (1479). Accepting the suggestion, the government put Dunhuang under the command of Handong Left Guard and appointed Zhike as the Commander responsible for strengthening the defense capability in Dunhuang. In the 11th year of Zhengde Era (1516), after Kumul was controlled by the Turfan, Dunhuang became the frontline against the Turfan. But Qitaili, Zhike's son, was too weak to resist invasion so that he had to move to Suzhou. His two subordinates, Tiemuge and Tuba, occupied Dunhuang and surrendered soon after. The Turfan tribe grew so powerful that they controlled the western part of the Hexi area and became a separatist force against the Ming Dynasty. In the 3rd year of Jiajing Era (1524), unable to expel the Turfanians out of the Hexi Corridor, the Ming government had no choice but to close the Jiayu Pass, which meant the central government abandoned ruling the territory west of that area. In 1528, dissatisfied with the rule by Turfan, Tiemuge and Tuba led his 5,400 followers back to east

力的膨胀，以至于控制了河西西部的广大地区，形成了与明政府相抗衡的割据势力。明政府无力应付，只好于嘉靖三年（1524 年）正式关闭了嘉峪关，放弃了对关外的控制。虽然帖木哥和土巴二人归附了吐鲁番，但由于他们不满吐鲁番的统治，于嘉靖七年（1528 年）率部众 5400 余人回归关内，敦煌完全被吐鲁番占领。

1644 年，明朝灭亡，清军入关，并定都北京。康熙五十四年（1715 年），清朝出师征讨嘉峪关以西地区，并在关外设置了赤金、靖逆二卫。此时，敦煌也被清政府从吐鲁番的控制下夺回，又回到了中央政府管辖之下。雍正元年（1723 年），清朝在敦煌设置沙州所，属安西同知所管，这是敦煌重新开发的开始。雍正三年（1725 年），川陕总督岳钟琪巡边至敦煌，针对敦煌重要的地理位置，建议清政府将沙州所升格为沙州

of the Jiayu Pass, whereupon Dunhuang was completely occupied by the Turfanians.

In 1644, the Ming Dynasty perished. Troops from the Qing, a Manchu regime from northeastern China, entered the Shanhai Pass and made Beijing the capital of the Qing Dynasty. In the 54th year of Emperor Kangxi (1715), the Qing government sent out troops to reclaim the western areas as far as the Jiayu Pass and set up Chijin and Jingni Guards. Meanwhile, Dunhuang returned to the administration of the imperial government. In the 1st year of Emperor Yongzheng (1723), the Qing government established Shazhou Post in Dunhuang, managed by the Vice Prefectural Magistrate of Anxi, which marked the beginning of revitalizing Dunhuang. In 1725, Dunhuang was inspected by Yue Zhongqi, the Governor-General of Sichuan and Shaanxi Provinces. Considering its important geographic location, the central government upgraded Shazhou Post to Shazhou Guard[①] under his suggestion. Yue Zhongqi then gathered more than 2,000 unemployed people to reclaim wasteland in Dunhuang. Aiming to carry out the *tuntian* policy smoothly, the Qing government adopted a series of proactive measures. First, prefectures or counties along the road to Dunhuang were required to provide food for people who were willing to cultivate the wasteland areas. Second,

① The guard-post (*wei-suo*) system was an important military system created in the Ming Dynasty. Guard was a military unit commanding 5,600 soldiers; post was the subordinate unit of a guard.

卫,得到了清政府的许可。岳钟琪还招揽无业贫民2000余户前往敦煌开垦荒地。为了搞好敦煌的实边屯田工作，清政府采取了一系列积极措施。首先,对于前往屯田的农户,沿途州县要给予口粮。而当实边户民到了敦煌后，又先把他们安置在空闲的营房里暂住,随即按户发给房价银三两,并命令地方政府于城外每户给空地二分四厘,各盖房二间。经过以上措施的实施执行，广大移民者就能够安心开发敦煌了。接着又按照壮劳力为户的单位，每户授田50亩,这样就可重新开垦和扩大耕地面积12万余亩。随着对土地的精心耕种，敦煌当地粮食产量也增加了。所种的小麦,每播种一斗,可以收获一石三四斗不等。当时,清政府又在党河东、西两岸共开大渠5道,计长140里,支渠与毛渠纵横交织。这样就使得新开垦的10万多亩良田都可以得到水利灌溉，敦煌绿洲又重新繁荣起来了。就是在这一年,党河水暴涨,沙州卫城被党河水侵蚀,东墙塌陷。清政府派遣光禄少卿汪隆前往敦煌，负责在党河东岸另筑沙州城。据记载,新建的卫城“周

after arriving in Dunhuang, these people were assigned empty barracks to live in and then each household was given money to build a house of their own in the area allocated by the local government, which helped the migrants work there without difficulty. Third, based on the number of able-bodied laborers, each household was allocated a field of about 50 *mu*. Thus the wasteland of nearly 120,000 *mu* could be cultivated. Gradually, grain yields in Dunhuang increased. At the same time, the government built five major canals about 140 *li* long along the eastern and western banks of the Danghe River, interwoven with a number of branch canals, which guaranteed irrigation to more than 100,000 *mu* of the newly-cultivated fertile farmland. As a result, Dunhuang prospered once again. But it was in this year that the Danghe River flooded, destroying the eastern walls of protective town of Shazhou. The Qing government dispatched the Vice Minister of the Court of Imperial Entertainments named Wang Long to be in charge of rebuilding Shazhou along the eastern bank of the Danghe River. It was recorded that the newly-built protective town was grand and magnificent. It was more than 1.5 kilomters long in perimeter and 6.5 meters high. The base part was 7.7 meters and the top part 3.3 meters wide, with additional walls of 1.7 meters high. In the process of

三里三分，高一丈九尺六寸，基宽二丈三尺，顶宽一丈，堞墙高五尺"，气势宏伟。在整个修城过程中，由于汪隆恪尽职守，能体察民情，故百姓较能出力，使修城工程顺利完工。乾隆二十五年(1760年)，清政府改沙州卫为敦煌县。在改县的同时，还加强了军事建设，设置了沙州巡防营，隶属肃州镇，设参将统领。

清政府在加强敦煌政治、经济、军事建设的同时，也加强了文化教育建设。乾隆二十四年(1759年)，河北宛平县举人曾希孔任敦煌知县，首先举办学校，倡建鸣沙书院。书院选址于县城关东北部，曾希孔亲自督建。乾隆二十五年，书院正式建成，开始招生工作。道光十九年(1839年)，敦煌人雷起稼，年仅20岁，就得中

reconstructing the town, Wang Long could fulfill his duties of serving the people and understanding their needs, which helped him win the trust of local residents. In the 25th year of Qianlong Era (1760), Shazhou Guard was renamed Dunhuang County equipped with a Brigade (*ying* in Chinese), a basic operational unit of the Green Standards to defend the local people, under command of an Assistant Regional Commander.

In addition to advancing the political, economic and military construction of Dunhuang, the Qing government attached great importance to the development of education. In the 24th year of Qianlong Era (1759), Zeng Xikong, the Magistrate of Dunhuang, advocated to establish the Mingsha Academy in the northeast of the county. The next year, the Academy began to enroll students. In the 19th year of Daoguang Era (1839), local citizen Lei Qijia succeeded in passing the imperial examinations and obtained the title of *juren*① at the age of 20. He was then recommended as a teacher of aristocratic children in Beijing. Five years later, he came back to Shazhou in the name of Magistrate, waiting for new appointment from the central government. Soon he took up the post of a lecturer at the Mingsha Academy. During twenty years of his teaching, he made great efforts to cultivate the

① The term *juren* was first used during the Han Dynasty for recommendees selected by the provincial authorities. During the Sui and Tang dynasties, it was used for candidates sent in by the prefectures, districts, various schools and the Directorate of Education, and who participated in the centrally organized examination in the imperial capital. During the Ming and Qing periods, the title of *juren* was awarded to graduates of the provincial examination.

举人，并留京充任教授皇家子弟的学官。5年后期满，以知县的身份依例归乡等待清朝政府的重新任命。不久，他就出任鸣沙书院主讲，任教20余年，尤以培养地方士风为己任，勤诲不倦，奖掖后进。一时间，敦煌人才辈出。如举人张克宽、雷起鸿、祁士麟、王化通，皆出于门下。鸣沙书院延至解放时，共经历了189个春秋，培养出了一大批人才。虽然敦煌的经济和文化在清朝略有恢复，再也没有能够恢复到汉唐时的盛况(图42)。

local intellectual ethos and support the younger generation. Influenced by him, many talented people emerged in Dunhuang, such as Zhang Kekuan, Lei Qihong, Qi Shilin, and Wang Huatong, all of whom were students of Lei Qijia. The Mingsha Academy had been cultivating young minds for 189 years until 1949. However, in spite of modest gains in its economy and culture in the Qing Dynasty, it was nevertheless impossible for Dunhuang to regain its former golden age as experienced in the Han and Tang dynasties (Fig.42).

图42　莫高窟三层楼　清
Fig.42　Three-Storey Tower, Mogao Caves　Qing Dynasty

丝路明珠：敦煌

Dunhuang: Pearl of the Silk Road

古代都会城市敦煌

The Ancient Metropolis of Dunhuang

在西汉开通丝绸之路后，由于得天独厚的地理位置，敦煌很快就成为中西交通线上的重要枢纽。在东西方通过丝路互通有无的同时，作为丝路重镇的敦煌，其作为丝路贸易中转站的地位也日益巩固和发展。丝路贸易的繁荣不仅促进了敦煌的商业发展，敦煌的手工业也迅速发展起来。此外，由于地近西域，中央王朝在经营西域时，敦煌的地域优势更加得以凸现。所以，在中国历史上，敦煌不仅是交通枢纽和商业城市，而且在相当长的时间里，敦煌作为军事重镇的特点也非常突出。

After the opening of the Silk Road in the Western Han Dynasty, Dunhuang quickly became a transportation junction between China and the West due to its unique geographical location. As a communication and transit hub along the Silk Road, Dunhuang became increasingly important. The prosperity of trade along the Silk Road promoted the development of commerce and skilled trade in Dunhuang. In addition, since Dunhuang was located near the Western Regions, its geographical advantage was highlighted even more during imperial China's administration of the Western Regions. Therefore, in Chinese history, Dunhuang was not only a transportation hub and trading center, but an important military town as well.

交通枢纽
A Transportation Hub

丝绸之路是一条横贯欧亚大陆的著名通道。它东起西汉的首都长安(今西安)或东汉的首都洛阳,西至罗马,将沿线各个国家和地区的政治、经济、文化中心连接起来。丝绸之路是中外经济文化交流的通途、友好交往的大道。东罗马、大食(位于阿拉伯半岛)、印度(唐代称为天竺)、波斯等许多西方国家,都通过丝绸之路与中国建立了密切的联系。东罗马、大食等地生产的玻璃、药材、犀角、象牙、香料等特产,由使者和胡商带到中国,以换取丝绸、茶叶、瓷器等货物,中国的造纸技术也是由他们传至大食,并最终传到了欧洲(图 43)。产生于印度的佛教,首先被传到西域,再通过西域传播到中国内地,所经过的路线就是历史上著名的丝绸之路。而属于东罗马基督教一支的景教,也在唐代

The Silk Road was an important route connecting Europe and Asia. It began from Chang'an (present-day Xi'an), the capital city of the Western Han Dynasty, or Luoyang, the capital city of the Eastern Han Dynasty, in the east. It stretched all the way to Rome in the west, connecting the political, economic and cultural centers in many countries and regions along its routes. The Silk Road was a route connecting China and Western countries for cultural exchanges and friendly contacts. The Eastern Roman Empire, the Arab Empire (located in the Arabian Peninsula), India (known as Tianzhu in the Tang Dynasty), Persia, and many other Western countries established close ties with China through the Silk Road. Glass, medicine, rhinoceros horn, ivory, spices, and other specialty products from the Eastern Roman Empire, the Arab Empire, and other countries were brought to China by the envoys and traders in the Western Regions and exchanged for silk, tea, porcelain, and other goods. China's paper-making technology was also introduced to the Arab Empire, and eventually spread to Europe (Fig.43). It was through the well-known Silk Road that Buddhism was first brought to the Western Regions from India, and then spread to the

图 43　莫高窟第 103 窟　溪山行旅　盛唐

Fig.43　Traders Travelling in the Xishan Mountains, Mogao Cave 103　High Tang

由波斯人沿丝绸之路传入长安。今陕西省碑林博物馆中唐德宗时所立的《大秦景教流行中国碑》，详细地记载了这一文化传入中国的经过。

根据自然及历史条件，丝绸之路可以划分为东、中、西三段。丝路东段东起长安或洛阳，西至敦煌地区的阳关和玉门关；而从敦煌出玉门关、阳关，西至葱岭间的道路属于丝路中段；葱岭以西经

Central Plains of China. Nestorianism, a sect of Eastern Roman Christianity was also introduced to Chang'an in the Tang Dynasty by the Persians along the Silk Road. The process of the introduction of Nestorianism into China was recorded in detail on the Nestorian Monument in China erected by Emperor Dezong of the Tang Dynasty. It is now located in Xi'an Beilin Museum (also known as Stele Forest) in Shaanxi Province.

Owing to geographical and historical conditions, the Silk Road can be divided into the eastern and western sections, and the section in between. The eastern section stretched from Chang'an or Luoyang in the east to the Yangguan Pass and the Yumen Pass in Dunhuang in the

中亚、西亚直至欧洲的道路和南至南亚巴基斯坦、印度的道路统称为西段(图44)。丝绸之路的东段和中段基本上都在中国的版图内,与我国及敦煌的历史联系最紧密。敦煌地处河西走廊西端,陆上丝绸之路主干道通过这里,使得敦煌在古代中西文化交流史上扮演着重要的角色。

丝绸是我国古代劳动人民的伟大发明和创

west. The section in between covered the area from the Yangguan Pass and the Yumen Pass to the Congling Range (present-day Pamirs) in the west. The western section consisted of two routes. The one extended from west of the Congling Range through Central and Western Asia all the way to Europe; the other extended from west of the Congling Range through Central Asia to Pakistan and India in South Asia (Fig.44). The eastern section and the section in between were basically within Chinese territory, having the closest historical ties with China. Dunhuang is located on the western end of the Hexi Corridor where the overland Silk Road passed through, thus Dunhuang played an important role in the ancient history of cultural exchange.

图44 阳关古道(邵如林 摄)

Fig.44 Ancient Path to the Yangguan Pass (Photo by Shao Rulin)

造，至晚在3000多年以前的殷商时代，我国劳动人民就已经能够用蚕丝织成精美的丝绸。20世纪，考古学家在德国的一座克尔特人首领墓葬（公元前6世纪）中发现了丝绸织物残片；在苏联阿尔泰区巴泽雷克的几座墓葬中，也出土了中国的丝织物。这些墓葬属于公元前5世纪，即相当于我国的战国初期。在阿尔泰巴泽雷克古墓（公元前10世纪中叶至公元前3世纪）曾发现保存完好的中国凤凰刺绣和山字纹铜镜。中国中原地区的丝绸和其他物品在西欧的出现，说明上古时期中西方已经存在经济文化交流。游牧于黑海、里海、咸海一带的斯基泰人和其他游牧民族是早期欧亚交流的开拓者和先行者。而早在公元前334年，即希腊–马其顿国王亚历山大东征之前，远在欧亚大陆两端的两大文明中心——希腊和中国之间就互有传

Silk is a great invention by the people of ancient China. As early as the Shang Dynasty (1600 BC–1046 BC), nearly three thousand years ago, Chinese people used silkworm cocoon filaments to make fine silk. In the 20th century, archaeologists found pieces of silk fabric in a Celtic chieftain's tomb (in the 6th century BC) in Germany. Chinese silk was also unearthed from the Pazyryk Cemetery in the Altai region in Russia, which dates back to the 5th century BC, equivalent to the early Warring States period (475 BC–221 BC) in Chinese history. In the Pazyryk Cemetery (in use roughly from the middle of the 10th to the 3rd century BC) were discovered well-preserved Chinese embroideries about phoenix and a copper mirror with a heraldic symbol of a mountain on it. Silk and other goods from Central Plains in China found in Western Europe indicate that cultural and economic exchange between China and Western countries already existed in ancient times. The early pioneers of Eurasian exchange were nomadic Scythians as well as other nomadic peoples from the Black Sea, the Caspian Sea, and the Aral Sea. As early as 334 BC, before the conquest of Alexander the Great, China and Greece, the two major centers of civilization on the Eurasian continent, had some knowledge of each other. According to Roman geographer Strabo's works, China was called Seres by the Greeks around the 3rd century BC. "Seres" came from the Greek word "Ser," meaning "silk," and "Seres" thus referred to "the country

闻。据古罗马地理学家斯特拉波的著作，大约在公元前3世纪，中国就被希腊人称为“赛里斯”。“赛里斯”是由希腊“赛尔”一词转化而来，“赛尔”是蚕丝的意思，“赛里斯”即是“丝国”。这反映了我国早在公元前在与西方各国的交往中，就以丝织物作为向外输出的重要商品。

从远古时期，作为丝绸之路所经过的西域即我国的新疆地区，便和内地发生了紧密的联系。我国古代文献中，多次提到黄帝涉流沙、登昆仑的事迹。据学者考证，此处的昆仑即今天的和田南山一带。古籍中还记载了传说中的尧曾越过塔克拉玛干沙漠，跨越昆仑山到葱岭以西的龟山，会见了西王母。所谓西王母，实际是西域地区处于母系氏族社会时的一个以虎豹为图腾的部落女领袖（图45）。大禹为了向西王国学习，也曾亲自到过西域地区。而成书于战国的《穆天子传》更详细地记载了周穆王游历西域地区的情景。周穆王自宗周（即今西安）出

of silk." This clearly shows that Chinese silk was an important trading commodity with Western countries before the Christian era.

From ancient times, the Western Regions where the Silk Road passed through, particularly the present Xinjiang region, had been in close contact with China's interior. In ancient Chinese literature, it was repeatedly mentioned that Yellow Emperor crossed the desert and climbed the Kunlun Mountains. It is verified by scholars that the Kunlun Mountains in documents are the present-day Nanshan area in Hetian (Khotan), Xinjiang. It was also recorded that Emperor Yao, a Chinese legendary ruler, crossed the Taklamakan Desert, the Kunlun Mountains, and reached the Guishan Mountain located in the west of the Pamirs, where he met Queen Mother of the West, a female leader of a matriarchal tribe from the Western Regions who worshiped tigers and leopards (Fig.45). In order to learn from the Kingdom of the West, Emperor Yu personally visited the Western Regions. In the *Tale of King Mu*, compiled in the Warring States Period, there are detailed records about his travels to the Western Regions. Setting out from Zongzhou (present-day Xi'an), King Mu of Zhou traveled across present-day Xinjiang, over the Pamirs to the Kyrgyz steppes, and returned back to the interior China. These journeys mentioned in ancient Chinese texts are brief, and the

图 45　莫高窟第 305 窟　帝释天妃(西王母)　隋

Fig.45　Queen Mother of the West, Mogao Cave 305　Sui Dynasty

发，经过今新疆各地，翻越了帕米尔高原，直到吉尔吉斯大草原；又从吉尔吉斯大草原返回内地。尽管我国古籍中记载上述情况十分简略，甚至其中还掺杂着不少神话，但是，它却反映了一个基本事实，即我国古代新疆地区与内地之间早就相通，彼此联系十分紧密。河南安阳殷墟妇好墓曾出土了商代的和

accounts are even interspersed with numerous myths, but they still reflect a basic fact that Xinjiang in the past had long been in communication and close contact with the Central Plains. Khotanses jade from the Shang Dynasty was unearthed in the tomb of the Fuhao in Anyang in Henan Province. According to pre-Qin Dynasty classics, jade transported from the Western Regions was called "jade from mountains of the Yushi." Yushi meant the Yuezhi, which showed that the Yuezhi nomads roaming between Dunhuang and the Qilian Mountains had been transporting jade to the Central Plains quite some time

田玉，而在先秦的典籍中，把西域运来的玉称之为“禺氏边山之玉”。“禺氏”即月氏，表明在中原和西域直接沟通以前的相当长一段时间里，游牧于敦煌、祁连山之间的月氏人，扮演着向中原传输玉石的角色。由此可见，在张骞通西域前，丝绸之路已出现。但最初出现的丝绸之路，常常因一些民族或国家的纠纷和战争而中断。即使它有时相通，也因山川阻隔，道路遥远，加之缺乏食宿和安全保障而时陷停顿。所以，只有到了张骞通西域后，由于中国汉朝政府在西域地区采取了各种有力措施并和帕米尔以西各国建立起了友好关系，才使得这条横贯亚洲的通道获得了发展，从而出现了空前的繁荣局面。

在周秦时期，月氏、乌孙、匈奴和诸羌先后居住在河西等地，对这一地区的开拓起了很大作用。特别是公元前 209 年，匈奴

before there was direct contact between interior China and the Western Regions. Thus, before Zhang Qian was sent to the Western Regions, the Silk Road was already in existence. However, in the beginning, the routes of the Silk Road were not well-connected because of tribal disputes and warfare among states. Even during times of peace, the routes were still hindered by mountains and rivers, long distances, and the lack of accommodation or security. Therefore, after Zhang Qian had successfully gone to the Western Regions as an imperial envoy of the Han Dynasty, the Han government took various effective measures for opening up the Western Regions; friendly relations were established with states west of the Pamirs, which contributed to unprecedented development and prosperity along the Silk Road.

During the Zhou (1046 BC–256 BC) and Qin (221 BC–206 BC) dynasties, the Hexi area was inhabited by the Yuezhi, the Wusun, the Xiongnu, and the Qiang peoples, who all contributed to the development of the region. Particularly, 209 BC marked a transition of the Xiongnu from a primitive society to one with social classes. The Xiongnu became more powerful after establishing a slavery system and greatly threatened the Wusun and the Yuezhi living in the Hexi area. In the 3rd year of Qianyuan Era of Emperor Wen of the Han Dynasty (177 BC), the Yuezhi were defeated by the Xiongnu, and were forced to move westward from the Hexi Corridor to the Ili River Basin in

从原始社会过渡到阶级社会，建立奴隶制政权之后更加强大，居住在河西一带的月氏和乌孙的势力范围受到了匈奴的极大挤压。汉文帝前元三年（前 177 年），月氏人被匈奴打败，被迫从河西走廊西迁到今天新疆的伊犁河流域。汉文帝后元三年（前 161 年）左右，乌孙联合匈奴打败月氏并在伊利河流域建立了乌孙国。由于月氏的西迁，匈奴随即进入河西地区，占领了月氏和乌孙故地，控制了河西走廊的西部，同时也控制了楼兰及西域部分地区。而汉武帝刘彻为了联络月氏、乌孙抗击匈奴，先后两次派遣张骞出使西域。武帝建元二年（前 139 年），张骞第一次出使西域，曾到达了大宛（今费尔干纳）、康居（今撒马尔罕）和居住在阿姆河北岸的大月氏等地。但大月氏此时已经占领了大夏的故地，生活稳定，不愿返回河西与匈奴对抗。张骞虽然没有完成联合大月氏夹击匈奴的原

Xinjiang. In the 3rd year of Houyuan Era of Emperor Wen (161 BC), the Wusun joined forces with the Xiongnu to defeat the Yuezhi and the State of Wusun was then established in the Ili River Basin. As soon as the Yuezhi moved out of the Hexi area, the Xiongnu immediately moved in, occupying the place where the Yuezhi and the Wusun had lived. The Xiongnu controlled a vast land including the western part of the Hexi Corridor, Loulan, and part of the Western Regions. In order to fight against the Xiongnu, Emperor Wu of the Han Dynasty sent Zhang Qian to the Western Regions twice in an attempt to unite the Yuezhi and the Wusun. In the 2nd year of Jianyuan Era of Emperor Wu (139 BC), Zhang Qian was sent to the Western Regions for the first time. He went to Dayuan (present-day Fergana), Kangju (present-day Samarkand) and places on the north bank of the Amu Darya inhabited by the Greater Yuezhi. The Greater Yuezhi, however, were unwilling to return to the Hexi Corridor to fight against the Xiongnu for they had occupied the place where the Bactrians had inhabited and were living a stable life then. Although the plan to seek a military alliance with the Greater Yuezhi against the Xiongnu failed, Zhang Qian went back with vital and detailed information about the west area of the Xiongnu and the states in the Western Regions, which proved helpful for the victory of Huo Qubing's military action in the Hexi Corridor. Zhang Qian was dispatched to the Western

定计划,却将西域各国及匈奴西部的具体情况带回了西汉,为霍去病夺取河西走廊的军事行动提供了重要的情报。武帝元狩四年(前119年),张骞再度出使西域,又到达了乌孙地区,并派遣使者到达了中亚各地。张骞两次出使西域,历时十余年,行程万余里,沿途历尽艰险,备尝苦楚。张骞率先出使西域的壮举,在历史上首次打通了直接联系中原和西域各国的丝绸之路。因此,史书上把张骞开通西汉与西域交流一事,形象地称之为"凿空"。而在张骞所开辟的连接中西交流的道路上,敦煌是最为重要的基地之一。

张骞"凿空"西域,以亲身经历和实践,发现和考察了被匈奴中断和阻塞的丝绸之路,详细记载了丝绸之路的具体路线和行经地点,以及详细报告了中亚各国山川、地形、风土人情、物产等自然和社会情况,这给当时的中国人开辟了一片知

Regions for a second time in the 4th year of Yuanshou Era of Emperor Wu (119 BC). He reached the area where the Wusun lived and sent messengers to Central Asia. Zhang Qian's two diplomatic missions to the Western Regions lasted more than ten years, covering more than 5,000 kilometers. Despite numerous difficulties and trials along the way, he was the first Chinese person sent on a mission to the Western Regions, opening up the Silk Road directly connecting the Central Plains with the states in the Western Regions for the first time in history. Therefore, Zhang Qian's contribution was vividly called *zaokong* (meaning exploration of an unknown place in ancient China) in historical texts. Dunhuang was one of the most important bases along the route Zhang Qian opened to connect the Central Plains with the Western Regions.

On his mission to the Western Regions and from his personal experience, Zhang Qian explored and studied the Silk Road which had been obstructed by the Xiongnu. He made detailed records of the specific routes of the Silk Road and the places along the way. He also reported at length the mountains, terrains, natural resources, customs, and other geographical and social conditions of the Central Asian countries, opening up a new world of knowledge for Chinese people at that time. In addition, Zhang Qian also made possible direct communication between China and Central Asia, as well as India, which put an end to the

识的新天地。此外，张骞的壮举还沟通了中国与中亚地区以及印度等国的直接联系，结束了中国靠传闻猜想外部世界的历史，进一步激发了与外部世界交往的热情。自从张骞通西域后，一时之间，丝绸之路呈现出了空前的繁荣状况。据史书记载，张骞开通西域后，汉朝赴西域的使者，“相望于道”，“一辈大者数百，少者百余人”。一年之中，“使多者十余，少者五六辈”。而出使西域的国家，“远者八九岁，近者数岁而反”。那么多的人到西域去，其中有的是真正的汉使，但更多的却是借着汉使的名义赴西域去从事贸易的商人。与此同时，从西域来汉朝的“使者”也很多，他们当中有真正的使臣，而更多的也是以使者身份，假借“贡献”为名的商人。由于张骞两次出使西域，在西域各地留下了深刻印象，所以，即使在他死后，被派往西域的汉朝使者，为了取得西域各族和各个国家的信任，仍然打着张骞的旗号。

西汉时最初往西方各地所走路线，主要是长安出发，经关

era of guesswork on China's part regarding the histories of other countries. The Chinese became more interested in interaction with the outside world, and the Silk Road began to show unprecedented prosperity. According to historical records, after Zhang Qian's opening up of the Western Regions, the Western Han Dynasty sent hundreds of envoys to get there. Generally, it took eight or nine years to have a journey to the farthest reaches of the Western Regions and back. Among the travelers, some were envoys dispatched by the Emperors of the Han government, while some were merchants going to trade in the Western Regions. Likewise, among the envoys from the Western Regions, most of them were traders in the name of paying tributes except some real envoys. Since Zhang Qian's two diplomatic missions made a deep impact on the states in the Western Regions, the envoys sent to the Western Regions continued in Zhang Qian's name after his death in order to win the trust of the peoples there.

During the Western Han Dynasty (206 BC–AD 25), the route to the Western Regions started from Chang'an, the capital city of the Han Dynasty, via the Guanlong Circuit into the Hexi Corridor. The Hexi Corridor is an important passage of the Silk Road, stretching from the Wushao Mountain in the east to Dunhuang in the west. To the

陇道进入河西走廊。河西走廊东起乌鞘岭，西至敦煌，是丝绸之路的要道。河西走廊以北是合黎山、龙首山，南沿祁连山，中间形成了一条天然平坦的通道。武威是丝绸之路向西进入河西走廊的第一个重要城市，也是一个重要的贸易集散地。武威原是匈奴休屠王的驻牧地，建有盖臧城，汉代称为姑臧。武威地扼河西走廊东口，地势重要，在历史上是兵家必争之地。同时，它又是丝绸之路的要冲，商业贸易的重镇。从武威西经张掖、酒泉等地到达敦煌。由敦煌向西，丝绸之路分为南北两道。出设置于敦煌的阳关，至楼兰(今新疆罗布泊西)，然后沿今新疆塔克拉玛干沙漠南侧的昆仑山北坡向西，经过且末、于阗、莎车等地，然后到达葱岭。这条路线称为南道。葱岭，即今天的帕米尔地区，

north of the Corridor are the Heli Mountain and the Longshou Mountain, and to the south are the Qilian Mountains; there is a natural flat valley passage in between. Wuwei is the first major city west along the Silk Road into the Hexi Corridor and it has been an important trading center and town of great military importance historically. Originally, Wuwei was in the domain of Prince Xiuchu of the Xiongnu, where Gaizang Town, called Guzang in the Han Dynasty, was built. Wuwei had been the military place for which many states or tribes struggled because of its strategic location at the eastern end of the Hexi Corridor. Meanwhile, Wuwei was the gateway of the Silk Road and the crucial town for commerce as well. People could start from Wuwei, and continued westward via Zhangye and Jiuquan to Dunhuang. The road extended westward from Dunhuang and branched into the northern and the southern routes. The southern route stretched from the Yangguan Pass to Loulan (west of present-day Lop Nor in Xinjiang), and then extended westward along the northern slope of the Kunlun Mountains south of the Taklamakan Desert in Xinjiang, and passed through Qiemo, Khotan, and Shache[1] before finally reached the Congling Range (present-day Pamirs, which was under the administration of Protectorate of the Western Regions in the Western Han Dynasty). According to the *Geography of the*

① Shache is also known as Yarkand.

在西汉属西域都护府所管之地。《西河旧事》载："葱岭其山高大，上悉生葱，故以名焉"。两汉时期,先后有几个国家活动于此,是经丝绸之路中段南道去中亚、西亚和南亚的咽喉要地。这里峡谷遍布,沟壑纵横,冰川雪峰,山高水深。有因海拔高而空气稀薄的大头痛山、小头痛山,有山高陡峭难行的乏驴岭。尤其是兴都库什山间的悬崖，幽谷险峻,道路不通,来往商旅往往通过栈道行进。栈道下临不测之深渊,人们通行的时候,"以绳索相持而度",《汉书·西域传》记载:"畜坠未半阬谷尽靡碎，人堕势不得相收视，险阻危害,不可胜言。"但这种险峻的地理环境并没有阻止东西方民族的文化交流,生活在帕米尔高原的各族人民在汉代就已开发了这个世界屋脊,为开拓东西道路交通创造了条件。

West of the Yellow River, Congling Range received its name for towering mountains with forested green onions. During the Western and the Eastern Han dynasties, Congling Range which several states occupied successively was the key junction on the southern route of the in-between section of the Silk Road to Central, West, and South Asia. It was characterized by a crisscross network of ravines, canyons, high mountains, deep valleys, and glaciers. There were the Big Toutong Mountain, and the Small Toutong Mountain (*Toutong* in Chinese means headache), both well-known for the high altitude and thin air, as well as the Falü Ridge (*Falü* in Chinese means exhausting a donkey) noted for its high mountains and steep slopes. In particular, the Hindu Kush Mountains were a barrier for its steep valleys and towering cliffs, making it impassable for merchants to travel along. People had to go along plank roads built along the face of a cliff over deep and unknown valleys. The ominous danger of walking along the plank road was recorded vividly in the *Book of Han: Traditions of the Western Regions* that the animals would crash into pieces before touching the bottom of the valley and it was impossible to save the person who fell down the valley. It's beyond one's words to describe the danger there. But such harsh geographic conditions did not hinder cultural exchange between the East and the West. Groups of people living in the Pamirs cultivated this roof of the world in the Han Dynasty, creating conditions for the development of transportation between the Central Plains and the Western Regions.

在丝绸之路开通之初，由于匈奴对北线的阻扰，所以南道比较畅通。至汉宣帝时期，匈奴郅支单于被汉朝击败，匈奴对西域北部地区的威胁被消除，丝路北道也畅通起来。之后，汉王朝除任命郑吉管理南道各地外，还兼护北道各地，因而称为“都护”。这是汉朝廷设在当地维持地方秩序、保护交通安全的最高军政长官，也是中国历史上最早出现的“都护”名称。丝绸之路北道出玉门关穿白龙堆沙漠的楼兰故城（位于罗布泊西北），至车师前王庭（即高昌，今吐鲁番），沿塔克拉玛干沙漠北侧的天山南坡向西，经龟兹（今库车）、疏勒（今喀什）等地，与南道会合，然后翻越葱岭，继续西行。由葱岭西行可至大月氏、康居、奄蔡、安息（今伊朗），最远可达大秦（罗马帝国）设在埃及的亚

In the initial years of the Silk Road's opening, the northern route of the Silk Road was blocked by the Xiongnu, while the southern route was comparatively smooth. By the reign of Emperor Xuan of the Han Dynasty, the Xiongnu, under their leader Zhizhi Chanyu, had been defeated and their threat to the northern part of the Western Regions was eliminated, making the northern route of the Silk Road open and clear. After that, Zheng Ji, a general in the Han Dynasty, was appointed by the imperial court to be in charge of the areas along the northern and southern routes of the Silk Road. Thus the title Protector-General① appeared for the first time in Chinese history. It was the title with the highest military and political position, responsible for maintaining local order and security for traffic. The northern route of Silk Road started from the Yumen Pass, then went through the old city of Loulan in the Bailongdui Desert (located in northwest of Lop Nur) to the court of Nearer Jushi (also called Gaochang, present-day Turfan). Then it extended west along the southern slope of the Tianshan Mountains north of the Taklamakan Desert, via Qiuci (present-day Kucha) and Shule (present-day Kashgar), merging with the southern route of the Silk Road, and passed through the Congling Range. Then it continued to stretch westward through the Greater Yuezhi, Kangju, Yancai, Anxi (present-day Iran) to

---

① Protector-General means *duhu* in Chinese. *Du* means both or all, and *hu* means protection.

历山大城。汉代道路的布局和走向,不仅为中国古代丝绸之路的基本格局奠定了基础,也是中国丝绸之路交通的格局和内涵。沿着张骞所凿空的这条丝绸之路,中国的丝绸源源不断地运往西方,成为罗马帝国时髦的服装原料。同时,西方的珍禽异兽、宗教思想也陆续流入中原。位于丝绸之路咽喉之地的敦煌,由于得天独厚的地域优势,很快就成为东西方的贸易中心和商品中转站。

随着中西交往的发展,为了适应中西交通发展的需要,新北道的开辟也就成为历史的必然趋势。汉朝对匈奴作战的持续胜利,也为新北道的开辟提供了必要的保障。公元前67年,郑吉破车师,并将其分为前、后王国。此后,由楼兰向西北去车师前国的路线经常使用,由车师前国亦可折向西南达到焉耆。这条北道因经楼兰古国,又有楼兰故道之称。由此道往焉耆、龟兹、疏

Alexandria in Egypt. The overall arrangement or layout of the routes in the Han Dynasty laid the foundation for the basic structure of both the ancient Silk Road and transportation routes for silk trade in China. China's silk was continuously transported to the West via the overland Silk Road opened up by Zhang Qian, and was sold as fashionable luxury fabric for attire in the Roman Empire. In turn, exotic animals and religious beliefs of the West were also brought to China's Central Plains. Due to the unique geographical location along the Silk Road, Dunhuang quickly became the trade center and transfer station of commodities between China and the West.

With the development of exchanges between China and the West, an inevitable need arose for opening up a new northern route of the Silk Road to meet transportation demands. The Han Dynasty's continual victories over the Xiongnu provided the necessary guarantee for the opening up of the new northern route. In 67 BC, Protector-General Zheng Ji defeated the State of Jushi and divided it into the Nearer Jushi and the Further Jushi. Later, the route northwestward from Loulan to the Nearer Jushi was frequently used and it curved southwestward from the Nearer Jushi to Yanqi. This route was also called the Ancient Loulan Passage as it passed through ancient Kingdom of Loulan. It was a shorter route to Yanqi, Qiuci, Shule, and other destinations. But going out of the Yumen Pass, the route ran across the Bailongdui Desert

勒等地的路程虽短，但由敦煌出玉门关后，必须要经过极度难行的白龙堆沙漠。白龙堆沙漠不仅干旱无水，而且风沙呼啸，行人极易迷失方向。所以，人们都尽量避开白龙堆沙漠。汉平帝时，戊己校尉徐普发现从车师后国经五船北达玉门关，既可避开白龙堆沙漠，又可缩短里程和时间，于是他就建议西汉朝廷开辟了这一道路。但所谓的开道，并不是指修建道路，而是修建并驻守驿站烽燧等。新北道从敦煌出发，不经白龙堆沙漠和楼兰，而径向西北，经五船北，可抵车师。由此向西到焉耆、龟兹，可以和原来的丝绸之路北道会合。这样一来，原来的北道就成了实际上的中道。

新北道的开通，加强了西汉与西域各国的联系。到了王莽建立新朝之后，由于对西域少数民族的政策不当，导致中原王朝与西域诸国的关系中断，通往西域的道路也难以通行。东汉时，窦宪率军北伐，打败了北匈奴，而班

where people easily got lost because of an extremely arid climate with strong sand storms. As a result, travelers tried to avoid the desert. During the reign of Emperor Ping of the Han Dynasty, Xu Pu, the *Wuji* Colonel, explored a shorter route stretching from the Further Jushi, passing through north of Wuchuan before arriving at the Yumen Pass. More importantly, the desert would be avoided. He recommended the imperial court to open up this route, which indicated the construction of beacons and watchtowers and stationing troops along the route instead of the building of an actual road simply. The new northern route started from Dunhuang, bypassed Bailongdui Desert and Loulan, then extended northwest through the north of Wuchuan to Jushi. From there it stretched westward to Yanqi and Qiuci, merging with the original northern route. In that way, the original northern route became the middle route of the Silk Road.

The opening of the new northern route strengthened communication between the Western Han Dynasty and the states in the Western Regions. But after the establishment of the Xin Dynasty (AD 9–23) by the usurper Wang Mang, such contact was broken off due to policies against the ethnic groups in the Western Regions, resulting in great difficulties traveling to those areas. During the Eastern Han Dynasty (AD 25–220), General Dou Xian defeated the Northern Xiongnu.

超父子又重新经营西域，使得西域诸国重新归附汉朝，新北道再次得以畅通。为了保障新北道的安全和畅通，汉顺帝永建六年（131 年），汉政府在西域的伊吾设伊吾司马，进行屯田和戍守。

东汉末年的黄巾起义之后，中原地区的地方势力相互攻伐不休，社会经济受到了极大破坏，西域与中原之间联系的丝绸之路交通也暂时中断。曹魏政权建立之后，通过实行屯田等措施以发展经济，同时还注意发展交通，逐渐成为三国时期实力最为强盛的政权。魏文帝黄初三年（222 年），西域的鄯善、龟兹、于阗等国遣使通魏，标志着自东汉末年以来中断数十年的丝路交通重新得以恢复。随着丝绸之路交通的恢复，中西政治交往、经济文化交流日益增多，敦煌在丝绸之路上的地位也显得日益重要。《三国

Under the management of General Ban Chao and his son, the states in the Western Regions showed allegiance to the imperial government again and the new northern route was resumed. In the 6th year of Yongjian Era of Emperor Shun (131), to ensure the continued safety of the route, the Han Dynasty appointed the Commander in Yiwu to have garrison troops stationed there and to open up wasteland.

Local forces in the Central Plains went through endless conflicts after the Yellow Turban Rebellion towards the end of the Eastern Han Dynasty. Consequently, the economy was greatly damaged and traffic along the Silk Road was temporarily disrupted. During the Three Kingdoms period (220–280), thanks to measures taken to develop the economy and transportation, the Kingdom of Wei (220–265) became the most powerful. In the 3rd year of Huangchu Era of Emperor Wen (222), emissaries from Shanshan, Qiuci, Khotan, and other states in the Western Regions were sent to the Kingdom of Wei, marking the restart of the Silk Road after it had been blocked for several decades since the end of the Eastern Han Dynasty. With the restoration of overland traffic on the Silk Road, there was an increase in political, economic, and cultural exchange between the Central Plains and the Western Regions. Thus, Dunhuang was becoming increasingly important along the Silk Road. According to the *Brief Records of the Kingdom of Wei: the Peoples of the Western Regions*, Dunhuang was specifically mentioned in the records of the Silk Road at that time: "There was two, now three routes from the Yumen Pass in

志》引《魏略·西戎传》在记载此时的丝绸之路时，着重提及敦煌："从敦煌玉门关入西域，前有二道，今有三道。从玉门关西出，经婼羌转西，越葱领（岭），经县度，入大月氏，为南道。从玉门关西出，发都护井，回三陇沙北头，经居卢仓，从沙西井转西北，过龙堆，到故楼兰，转西诣龟兹，至葱领（岭），为中道。从玉门关西北出，经横坑，辟三陇沙及龙堆，出五船北，到车师界戊己校尉所治高昌，转西与中道合龟兹，为新道。"由此可见，中原经河西走廊进入西域的丝绸之路，自敦煌一分为三，敦煌成为丝绸之路上当之无愧的咽喉要地。

魏晋南北朝时期是

Dunhuang to the Western Regions. The southern route starts westward from the Yumen Pass, and goes to the Greater Yuezhi, via Ruoqiang, the Congling Range, and the Xuandu Mountain. The middle route stretches westward from the Yumen Pass, passing through Duhujing, the northern end of Sanlongsha, the Julu Warehouse, moving northwestward from Shaxijing, across Bailongdui Desert, to the old Loulan, and then running westward to Qiuci and finally to the Congling Range. The new route still starts from the Yumen Pass, passing through Hengkeng, bypassing the Sanlongsha and Bailongdui Desert, taking an exit in the north of Wuchuan, going to Gaochang (the command of the *Wuji* Colonel), then running westward to merge with the middle route at Qiuci." Based on the information from this text, the Silk Road via the Hexi Corridor connecting the Central Plains and the Western Regions split into three routes from Dunhuang, making Dunhuang the hub.

The Wei, Jin (265–420), and Northern and Southern dynasties (420–589) witnessed extensive turmoil in Chinese history, causing the people living in the northern areas to suffer tremendously. When separatist regimes were attacking each other, the traffic around these territories was blocked; by contrast, the Hexi area remained stable thanks to its geographical advantages. Although the Five Liangs[①] arose in succession in the Hexi area, it was

① Five Liangs (304–439) refer to the Former Liang, the Later Liang, the Southern Liang, the Western Liang, and the Northern Liang.

我国历史上著名的历史大动荡时期，北方地区的广大人民遭受了巨大的苦难。在各个割据政权频繁相互攻伐的情况下，各地的交通经常被隔断，但此时河西一带却由于地域的关系保持了难得的安定。虽然在河西地区曾相继兴起五凉政权，但相对而言，这里的战争较少，社会秩序比较安定，经由敦煌的丝绸之路仍是中西交通的主干道。建兴二十三年(335年)，前凉张骏派杨宣率兵越流沙，至龟兹、鄯善，西域诸国望风归附，并纷纷遣使入贡。杨宣入西域，走的正是经敦煌出玉门关，然后转向通往西域的南道。建元十八年(382年)，前秦苻坚派吕光等进击西域诸国中不肯归附者。吕光出长安后，经敦煌，西出流沙，转入北道，经高昌、焉耆，至龟兹，大破龟兹、温宿等国，入龟兹改立其王，西域降附的国家有30多个。北凉永安四年(404年)，后秦京兆僧人智猛召集志同道合的僧人15人，入天竺(今印度)求法。他所走的路线也是由长安出发，西行进入河西走廊，经凉州、张掖、酒泉到达敦煌(图46)。由敦煌的

relatively peaceful then. The Silk Road via Dunhuang was still the main artery connecting China and the West. In the 23rd year of Jianxing Era (335), Zhang Jun from the Former Liang arranged Yang Xuan to lead the army across the desert to Qiuci and Shanshan, which induced some of the other states in the Western Regions to send envoys to pay tribute to the Former Liang. In this expedition, Yang Xuan took the southern route of the Silk Road to the Western Regions. In the 18th year of Jianyuan Era (382), Fu Jian from the Former Qin sent Lü Guang to conquer the states in the Western Regions whose rulers refused to surrender. Lü Guang set out from Chang'an, passing through Dunhuang, continuing westward via the desert, and then taking the northern route through Gaochang and Yanqi to Qiuci. Along the way, he conquered Qiuci, Wensu, and other states, making about 30 states in the Western Regions surrender to the Former Qin. In the 4th year of Yong'an Era of the Northern Liang (404), Zhimeng, a monk from the Later Qin, gathered another 15 like-minded monks to go to Tianzhu (present-day India) in seek of Buddhist knowledge. They started their journey from Chang'an, and headed westbound into the Hexi Corridor, passing through Liangzhou, Zhangye, Jiuquan before arriving in Dunhuang (Fig.46). Then they traveled westward from the Yangguan Pass,

图 46　莫高窟第 275 窟　交脚弥勒　北凉
Fig.46　Maitreya in Cross-Ankled Position, Mogao Cave 275　Northern Liang

阳关西行，越过沙漠后，经过鄯善、龟兹、于阗等国到达天竺，并最终由天竺沿原路返回凉州。

隋唐时期，尤其是唐朝贞观、开元、天宝年间是丝路交通繁荣昌盛时期。自长安开远门外至天山南北、葱岭内外，烽戍驿站，万里相继。水路关隘各有查禁，行人往来皆有凭证，正所谓“驿使验符券，传送据递牒，军防丁夫有总历，自余各请过所而度”。这都标志着丝绸之路的发达和繁荣。极盛时期的唐代长安，曾与数百个国家和地区保持着友好交往关系，丝绸之路便是当时中国与西方各国联系的主要纽带。唐人张籍在《凉州词》中曰：“边城暮雨雁飞低，芦笋初生渐欲齐。无数铃声遥过碛，应驮白练到安西。”形象而生动地描写了当时载运丝绸的骆驼大队于暮色苍茫中穿越大漠，向西方跋涉的壮观场面(图47)。

对于隋唐时期的丝绸之路的具体走向，《隋书·裴矩

crossing the desert, Shanshan, Qiuci, and Khotan to Tianzhu, and eventually returning to Liangzhou via the same route.

The Silk Road enjoyed a period of prosperity during the Sui (581–618) and Tang (618–907) dynasties, especially in the eras of Zhenguan (627–649), Kaiyuan (713–741), and Tianbao (742–756) in the Tang Dynasty. There were beacons, watchtowers, and postal relay stations along the Road from Kaiyuan Gate in Chang'an all the way to the northern and southern sides of the Tianshan Mountains as well as both inside and outside the Congling Range. Strict and careful checks were done when people went through the passes along the Silk Road, and passengers were required to show credentials or official passes, which marked the pinnacle of the Silk Road. During the High Tang, Chang'an maintained friendly relations with hundreds of countries and regions around the world, and the Silk Road was the main link between China and other countries in the West. Zhang Ji, a poet from the Tang Dynasty, wrote in his poem "Ode to Liangzhou," "A group of wild geese flew over the frontier in the rain, newborn asparagus pushed forth their shoots / Countless sound of bells came from the camels crossing the desert, carrying silk to Anxi." The poem depicted a vivid image of a caravan carrying silk and crossing the desert to the West in the gathering dusk (Fig.47).

The *Book of Sui*: *Biography of Pei Ju*

图 47　莫高窟第 217 窟　法华经变化城喻品　盛唐

Fig.47　*Lotus Sutra* Illustration , Mogao Cave 217　High Tang

传》引裴矩撰《西域图记·序》对当时的丝路三道作了一个较为明晰的叙述："发自敦煌，至于西海，凡为三道，各有襟带。北道从伊吾，经蒲类海铁勒部，突厥可汗庭，度北流河水，至拂菻国，达于西海；其中道从高昌、焉耆、龟兹、疏勒，度葱岭，又经钹汗、苏对沙那国、康国、曹国、何国、大小安国、穆国，至波斯，达于西海；其南道从鄯善、于阗、朱俱波、喝槃陀，度葱岭，又经护密、吐火罗、挹怛、忛延、漕国至北婆罗门，达于西海……故知伊吾、高昌、鄯善，并西域之门户也，总凑敦煌，是其咽喉之地。"从这条记述中可以清楚地看到，隋唐时期敦煌在丝路上的重要地位。而经过长时间的发展，两汉时期的新北道已与最初西汉时期开拓的南北两道并驾齐驱，成为一条重要商道(图 48)。

cited the *Preface to Maps and Notes on the Western Regions* by Pei Ju, who described in detail three specific extensions of the Silk Road during the Sui and Tang dynasties: "The Silk Road starts from Dunhuang and reaches the Western Sea (Mediterranean); it consists of three routes with their own subdivisions. The northern route extends from Yiwu, passes through the Tiele tribe on the Pulei Lake, the Turkic Khaganate, across the Beiliu River, to the Byzantine Empire and finally reaches the Western Sea. The middle route stretches over from Gaochang, passing through Yanqi, Qiuci, Shule, the Congling Range, running further to the states of Pohan[1], Sutrushana, Samarkand, Kebud, Kushānika, Bukhara, Murv to Persia, finally reaching the Western Sea. The southern route starts from Shanshan, passing through the states of Khotan, Zhujubo, and Hepantuo, over the Congling Range, proceeding to Humi, Tokharoi, Yida, Fanyan and Kabouldan, going to northern India, and ending at the Western Sea... Therefore, the Silk Road starts off from Yiwu, Gaochang, and Shanshan as portals to the Western Regions, but they all come together at Dunhuang, which is a strategic passageway of the Silk Road." The above records are clear proof of the crucial position Dunhuang enjoyed in the Sui and Tang dynasties. After long years of development, the new northern route opened in the Han Dynasty as well as the old northern and southern routes created in the

① Pohan was also known as Dayuan in the Han Dynasty.

图 48　莫高窟第 103 窟　维摩诘　盛唐
Fig.48　Image of Vimalakirti，Mogao Cave 103　High Tang

唐朝时的丝路北道，由敦煌向北，经柔远守捉所在的伊州柔远县，越莫贺延碛至伊州治所伊吾。然后再北越天山，到达天山北麓伊吾军驻所甘露川（今新疆巴里坤县），经蒲类(今新疆木垒县)，沿天山北麓西至北庭都护府治庭州（今新疆吉木萨尔县北庭古城)。由庭州西经沙钵城守捉（吉木萨尔县双岔河子村)、冯洛守捉(今新疆阜康县紫泥泉)、耶勒城守捉（今新疆阜康市东的土墩子)、俱六守捉(今米泉区甘家堡）至轮台县（今乌鲁木齐市)。自轮台西行，经张堡城守捉(今新疆昌吉县境)，渡里移德建河(剑河)到乌宰守捉(今新疆玛纳斯县)，再渡叶叶河（玛纳斯河）至叶河守捉。渡黑水至黑水守捉(在新疆乌苏市老西湖附近)，又经东林守捉、西林守捉（在今新疆乌苏市境)，渡石漆河（今新疆精河)，逾车岭至弓月城（今新疆伊

Western Han Dynasty became important commercial roads (Fig.48).

The northern route of Silk Road during the Tang Dynasty extended northward from Dunhuang, via Rouyuan County in Yizhou, across the Moheyan Desert to Yiwu, then over the north side of the Tianshan Mountains to Ganlu Valley (present-day Balikun County in Xinjiang) where the Yiwu Army was stationed. Then it went through Pulei (present-day Mulei County in Xinjiang), and moved further westward along the north side of the Tianshan Mountains to Tingzhou (ancient Beiting Town in present-day Jimusa'er County in Xinjiang). Then it went from the west of Tingzhou through the Defense Detachments of Shabo (present-day Shuangchahezi village in Jimusa'er County), Fengluo (Zini Spring in present-day Fukang County in Xinjiang), Yele (present-day Tudunzi in the east of Fukang County), and Juliu (present-day Ganjiabao in Miquan County), and then to Luntai County (present-day Urumqi). The route continued westward from Luntai, going through Defense Detachment of Zhangbao Town (present-day Changji County in Xinjiang), the Jianhe River, Defense Detachement of Wuzai (present-day Manasi County in Xinjing), the Yeye River (now called Manasi River) to Defense Detachment of Yehe, where it went further across the Heishui River, Defense Detachment of Heishui (near old West Lake in Wusu City in Xinjiang), Defense Detachments of Donglin and Xilin (in present-day Wusu City), and ran across the Shiqi River

宁县吐鲁番圩子古城)。再过思浑川渡伊丽河,西行经热海北岸,到达碎叶城。碎叶是唐朝西部地区重要的政治和交通中心,不但置有碎叶镇,还驻守有保大军。唐高宗调露元年(679年),裴行俭送波斯王子泥涅斯回国时,也送到碎叶。长安元年(701年),我国著名诗人李白出生于此,而安西都护王方翼和杜怀宝曾一度镇守在这里。丝路中道自安西出敦煌的玉门关,经莫贺延碛(哈顺沙漠)南缘,至吐鲁番盆地西州治所高昌。再沿天山南麓向西南至焉耆,出焉耆向西经铁门关至安西都护府治龟兹(今新疆库车),又出拓厥关,经苦井(今新和县西)至拨换城(今阿克苏)。又西北渡拨换河小石城,至大石城(今乌什城)。复经粟楼峰(今乌什县别迭里)、拨达岭(今别迭里山口),至顿多城(赤谷城)。又西北渡真珠河(即那林河),过乏驴岭,沿碎叶水至热海(今伊塞克湖),经裴罗

(present-day Jinghe River in Xinjiang), and the Cheling Mountain before reaching Gongyue Town (the ancient Weizi Town in Turfan, Xinjiang). After that it extended to Sihun Valley, and the Yili River, stretching westward to the north of Rehai Lake before reaching Suyab (*Suiye* in Chinese) which was an important political and transportation center in the Western Regions during the Tang Dynasty. In Suyab was established the Suyab Garrison and stationed Baoda Army. It was the place where Pei Xingjian said goodbye to Nines, Prince of Persia, on his return trip back home in the 1st year of Diaolu Era (679). Suyab was also the birthplace of Li Bai, a famous poet from the Tang Dynasty. Wang Fangyi and Du Huaibao, Protector-Generals of Anxi, also served there. The middle route of Silk Road started from Anxi out of the Yumen Pass in Dunhuang, extending along the southern rim of Moheyan Desert (present-day Hashun Desert) to Gaochang (the seat of local government of Xizhou Prefecture) in the Turfan Basin and going southwestward from the south side of the Tianshan Mountains to Yanqi, where it continued westward across the Tiemen Pass to Qiuci (present-day Kucha in Xinjiang), the seat of the Protectorate of Anxi, and then went out of the Tuojue Pass, through Kujing (west of present-day Xinhe County) to Bohuan Town (present-day Aksu). From there it went through the Town of Little Stone northwest of the Bohuan River, then extended to the Town of Big Stone (present-day Wushi Town), and went through Sulou Peak (present-day

将军城，至碎叶城。丝路南道自沙州寿昌县西40里到达西汉时期所置的阳关故城，沿罗布泊南岸西行，至汉代的伊循城，又西行80里到达石城镇，即汉代的楼兰国，也就是鄯善(若羌)。又西行200里至新城，又西行经特勒井，渡且末河，经500里至播仙镇(原且末城)，又西行经悉利支井、祆井、勿遮水、杜堡、彭怀堡、坎城守捉，最终到达于阗。

由此可以看出，虽然汉唐以来丝绸之路的具体路线有所变动，但不管是两汉时的南、北两道，还是两汉以后的南、中、北三道，敦煌都是丝绸之路分道的起点和合道的汇集点。古代的中外使者、商队、僧徒西去东来，都必须经过敦煌。也正是因为如此，《隋书·裴矩传》中才会将其形象地比喻为丝绸之路的咽喉。

Biedieli Mountain), the Boda Mountian (entrance to the present Biedieli Mountain) to Dunduo Town (also called Chigu Town), then went across the Zhenzhu River (also called the Nalin River) and the Falü Ridge. From there it went along the Suyab River to Rehai Lake (present-day Issyk-Kul Lake), and proceeded to the Town of General Peiluo and finally reached Suyab Town. The southern route of Silk Road started from the west away from Shouchang County of Shazhou to the old town of Yangguan established in the Western Han Dynasty. Then it went westward along the south bank of Lop Nur, to Yixun Town in the Han Dynasty, and continued running 80 *li* onto the Shicheng Town, namely Loulan Kingdom in the Han Dynasty, or Shanshan (also called Ruoqiang). Then it stretched 200 *li* westward to Xincheng Town, Telejing, the Qiemo River, going another 500 *li* before reaching Boxian Town (the previous Qiemo Town). Finally it reached Khotan after crossing Xilizhijing, Xianjing, the Wuzhe River, Dubao Castle, Penghuai Castle, and Defense Detachment of Kancheng.

As can be seen from the above detailed descriptions, the extensions of the Silk Road in the Han Dynasty were different from those of the Tang Dynasty. However, no matter how changeable the routes of the Silk Road were, Dunhuang was always the starting as well as converging point of the divisions of the Silk Road. It was the place which envoys, merchants, and monastics from China and other countries must pass through. That is why Dunhuang was figuratively depicted as the "neck" of the Silk Road in the *Book of Sui*: *Biography of Pei Ju*.

商业都会

A Trading Center

自从汉代开通丝绸之路以后，中亚粟特地区的胡商即一批批沿着丝绸之路，途经敦煌而进入中国腹地。由于敦煌特殊的地理位置，成就了其荟萃中西的伟大成就。原早在东汉时，敦煌已经被当时的学者称作“华戎所交一都会”,成为著名的国际贸易都市。即使是十六国大动乱时期，仍有大量中亚胡商活跃在敦煌。尤其是进入唐朝，随着丝绸之路的畅通与繁荣，中亚胡人的东徙浪潮益发高涨（图49)。唐玄宗天宝年间,敦煌地区更是出现了一个由粟特人组成的从化乡,这些胡人成为唐朝的正式编户。而这些活跃在丝绸之路上的胡商将中国的丝绸、瓷器、造纸及雕版技术带到中亚、西亚和欧洲,同时也将西域及西方出产的

After the opening up of the Silk Road in the Han Dynasty, a great number of merchants from the Sogdian area in Central Asia entered China's interior through Dunhuang. Due to its special geographic location, Dunhuang made great achievements in connecting China and the West. As early as in the Eastern Han Dynasty, Dunhuang was regarded by scholars as a "metropolis connecting China and the West," namely, a renowned center for international trade. Although China was in chaos during the period of the Sixteen Kingdoms, many traders and merchants from Central Asia were still active in doing business in Dunhuang. Particularly, with the development and prosperity of the Silk Road in the Tang Dynasty, more and more people migrated eastward from Central Asia (Fig.49). During the Tianbao Era of Emperor Xuanzong in the Tang Dynasty, a township named Conghua was set up, in which Sogdian people officially registered households. It was those Western merchants working along the Silk Road who not only introduced Chinese silk, porcelain, papermaking, and block printing to Central Asia, West Asia, and Europe, but also brought horses, camels, grapes, alfalfa, and coloured glaze techniques as well as Western music, dance, and acrobatics into China's interior. Such business

图 49　西安出土的胡人俑
Fig.49　Figurine of Hu Tribesman Unearthed in Xi'an

良马、骆驼、葡萄、苜蓿、琉璃及胡乐胡舞、杂技百戏等源源不断地传入内地。中亚胡人的商业活动刺激了包括敦煌在内的整个河陇地区的发展和繁荣。

活跃在丝绸之路上的胡商，主要来自中亚地区以康国为中心的若干小国。根据中外史料记载，粟特人在公元前5—6世纪时已经出现，是世代繁衍聚居在锡尔河与阿姆河流域的古老民族，曾先后隶属于波斯阿赫明尼德王朝、希腊亚历山大帝国和塞琉古帝国。而秦汉之际被匈奴驱逐出河西地区的月氏人持续西迁，最终迁徙到了中亚的粟特地区。西迁中亚的月氏人建立了自己的政权，这就是曾经称雄中亚、南亚的贵霜帝国。一部分追随不及的小股月氏人，留下来和河西南山的羌人汇合，称为小月氏。后来，强大一时的贵霜帝国发生了内乱，最终形成了多个国家。各个国家的民众就以各自所在国名为姓，如康、安、曹、米、史、何、罗、石、贺等。由于西迁的月氏人的祖先原来居住在河西祁连山麓的昭武城，所以隋唐时

activities stimulated the development and prosperity of Hexi and Longyou areas, including Dunhuang.

These merchants were mainly from small states centred around Samarkand in Central Asia. According to historical records, the Sogdians, emerging sometime during the 5th to 6th century BC, were an ancient people living in the basins of the Syr Darya and the Amu Darya, and were later controlled by the Persian Achaemenid Empire, Alexander the Great's Hellenistic Empire and the Greek Seleucid Dynasty successively. At the transition between the Qin and the Han dynasties, some of the Yuezhi people were expelled westward from the Hexi area by the Xiongnu, finally arriving in the Sogdian area. They established their own regime called the Kushan Empire, ruling areas in Central Asia and South Asia at the time. The rest of the Yuezhi who stayed merged with the Qiang people around the Nanshan Mountain in the Hexi area, also known as the Lesser Yuezhi. Later, the once powerful Kushan Empire disintegrated into many small states. People in such states took the name of their country as their family names such as Kang (kāng), An (ān), Cao (cáo), Mi (mǐ), Shi (shǐ), He (hé), Luo(luó), Shi (shí) and He (hè). Because the forefathers of these Yuezhi people in the Kushan Empire originally lived in Zhaowu Town located at the foot of

期的史书中把这些中亚胡人称作“昭武九姓”，也称为粟特人。

在未迁入中亚之前，月氏人就曾控扼河西的孔道，进行丝绸和珠玉的转运贸易。“月氏”也就是管仲所说的“禺氏之玉”的“禺氏”，反映出月氏本来就是一个有着经商传统的民族。迁到中亚后，月氏人保持了善于经营商业的特点。《史记·大宛列传》记载他们“善市贾，争分铢”，也就是说他们善于经商，而且对于商业利益分毫必争。粟特人保持了其先祖选择职业的特点，经营兴利以谋生。粟特人有一个风俗，在孩子出生以后，父母要在孩子口上涂蜜、手上涂胶，就是期望孩子长大以后做生意时，能做到口似蜜，而钱赚到手后则会粘在手上，不再溜走。

丝绸之路开通以后，粟特地区与中原的民间交往进一步得到加强，大量粟特人前来中国。根据规定，西汉地方政府要为往来的胡商沿途提供食

the Qilian Mountains in the Hexi Corridor, they were named the Nine Zhaowu Clans, also called Sogdians in the history books from the Sui and Tang dynasties.

Before migrating into Central Asia, the Yuezhi had controlled the passageway to the Hexi Corridor for transferring silk, pearls, and jade. The Yuezhi were the people of Yushi in “the jade from Yushi” mentioned by Guan Zhong[1], showing they had been a nomadic people with a tradition of doing business. When in Central Asia, the Yuezhi retained their trading customs as before. It was recorded in the *Records of the Grand Historian: Dayuan* that they were skilled merchants and quite competitive for dimes and nickels. They inherited the features of their old generations to choose trading as their career. They even had a custom that after a baby was born, his parents would put honey in his mouth and glue on his hands, expecting their child could be honey-mouthed and hold onto money firmly while doing business after he grew up.

After the opening up of the Silk Road, non-governmental contact between the Central Plains and the Sogdian region increased. A great number of Sogdians came to China. According to Western Han Dynasty

---

① Guan Zhong was a celebrated chancellor and reformer of the State of Qi during the Spring and Autumn period.

宿。由于前往汉朝的胡商数量太大，以至于出现了敦煌和酒泉郡及丝绸之路南道上的 8 国不堪重负的情景。魏晋南北朝时期，也有很多中亚的胡人来到中国，其中有参与政治活动的官员、传播佛法的高僧，但更多的还是为兴利贸贩的商人。从河西的敦煌到东汉的都城洛阳，到处都可以见到中亚胡商活动的足迹。隋朝统一之后，粟特地区与中原的联系得到进一步加强。他们不但以昭武诸国的名义频繁遣使，同时民间的往来更为常见。或者由于经商的需要，或者为了移民，或者两者合二为一，大批粟特人涌入中原。在新疆塔里木盆地周边地区，此时已经开始形成一系列粟特人聚落。至隋炀帝时，裴矩根据前往张掖贸易的西域胡商所述，撰成《西域图纪》。他在此书的序言中指出："发自敦煌，至于西海，凡

regulations, local governments along the Silk Road were required to supply room and board for merchants from Central Asia. Consequently, an influx of traders into China caused Jiuquan and Dunhuang prefectures as well as other eight states along the southern route of the Silk Road unable to afford the demand. During the period of the Wei, Jin, and Northern and Southern dynasties, large amounts of people from Central Asia came to China, among whom some were officials involved in diplomatic and political activities, and some were eminent monks disseminating Buddhist teachings, but most were merchants hoping to earn huge profits. From Dunhuang in the Hexi area to Luoyang, the capital city of the Eastern Han Dynasty, traders from Central Asia could be seen everywhere. The relationship between the Central Plains and the Sogdian region was further strengthened after the unification of the Sui Dynasty. During that period, the Sogdians not only frequently dispatched envoys to China, but also strengthened non-governmental contacts. A large number of Sogdian people poured into China, with some being envoys representing the states of Zhaowu, some being involved in business or immigration, or both. At the time, the Sogdians had settled in the areas surrounding the Tarim Basin. During the reign of Emperor Yang of the Sui Dynasty, an official and geographer Pei Ju wrote his *Maps of and Notes on the Western Regions* based on information from merchants of the Western Regions who traded in Zhangye. In its preface, he stated, "The Silk Road starts from

为三道，各有襟带。”而三大商道中的中道，主要所经过的就是粟特地区。根据记载，在裴矩主持张掖互市期间，曾有大量的粟特人前往张掖及凉州贸易。

敦煌是胡商进入河西和中原地区的门户，从汉代以来此地即为“华戎所交一都会”，胡商在敦煌的商业活动受到当地政府的支持和保护。如三国时仓慈出任敦煌太守，就大力打击欺诈胡商的地方豪强，保护过往商人的安全，制定各种政策以方便胡商前往洛阳和内地贸易。所以，当仓慈死后，胡商才会聚集在戊己校尉及长史的办公地点，为仓慈举行哀悼仪式。敦煌文书《沙州都督府图经》里记载敦煌西北100多里的地方有一处兴胡泊，“其水咸苦”。经玉门

Dunhuang and reaches the Western Sea (Mediterranean); it consists of three routes with their own subdivisions.” Here the middle route of the three mainly extended through the Sogdian region. It was also recorded that when Pei Ju was in management of frontier trade, numerous Sogdians headed for Zhangye and Liangzhou to do business.

Dunhuang had long been the gateway for traders entering the Central Plains via the Hexi area. Since the Han Dynasty it had been regarded as “a metropolis connecting China and the West,” where the business activities of merchants were protected or supported by the local government. For example, Cang Ci, the Governor of Dunhuang Prefecture in the period of Three Kingdoms, clamped down on the powerful landlords who cheated Western traders, so as to protect the security of the merchants. He implemented a series of measures ensuring smooth, accessible trade for merchants heading to Luoyang and other places within China's interior. After his death, Western merchants spontaneously arranged a memorial ceremony for him, as a sign of their esteem and appreciation. It was recorded in the *Pictorial Records of Superior Prefecture of Shazhou* that there was a place named Xinghu[①] Lake with salty and bitter water, 100 *li* away from the northwest of Dunhuang. It received its name because all

① *Xing* means being prosperous, and *hu* refers to people from the Western Regions and particularly the Sogdians.

关东来敦煌或西去西域的中亚胡商，都要在此停留以休整，故得名。西晋永嘉六年(312年)二月，在粟特商团首领纳尼班达写往萨马尔罕的粟特文信件中，详细叙述了该商团的活动："阿尔梅特萨斯在酒泉一切顺利，阿尔萨斯在姑臧也一切顺利……自从有位粟特人内地来此已三年，那时我正为古塔门萨斯准备行装前往淮阳"，"我们从敦煌前往金城去销售大麻纺织品、毛毡……我们希望金城至敦煌时的商业信誉，尽可能长期得到维持。自从我派沙拉和法拉扎德去内地，至今已有八年，三年前他们曾来过信……我派另一名叫阿尔提赫凡达的人去内地，又已过去四年，因为商队是从姑臧启程的，故他们在第六个月才到达洛阳……我又派纳尼安去敦煌"。这个粟特商团规模很大，他们从敦煌

merchants from Central Asia who travelled eastward to Dunhuang through the Yumen Pass or returned westward to the Western Regions stopped to rest there. In February of the 6th year of Yongjia Era of the Western Jin (312), in the letters written by Nerney Ban Tak, the head of a Sogdian merchants group, to Samarkand, their activities were described in detail. "All is smooth for Almetsass in Jiuquan, and so is for Alsace in Guzang[①] ... It was heard that a Sogdian businessman has been here from the Central Plains for three years and I was then preparing luggage for Gutmensars who would go to Huaiyang.[②]" "We travelled from Dunhuang to Jincheng to trade hemp textiles, felt, and other goods. We hope the business reputation between these two cities can last as long as possible. It has been eight years since I sent Sara and Farazadeh to the Central Plains. Three years ago, they sent me a letter ... Four years ago, I sent another man named Aratihovatar, who started from Guzang and arrived in Luoyang six months later ... I sent Nanien to Dunhuang." Based on the contents of these letters, it can be seen that this merchants group was a large enterprise with the purpose of selling hemp textiles in Jincheng (present-day Lanzhou). They hoped to maintain long-term commercial stability between Dunhuang and

---

① Guzang refers to present-day Wuwei in Gansu.

② Huaiyang refers to a county in present-day Henan.

派遣商队前往金城（今兰州）销售大麻纺织品，并希望维持敦煌至金城一线的长期商业稳定，可见当时敦煌在丝绸之路上的贸易集散地的重要地位。

到了唐代，随着敦煌商业经济的发展，有更多的粟特人进入敦煌境内进行商业活动，成为敦煌贸易市场的主体。据敦煌文献记载，敦煌所属的石城镇就是由粟特人所建。石城镇本是汉代鄯善国的鄯善城，由于隋朝末年天下大乱，所以此城被废弃。到了唐朝贞观年间，康国大首领康艳典东行入唐，居住在此城。因为有大批胡人随之而来，所以石城镇就成为粟特人在敦煌的一大据点。康艳典为康国胡商的大首领，前来石城镇居住显然是出自商业利益上的考虑。康艳典以石城镇为据点，先后修建了新城、蒲桃城、萨毗城等城镇，而这些城镇都应是粟特商人的商业据点。唐中

Jincheng, demonstrating Dunhuang's importance as an entrepôt along the Silk Road.

In the Tang Dynasty, with the development of the commercial economy in Dunhuang, an increasing number of Sogdians went there for business, becoming the main body of the trade market. According to Dunhuang documents, the Shicheng Town under the command of Dunhuang was established by the Sogdians. It was originally known as Shanshan Town during the Han Dynasty, but was deserted because of the turmoil in the final years of the Sui Dynasty. During the Zhenguan Era of the Tang Dynasty, Kang Yandian, the leader of Samarkand, travelled eastward to live in the Shicheng Town. As more and more Sogdians settled there, the Shicheng Town became a major base for them. As the head of the Hu merchants in Samarkand, Kang Yandian's settlement was for commercial benefits. Based on the Shicheng Town, he built the towns of Xincheng, Putao, and Sapi one after another, all of which later developed into bases for business of Sogdians. During the Jinglong Era (707–710) of Emperor Zhongzong of the Tang Dynasty, fleeing civil strife from the Western Turks, Sogdian people living in Central Asia poured into Dunhuang, many of whom settled there for trade. Such ambitious people not only engaged in a variety of trades, but also served as officials managing the markets, reflecting their traditional quality of being talented in business. In order to efficiently facilitate the management of the Sogdians, the Tang government established

宗景龙年间（707—710年），由于受西突厥内乱的影响，生活在中亚地区的粟特人大量涌入敦煌。很多粟特人为了从事贸易活动的便利，干脆定居在敦煌。粟特人在敦煌的活动很活跃，不但从事各种商业贸易活动，而且有的粟特人还担任了管理市场的官员，充分体现了粟特人精于经营的特点。为了便于管理这些粟特人，唐政府专门在敦煌县设立了从化乡，成为敦煌十三乡之一。从化乡位于敦煌东门外一里左右的祆神祠附近，而紧邻设置在城东200步的州城驿。这里是一处陆路交通枢纽，不管是进入唐朝内地，还是出往西域，都要以此为起点。这些粟特人定居在紧邻敦煌交通中心的要冲之地，极大地便利了他们的经商活动。

昭武九姓胡人中盛行火祆教。火祆教以崇拜光明和善良为其教旨，由此拜日、月、星辰，总为拜天，故初传中国时多称为祀天神、拜胡天。由于其还认为火是光明和善良的代表，故也拜火。在公元226年前后，波斯王国定火祆教为国教，于是在中亚诸国得到了广泛的传播。昭武九

Conghua Township, one of the 13 townships in Dunhuang County. Conghua Township, located near the Zoroastrian Temple about one *li* away from the East Gate of Dunhuang and adjacent to Zhoucheng post, was a traffic hub, through which people could enter the Central Plains or the Western Regions. The settlement of Sogdian immigrants in such an important traffic center greatly facilitated their business activities.

Zoroastrianism was prevalent among the people of the Nine Zhaowu Clans. Zoroastrianism held the worship of brightness and goodness as its dogma, thus it worshipped heavenly bodies such as the sun, the moon, and the stars. When introduced into China, Zoroastrianism was called Sitianshen or Baihutian, which meant "offering sacrifices to Heaven." Meanwhile, it took fire as an entity of brightness and goodness, so it worshiped fire as well. Around 226, Zoroastrianism was established as the official religion in the Persian Empire; it then spread widely among countries in Central Asia including the homelands of the Nine Zhaowu Clans, among whom the Zoroastrian temples where religious ceremonies were held had a lofty position. With the immigration of people from those countries, Zoroastrianism was introduced into China. During the Wei and Jin dynasties, it was in the Hexi area that

姓各国也随之奉行此教，而举行祭祆活动的祆祠在昭武九姓各国中具有崇高地位。随着九姓胡人的东来，火祆教也随之传入中国。魏晋以来，河西是胡商最集中的地区，祆教在这里传播也较早。到了唐代，河西地区的火祆祠明显增加。根据敦煌写本《沙州图经》记载，敦煌也有"祆神"祠。敦煌的祆神祠，在城东一里左右。祆祠的方圆有100多步，里面绘有祆教天神画像20龛。敦煌写本P.2748号《敦煌廿咏》"安城祆咏"中，有"版筑安城日，神祠与此兴"的记载，可知敦煌祆祠又名安城，即上述州东的祆神祠。964年的《归义军酒司酒账》中就记载到此年的四月二十日，城东赛祆神所用酒的数量，证明此祆祠直到10世纪后期仍在使用。而一度属唐沙州管辖的鄯善石城地区，也建有祆舍。

在敦煌石窟壁画中我们也经常可以看到中亚粟特商人的形象。如敦煌莫高窟第296窟窟顶北披有北周时期

Hu merchants were most concentrated, and as a result, Zoroastrianism was introduced there the earliest. In the Tang Dynasty, more and more Zoroastrian temples were erected. According to the *Pictorial Records of Shazhou*, there was a Zoroastrian temple in Dunhuang, which was situated about one *li* away from the east of Dunhuang. The temple had a radius of about 100 *bu*, and in it stood 20 statues of gods from Zoroastrianism. In "Twenty Poems of Dunhuang" (Dunhuang manuscripts P.2748), a similar record can also be found with the name "Ancheng," which referred to the Zoroastrian temple mentioned above in Dunhuang. In addition, quantity of wine used in the Zoroastrian temple until the 20th of April of 964 was recorded in *Account Book of Wine in the Guiyijun Period* in the same year, which proved that the Zoroastrian temple had been in use until the late of the 10th century. Meanwhile, a Zoroastrian temple could be found in the Shicheng Town of Shanshan under the administration of Shazhou as well.

The images of Sogdians from Central Asia could be seen frequently in the murals of Dunhuang. For instance, the *Punya-ksetra* (*Field of Merit*) *Illustration Painting* in Mogao Cave 296 painted during the Northern Zhou Dynasty depicts a small bridge with two pack horses carrying bundles of products, followed by four Han merchants; at the other end of the bridge are two Hu traders. One has a high-bridged nose and deep-set eyes, wearing

所绘制的《福田经变》。画上描绘了一座小桥，桥上有两匹驮着商品包裹的马，后面是4个汉族模样的商人。而桥的另一侧则画有一个头戴尖顶帽、深目高鼻的胡商牵着两峰骆驼，正准备过桥，骆驼身上驮着高大的货包。另一个胡商赶着两头驮着货物的毛驴相随。莫高窟第420窟窟顶东披是隋代所绘制的《观世音菩萨普门品》，讲的是胡商出行前跪地求观世音菩萨保佑一路平安。商队启程后，赶着一队驮着货物的骆驼、毛驴翻山越岭。当商队下到山谷休息时，忽然一群穿戴盔甲的强盗骑马冲杀过来。商人仓促应战，寡不敌众，全部被俘。正在这时，观音显灵，于是胡商最终得救。而莫高窟中所绘胡商形象最为传神的当属第45窟的“胡商遇盗图”。画面是山间一伙强盗手持长刀劫持了一群胡商，胡商将货物卸到地上，向强盗求饶。

a peaked cap. He is about to cross the bridge by pulling two camels laden with cargos, while the other Hu trader follows him by leading two donkeys carrying goods. On the eastern slope of the ceiling of Cave 420 is the *Chapter of the Universal Gate of Avalokitesvara Bodhisattva* painted in the Sui Dynasty, which depicts a group of Hu merchants kneeling in prayer to Avalokitesvara for a safe journey. According to the sutra, a trade caravan crossed hills and valleys with their camels and donkeys carrying goods. When they stopped to rest in a valley, armed bandits on horseback rushed towards them. Caught unawared, all of the merchants were captured. At that very moment, Avalokitesvara appeared and saved them. The most vivid image of Hu traders can be seen in the *Hu Merchants Encountering Bandits Narrative Painting* in Mogao Cave 45. It depicts a group of bandits with long knives in their hands attacked Hu traders, who then beg for mercy after depositing the goods on the ground. These merchants are depicted with the distinctive characteristics of people in Central Asia at the time—deep-set eyes, high-bridged noses, as well as curly hair and thick beards. Their leader stands at the front of the caravan, wearing a long green robe and a peaked felt cap. He is followed by other merchants in long robes with round collars, some wearing felt caps, and some turbans. The last trader in a red robe leads two donkeys laden with goods. All the merchants appear frightened, putting their palms together devoutly to ask for help from Avalokitesvara

这些商人都深目高鼻、发卷髯浓，具有十分鲜明的中亚特色。站在最前面的商队首领头戴高顶毡帽，身着绿色长衫。其身后的胡商有的头戴毡帽，有的以长巾缠头，多穿圆领长衫。最后穿红袍的商人，牵引着两头驮满货物的毛驴。这些胡商神色慌张，双手合十，请求观世音菩萨解救(图 50)。这种高高的尖顶毡帽，是胡人常戴的一种帽子。而这些商人深目、高鼻等特征，表明他们正是当时敦煌人常常见到的粟特商人形象。

吐蕃占领敦煌之后，在行政建制上废除唐朝的乡里制，而设置擘三、僧尼、行人、阿骨萨、丝绵等部落。敦煌地区的粟特人主要集中于丝绵部落和行人部落。丝绵部落分布在敦煌城内及城周围的百尺村附近，主要从事丝绸生产和手工业蚕坊。在吐蕃占领敦煌之前，粟特人在敦煌的商业贸易和手工业领域中就十分活跃，所以吐蕃统治者就将他们安置在丝棉部落，主要从事丝绸及布等商品的生产和销售。此外，还有很多粟特人沦为敦煌各寺院的寺户，在寺院中担当各种杂役。从他们所从事的差役种类看，粟特人所从事的

(Fig.50). These people with their distinctive features and clothing reflect the image of Sogdian traders as viewed by Dunhuang people at the time.

After Dunhuang was occupied by the Tubo, the township and village administrative system in effect under the Tang Dynasty was abolished. Instead, a quasi-tribal system was established, such as *qingsan* tribe, the tribe of the Sangha, the tribe for military defense, *Agusa* tribe, the tribe for farming, sericulture, and production, and so on. The Sogdian people in Dunhuang mainly belonged to the tribes for farming, sericulture and production, and military defense, the former of which was located inside or around Dunhuang and engaged in silk production and silkworm-raising workshops. The Sogdians had been active in commercial activity and skilled trades before the occupation of Dunhuang by the Tubo, and thus the new rulers placed them in the tribe for farming, sericulture, and production to handle the production and sale of silk and finished cloth. In addition, some Sogdians became the households doing chores in temples. Their pursuits showed that Sogdian people undertook various occupations, instead of being confined to commercial affairs as before. For example, some were skilled craftsmen,

图 50　莫高窟第 45 窟　胡商遇盗图　盛唐

Fig.50　Hu Merchants Encountering Bandits Narrative Painting, Mogao Cave 45　High Tang

职业已经不像以前仅限于商业，而是广泛分布于敦煌社会的各个行业。有些属于有一定技能的手工业者，如木匠、毡匠、酒户、塑匠以及车头等，有的则从事农牧业生产，如舂稻、修仓、放羊等。除从事商业、手工业及农牧业生产以外，还有一部分粟特人在吐蕃政权中任职。康秀华是位粟特商人，主要从事经营胡粉生意。他为了抄写一部经书，一次就向寺院施舍了粟 150 石、银器 35 两，另外还有相当于 300 石麦子的胡粉，总价值相当于 10 匹马，或者 30 头牛，足见其家境的

such as carpenters, felt workers, wine producers, Buddhist statue sculptors and wagon makers; some were engaged in agricultural production and animal husbandry, including rice threshing, storehouse maintenance and repair, and sheep herding. Additionally, some even took up governmental posts in the Tubo regime. For instance, Kang Xiuhua, a Sogdian merchant engaged in the Hu powder business, was appointed as the Commissioner of a tribe to manage Sogdian affairs in Dunhuang because of his wealth. In

殷实。因为家富于财，所以被吐蕃统治者任命为部落使，以管理敦煌当地粟特人的相关事务。

晚唐五代归义军时期，敦煌仍居住有大量的粟特人。他们担任归义军政权中的各级官吏，其中著名的人物有归义军第一任节度副使安景旻等。914年之后，粟特人曹议金更是取代张氏家族掌握了归义军政权。除出任归义军地方政府官员外，粟特人还出任了归义军佛教教团上到都僧统下到一般僧众的各级僧官。晚唐到五代，敦煌的村落中有很多以粟特人为主建立的村落，如安家庄、曹家庄、史家庄、康家庄、罗家庄、翟家庄等。

粟特人好饮酒，西域所出产的名酒“三勒浆”就是他们的杰作。而粟特人所信仰的祆教在举行宗教仪式时常常要用到酒。所以，唐宋时期，粟特人在敦煌开设了不少以自己姓氏命名的酒店，如曹家酒店、安家酒店、罗家酒店等(图51)。这些酒店是粟特人活动的重要场所。敦煌文献S.

order to copy a sutra, he donated 150 *dan* of millet, 35 *liang*[1] of silverware and plenty of Hu powder (equal to 300 *dan* of wheat) to the local temple, the value of which was equal to 10 horses or 30 cattle.

During the periods of the Late Tang, the Five Dynasties (907–960), and the *Guiyijun* regime (851–1036), considerable numbers of Sogdians continued to settle in Dunhuang. They held governmental posts in all levels in the *Guiyijun* regime, such as An Jingmin, the first Vice Military Commissioner of *Guiyijun* Force. After 914, Cao Yijin, from a Sogidan family, even took the place of Zhang's family and became the ruler of the *Guiyijun* regime. Sogdians also took up posts as clerics in all levels in the Buddhist Khalsa. During the periods of the Late Tang and the Five Dynasties, there appeared many villages mainly with Sogdian residents in Dunhuang, such as the An, Cao, Shi, Kang, Luo, and Zhai villages.

Sogdians preferred to drink wine, Sanlejiang being the most popular wine produced by them in the Western Regions. Wine was always used in the religious ceremonies of Zoroastrianism. Therefore, in the Tang and Song (960–1279) dynasties, there were many wine shops that bore

① *Dan* and *liang* are Chinese weight units. *Dan* is a unit of dry measure for grain and 1 *liang* equals to 50 grams.

图 51　莫高窟第 61 窟　酒肆　五代

Fig.51　Wine shop, Mogao Cave 61　Five Dynasties

2894《壬申年(972 年)十二月社司转帖》就出现了很多以曹、安、史、康、石、罗、白、米、何等为姓的粟特人名。按照社司的规定,他们分别被约到曹家酒店、安家酒店和罗家酒店聚齐，进行相关活动。此外，社司还规定对于迟到之人,要进行罚酒的惩罚。

敦煌地区销售的很多商品实际上本地并不生产,而是由粟特人转运而来。商品的产地真可谓天南海北,相距何止万里,而正是

Sogdian surnames, such as Cao, An, and Luo (Fig.51). These wine shops became important places for their gatherings. As recorded in *Notice by Leader of the Local Community in December, 972* (Dunhuang documents S.2894), many Sogdian people with the family names of Cao, An, Shi, Kang, Shi, Luo, Bai, Mi, and He were invited to Cao's, An's, and Luo's wine shops for various activities. If someone was late, the punishment was to drink more wine.

In fact, many commodities sold in

因为敦煌独特的地理位置，才使它们汇聚一地。敦煌当地市场上有从西域地区进口的蕃锦、胡锦、波斯锦等，还有出产于朝鲜的高丽锦，其中胡锦包括了粟特锦和拜占庭锦。铁器主要来自中亚、伊州、甘州和中原地区，有胡锁、汉锁等各种铁器。银器有来自于中原的银碗、东罗马的银盏和粟特地区金花银盘、金花银瓶等。珠宝中有从南亚、东罗马或者中原进口的珊瑚、珍珠，有波斯出产的琉璃、玛瑙、琥珀，有于阗出产的瑟瑟和玉器等。毛织品中有从于阗进口的花毯、毛褥以及从粟特地区进口的红绣毯和西川、南山进口的褐。敦煌药材市场上常见的有出产于西域的胡椒、高良姜、诃梨勒等，也有出产于中原的人参、橘皮、芍药等；而敦煌市场上的硇砂主要出产于粟特的康国，应当说敦煌药材市场

Dunhuang were not produced locally. Instead, they were imported by the Sogdians. It was Dunhuang's unique geographical situation that allowed commodities from different places to converge in one location. For example, the woven silk brocade sold in the markets was from different places, such as the Tubo, Sogdia, Byzantium, Persia, and Goryeo. Ironware, including locks made by both Sogdians and ethnic Han came mainly from Central Asia, Yizhou, Ganzhou, and the Central Plains. Silverware available included silver bowls from the Central Plains, silver cups and vases from the Byzantine Empire, and silver plates and bottles inlaid with gold flowers from Sogdia. As for jewelry, there were pearls and coral from South Asia, Byzantine Empire, and the Central Plains; azurite, agate, and amber from Persia; and gems and jadeware from Khotan. Woollen goods in cluded tapestries and mattresses from Khotan; red embroidered carpets from Sogdia; and coarse wo ven cloth from Xichuan and Nanshan. Besides, imported into Dunhuang were medicinal materials such as pepper, galangal, and haritaki (myrobalan) from the Western Regions; ginseng, orange peel, Chinese herbaceous peony from the Central Plains; and sal ammoniac from Samarkand in the Sogdian region. In regard to everyday foodstuffs, granulated sugar and spices came from India, and liquor, melons, jujubes, Hulinzi (a kind of fruit), and wine came from Central Asia. Weapons were mainly from the Uyghur and Tartar areas. Among the imported commodities, the most distinctive items were Hu powder, cotton cloth,

上的大部分药材主要靠进口所得。生活用品有从印度等地进口的砂糖，有从中亚进口的胡酒、大食瓜、胡枣、胡林子、葡萄酒，还有从回鹘和鞑靼地区进口的兵器及从印度进口的香料等。在众多的外来商品中，胡粉、棉布、玉器、珠宝等商品最具特色。据姜伯勤先生研究，胡粉是一种价格昂贵的高级化妆品；同时也是当时敦煌地区民众开窟造像绘制壁画使用的一种比较常见的颜料。至于胡粉的产地，敦煌文献中没有明确的记载，但是有一点可以肯定，即胡粉应产于西域地区。胡粉既使用于画窟画幡，又用于民众女性的化妆，同时胡粉还用于入药，以解果菜毒，故其用量很大。棉布是敦煌籍账文献中最常见的纺织品。唐代敦煌地区种植棉花，棉布中的官布是作为一种常收地税而附着于土地上，但是敦煌当地出产的棉布无论从质地还是从产量上说，还不能满足需要，故经常需要从西州地区进口为数不少的棉花或棉织品。西州的棉布以其质地精良而备受敦煌民众的青睐，从敦煌籍账文书的记载中可以看出，西州出产的棉布在敦煌市场上不但数量多，而且多作为礼品在重要场合使用。敦煌地区本身不产玉，出现于敦煌贸易市场上的玉及玉器大部分是于阗等地

jade, and jewelry. Based on research from Jiang Boqin, Hu powder was a ground mineral used as both an expensive cosmetic as well as a common pigment for painting murals; it was also used in medicine to "detoxify" fruits and vegetables. Thus it was used in large quantities. No records of its original place were known, but one thing that remained certain was Hu powder was produced in the Western Regions. Cotton fabric was the most common textile recorded in Dunhuang documents. During the Tang Dynasty, cotton was planted in Dunhuang, and the official cloth was regarded as a tax attached to the land, but the amount needed for cotton cloth could not meet demand because of its poor quality and low quantity. As a result, it was imported from the Xizhou area and was preferred by people in Dunhuang for its excellent quality. It was recorded that cotton cloth produced in Xizhou was widely available in markets, and was commonly used as gifts on important occasions. No semi-precious stones were produced in Dunhuang, so most jadeware or carved hardstone in markets were imported from Khotan. Popular imported objects included azurite, agate, and coral. Azurite,

进口的。传入敦煌贸易市场的珠宝比较常见，有琉璃、玛瑙、珊瑚等。琉璃原产地是波斯，是波斯倾销唐代中国市场的主要商品；珊瑚主要出产于中国南部沿海地区和南亚地区，是敦煌地区的典型进口商品，反映敦煌对外贸易的范围之广。

敦煌对外商业贸易的地区范围非常广泛，种类丰富，东到中原及朝鲜，南到吐蕃和印度，西到波斯、印度和东罗马。于阗出产的锦、毯及玉石，西州出产的棉布，最受敦煌人的青睐，除了部分作为自用外，大部分易手售往中原等其他地区，从中转贩运的贸易中获利(图 52)。敦煌与于阗、西州回鹘之间的商业贸易大量是丝绸与珠宝、棉布之间的贸易，敦煌从于阗、西州进口的玉石、棉布中有相当部分又被转售其他地区，特别是作为礼品进献给中原、甘州回鹘政权的上层贵族，用于沟通双方感情，加强相互间的联系。敦煌“地不产珍，献无奇玩”，连向中原王朝进贡诸物都不是当地所产。因此，敦煌市场上的商品大都靠从外地进口，

originally mined in Persia, was a major exported commodity from Persia to China in the Tang Dynasty, and coral was mainly produced in the southern coastal areas of China and South Asia, which reflected how wide the extent of foreign trade was.

The foreign trade sources in Dunhuang were extensive, spanning eastward to the Central Plains and Goryeo, southward to the Tubo and India, and westward to Persia, India, and Byzantine Empire. The commodities were also rich in diversity. Brocade, blankets, and jade from Khotan, and cotton cloth from Xizhou were favored by people in Dunhuang. As for these commodities, most of them were resold to other places so as to gain profits again (Fig.52). The trade between Dunhuang and Khotan and Xizhou Uyghurs focused on exchange between silk and gems as well as cotton cloth, while the goods from Khotan and Xizhou would be resold and sometimes were used as tributes presented to the central government and nobles of the Ganzhou Uyghurs regime to strengthen relationships with each other. Based on the above mentioned, it is clear that no rare or precious goods were produced in Dunhuang locally, and even the tributes presented to the central government were the ones imported from other places. It was worthy of the name of the chief center for trade. The pigment of ultramarine from azurite was only produced in Central Asia; azurite blue and malachite green came

图 52 莫高窟第 61 窟 商旅行人 五代

Fig.52 Traveling Merchants, Mogao Cave 61 Five Dynasties

进行中转贸易。作为颜料的金青只有中亚地区出产，而石青、石绿主要来自于吐蕃地区，为佛像镀金用的水银也是从西域进口。棉布主要是由西州进口，种类有西州布、安西氎、官布以及粗氎、细氎、立机氎、白氎等。由于敦煌的这种国际化程度，外来商品充斥整个敦煌贸易市场，对敦煌民风民俗影响很大。胡食、胡服、胡风盛行。如招待客人时，吃的有胡饼(有油胡饼、肉胡饼)，饮用的有胡酒，演奏的有胡腾、胡旋舞，连交流用语也兼用胡语。

from the Tubo, and even silver mercury used for gilding statues of the Buddha was from the Western Regions. Cotton cloth in a wide range of varieties was mainly imported from Xizhou. Due to the cosmopolitan nature of Dunhuang, the markets were filled with foreign goods, which had a great impact on local traditions and customs. Western food, clothing, and lifestyles were prevalent. For example, when serving guests, people would speak the Hu language, eat Hu flat cakes with meat or oil, drink Hu wine, and perform *huteng* and *huxuan* dances.

唐代，敦煌在成为西北地区贸易中心的同时，本地的经济，尤其是畜牧业和手工业，都发展到了一个较高的水平。敦煌地区降水稀少，祁连山融化的雪水成为敦煌绿洲的命脉。由于气候干旱，林木生长条件较差，故多草类植被，所以敦煌天然适合放牧。唐五代敦煌地区上至地方政府，下至寺院、普通百姓，都喂养牲畜，但是能代表唐及五代敦煌地区畜牧业水平的还是官方养殖。当地政府设立主管畜牧业的专门机构，负责对所养牲畜的管理，反映了政府对畜牧业的重视和控制的严格。根据敦煌文书记载，政府所经营的畜牧业所养的牲畜有羊、马、驼等。敦煌地区发达的畜牧业对当地的民间信仰产生了重大的影响，出现了各种的畜神。晚唐时期的敦煌地方政府将赛驼马神等活动纳入政府管理的范围，反映了政府对畜牧业的重视。

唐及五代时，敦煌手工业划分非常细致，手工业行

During the Tang Dynasty, as a trading center in the northwestern region, the economy in Dunhuang, especially animal husbandry and artisan crafts, developed greatly. Due to the shortage of rainfall in Dunhuang, melting glaciers from the Qilian Mountains became the lifeblood for local people. Its arid climate resulted in poor conditions for trees but was fit for grasses suitable for grazing. Therefore, all ranks of society in Dunhuang, from the government to the clergy down to the common people, raised domestic grazing animals. The local government set up a special organization to strictly manage animal husbandry, indicating it paid close attention to this enterprise and representing the standard of development of animal husbandry in Dunhuang. According to Dunhuang manuscripts, the grazing animals raised by government were mainly sheep, horses and camels. Advanced animal husbandry influenced folk beliefs among people in Dunhuang, resulting in the appearance of many animal deities. During the Late Tang, the local government organized the activity of worshiping the gods for blessing horses and camels, showing the importance of animal husbandry at the time.

During the Tang Dynasty and the Five Dynasties, the division of skilled labor in Dunhuang was precise and complete, indicating that trades and handicrafts were well developed. For example, based on the titles of craftsmen, there were wine maker, miller, oil

业间很细的划分反映了当时手工业的发展水平。从手工业的工匠名称看，有粮油等食品加工手工业，酿酒业的官酒户、酒店，粮食加工的碨户，油料加工业的梁户；有纺织业的棉纺加工中的洗緤博士、染匠、褐袋匠等，丝织业中的桑匠，毛纺业中的毡匠；皮革制造业中的皮匠、皮条匠、缝皮匠、靴匠等；冶铁业中的铁匠、泻匠、锅子匠等；建筑业中的泥匠、木匠；造纸业中的纸匠；兵器制造业中的弓匠、箭匠、弩匠等。行业种类齐全，分工细致。归义军政权名义上附属唐中原王朝，是中原王朝管辖下的行政建制，实质上是半独立政权。中原对敦煌控制松散，鞭长莫及。特别到五代和宋初，归义军成为一个完全独立的政权。由于少数民族政权的阻隔，到达敦煌的中原商品不但数量极少、满足不了当地的需要，而且价格昂贵。在这种背景下，必须建立种类比较齐全的手工业，以适应官府、民众、寺院的各种需

presser, cotton cloth washer, cloth dyer, coarse cotton maker, silk maker, felt maker, furrier, shoemaker, blacksmith, castiron molder, pan maker, mason, carpenter, paper maker, bowyer, arrow maker and crossbow maker. All these reflect the rich variety and precise division of skilled labor at the time. The *Guiyijun* regime, a regional administrative organization under the guidance of the central government, was in fact a semi-independent regime in the Tang Dynasty, and even completely dependent in Five Dynasties and the early Song owing to the loose management from the Central Plains for its long distance. Due to interference from tribal regimes and warring nomads, commodities sent from the Central Plains to Dunhuang were expensive and could not meet locals' demand. Under such circumstances, comprehensive handicraft trades were developed to fit various demands from governmental officials, the monastic community, and the local populace. In particular, during the Tang and the Five Dynasties, Buddhism was the dominant religion in Dunhuang, and adherents were keen on building cave temples for worship, creating classes of artisans such as painters and sculptors. Additionally, advanced animal husbandry and cotton cultivation created new jobs, such as furriers and cotton cloth washers. At the time, the skilled trades in Dunhuang had enormous effects on the Hexi area, neighboring regimes, and even the Central

求。唐及五代敦煌佛教兴盛，修寺造窟成风，由此而兴起了画匠、塑匠为主的伎术院、塑行等特殊手工业行业，而且经久不衰。唐及五代敦煌畜牧业发达，棉花普遍种植，故有皮匠、洗緤博士出现。唐及五代敦煌手工业对河西各地、周边政权及中原手工业有很大影响。归义军政权往西州、伊州、甘州及于阗的使节中就有许多工匠在内。元朝占取河西后，敦煌人户被大量迁到甘州、肃州，部分工匠又从甘州徙至襄阳府，对中原手工业亦产生了重要影响。

在归义军统治时期，敦煌地区与外界的商业贸易，除了旧有的由商人进行转运贸易外，又增加了一种新的形式——贡使贸易。晚唐及五代敦煌归义军时期对外贸易相当频繁，经常向中原地区和西域及周边诸政权派遣使团。这些使团规模大、人员庞杂，有官员也有一般随员，还有相当多的商人和僧侣。在一般情况下，使团成员都要携带一些纺织品或其他质轻价高的物品

Plains. For example, many envoys dispatched to Xizhou, Yizhou, Ganzhou, and Khotan were skilled craftsmen. After the Hexi area was controlled by the Yuan Dynasty (1206–1368), numerous households in Dunhuang relocated to Ganzhou, Suzhou, and then some to Xiangyang Prefecture, which influenced the skilled trades in the Central Plains greatly.

During the period of the *Guiyijun* regime, in addition to trans-shipment trade by merchants, there existed a new way — tributary trade —for commercial exchange between Dunhuang and the outside world. At the time, the *Guiyijun* government frequently dispatched missions to the Central Plains, the Western Regions, and smaller separate states. The missions were always large-scale with officials, entourages, merchants, and monks. Generally, members of these missions would trade textiles or other goods in light weight and at high prices to merchants in other states. Meanwhile, when they returned, they brought back products and sold them in markets in Dunhuang or resold them to other places via Dunhuang. As a local regime, the *Guiyijun* regime frequently sent missions for tribute to the central government, which made tributary trade possible. The numerous and diverse tributary items included horses, jade, ammonium chloride, antelope horns, and silk fabrics mainly from Dunhuang or other states. For example, in the early 10th

去贩卖，同时将其他地方的物产贩到敦煌市场出售，或经敦煌再转售到其他地方。归义军作为一个地方政权，常常要向中央政府派遣使团进贡，这就为贡使贸易提供了可能。归义军向中央政府进贡的物品一般以敦煌本地及外来的特产为主，主要包括马匹、玉器、硇砂、羚羊角、丝织品等，物品的数量有时非常巨大。10世纪前期，归义军节度使曹议金一次就向后唐政府进贡马400匹、玉1团，次年又进贡马75匹、玉36团，可见进贡的规模之大(图53)。在向中央政府进贡的同时，中央政府通常要向他们回赐物品，回赐的物品以丝织品居多。这正是敦煌地区与西方进行贸易的重要商品，而且回赐物品的价值往往要高出进贡物品的很多倍。敦煌地方政权通过这种方式，获利丰厚，所以乐此不疲。另外，中央政府会按使团人数的多少，额外给予奖赏。所以，敦煌地方政府向中原所派遣的使团人数通常也比较庞大。通过这种贡使贸易，中央政权得到万国来朝的政治繁荣局面，而敦煌地方则取得丰厚的利益回报，双方各取所需。在使团作为一个整体同中央政权进行贸易的同时，使

century, tributes provided by Cao Yijin, the Military Commissioner of *Guiyijun* Force, consisted of 400 horses and a large piece of jade, and in the following year, 75 horses and 36 pieces of jade were provided, indicating how massive the tribute could be (Fig.53). The central government would then grant other goods in return, usually including silk fabric, which was an important commodity of Dunhuang to exchange with the Western states. Generally, the value of the products given in return by the central government was many times more than the tributes presented, providing a lucrative opportunity for Dunhuang to earn profits. Besides, the central government would give additional award according to the number of the tribute mission's members, resulting in the local government of Dunhuang sending large-scale missions to the Central Plains. By means of the tributary trade, the central government witnessed its own political prosperity by receiving tributes from hundreds of states or kingdoms on the one hand, and Dunhuang earned generous benefits on the other hand. While the delegation was trading with the central government, individual members of the mission would trade one-on-one with the populace in the Central Plains. In this way, abundant

图 53　莫高窟第 100 窟　曹议金出行图(部分)　五代

Fig.53　Section of *Procession of Cao Yijin*, Mogao Cave 100　Five Dynasties

团成员也会作为个体，单独同中原的百姓进行贸易。这样，通过派遣使团这种政治行为掩盖下的商业贸易形式，敦煌地区所出现的许多外来的商品，源源不断地流入中原地区。

在归义军统治敦煌时期，敦煌的对外商业贸易再

Western commodities in Dunhuang steadily found their way into the interior of China.

During the period of the *Guiyijun* regime, foreign trade in Dunhuang boomed again. However, during the early years of the Northern Song Dynasty (960–1127), the position of Dunhuang was greatly weakened, because the Silk Road was cut off by the Western Xia (1038–1227). Meanwhile, the economic center of the Song Dynasty moved southward.

度繁荣。至北宋初年,丝绸之路被西夏隔断，敦煌的地位被极大地削弱。由于陆上丝绸之路的隔绝，同时由于宋代经济中心南移，一条新的丝绸之路——海上丝绸之路兴起了。海路的兴起取代了陆上丝绸之路的地位。此后，虽然元朝时联系中西方经济

A new silk road—the Maritime Silk Road—arose, replacing the overland Silk Road. Although the road connecting economic and cultural exchange between the East and the West was rebuilt in the Yuan Dynasty, the overland trade via Dunhuang could not be revived to its previous pinnacle as it was in the Han and Tang dynasties. As a result, Dunhuang no longer enjoyed its former prosperity as an international metropolis.

文化交流的道路重新被打通，但经由敦煌的陆路的贸易再也没有恢复到汉唐的盛况。从此，敦煌再也不复国际大都市的繁荣景象了。随着经济的衰退，敦煌地区的宗教文化水平急剧下降。具体到莫高窟的艺术作品，元朝时期的技艺水平与唐朝相比已大为逊色(图 54)。

Equally, along with the economic recession, religious culture in Dunhuang declined sharply. Looking at the Mogao Caves as an example, it is evident that the skill embodied in works created during the Yuan Dynasty was far inferior to that of the Tang Dynasty (Fig.54).

图 54 莫高窟第 3 窟 飞天 元

Fig.54 Flying Apsara, Mogao Cave 3 Yuan Dynasty

军事重镇
A Garrison Town

丝绸之路开通后，河西走廊的地位益显重要，也越发得到汉政府的重视。为了避免漠北的匈奴和湟水地区的羌族联合，元鼎五年（前112年）十月，汉武帝曾率数万骑兵巡视西北边防，并于次年十月击败西羌，羌人被迫退到湟水以西。此后，汉武帝设置护羌校尉以管理羌人事务，这也就消除了西羌对丝绸之路的威胁。在河西地区，汉武帝一方面凭借着险峻的山势设立军事要塞，另一方面针对河西地广人稀的实际情况，迁徙汉人前往充实边境。元封五年（前106年）至元封六年（前105年）左右，汉武帝从武威郡、酒泉郡中分出部分地域设置张掖郡、敦煌郡。敦煌、酒泉、

Since the inception of the Silk Road, the Hexi Corridor played an increasingly significant role in the region, receiving great attention during the Han Dynasty. To avoid an alliance between the Xiongnu in north of the Gobi Desert and the Qiang in the Huangshui area, Emperor Wu of the Han Dynasty led a massive cavalry numbering tens of thousands on a scouting expedition to the northwestern frontier in October of the 5th year of Yuanding Era (112 BC). They defeated the Qiang in October of the following year, forcing them to fall back to the west of the Huangshui River. Hereafter, Emperor Wu established the Commandant of the Qiang Tribe to administer the affairs of the Qiang, eliminating the threat to the Silk Road. In the Hexi area, on the one hand, Emperor Wu built military forts along precipitous mountains; on the other hand, he ordered the ethnic Han to migrate to the Hexi area, covering a vast territory with a sparse population, to consolidate the border defense. During the period from the 5th to 6th year of Yuanfeng Era (106 BC–105 BC), Emperor Wu zoned some areas from Wuwei and Jiuquan Prefectures, and then established Zhangye and Dunhuang Prefectures there. These four prefectures were historically known as the Four Prefectures in the Hexi Area. Additionally, an army of approximately 5,000 men was garrisoned north of Jiuquan under the

张掖、武威也就是历史上著名的河西四郡。此外，汉武帝还派遣李陵率军5000人屯兵今酒泉北部地区，教授当地人民骑马射箭的技能。这些措施在巩固汉朝西北边防、保障丝绸之路安全畅通等方面都起到了重要的作用。

随着西域和汉朝联系的加强及道路的畅通，双方之间的贸易往来日益密切。而处于前哨位置的敦煌之战略地位也越来越重要。西汉与西域开展贸易交往之后，大宛等国贪图财物，对汉朝和西域诸国的使团横征暴敛，阻挠了双方关系的进一步发展。此时，汉朝出于抵御匈奴等势力的考虑，需要大量品种优质的战马。而大宛出产骏马，也就是历史上著名的“天马”，也被称作“汗血宝马”。汉武帝命使者前往大宛征求，但为大宛所拒绝。使臣返回长安后，告诉汉武帝大宛的贰师城出产好马，但他们把好马藏匿起来而不肯给汉使。此后，

command of General Li Ling, who taught horseback riding and archery skills to the local people. All these measures played an important part in consolidating the northwestern frontier defense and guaranteeing security and peace along the Silk Road.

As the contact between the Han Dynasty and the Western Regions was strengthened and the communication between these areas was unblocked, trade between the two sides became increasingly close. Thus the strategic position of Dunhuang, as an outpost in the western border, was becoming increasingly important as well. After the Western Han Dynasty established trade relations with the Western Regions, Dayuan, an ancient state in Western Regions, and its neighboring countries extorted excessive taxes and levies from the missions of the Han Dynasty and other states in the Western Regions, which obstructed the further development of relations between the two sides. As the central government of Han needed battle horses to resist the Xiongnu, they sought out Dayuan for their tall and powerful steeds, known as Ferghana horses, also called “Heavenly Horses” or “Blood-Sweating Horses.” Emperor Wu sent envoys to Dayuan to purchase the horses, but the sale was refused. The envoys went back to the Central Plains and reported to the emperor that Ershi Town, the capital of Dayuan, was the place of fine horses, but Dayuan had rebuffed their offer. The Emperor then sent envoys to Dayuan once

汉武帝再次派遣使者持千金和金马前往大宛购买骏马,但还是没有谈判成功。而当汉朝使臣离开后,大宛的大臣又下令其东部边境的守将攻杀汉使,并将其携带的财物洗劫一空。由此,导致了西汉对大宛的征伐。

太初元年(前 104 年),汉武帝任命李广利为贰师将军,发骑兵 6000 余骑,步兵数万人以讨伐大宛。李广利率军由长安出发,经长途跋涉后到达敦煌。在敦煌稍事休整后,汉军随即出玉门关,西行过罗布泊,沿丝绸之路北道西进。但由于路途中的诸国拒绝为李广利提供物资供给,当汉军到达郁成时,军队只剩下了数千人,结果被郁成王打得大败。在迫不得已的情况下,李广利领军东撤,并于太初二年(前 105 年)返回敦煌,士卒只剩下原来的十之一二左右。于是,李广利就上书汉武帝,认为此次出征由于道路太远,导致军粮无法正常供应,所以士卒们怕的不是打仗,而是缺粮;此外,由于所带士兵太少,还不足以攻下大宛。由此,李广利希望汉武帝暂且罢兵,等调遣大军之后才能再次出兵。汉武帝看到李广利的上书后勃然

more with gold as payment for the horses, but this negotiation broke down as well. Further exacerbating the situation, when the envoys left, the ministers of Dayuan ordered the general garrisoned in the eastern border to kill the envoys and rob them of their gold and belongings, which resulted in the Western Han Dynasty's conquest of Dayuan.

In the 1st year of Taichu Era (104 BC), Emperor Wu appointed Li Guangli as the General against Ershi to lead more than 6,000 horsemen and tens of thousands of infantry soldiers to conquer Dayuan. General Li set out from Chang'an and marched an enormous distance to Dunhuang. After resting and reorganization, the army departed from the Yumen Pass and moved westwards to Lop Nor, marching westwards along the northern route of the Silk Road. Due to a shortage of supplies from states along the way, General Li lost many men when arriving at Yucheng, located on the eastern border of Dayuan. There he faced a crushing defeat, forcing his retreat to Dunhuang in 105 BC with only about ten percent of his army left. General Li reported to Emperor Wu they were defeated from a lack of military provisions, not from fear of fighting against the enemy; moreover,

大怒，马上派遣使者关闭玉门关，宣布征讨大宛的军队如果敢入玉门关就格杀勿论。李广利不敢入关，但由于玉门关以西的大片土地仍属敦煌郡所管，所以留在敦煌也不算违背汉武帝的命令。而在这年夏天，西汉在与匈奴的战争中失利，损失士卒两万余人。当时西汉朝中的大臣都认为应该放弃继续进攻大宛，专心对付匈奴。而汉武帝认为既然已经讨伐大宛，如果不能取胜大宛这个小国，不仅得不到大宛的骏马，还会导致西汉在西域的威信丧失殆尽。于是，汉武帝给留在敦煌的李广利派遣援军。据《史记·大宛列传》记载，此次出征场面十分壮观："（汉武帝）赦囚徒材官，益发恶少年及边骑，岁余而出敦煌者六万人，负私从者不与。牛十万，马三万余匹，驴骡橐它以万数。多赍粮，兵弩甚设，天下骚动，传相奉伐宛，凡五十余校

the number of troops was insufficient to capture Dayuan. Thus he suggested that they withdraw the troops first and then set out on another campaign after recruiting enough soldiers. Emperor Wu was enraged, responding with an order to close the Yumen Pass and announcing that any soldier who entered the pass would be killed. General Li did not dare to retreat into the pass, but because the vast area to the west of the Yumen Pass was still under the administration of Dunhuang Prefecture, it was not against the emperor's order to stay in Dunhuang. In the summer of that year, the Han troops were defeated by the Xiongnu, losing roughly 20,000 soldiers. Consequently, a number of ministers agreed that they should cease attacks against Dayuan, and resisted the Xiongnu with all forces instead. However, Emperor Wu believed that if they gave up halfway and could not capture a small state such as Dayuan, they would not only lose the coveted horses, but also undermine their own prestige in the Western Regions. As a consequence, he dispatched reinforcements to General Li Guangli. The event was recorded in the *Records of the Grand Historian: Dayuan*[①].

① In the original text, the content recorded in the *Records of the Grand Historian: Dayuan* is further explained in modern Chinese in the following paragraph. The translated text just offers the content once.

尉。宛王城中无井，皆汲城外流水，于是乃遣水工徙其城下水空以空其城。益发戍甲卒十八万，酒泉、张掖北置居延、休屠以卫酒泉，而发天下七科适，乃载糒给贰师。转车人徒相连属至敦煌。”

此次出征，汉武帝一方面赦免了囚徒，让他们充当步兵，另外，还进一步征发了少年豪杰及边骑。一年多的时间里，到达敦煌的军队有6万余人，而携带私人装备从军者还不在此范围内。为了避免再次出现乏粮的覆辙，此次出征西汉政府动用了牛10万头，马3万余匹，驴骡万余头以运送军粮。由于得到大宛王城中没有水井，而只能到城外汲取河水的情报，汉武帝还派遣了水工随军，计划断绝城内的水源。此外，汉武帝还征发有罪之官吏、亡命、赘婿、商人等具有7种身份之人为李广利运送军粮。由于此次出征军势强大，沿途小国纷纷出迎并主动为汉军提供补给，所以到达大宛的军队有3万多

To win the battle, some prisoners were absolved by Emperor Wu to serve as soldiers, and many young men with excellent ability and horsemen were recruited for the army. The troops sent to Dunhuang numbered more than 60,000 within one year, which did not include the campaigners taking their own equipment at their own volition. To avoid repeating their mistake, the central government used 100,000 cattle, more than 30,000 horses, and thousands of mules and donkeys to deliver the supplies. At the time, the whole country was shocked at the scale of army. It was said that the number of commandants attacking Dayuan reached to fifty. Based on the information that there was no well in the capital of Dayuan and that people had to draw water outside the town, Emperor Wu sent irrigation workers with the army, planning to cut off the water source of the capital. The Han government also dispatched 180,000 soldiers in armours, garrisoned in Jiuquan and Zhangye. The other two counties, Juyan and Xiuchu, were established to guard Jiuquan Prefecture. In addition, the court recruited seven groups of people of the lower classes or bad reputation to transport army provisions for General Li, such as condemned officials, fugitives, son-in-laws living with their wives' family, businessmen and so on. The endless stream of transshipment stretched to Dunhuang. Seeing the powerful military force of the Han Dynasty, small states along the Silk Road all received

人。大宛在困守40余日后，被迫与李广利谈判，提出只要汉军不再进攻，大宛将允许汉军随意挑选好马，并愿意为汉军提供补给。李广利答应了大宛的条件，挑选了好马数十匹，中马和母马3000余匹。此外，还将大宛大臣中亲汉的昧蔡立为大宛王，与其结盟后罢兵。而汉武帝在获得大宛的天马后亲自做天马之歌，对此事进行歌颂，歌词中唱道："天马来，从西极。徙流沙，九夷服……天马来，历无草。经千里，循东道。"喜悦之情溢于言表。

李广利两次讨伐大宛，都是在敦煌屯军进发，可见在汉武帝时期设置敦煌郡之后，敦煌已经成为西汉开拓西域的前沿基地。既然敦煌的军事地位如此重要，那么西汉政府自然会格外重视增强敦煌的军事防御能力。在汉武帝设置敦煌郡以前，汉政府就曾经设置

the army and provided supplies to them. When General Li's army arrived in Dayuan, there were still approximately 30,000 soldiers. After a 40-day siege, Dayuan was forced to negotiate with the Han Dynasty. If the Han forces stopped the attack, Dayuan would allow them to select horses at will and provide them with supplies; General Li accepted the offer and appointed one of the pro-Han nobles in Dayuan named Mei Cai as their new king, thus cooperating with Dayuan and then leaving with dozens of best horses, and approximately 3,000 moderate horses and mares. Emperor Wu was so delighted that he wrote "Ode to the Heavenly Horse Ⅲ" to praise this event. "The Heavenly Horse came from the remote west; Crossing the desert, making all ethnic people convinced. ... The Heavenly Horse came across the grassless road; Passing through a thousand miles along the eastern route." The song reflected how pleasant Emperor Wu was after getting such fine horses.

General Li Guangli's two conquests to Dayuan were centered on Dunhuang where they first stationed the army and then set out. After Emperor Wu established Dunhuang as a prefecture, it became the Western Han Dynasty's boundary for exploring Western Regions. Since Dunhuang was an important military town, the government took much effort to strengthen its military defenses. Previously, the Han Dynasty had established a military organization—the Commandant of Yumen in Jiuquan Prefecture—to govern the Dunhuang area. After Dunhuang

"酒泉玉门都尉"的军事机构以管理敦煌地区。而在设置敦煌郡之后，下置敦煌、龙勒、效谷、广至、冥安、渊泉6县，由敦煌太守总领军政，并置都尉专掌军防。此外，还建立了由屯兵、屯田、军需、邮传、候望等系统构成的完整的军事体系。

敦煌太守是敦煌地区最高军政长官，下置玉门、阳关、中部、宜禾4个都尉府。其下又分别设候塞、部、亭燧等军事机构，所在的障燧是守军驻扎之所，由都尉、候、塞尉、候长、燧长各级武官带领戍卒和燧卒戍守。为了保卫敦煌的安全，汉朝在敦煌北部边境沿疏勒河、长城一线设置了玉门、中部、宜禾三都尉，各自建筑障、候塞等军事设施。玉门都尉的治所在今天敦煌西北70公里处的小方盘城，下置大煎候、玉门两候官，东与中部都尉平望候官朱爵燧防区相接。玉门都尉的辖区内，

was set up as a prefecture, the central government created six counties under its administration: Dunhuang, Longle, Xiaogu, Guangzhi, Ming'an, and Yuanquan. The Governor of Dunhuang Prefecture managed military and political affairs, while the Commandant was in charge of the military defense. At the same time, the government also established an elaborate military system, consisting of garrison troops, station peasants, troops for military supplies, post stations, patrols, and sentries.

The Governor of Dunhuang Prefecture was the highest level military and political officer in this area, with four military commands under his supervision, including Yumen, Yangguan, Zhongbu, and Yihe. Each military commandery government had its own subsidiary military organizations, including forts, beacon towers and watchtowers. These organizations stationed troops in the watchtowers, garrisoned by different levels of military officers and soldiers. To guarantee the security of Dunhuang, the government established Commandants of Yumen, Zhongbu, and Yihe, and built barriers and watchtowers at the northern border of Dunhuang along the Shule River and the Han Great Wall. The seat of the Commandant of Yumen was located at the Small Fangpan Warehouse, 70 kilometers northwest of present-day Dunhuang, with two military officials under its supervision. The eastern jurisdiction of the Commandant of Yumen was connected with the garrison area of Zhongbu. In the jurisdiction of the Commandant of Yumen,

今天现存的汉代烽燧遗址有 31 座(图 55)。阳关都尉的治所在阳关,位于敦煌城南 30 公里的南湖乡古董滩上,负责防卫南湖至敦煌城之间的区域,现存汉代烽燧 10 余座。中部都尉又称步广尉,防卫敦煌北部边境的中段,其下设平望、破胡、吞胡、步广、万岁 5 个候官,其治所在步广候官。中部都尉

there remain 31 ruins of beacon towers in the Han Dynasty (Fig.55). The seat of Commandant of Yangguan, located in Gudongtan of Nanhu Village, 30 kilometers to the south of Dunhuang, was responsible for the defense of the area from Nanhu Village to Dunhuang. Presently there remain 10 beacon tower ruins from the Han Dynasty. The Commandant of Zhongbu with the seat in Buguang, defended the middle section of the northern border of Dunhuang with five fortifications under its supervision, including Pingwang, Pohu, Tunhu, Buguang and Wansui. The eastern area of its jurisdiction connected with the Linjie garrison area of Yihe; presently there are 34 extant ruins of beacon towers built in the Han Dynasty. In addition,

图 55 汉代烽燧中用于告警的积薪(邵如林 摄)
Fig.55 Watchtower Firewood Used in the Han Dynasty (Photo by Shao Rulin)

的防守区域东与宜禾都尉宜禾候官临介燧防区相连，现存汉燧34座。宜禾都尉防卫敦煌东北边境的长城一线，下置宜禾、鱼泽、昆仑、美稷、广汉5个候官，治昆仑障，东部与酒泉郡西部都尉防区相接，现存烽燧38座。玉门、中部、宜禾三都尉府之间以烽燧彼此连接，构成了敦煌城北方的屏障，同时又与设置于敦煌城西的阳关遥相呼应。从这个意义上说，在军事上，敦煌既是汉长城西段的堡垒，又是汉朝西进的战略基地，维系着河西乃至秦陇腹地的安危。

除了设置玉门、阳关等4都尉府外，西汉政府还在敦煌境内修筑了长城。敦煌郡内的长城是从东边酒泉郡延伸而来的，大约完成于西汉元封年间(前110~前104年)。元封年间，汉朝将设置在敦煌北部的玉门、中部、宜禾三都尉沿疏勒河南岸所构筑烽燧通过长墙连接起来，被称为长城，也叫边塞、边墙。敦煌郡境内

the Commandant of Yihe with the seat in Kunlun fort defended the northeastern border of Dunhuang along the Han Great Wall, governing five fortifications, including Yihe, Yuze, Kunlun, Meiji, and Guanghan. Its eastern part connected with the area of the Western Commandant of Jiuquan Prefecture. Thirty-eight beacon tower ruins from the Han Dynasty still remain today. The headquaters of Commandants of Yumen, Zhongbu, and Yihe were connected to each other by the watchtowers and fortifications, forming the defensive system to the north of Dunhuang, and coordinating with the Yangguan Pass to the west of Dunhuang. Thus, Dunhuang was a stronghold of the western section of the Han Great Wall during the Han Dynasty, and also the strategic base of westward expansion for the central government, maintaining the security of the Hexi area, and even of the hinterlands of the Qinlong area①.

The Western Han Dynasty built the Han Great Wall within Dunhuang in Yuanfeng Era (110 BC–104 BC), extending it from Jiuquan Prefecture in the east. During this period, the government connected beacon towers built along the Shule River in Yumen, Zhongbu, and Yihe with long walls, which were called the Great Wall, or frontier walls, or frontier fortress. This section of the Han Great Wall

① Qinlong area includes the Qinling Mountains and the Longshan Mountain.

的长城从冥泽西南岸起，向西延伸到小方盘城以西，东西长约300公里。长城上每个烽燧之间相距2里到10里不等。据李正宇先生估算，在300公里的长城沿线当有烽燧120座以上。根据汉制，每个烽燧设有燧长、属吏，及燧卒10余人，再加上都尉府及候官的长官、属吏及兵卒、后勤人员，汉代敦煌郡仅长城一线部署的兵力大约在2000人以上。在西汉时期，这是一支相当强大的军事力量，又是一支相当大的屯垦力量，为敦煌的军事防御能力的加强和农业的发展作过重要的贡献。

担任长城及长城沿线诸烽燧戍守任务的士卒，在性质上属军事系统，但在建制上不同于野战部队，具有明显的地方化特征。在一般情况下，不承担境外的征战任务，只是在特殊情况下才部

was about 300 kilometers long, stretching westward from the southwestern bank of the Mingze River to the west of the Small Fangpan Warehouse. The distance between the two beacon towers ranged from 2 *li* to 10 *li*. According to the historian Li Zhengyu's estimation, there were over 120 beacon towers covering 300 kilometers of the Han Great Wall. Based on regulation from the Han Dynasty, roughly ten people were stationed at each beacon tower, including the beacon officer, subordinate officials, and beacon soldiers. In addition, along with the officials from the commands of the Commandants and fortifications, garrison soldiers, and support crews, over 2,000 armed soldiers were stationed along the Han Great Wall in Dunhuang Prefecture during the Western Han Dynasty. It was a strong military force as well as a powerful group to open up wasteland, making significant contributions to the military defense and the agricultural development of Dunhuang.

The soldiers who guarded the beacon towers possessed distinct characteristics different from the field troops. Generally, they did not undertake military missions to other regions, and only went out to battle under special circumstances. Other than security and defense tasks, the garrison troops also had to reclaim wasteland and repair beacon towers or fortifications in the frontier. Historical records show that before the 4th year of the Yuanding Era (113 BC), wasteland reclamation had been carried out in Dunhuang as well as other

分奉调出征。戍守部队除了担任警戒、防御等任务外，平时还担负着屯田及修缮塞障等任务。据文献记载，在元鼎四年（前 113 年）之前，敦煌等地就已经开始屯田的工作了。西汉王朝在敦煌及河西其他地区的屯田，最早就是由这些戍卒进行的。所以，屯田活动必须随着边地障塞亭燧的设置、防御组织的建立而开展。元封三年（前 108 年），汉朝的边塞由酒泉延伸至玉门关。所以，学者多将此年视为敦煌有计划进行屯田的开始。西汉敦煌屯田主要有三个地区：其一，在玉门关外大煎都候官辖区，也就是今天敦煌市榆树泉盆地东部。这里地势平坦，水源充沛，适宜于农业种植。其二，在宜禾都尉辖区的宜禾、鱼泽候官区，即今天瓜州、敦煌两县、市交界一带。其三，在阳关都尉所属渥洼水西岸地区。这一带曾发现汉代的田垄、房基、墓葬等遗迹及石磨、石臼、陶器等遗物。这些遗

locations. This was first done by garrison soldiers, that is to say, the opening up of wasteland was launched in tandem with the establishment of fortifications and beacon towers and the defense equipment. In the 3rd year of Yuanfeng Era (108 BC), the frontier fortresses of the Han Dynasty stretched from Jiuquan to the Yumen Pass; thus numerous scholars regard this year as the starting point of planned wasteland reclamation in Dunhuang. The main area for reclamation in Dunhuang in the Western Han Dynasty included three districts. The first was the jurisdiction of the Dajiandu fortification outside the Yumen Pass (the area east of the Yushuquan Basin in present-day Dunhuang), which was suitable for farming because of its flat land and abundant water resource. The second was the jurisdiction of Yihe and Yuze fortifications (the intersection of present-day Guazhou County and Dunhuang City), which was supervised by the Commandant of Yihe. The third was the western bank of the Wowa River, which was under the management of the Commandant of Yangguan. Considerable numbers of relics have been excavated in these areas, including ridges in fields, foundations of houses, tombs, stone mills, stone mortars, and pottery, revealing the situation of land cultivation and garrison posts at the time. With the extension of the reclaimed wasteland, the Western Han Dynasty moved in migrants from the Central Plains, sent exiles there to

迹和遗物，反映了当时戍守和屯田情况。随着屯田规模的扩大，西汉又从内地多次迁来移民，发配流犯，充实军屯，并设置农都尉专门管理军屯事务。而屯田工作的展开，在敦煌逐渐形成了一片片农耕绿洲，使各级地方政权的统治得以进一步巩固。

西汉王朝利用大批戍田卒在敦煌屯田，属于国家经营的与军事有关的生产活动。屯田所需的土地以及农具、籽种、耕牛和田卒生活所需，均由国家供给。而戍田卒在屯田上的劳动是在给国家服徭役，所以屯田生产的收获物全部要上缴国家。汉朝在敦煌的屯田活动，不仅为敦煌当地的守军提供了充足的军粮供应，同时，也促使敦煌地区的农业生产水平得到了迅速的提高。由于敦煌地处中原通往西域的咽喉之地，所以西汉在敦煌的屯田活动一直没有停止。根据敦煌马圈口所获汉简的记载，居摄三年(公元8年)三月，敦煌郡效谷县益寿里的邓尊曾将大煎都屯田所获的粮食运送到郡仓。这也就证明，

replenish the station troops, and appointed the Commandant for Agriculture to administrate the land-reclamation and garrison affairs for the army units. Thus with the implementation of land-reclamation, patches of farming oases were formed in Dunhuang, and the rule by local authorities at different levels was consolidated.

The opening up of wasteland by the large numbers of garrison troops sent by the Western Han fell under the realm of the central government's military operations. All the land, farm tools, seed, cattle, and provisions for soldiers were provided by the government. The soldiers' production was counted as corvée labor, requiring all crops to be handed over to the government. Such crops not only provided army provisions for the local defense troops, but also enhanced agricultural production in Dunhuang. Because of its location at the crossroads between the Central Plains and the Western Regions, land-reclamation in Dunhuang never ceased during the Western Han period. According to historical records from Han bamboo slips in Dunhuang, in March of the 3rd year of Jushe Era (AD 8), Deng Zun from Yishou Village of Xiaogu County in Dunhuang Prefecture transported grain harvested from the troops' farmland to the prefecture's storehouse. This proves that the reclamation of wasteland in the Western Han Dynasty continued at least to the reign

西汉的屯田最起码持续到了王莽时期。

公元8年，王莽取代西汉，建立新朝。王莽篡位后，收回了西汉赐予西域各国国王的王印，而将他们统统降为侯，并重新颁印。这就引起了西域诸国的怨恨。他们纷纷与新朝断绝关系，转而投靠匈奴。但由于匈奴对西域诸国征收很重的赋税，诸国不堪重负，在东汉光武帝刘秀建武年间，诸国遣使东汉请求内属，并希望东汉能够派遣西域都护前往管理。刘秀认识到天下初定，东汉还没有能力经营西域，最终拒绝了诸国的请求。永平年间，北匈奴胁迫西域诸国并寇扰河西郡县，造成了敦煌等地"城门昼闭"的严重后果。为了解除北匈奴对东汉西北地区的威胁，明帝永平十六年(73年)，东汉政府北征匈奴，夺取了伊吾卢之地，并在此设置宜禾都尉以进行屯田，重新

of Wang Mang.

In AD 8, Wang Mang usurped the throne from the Western Han Dynasty and made himself the emperor of the Xin Dynasty. He took back the imperial seals from states in the Western Regions, which had been granted by the Western Han government, and demoted the princes to marquesses, causing these states to hold a grudge against him. They ended all relations with the new dynasty and sought refuge with the Xiongnu. However, having suffered from heavy taxes levied by the Xiongnu, the states in the Western Regions could no longer shoulder the burden. So during the period of Jianwu Era of Emperor Guangwu of the Eastern Han Dynasty, they then dispatched envoys to the central government to surrender, hoping the central government would in turn send the Protector-General of the Western Regions to govern the area. Liu Xiu, the founder of the Eastern Han Dynasty, realized that the country was merely at the beginning of appeasing the chaos and that the government did not possess the ability to manage affairs in the Western Regions, so he declined the request. During the period of Yongping Era, the Northern Xiongnu coerced the states in the Western Regions into attacking prefectures and counties in the Hexi area. The seriousness of the situation caused Dunhuang and other places to close the town gates during the daytime. In order to relieve the Northern Xiongnu's threat to the northwestern area of the Eastern Han Dynasty, in the 16th year of Yongping Era (AD 73), Emperor Ming sent

开始了对西域的经营。于阗等国国王皆派遣子弟前往洛阳充当宫廷宿卫，以表示对东汉王朝的归附。东汉重新恢复中央王朝在西域的权威之初，明帝派遣中郎将居住在敦煌，管理西域事务。永平十七年(74年)十一月，东汉政府又派遣奉车都尉窦固、驸马都尉耿秉、骑都尉刘张出敦煌昆仑塞，在蒲类海击破了白山虏，既解除了来自北面的匈奴对伊吾的威胁，又打通了通往车师的道路。随后，汉政府在西域设置了西域都护和戊己校尉的管理机构，其中副校尉就设置在车师。

明帝死后，与北匈奴勾结的焉耆、龟兹等国攻杀了西域都护陈睦，而匈奴和车师则围攻驻守在柳中的己校尉关宠，被关宠击退。此后，匈奴又联合龟兹进攻驻守在疏勒的戊校尉耿恭。经数月苦战，疏勒城内的汉军仅剩下数十人。匈奴单于知道城内已

troops to conquer the Xiongnu, and captured Yiwulu. They then set up the Commandant of Yihe there to charge garrison troops for opening up wasteland, marking the restart of the central government's administration in the Western Regions. The rulers of states such as Khotan sent their relatives to Luoyang to join the army of the palace, indicating surrender to the central government. During the early days when the Eastern Han Dynasty regained authority in the Western Regions, Emperor Ming sent commander to Dunhuang to manage affairs in the Western Regions. In November of AD 74, the government also sent Dou Gu, the Commandant of Chariots, Geng Bing, the Commandant of Attendant Cavalry, and Liu Zhang, the Commandant of Cavalry, to start an attack out of the Kunlun fort in Dunhuang and defeated the Xiongnu at Pulei Lake, ending the Xiongnu's threat to Yiwu and opening the route to the State of Jushi. Soon afterwards, the Eastern Han Dynasty established administrative bodies including the Protector-General of the Western Regions and *Wuji* Colonel in the Western Regions, in which the office of Vice Colonel was in Jushi.

After the death of Emperor Ming, Yanqi and Qiuci in cooperation with the Northern Xiongnu, attacked and killed Chen Mu, the Protector-General of the Western Regions. Meanwhile, the Xiongnu allied with Jushi to surround Guan Chong, the *Ji* Colonel, who garrisoned Liuzhong, but they were defeated.

弹尽粮绝，想要招降耿恭，许诺如果耿恭投降，就封其为白屋王并将女儿嫁给他。耿恭将匈奴的使者诱到城上，"手击杀之，炙诸城上"，使者的官属无可奈何，只能哭号而去。关宠被匈奴、车师围攻后，曾派遣使者返回东汉求救。汉政府派遣征西将军耿秉屯酒泉，并代理酒泉太守；派遣秦彭、王蒙及皇甫援等人调发敦煌、张掖、酒泉三军及鄯善兵，合计7000余人前往救援。建初元年(76年)正月，援军与据守柳中的汉军会合，在交河城大败匈奴和车师。此时关宠已死，王蒙等人就想引兵东返。此前耿恭所派遣至敦煌运送士卒冬装的范羌，正在王蒙军中。他认为应该前往疏勒救援耿恭，但诸将皆不敢孤军深入。范羌只能领兵2000人，沿天山北麓前往救援。而在救援的路上，援军又遇上了丈余深

After that, the Xiongnu united with Qiuci again and attacked Geng Gong, the *Wu* Colonel, who garrisoned Shule. After several months of fighting, only a few dozens of Han soldiers were left in Shule Town. Learning that the Han army had run out of ammunition and food supplies, the chieftain of the Xiongnu wanted to bid Geng Gong to surrender, promising that if General Geng gave in, he would confer the title of Prince of Baiwu upon Geng and wed his daughter to him. However, General Geng refused by killing the envoy on the gate tower, causing the followers of the envoy to leave, crying in anger. After being besieged by the Xiongnu and Jushi, Guan Chong sent messengers back to the imperial court and asked for reinforcements. The central government dispatched General Geng Bing to Jiuquan, acting as the Governor of Jiuquan Prefecture. The government also sent Qin Peng, Wang Meng, and Huangfu Yuan to dispatch armies numbering some 7,000 soldiers from Dunhuang, Zhangye, Jiuquan, and Shanshan to help in the rescue. In January of the 1st year of Jianchu Era (AD 76), the reinforcements rendezvoused with the army stationed in Liuzhong, dcfcating the Xiongnu and Jushi in Jiaohe Town. When Guan Chong died, Wang Meng wanted to return eastwards. But Fan Qiang, who had been dispatched to deliver winter clothing to soldiers in Dunhuang by General Geng Gong, was staying at General Wang Meng's army. Fan believed they should head for Shule to rescue General Geng. However, the generals were reluctant to penetrate into enemy territory; as a

的大雪，所以路途极其艰难。他们到达时正好是晚上，城内的士卒听到军队行进的声响，就以为是匈奴又来侵犯，都大惊失色。范羌远远地高声大喊："我范羌也，汉遣军迎校尉耳。"城中的士卒皆大呼万岁，声震天地。在从疏勒撤退的路上，汉军遭到了匈奴的连续追击，将士只能且战且退。由于镇守疏勒的将士受围困期间饥饿劳累过度，再加上连续作战，所以从疏勒返回时还有 26 人，但当三月到达玉门关时，最终只剩下了 13 人。

和帝永元元年(89 年)，大将军窦宪大破匈奴。永元二年，窦宪派遣西域副校尉阎槃率领 2000 余骑，收复了此前被匈奴占领的伊吾地。永元三年，班超遂定西域，汉政府即以班超为西域都护，驻守在龟兹。此外，还复置了戊己校尉，领兵 500 人，驻守在车师前部的高昌壁。永元六年(94 年)，班超击败焉耆，于是，西域 50 余

result, Fan Qiang led 2,000 soldiers for the rescue mission along the northern foot of the Tianshan Mountains. On the way, they encountered heavy snow, making their journey long and difficult. They finally reached Shule at night. Hearing the sound of marching, the soldiers in the town mistook it as the Xiongnu's invasion and were in great panic. Fan Qiang shouted loudly, "I am Fan Qiang, and now leading the soldiers to greet the Colonel!" The soldiers in the town were overjoyed and shouted, "Long live the Emperor!" On their way back from Shule, the Han Dynasty's army were pursued and attacked by the Xiongnu; the soldiers had to carry on the fight while retreating. Because of hunger and successive fighting while being besieged, only 26 soldiers who had garrisoned Shule returned, but when they withdrew to the Yumen Pass, only 13 of them were left alive.

In the 1st year of Yongyuan Era of Emperor He (AD 89), the General-in-Chief named Dou Xian inflicted a crushing defeat to the Xiongnu. The following year, General Dou dispatched Yan Pan, the Vice Colonel of the Western Regions, to lead 2,000 cavalrymen, recapturing Yiwu which had been occupied by the Xiongnu. In AD 91, General Ban Chao pacified the Western Regions, and was appointed as the Protector-General of the Western Regions and stationed at Qiuci. In addition, the government re-established *Wuji* Colonel, leading 500 soldiers and garrison

国全部纳质内属。但在安帝永初元年（107年），西域诸国频频围攻都护任尚、段禧等人。东汉政府认为中央王朝距西域路途太远，且地形凶险，难以及时派兵应援，所以安帝下诏罢除西域都护，再次断绝了与西域的关系。此后数十年间，北匈奴联合西域诸国，频繁侵扰西北边境。

元初六年（119年），敦煌太守曹宗认为西域诸国的威胁太大，在获得中央政府的许可后，派遣长史索班率1000余人屯守于伊吾，以招揽西域。不久，车师前王和鄯善王就前来归附。对于东汉的介入，匈奴当然不能容忍，在联合车师后部王攻陷伊吾、杀索班后，又击走了车师前王。面对匈奴的巨大压力，鄯善急忙向曹宗求救。曹宗上书朝廷，希望东汉王朝能够出兵攻打匈奴，为索班报仇雪恨。此外，他还建议应

troops in Gaochangbi of the Nearer Jushi. In AD 94, General Ban defeated the State of Yanqi, which resulted in about 50 states in the Western Regions paying allegiance to the Eastern Han Dynasty. However, in the 1st year of Yongchu Era of Emperor An (107), the Protector-Generals Ren Shang and Duan Xi were frequently besieged by the states in the Western Regions. Emperor An had to issue an imperial edict to abandon Protectorate of the Western Regions considering the long distance and rough overland terrain between the central government and the Western Regions and inability to send reinforcements. This meant the Han Dynasty severed relations with the Western Regions once again. During the following decades, the Northern Xiongnu allied with other states in the Western Regions to frequently invade and harass the northwestern border of the Han Dynasty.

In the 6th year of Yuanchu Era (119), Cao Zong, the Governor of Dunhuang Prefecture, believing they were under great threat from the states in the Western Regions, dispatched Suo Ban, the Chief Official, to lead 1,000 soldiers to garrison Yiwu with the permission of the central government. Soon after, the kings of the Nearer Jushi and the Kingdom of Shanshan surrendered to the Han Dynasty. Of course, the Xiongnu could not allow the Han Dynasty to expand its influence over the Western Regions, so allying with the Further Jushi, they captured Yiwu, killed Suo Ban and drove off the King of the Nearer Jushi. In the face of great pressure from the Xiongnu, Shanshan

该进一步经营西域。曹宗的主张没有得到当时掌握实权的邓太后的赞同，面对匈奴咄咄逼人的气焰，东汉政府只是在敦煌设置了西域副都护，其领兵仅仅 300 人，所以对于西域只能是名义上的统辖，而不能有实际的举措。由于此后匈奴和车师接连寇扰河西，东汉无力抵御，所以朝中有大臣甚至主张关闭玉门关和阳关，以绝后患。

为了应对北匈奴联结西域诸国威胁东汉西北边防，延光二年(123 年)，敦煌太守张珰上书提出了相应的三条计策。张珰指出，匈奴派遣呼衍王控制西域，其经常巡视于蒲类海和秦海之间，利用西域的势力危害东汉。如果以酒泉属国派遣士卒 2000 余人，集结于敦煌的昆仑塞，首先进击呼衍王，这样就断绝了匈奴在西域统治的根本，这是应付当前局面的上策。如果

asked Cao Zong to send reinforcements. Cao Zong submitted a statement to the central government, hoping that the government could send an army to attack the Xiongnu and avenge Suo Ban's death. He also suggested the government enhance its control over the Western Regions. However, Cao's suggestions were not taken by Empress Dowager Deng, who grasped the real power of the Han Dynasty. So, facing the fierce Xiongnu, the Han Dynasty merely established the position of Vice Protector-General of the Western Regions in Dunhuang, with only 300 soldiers garrisoning there. This action could be seen as merely a partial control of the Western Regions, not an actual effective measure. Thus, the Eastern Han Dynasty could not resist being constantly harassed and invaded by the Xiongnu and Jushi in the Hexi area. Many ministers even proposed closing down the Yumen Pass and the Yangguan Pass so as to spare further trouble.

In order to deal with the situation of the Northern Xiongnu allying with states in the Western Regions to harass the northwestern border of the Eastern Han Dynasty, in the 2nd year of Yanguang Era (123), Zhang Dang, the Governor of Dunhuang Prefecture, put forward a proposal with three plans to the central government. He pointed out that the Xiongnu had dispatched Prince Huyan to make regular inspection tours between Pulei Lake and Qinhai Lake, which threatened the security of the Eastern Han Dynasty. Thus, the best plan would be to let the vassal state in Jiuquan dispatch approximately

不能出兵，可以向柳中派遣军司马，另外再派遣将士 500 人防护，其所需的物资可以由敦煌等 4 郡供应，这是中策。如果这样还不行，就只能放弃交河城，将鄯善国的民众迁徙到玉门关以内，此乃下策。张珰的奏表到达洛阳之后，东汉政府就在朝堂上讨论他的建议。尚书陈忠上疏指出，匈奴是汉王朝的最大外患，所以汉武帝时锐意经营河西及西域，设置河西四郡断绝了匈奴和南羌的联系，西域 36 国归附西汉，这样就等于切断了匈奴的右臂，从而极大地削弱了匈奴的势力。而目前北匈奴已经攻破车师，势必要向南攻击鄯善；如果弃而不救，西域诸国就会重新跟随匈奴。这样的话，北匈奴一方面可以获得丰厚的经济来源，另一方面又可以再次与南羌取得联系，那么河西四郡就危在旦夕了。而如果河西四郡危

2,000 soldiers and garrison troops to gather in the Kunlun fort in Dunhuang so as to attack Prince Huyan first, destroying the center of the Xiongnu's power in the Western Regions. If the government could not send out an army for battle, the second-best plan would be to dispatch the Assistant Commander with 500 soldiers to garrison Liuzhong; military supplies could be provided by the four prefectures including Dunhuang. If these two plans did not work, giving up Jiaohe Town and relocating people in Shanshan within the Yumen Pass would be the last option. When Zhang's petition was sent to the Han court, the ministers in the central government discussed his suggestions. The minister Chen Zhong pointed out that the Xiongnu had been the largest foreign aggressor to the Han Dynasty, thus during the reign of Emperor Wu, he had managed the affairs in the Hexi area and the Western Regions with keen determination by creating the Four Prefectures in the Hexi Area, cutting off relations between the Xiongnu and the Southern Qiang. Thereafter, 36 states in the Western Regions had all surrendered to the Han Dynasty, weakening the power of the Xiongnu. Chen Zhong said that the Northern Xiongnu had conquered Jushi, and then headed southward to attack Shanshan. If Shanshan could not be secured by the government, the states in the Western Regions would have to surrender themselves to the rule of the Xiongnu. If this happened, the Northern Xiongnu would not only get access to great economic resources but also restore contact with the Southern Qiang. The Four Prefectures in the

急，则不得不救，等到那时候所付出的代价必然会比现在经营西域大得多。目前情况下，西北边境守御装备比较落后，而内地郡县又不修武备，造成了敦煌孤危的局势。所以当西域诸国向敦煌告急时，敦煌太守也无能为力。这样下去，对内来说不能安抚军民，对外来说不能对蛮夷产生震慑作用。所以，应该在敦煌设置校尉，还应该增加在河西四郡的驻军，以经营西域诸国，这样才能威慑匈奴。汉朝政府最终采取了张珰提出的中策，派遣了班超之子班勇为西域长史，率军500人，屯守柳中。很快，班勇就先后击败车师和焉耆。于是，龟兹、疏勒、于阗、莎车等国皆来归附。

由于代替西域都护主管西域事务的护西域副校尉长驻敦煌，敦煌太守成为汉朝在西域地区采取军事行动的实际负责人。据《后汉书·西域传》记载，东汉顺帝阳嘉四年（135年）春，北匈奴呼衍王由于不满车师归附东汉，

Hexi Area would be on the verge of destruction. At the time, the government would pay a higher price for rescuing the prefectures than for managing the Western Regions. In addition, military equipment for the northwestern garrison troops was outdated, and the prefectures did not pay close attention to its weapons and military provisions, causing a dangerous situation for Dunhuang. As a result, when the states in the Western Regions reported an emergency to Dunhuang, the Governor of Dunhuang Prefecture could do little to help. Chen Zhong viewed if things continued in this way, it would go against pacifying the troops and the populace; nor could it overwhelm the tribal peoples in the Western Regions. He suggested that it be possible for the central government to appoint a Colonel in Dunhuang and increase garrison troops in the Four Prefectures in the Hexi Area to intimidate the Xiongnu. Finally, the Emperor accepted Zhang Dang's proposal and appointed Ban Yong, the son of Ban Chao, as the Chief Official of the Western Regions, leading 500 soldiers to garrison Liuzhong. Soon after that, Ban Yong defeated Jushi and Yanqi, and consequently, the states of Qiuci, Shule, Khotan, and Shache all surrendered to the Eastern Han Dynasty.

Since the Vice Colonel of the Western Regions who had taken the place of the Protector-General of the Western Regions was stationed in Dunhuang, the Governor of

率军前往侵扰。顺帝认为车师等6国北面与匈奴接壤，是整个西域防御的屏障，如果车师被匈奴占领，则西域必然危急，所以命令敦煌太守裴岑调发郡国兵及玉门关候、伊吾司马之兵，共6300余人前往救援。汉军与匈奴军队战于勒山，汉军不利。永和二年(137年)秋，呼衍王又率军进攻车师后部，结果被裴岑击败。战后，裴岑特地在车师立碑以记功。清雍正七年(1729年)，大将军岳钟琪远征西塞，在巴尔库尔城西50里石人子发掘出《敦煌太守裴岑纪功碑》，后移置敦煌。据碑文的记载，阳嘉四年(135年)裴岑所率领的西征军中，敦煌郡兵就有3000余人，占据了总兵力的一半，是西征军的绝对主力。而这场战争由阳嘉四年(135年)持续到永和二年(137年)，也足见战争的激烈程度。

从上述史实可以看出，

Dunhuang Prefecture became the person in charge of military affairs in the Western Regions. According to the *Book of the Later Han: Traditions of the Western Regions*, in the spring of the 4th year of Yangjia Era of Emperor Shun of the Eastern Han Dynasty(135), Prince Huyan of the Northern Xiongnu, dissatisfied with Jushi's surrendering to the imperial court, led an army against it. Emperor Shun thought that the six states such as Jushi bordering the Xiongnu in the north were barriers for the Western Regions, so if Jushi was captured by the Xiongnu, the Western Regions would fall into an untenable situation. Consequently, the Emperor ordered Pei Cen, the Governor of Dunhuang Prefecture, to rescue Jushi with 6,300 soldiers from three forces, but the military operation at the Leshan Mountain was a failure. In the autumn of the 2nd year of Yonghe Era (137), Prince Huyan led the army to attack the Further Jushi, but was defeated by Pei Cen. After the battle, Pei Cen erected a monument recording the victory. In the 7th year of Emperor Yongzheng of the Qing Dynasty (1729), during an expedition to the western frontier fortresses, General-in-Chief Yue Zhongqi found the Monument of Pei Cen, the Governor of Dunhuang Prefecture, located 50 *li* west of Ba'erkuer Town and had it relocated to Dunhuang. According to the monument, in the 4th year of Yangjia Era (135), there were approximately 3,000 soldiers from Dunhuang Prefecture in Pei Cen's west expedition army, constituting half of the total strength and being the main force of the army.

从武帝派张骞通西域后的几百年间，汉政府破楼兰、姑师，伐大宛，与匈奴争车师，远征康居等，但凡征战，敦煌必为前线补给站。两汉和西域交通不下300年，其间维持正常关系者有200多年。随着使者的出塞入塞、戍卒屯田等，敦煌成了汉朝在西北地区经营的军事重镇。

北魏控制敦煌以后，在敦煌设镇，仍将敦煌作为经营西域的基地。5世纪40年代，北魏太武帝派成周公万度归率军连续出兵鄯善、焉耆、龟兹，控制了西域的大部分地区，丝绸之路南道重新得以畅通。据史书记载，此时自葱岭以西直至大秦（罗马帝国），“百国千城，莫不附焉，胡商贩客，日奔塞下”。但丝绸之路北道高昌以东还在游牧民族柔然的控制之下。柔然主要活动在北魏的北方，势力十分强大。到魏太武帝晚年，北魏在西域的优势地位已被柔然所动摇。到北魏献文帝时，敦煌以西、葱岭以东的广大地区都已臣服于

Moreover, the battle raged on until the year of 137, indicating the intensity of the battle.

It can be observed from the above mentioned historical facts that for centuries after Emperor Wu of the Han Dynasty sent the diplomat Zhang Qian to the Western Regions, when the Han government defeated Loulan, Gushi, and Dayuan, fought with the Xiongnu for Jushi, and conquered Kangju, Dunhuang had been the main supply depot for the frontlines in each battle. Communications between the Han Dynasty and the Western Regions lasted for more than 300 years, during which their relations remained friendly for roughly 200 years. With the entry and exit of ambassadors through the frontier passes, the stationing of garrison soldiers there, and reclamation of wasteland, Dunhuang became a significant garrison town for the Han Dynasty in governing the northwestern area.

After the Northern Wei Dynasty was founded, Dunhuang was established as a Garrison and was then regarded as the management base of the Western Regions. During the 440s, Emperor Taiwu of the Northern Wei Dynasty sent Wan Dugui, the Duke of Chengzhou, to attack Shanshan, Yanqi, and Qiuci. He then controlled most part of the Western Regions, allowing the reopening of the southern route of the Silk Road. According to historical records, the states west of the Congling Range all the way to the Roman Empire surrendered to the Northern

柔然。孝文帝延兴四年(474年)，北魏朝中的大臣屡次上言，建议放弃敦煌，但遭到了给事中韩秀的坚决反对。正是因为韩秀的不懈努力，最终得到了孝文帝的支持。北魏政府进一步提高了敦煌的建制级别，将敦煌镇升级为都大将，加强了敦煌的防守力量及利用敦煌经营西域的能力。

隋末天下大乱，河西的凉州和敦煌等地为李轨所占据。武德二年(619年)，安兴贵兄弟联络凉州等地的胡人起兵，执李轨归附唐朝，河西地区被纳入唐朝的势力范围，敦煌也被更名为瓜州。但由于此后瓜州刺史贺拔行威及敦煌当地人张护、李通等先后发动叛乱，所以一直到武德六年(623年)九月，唐朝在敦煌才建立起稳定的统治秩序。而此时瓜州已被肢解为瓜州和西沙州两个州，其中西沙州领敦煌、寿昌两县，治所敦煌。从敦煌改称西沙州看，此时唐政府已将敦煌视为

Wei Dynasty. Traders travelled along these areas frequently, but the northern route of the Silk Road, east of Gaochang, was still occupied by the Rouran who lived north of the Northern Wei and were influential in the area. The situation remained unchanged until the later years of Emperor Taiwu, when the central government's dominant position in the Western Regions was challenged by the Rouran Khanate. During the reign of Emperor Xianwen, the vast area from west of Dunhuang to east of the Congling Range was all controlled by Rouran. In the 4th year of Yanxing Era of Emperor Xiaowen (474), ministers frequently advised the government to abandon Dunhuang, but this was objected to by Han Xiu, the Supervising Secretary. Owing to Han Xiu's unremitting efforts, the Western Wei Dynasty further upgraded Dunhuang Garrison to a Senior Garrison, reinforcing the garrison strength and governing ability of Dunhuang.

The later years of the Sui Dynasty witnessed turmoil in China. Liangzhou and Dunhuang in the Hexi Corridor were occupied by Li Gui. In the 2nd year of Wude Era (619), An Xinggui and his brother allied with the ethnic groups in Liangzhou and captured Li Gui. The Hexi area was then brought under the control of the Tang Dynasty and Dunhuang was renamed Guazhou. Later, Heba Xingwei, the Prefect of Guazhou, together with local residents Zhang Hu and Li Tong, launched one rebellion after another. It was not until September in 623 that the Tang Dynasty recovered stable control over Dunhuang.

唐朝设在最西部的行政建制，也表明唐高祖李渊并没有继续西进以经营西域的雄心壮志。

武德九年(626 年)六月四日，李世民发动“玄武门之变”，取得了唐朝的最高权力。与李渊不同，李世民是一个具有雄才大略的皇帝。当时对唐朝威胁最大的敌对势力，就是建于漠北草原的东突厥汗国。而东突厥汗国此时还控制着西域北部的高昌及伊吾等地。贞观四年(630 年)，唐朝出兵漠北，消灭了东突厥汗国。东突厥所控制的伊吾，也在首领石万年的率领下归降唐朝。唐朝以其地设西伊州，后去“西”字。由于唐朝的势力已经挺进伊州，敦煌已非国家西境，所以在贞观七年(633 年)，敦煌正式更名为沙州。

贞观九年 (635 年)，唐朝又出兵青海，击败吐谷浑，使河西走廊不再受外部的干扰，步入稳步发展的轨道。而位于丝绸之路北道上

At the time, Guazhou had been divided into two prefectures—Guazhou and Xishazhou—in which Xishazhou governed Dunhuang and Shouchang counties. According to its renaming of Dunhuang, the Tang Dynasty apparently regarded Dunhuang as the westernmost administrative entity, and Emperor Gaozu of the Tang Dynasty expressed no ambition for further westward expansion to control the Western Regions.

On June 4th, 626, Li Shimin, the second Emperor of the Tang Dynasty, gained imperial power in the Xuanwu Gate Incident. Different from his father, Li Shimin (Emperor Taizong) was a ruler with great talent and bold vision. At the time, the biggest threat to the Tang was the Eastern Turkic Khanate in the prairie north of the Gobi Desert, which had already controlled the northern part of the Western Regions such as Gaochang and Yiwu. In the 4th year of Zhenguan (630), the Tang government dispatched troops to conquer and then wiped out the Eastern Turkic Khanate; Yiwu, led by its chief Shi Wannian, then surrendered to the Tang. The central government established the prefecture of Xiyizhou in Yiwu and later removed "*xi*" from the name. Thus, Dunhuang was no longer the westernmost border of China, and in the 7th year of Zhenguan Era (633), Xishazhou was renamed Shazhou.

In 635, the Tang Dynasty dispatched troops and defeated the Tuyuhun in Qinghai, protecting the Hexi Corridor from attacks and

的经济和军事重镇高昌，就成为唐朝进一步经略西域的障碍。此时，高昌在西突厥的唆使下，刻意挑拨薛延陀与唐朝的关系。在得到薛延陀可汗的汇报后，虽然有不少大臣反对，但唐太宗讨伐高昌的心意已决。贞观十三年(639年)十二月，唐太宗以吐鲁番的高昌王国阻隔丝绸之路北道经焉耆、高昌到敦煌的道路为由，派遣吏部尚书侯君集为交河道行军大总管，左屯卫大将军薛万钧与左屯卫将军姜行本为副总管，率兵讨伐高昌。

高昌王麴文泰得到唐朝发兵讨伐的消息后，对国人说："唐朝距离我们有7000里，其中还有2000里的沙碛。沙碛地无水草，冬天的时候寒风如刀，夏天的时候热风如烧，唐朝的大军怎么能越过沙碛呢！我以往入朝的时候，看到秦陇的北部地区非常萧条，远没有隋朝时富庶。现在唐军来讨伐我们，如果派遣的兵多，则其军粮肯定供应不上；如果唐军在3万以下，我们足以应付。所以，我们当以逸待劳，坐收

assisting the area in its development. As a result, Gaochang, a significant economic and military state on the northern route of the Silk Road, became an obstacle for the Tang Dynasty in further developing the Western Regions. At the time, Gaochang deliberately instigated relations between the Tang and the Syr-Tardush Khanate. After receiving a report from the Khan of Syr-Tardush Khanate, Emperor Taizong made up his mind to send armed forces to suppress Gaochang despite the objection from a number of his ministers. In December of the 13th year of Zhenguan Era (639), on the pretext that Gaochang cut off the Silk Road from Yanqi and Gaochang to Dunhuang, Emperor Taizong sent Hou Junji, the Regional Commander-in-Chief of the Jiaohe Circuit, assisted by General-in-Chief Xue Wanjun and General Jiang Xingben, to attack Gaochang.

Hearing this information, Qu Wentai, the King of Gaochang, said to his people, "The Tang Dynasty is 7,000 *li* away from Gaochang, and there is a 2,000-*li*-wide desert without water and any plant between the two countries. The wind is as sharp and severe as knives in winter and is as hot as fire in summer, so it is impossible for them to cross this harsh terrain. When I went to the Central Plains in the past, I found that the northern part of the Qinlong area was very desolate, far removed from the

其弊。如果他们屯兵城下，不过20天，粮食吃完后必定会撤退。然后我们就可以乘胜追击，所以没有什么好担心的。”但贞观十四年（640年）八月，侯君集所率的唐军已经越过敦煌西北的沙碛。麹文泰在无计可施的情况下，忧惧而死，其子麹智盛即位。麹智盛即位之后，将高昌主要兵力都抽调到高昌东部的军事重镇田地城以抵御唐军。

此次西征，唐军兵分两路，姜行本、牛进达为先锋，先出伊州，负责制造攻城的器械。唐朝为此次西征，专门抽调山东地区善于制造攻城器械的能工巧匠。他们跟随姜行本登上伊吾时罗漫山北麓的黑绀岭，砍伐山木以制造器械。他们屯集粮草，置办战马，制作兵器、战车、抛石机等攻城器械，有力地配合了前方部队的作战。而麹文泰发病死时，侯君集所率的唐军已经出伊州到达柳谷。唐军的间谍探知麹文泰马上就要下葬，到

prosperity of the Sui Dynasty. If the Tang dispatches troops to attack us, their military provisions will be in short supply; and if the soldiers are less than 30,000, our victory is certain. So we can just bide our time waiting for the exhausted enemy, and profit from their failure. Or even if they station troops outside the town, they will withdraw for lack of food in less than 20 days, and then we can follow up with victory. Therefore, there is nothing to worry about.” However, in August of 640, General Hou and his troops indeed crossed the desert northwest of Dunhuang. Qu Wentai died of distress and was succeeded by his son Qu Zhisheng. After that, Gaochang transferred its main forces to the important military town Tiandi, east of Gaochang, to defend against the Tang’s army.

In this battle, the army of the Tang Dynasty was divided into two branches in which Generals Jiang Xingben and Niu Jinda played a trailblazing role, setting out first from Yizhou and being responsible for creating the instruments for besieging the town. To guarantee this expedition, the Tang government deliberately transported skilled craftsmen from Shandong with the aim to manufacture weapons, chariots, catapults, and other instruments. They followed General Jiang to the Heigan Range at the northern foot of the Shiluoman Mountains and chop trees for making military equipment. These men also gathered grain, and collected battle steeds, effectively cooperating with the

时高昌的国人都会前往参加葬礼，所以，诸将都认为这是个发动袭击的好机会。而侯君集认为此次太宗讨伐高昌，是因为高昌没有尽到做臣子的礼节，如果唐军在其安葬时发动袭击，就失去了战争的正义性。于是唐军西进田地城。与高昌田地城的守军相比，唐军的武器装备更为先进。攻城器械中威力最大的当属推撞车和抛石车。推撞车由巨木制成，田地城泥质的城墙在它的撞击下，纷纷崩塌；而被抛石车抛出的巨石所击中的目标也“无不靡碎”。唐军的攻势从早上开始，到中午时分，田地城已被攻克，被俘虏的军民有 7000 多人，高昌的主力丧失殆尽。唐军趁胜进逼高昌的都城。此次攻城除利用了抛石车外，唐军还装备了高达 10 丈的瞭望楼。在瞭望楼的指导下，抛石车发挥了更大的威力，迫使高昌士兵纷纷逃入屋中以躲避巨石。在唐军锐不可当的进攻下，麹智盛被迫开门出降，被侯君

troops on the frontlines. When Qu Wentai was dead, General Hou had led the army to arrive in Liugu County. A spy of the Tang Dynasty learned that at the moment Qu Wentai was to be buried and all the people in Gaochang would be at the funeral. Most of the military officers considered it the best time to launch an attack, but General Hou disagreed since he viewed the battle would be dishonorable and unfair if they did so, because the real purpose of the expedition was to punish Gaochang who didn't fulfill the duty as a minister. Hence, the Tang troops marched westward to Tiandi Town in the State of Gaochang. Compared with the garrison troops in Tiandi Town, the army of the Tang was equipped with more advanced weapons, among which the battering arms made of wood and trebuchets were so powerful that the mud walls of Tiandi collapsed when hit, and all targets were smashed when hit by stones hurled by the catapults. Attack started in the morning, and by noon Tiandi Town was occupied by the Tang army, with roughly 7,000 soldiers and people captured, and the main force of the Gaochang Army was lost in the war. The Tang army seized the opportunity to approach the capital city of Gaochang. In next siege, the Tang also set up a watchtower with a height of 10 *zhang*. It assisted the performance of the catapults, forcing the enemy to take cover and escape indoors from the huge stones. Under relentless attack from the Tang army, Qu

集解送入京。在贞观十四年(640年)九月,唐太宗下诏改高昌为西州，把其纳入了唐朝的版图，并在此设置了安西都护府,以控制西域。这是唐朝进一步经营西域的重要一步。此外,唐朝还在天山北的今新疆吉木萨尔一带设庭州，行政建置均与内地州县相同。

清雍正年间，驻守巴里坤的宁远大将军岳钟琪在巴里坤松树塘附近，发现了为姜行本歌功颂德的《大唐左屯卫将军姜行本勒石纪功文》碑。雍正十一年(1733年)，岳钟琪为转运粮饷,命兵部员外郎阿炳安开辟了天山运道，并通过运道将碑运至天山顶。所以,在记述巴里坤当地名胜古迹的《镇西厅乡土志》中，称其为天山唐碑。中华民国二十年(1931年),马仲英攻陷哈密,天山庙亦被焚毁,石碑弃于野。中华民国三十六年（1947年),哈密地区的官员李朗星将此碑移至老城中山堂之西图书堂中。20世纪50年代,此碑

Zhisheng was forced to surrender and was sent to Chang'an escorted by General Hou. In September of 640, Emperor Taizong decreed that Gaochang would be renamed as Xizhou, where the Protectorate of Anxi was set up to manage the Western Regions, which indicated that Gaochang was then part of Tang's territory. This was a significant step for the Tang Dynasty to further its control over the Western Regions; in addition, the Tang also established prefecture of Tingzhou in presnt-day Jimusa'er of Xinjiang, whose administrative organization was similar to that of the Central Plains.

During the reign of Emperor Yongzheng of the Qing Dynasty (1723-1735), the General-in-Chief Yue Zhongqi found a stele commemorating General Jiang Xingben for his achievements, when he was garrisoned in Barkol. In 1733, in order to transfer provisions and funds for troops, General Yue ordered Abing'an, the Vice Director of the Ministry of War, to open up a passage in the Tianshan Mountains, and then carried this stele to the top of the mountain through the passage. Thus, according to the *Geography of Zhenxiting*, this stele was also known as the Tang Dynasty's Stele in Tianshan Mountains. In the 20th year of the Republic of China (1931), when Ma Zhongying, a military commander of the Kuomintang, captured Kumul City, the Tianshan Mountain Temple was destroyed in fire and the stele was abandoned in the

运至乌鲁木齐，现存新疆博物馆。在《大唐左屯卫将军姜行本勒石纪功文》中，除记述了姜行本的具体功绩外，还特别标出了姜行本统帅的主要将领。其中，沙州刺史、上柱国望都县开国侯刘德敏名列第一，而碑文的篆刻者为瓜州司法参军司马太真。这就证明在唐灭高昌的战役中，有敦煌、常乐地区的文武官员和士兵参加。敦煌又一次成为中原王朝进军西域的军事基地。

唐朝建立后，地处西域的焉耆奉唐朝为宗主国，常常遣使朝贡。但自从西突厥的大臣屈利啜为其弟娶焉耆王之女后，焉耆疏远了同唐朝的关系。贞观十八年（644 年），李世民命安西都护郭孝恪为西州道行军总管，率步骑 3000 人出银山道，前往讨伐。在唐朝大军压境的情况下，焉耆王弟栗婆准等三人前往西州归附。焉耆城四面皆环水，焉耆王自恃天险不设守备，郭孝恪趁夜色渡河，在破晓时分攻

wilderness. In 1947, an officer of the Kuomintang named Li Langxing transferred the stele to the western library of Zhongshan Hall, and in the 1950s it was carried to Urumqi. The stele is currently housed in the Xinjiang Museum. It not only records the specific exploits of General Jiang Xingben, but also lists the main officers under his command, including Liu Demin, the Prefect of Shazhou and Dynasty-founding District Marquess, whose name appears at the top of the list, and Sima Taizhen, the Administrator of Law, the person who engraved the stele. It also reveals that civil and military officers, and soldiers in Dunhuang and Changle took part in the battle when the Tang Dynasty conquered Gaochang. Dunhuang became an important military base for the government in the Central Plains to conquer the Western Regions once again.

After the establishment of the Tang Dynasty, the State of Yanqi in the Western Regions regarded the Tang as its superior, and often paid tribute to the central government. However, Yanqi became estranged from the Tang when Qu Lichuo, a minister of the Western Turks, asked the princess of Yanqi to marry his brother. In the 18th year of Zhenguan Era (644), Emperor Taizong appointed Guo Xiaoke, the Protector-General of Anxi, as the Regional Commander-in-Chief of the Xizhou Circuit to attack Yanqi with 3,000 soldiers. When the army was bearing down upon them, the king's brother Li Pozhun and two other

入焉耆王城，俘虏了焉耆王突骑支。郭孝恪撤兵三天之后，西突厥救援焉耆的大军才赶到。屈利啜派遣骑兵5000追击郭孝恪至银山，被郭孝恪大败。贞观二十二年(648年)，李世民又遣阿史那社尔讨伐龟兹。在此年的十二月，阿史那社尔攻陷了龟兹的王城，龟兹王布失毕带领少量的骑兵向西逃窜。沙州刺史苏海政、尚辇奉御薛万备率精骑急追布失毕600余里，并最终在拨换城将其擒获。永徽二年(651年)，西突厥首领阿史那贺鲁听到唐太宗去世的消息，起兵反叛，击败西突厥乙毘射匮可汗，自号沙钵罗可汗，建牙帐于双河及千泉，拥兵数十万。经过多次战争之后，显庆二年(657年)，唐朝彻底击败阿史那贺鲁，最终获得了西域的宗主权。次年五月，唐朝迁安西都护府于龟兹，并设立龟兹、于阗、焉耆、疏勒四镇，镇守并管理西域广大地区。

虽然西突厥的势力遭

officers went to Xizhou, surrendering to the Tang army. The Town of Yanqi was surrounded by water, thus, counting on this natural barrier, the King of Yanqi did not station troops there. General Guo crossed the river by moonlight, broke into the town at dawn, and captured the King. Reinforcements from the Western Turks didn't arrive in Yanqi until three days after General Guo withdrew his army. Qu Lichuo sent 5,000 cavalrymen in pursuit, attacking General Guo at the Silver Mountain, but they were defeated by Guo Xiaoke. In 648, Emperor Taizong dispatched General Ashina She'er to attack the State of Qiuci. In December, the general captured the capital town of Qiuci, and Bu Shibi, the King of Qiuci, escaped westwards with a small number of cavalrymen. Su Haizheng, the Regional Governor of Shazhou, and Xue Wanbei, the Chief Steward of Sedan-chair Service in the Palace Administration, led elite cavalrymen to chase the King of Qiuci for 600 *li*, finally capturing him in Bohuan Town. In the 2nd year of Yonghui Era (651), on learning of the death of Emperor Taizong, Ashina Helu, a chieftain of the Western Turks, launched a rebellion, killing Irbis Seguy Khan of the Western Turks and declaring himself Ishbara Khan in charge of hundreds of thousands of soldiers, with his capitals in Shuanghe and Qianquan. After several battles, the Tang Dynasty defeated Ashina Helu, gaining suzerainty over the Western Regions in the 2nd year of Xianqing Era (657). In May of 658, the

受了毁灭性的打击，但自龙朔二年（662年）开始，地处青藏高原的吐蕃王国开始与西突厥余部联合，同唐朝争夺对西域的控制权。在吐蕃的军事压力下，唐朝曾一度放弃对西域地区的控制，但自长寿元年（692年）王孝杰率军收复四镇，并发唐兵3万人镇守之后，唐朝在西域的控制力增强。从此以后，直到8世纪末的100年间，安西四镇的建制没有再动摇，西域基本上一直在唐朝的统治之下。

为了加强在西域的镇防能力，特别是针对吐蕃的威胁，唐朝在高宗上元二年和三年（675年、676年），把丝绸之路南道上的两个重镇——典合城和且末城，改称为石城镇和播仙镇，划归沙州直接管辖。这样就加强了丝绸之路南道的军事镇守能力，同时也标志着敦煌军事战略地位的提升。据史书及敦煌文献记载，在唐

Tang moved the headquarters of the Protectorate of Anxi to Qiuci and established four garrisons, including Qiuci, Yutian (Khotan), Yanqi, and Shule to garrison and govern the vast area of the Western Regions.

Although the Western Turks were dealt a destructive blow, the Tubo regime located on the Qinghai-Tibet Plateau had been allying with the remnants of the Western Turks to fight against the Tang Dynasty for control of the Western Regions since the 2nd year of Longshuo Era (662). Under military pressure from the Tubo, the Tang Dynasty had given up its control of the Western Regions for many years. But in the 1st year of Changshou Era (692), General Wang Xiaojie recaptured the Four Garrisons in Anxi and stationed 30,000 soldiers there, strengthening the Tang's control over the Western Regions. From then on, over the next hundred years, the administrative organization of the Four Garrisons in Anxi did not change, and the Western Regions were ruled mainly by the Tang Dynasty.

In order to strengthen its defense of the Western Regions, especially considering the threat from the Tubo, in the 2nd and the 3rd year of Shangyuan Era of Emperor Gaozong (675 and 676), two important towns—Dianhe and Qiemo along the southern route of the Silk Road—were renamed Shicheng Garrison and Boxian Garrison under the direct control of Shazhou. Through this, the military defense of the Tang Dynasty was strengthened on the southern route of the Silk Road. It also revealed that the strategic military

朝用兵西域和镇守西域的过程中，有不少沙州将士奔赴前线。比较著名的有正议大夫北庭副大都护瀚海军使兼营田支度等使阴嗣监及追擒龟兹王布失毕的沙州刺史苏海政，此外，还有游击将军上柱国西州岸头府果毅都尉张端、壮武将军行西州岸头府折冲兼豆卢军副使阴守忠等。景云二年(711年)，唐朝将旧陇右道分为陇右、河西两道。其中，河西道设置河西节度使，治凉州，统领赤水、大斗、建康、宁寇、玉门、墨离、豆卢、新泉等8军。设置于敦煌城内的豆卢军位置最西，可以为唐政府在西域东部地区的经营提供强有力的军事后盾。

“安史之乱”爆发后，唐政府抽调河西、安西、北庭等节度使属下的精锐前往中原平叛，造成了唐朝西北边防的空虚。唐代宗宝应元年(762年)，由于吐蕃和党项不断侵扰陇右诸州，当时唐朝又抽调大量安西和河西兵东去防守关中，这就给长期觊觎

position of Dunhuang had intensified. According to historical records and Dunhuang documents, when the Tang Dynasty dispatched troops to the Western Regions, a large number of officers and soldiers from Shazhou went to the frontlines, such as Yin Sijian, the Vice Grand Protector-General of Beiting, Military Commissioner of Hanhai Army, Commissioner of Agriculture and Finance, Su Haizheng, the Regional Governor of Shazhou, Zhang Duan, the Mobile Corps Commander, Vice Commandant of Assault-resisting Garrison, and Yin Shouzhong, the Vice Commissioner of Doulu Army. In the 2nd year of Jingyun Era (711), the Tang Dynasty branched out from old Longyou Circuit into Longyou Circuit and Hexi Circuit. In Hexi Circuit, the Military Commissioner of the Hexi Area was created with headquarters in Liangzhou, governing eight armies, including Chishui, Dadou, Jiankang, Ningkou, Yumen, Moli, Doulu and Xinquan. The Doulu Army was stationed in Dunhuang, the westernmost place of the eight armies, providing powerful military support for the central government's rule of the eastern area of the Western Regions.

After the outbreak of the An Lushan Rebellion, the Tang Dynasty transferred forces under the Military Commissioners of Hexi, Anxi, and Beiting to calm the rebellion in the Central Plains, leaving the northwestern border weakly defended. In the 1st year of Baoying Era of Emperor Daizong (762), the prefectures

河西地区的吐蕃可乘之机。广德元年(763年),吐蕃攻陷河、陇、秦、成、渭等州,入大散关后又攻陷了兰、廓、鄯、洮、岷等州,河西地区通往长安的陇右旧道被吐蕃割断。

广德二年(764年),吐蕃攻陷凉州。由于东归之路已被吐蕃切断,河西节度使杨志烈被迫率众逃奔甘州,后于永泰元年(765年)为沙陀所杀。大历元年(766年),河西节度使杨休明徙镇沙州,敦煌成为河西最高军政长官河西节度使的驻地。河西节度使退守沙州后,杨休明马上在敦煌当地做了"卸传甲帐,静侯田畴"的战略部署。为了抵御吐蕃的进攻,杨休明在大历二年(767年)左右前往安西征调兵马,准备凭借4镇留守的官兵和河西驻军残部与吐蕃决一死战。而在杨休明途经长泉时,被伊西庭节度留后周逸借助突厥之手所害。据敦

in Longyou area were frequently harassed by the Tubo and the Tanguts, and the Tang Dynasty again dispatched soldiers stationed in Anxi and Hexi to defend Guanzhong at the same time, providing an opportunity for the Tubo who had long coveted the Hexi area. In the 1st year of Guangde Era (763), the Tubo captured Hezhou, Longzhou, Qinzhou, Chengzhou, and Weizhou, marched into the Dasan Pass, and occupied Lanzhou, Kuozhou, Shanzhou, Taozhou, and Minzhou. As a result, the old Longyou Circuit allowing the Hexi area access to Chang'an was cut off by the Tubo.

In 764, the Tubo captured Liangzhou. Because the route for retreating eastwards had been cut off by the Tubo, Yang Zhilie, the Military Commissioner of the Hexi Area, was forced to escape to Ganzhou with his assistants, where he was killed in 765 by the Shatuo tribe, a branch of the Western Turks. In the 1st year of Dali Era (766), Yang Xiuming, the subsequent Military Commissioner of the Hexi Area, moved his headquarters to Shazhou, making Dunhuang the station with the highest ranking military and political official in the Hexi area. After withdrawing to Shazhou, Yang Xiuming immediately made a strategic plan. To resist attack from the Tubo, in 767, Yang Xiuming went to Anxi to demand supplies and soldiers, and decided to fight the Tubo to their ultimate defeat with the troops stationed in the Hexi area and four garrisons there. However, Yang was killed by the Turks when he was near Changquan. According

煌写本 P.2942《河西观察使判集·差郑支使望四镇索救援河西兵马一万人》记载，杨休明被害后，驻守在沙州的河西节度继续向四镇调兵，但由于周逸的从中作梗，沙州一直没有得到安西四镇的军事支持，这也为敦煌的陷落埋下了伏笔。贞元二年，在经历了长达 11 年的抵抗后，敦煌最终被吐蕃占领。但由于占领前，阎朝与吐蕃统治者达成了“毋徙它境”的协议；而根据敦煌文献记载，也确实可知在吐蕃占领之后，敦煌地区的人口没有出现大规模的外流，这就使得敦煌成为河西地区汉人和汉文化的中心。正是这样的原因，在经过吐蕃 60 年的统治之后，敦煌才能在张议潮的率领下，在河西地区率先揭竿而起，驱逐吐蕃统治者，并派遣使者奉十一州图籍归唐，成为我国历史上维护祖国统一的千古佳话。

唐宣宗大中五年（851 年），唐政府在敦煌设置归义军，敦煌再次成为藩镇的治所。张议潮除了担任归义军节度使外，还担负起河陇十一州观察使的重任。咸通七年(866 年)，张议潮多次派

to records from the *Verdict Collections of the Surveillance Commissioner of the Hexi Area* (Dunhuang manuscripts P.2942), after Yang's death, the new Military Commissioner of the Hexi Area stationed in Shazhou continued transferring troops from the four garrisons. But because of the obstruction from Zhou Yi, the Deputy Military Commissioner of Yizhou, Xizhou and Tingzhou, Shazhou could not get military support from four garrisons, foreshadowing the fall of Dunhuang. In the 2nd year of Zhenyuan Era (780), Dunhuang finally fell to the Tubo after 11 years of resistance. Luckily, due to an agreement reached before Dunhuang was occupied, the populace in Dunhuang was not forcibly relocated to other places, which was also recorded in Dunhuang documents. This allowed Dunhuang to become the center of the ethnic Han and Han culture in the Hexi area. Thus Dunhuang could take the lead in the Hexi area uprisings under the command of Zhang Yichao, despite nearly 60 years of rule by the Tubo. They drove out the Tubo, sending envoys to take a map and households registration of the 11 prefectures in the Hexi area back to the Tang government, which was an accomplishment praised far and wide for the reunification of China in history.

In the 5th year of Dazhong Era of

使者前往长安，汇报发生在河陇地区的重要事件，以显示其对上述地区的控制。但此时唐政府已经改变了此前利用归义军控制河陇的战略，而希望逐渐削弱归义军的势力。在张议潮控制河陇的意图与唐政府的战略发生冲突的情况下，咸通八年(867 年)，张议潮被唐政府征召入京。表面上看，张议潮入京后受到了唐政府的优待，但实际上，他充当的是人质的角色。此后，掌管敦煌等地事务的张淮深频繁遣使长安，希望获得唐政府的正式任命。虽然唐政府最终同意册封张淮深为节度使，但那已经是在唐僖宗文德元年（888 年），距张议潮入京已长达 21 年。就在这段时间里，河西地区陆续兴起了凉州唱末、甘州回鹘、肃州龙家等多个少数民族政权，归义军政权已经处于一个“四面六蕃围”的局面之下。同时，回鹘还从归义军手中

Emperor Xuanzong Ⅱ (851), the Tang Dynasty established the *Guiyijun* Force in Dunhuang, and again this place became the seat of a military governor. Zhang Yichao not only held the post of the Military Commissioner of the *Guiyijun* Force, but also was given the title of Surveillance Commissioner of 11 prefectures in the Hexi and Longyou areas. In the 7th year of Xiantong Era (866), Zhang Yichao sent envoys repeatedly to Chang'an to report important affairs occurring in the Hexi and Longyou areas, reflecting his power in these places. But the Tang government had changed its original strategy of controlling these areas through the *Guiyijun* regime; by contrast, the central government then wanted to weaken its power. Due to this conflict between the two, in 867, Zhang Yichao was summoned by the imperial court to Chang'an. Although on the surface it seemed that Zhang was given lavish treatment by the central government after entering the capital city, in reality he was held as a hostage. Zhang Huaishen, the nephew of Zhang Yichao, was in charge of the affairs in Dunhuang while Zhang Yichao was away, and sent envoys to Chang'an frequently, hoping for official approval as the head of *Guiyijun* regime. It was not until the 1st year of Wende Era of Emperor Xizong (888), however, 21 years after Zhang Yichao went to Chang'an, that Zhang Huaishen was appointed as the Military Commissioner of the *Guiyijun* Force by the central government. During this period, several powers from ethnic minorities rose up in the Hexi area, such as the Wamo in

夺得了伊州的控制权，归义军的辖区已由最初的十一州缩减为瓜、沙二州。五代和宋初，敦煌的归义军政权继续存在，并时常遣使中原政权，以获得他们的册封和赏赐。虽然在名义上曹氏归义军的创始人曹议金及其后代都接受中央王朝的册封，但中原和归义军之间存在多个少数民族政权，中央政府无法正式对敦煌进行管理，所以曹氏归义军所控制的瓜、沙二州实际上就是一个独立政权。由于具有独立性，所以曹氏归义军节度使的称号往往要高于中央政府的册封，甚至在曹氏晚期，节度使往往自称为王。

通过汉唐之际敦煌的历史，我们可以发现敦煌的军事重镇地位的获得与中央政府经营西域的战略密切相关，而在中央政府经营西域的

Liangzhou, the Uyghurs in Ganzhou, and the Long tribe in Suzhou, leaving the *Guiyijun* regime surrounded by them. Additionally, the Uyghurs wrested control of Yizhou away from the *Guiyijun* regime, and thus the area under *Guiyijun* regime's administration was reduced from eleven prefectures to two: Guazhou and Shazhou. During the Five Dynasties and the early years of the Song Dynasty, the *Guiyijun* regime in Dunhuang continued to exist and often sent envoys to the Central Plains to receive titles and awards from the imperial court. Officially, Cao Yijin, the succeeding Military Commissioner of the *Guiyijun* Force, and his descendants were all granted titles by the central imperial government. The *Guiyijun* regime under Cao's rule, however, was more independent for there were several tribal groups obstructing the central government's official administration in Dunhuang. For its independence, the title of Military Commissioner of the *Guiyijun* Force always ranked above other titles appointed by the central government. By the end of the reign of Cao's clan, the Military Commissioners had proclaimed themselves as Princes.

Throughout the history of Dunhuang during the Han and Tang dynasties, it is obvious that the position of Dunhuang as a military garrison was closely related to the central government's strategy of controlling over the Western Regions. During this time, Dunhuang usually played the role of military outpost and base of material supplies. From the Late Tang to the early Song, because of the shrinking of the central government's power

整体战略中，敦煌往往是作为军事前哨和物资供应基地的角色出现的。而自晚唐至宋初，由于中央政府势力的削弱及少数民族政权的存在，中央政府一直没能有力地控制河西、陇右等地，对西域地区的控制和经营更无从谈起。所以，敦煌的战略地位持续下降。

1036 年，西夏占领敦煌。此前，西夏已经灭亡了凉州的六谷蕃部和甘州的回鹘政权。所以，西夏对敦煌的占领也就标志着河西地区已全部为西夏所控制（图 56）。虽然据清人吴广成《西夏书事》的记载，李元昊在占领河西后，可能曾控制伊、西等地，但根据《宋史》的记载，西夏的西部边陲乃是敦煌。西夏在取得河西、稳固自己的后方之后，一直忙于同北宋的战争，所以并没有经营西域的雄心和力量。其设置于敦煌的军政机构最大的任务也就是保境安民而已，敦煌的军事地位并未因其地处边防而得以提升。

1206 年，成吉思汗建立起了一个空前强大的蒙古汗国。从蒙古国建立前的 1205 年到

and the rise of the ethnic tribal authorities, the central government did not have the ability to rule the Hexi and Longyou areas, much less control and management to the Western Regions. Thus the strategic position of Dunhuang continued to decline.

In 1036, the Western Xia captured Dunhuang. Prior to that, it had wiped out the Liugu Tribe in Liangzhou and the Uyghurs in Ganzhou. The occupation of Dunhuang indicated that the whole Hexi area was under the control of the Western Xia (Fig.56). According to the *Chronicles of the Western Xia* compiled by Wu Guangcheng in the Qing Dynasty, after Li Yuanhao, the founder of the Western Xia, captured the Hexi area, he also ruled Yizhou and Xizhou. But according to records from the *History of the Song Dynasty*, the western border of the Western Xia was still Dunhuang. After controlling the Hexi area, Li Yuanhao was busy fighting with the Northern Song Dynasty and did not have the ambition or determination to manage the Western Regions. The major aim of establishing military organization in Dunhuang was just to secure the defense and pacify the people, thus the military position of Dunhuang was not upgraded despite location as a boundary defense.

In 1206, Genghis Khan established the Mongol Empire, creating a land empire on an unprecedented scale. From 1205 to

图 56 莫高窟第 327 窟 飞天 西夏
Fig.56 Flying Apsaras, Mogao Cave 327 Western Xia

1209 年，蒙古大军曾三次征伐西夏。1226 年，成吉思汗在结束西征中亚的战争之后，再次率军对西夏发动猛烈的攻势。1227 年，在成吉思汗病逝数日后，蒙古军队杀死了已经投降的西夏国主，并攻陷了西夏的都城中兴府，西夏灭亡。西夏灭亡后，河西等地次第为蒙古军队所攻陷。而随着蒙古军队的

1209, the Mongolian army attacked the Western Xia three times. After finishing its conquest of Central Asia, Genghis Khan launched a fierce attack on the Western Xia in 1226. In 1227, several days after Genghis Khan's death, his army killed the emperor of the Western Xia who had already surrendered, and then captured its capital city, symbolizing the fall of the Western Xia. After that, the Hexi area and other places were occupied by the Mongols

不断征战，最终建立了疆域空前辽阔的元朝。由于交通重镇地位的丧失，敦煌在元帝国的版图中并不具有特殊的地位(图 57)。

洪武五年(1372 年)，明政府重修长城，冯胜在肃州以西 70 里处建嘉峪关，成

one by one. Through a series of conquests, the Mongols founded the Yuan Dynasty with unparalleled vast territory. Losing its position as an important traffic hub, Dunhuang no longer enjoyed a special position in the territory of the Yuan Dynasty (Fig.57).

In the 5th year of the Hongwu Era of Emperor Taizu of the Ming Dynasty (1372), the central government began to rebuild the

图 57　莫高窟第 332 窟女供养人　元

Fig.57　Painting of Female Donors, Mogao Cave 332　Yuan Dynasty

为明朝西部的边关，敦煌被弃置关外。虽然在永乐年间，明政府在敦煌设置了卫所，但并没有进行具体的军政管理，所以其对敦煌的控制只能停留在表面上。明朝中后期，由于中央政府无力介入西域事务，敦煌甚至沦为哈密和吐鲁番等地方势力角逐的战场。清雍正三年（1725年），清政府将沙州所升格为沙州卫，并进行了屯田等事务，使得敦煌的经济得以复苏。但由于远离边防，敦煌在军事上的战略意义已经完全丧失。

Great Wall, and Feng Sheng built the Jiayu Pass 70 *li* west of Suzhou as the western border of the country, leaving Dunhuang outside the Pass. Although the government established Guard or Post in Dunhuang during the period of Yongle Era, they did not fulfill any military and political administration there, showing that the control of Dunhuang was no longer significant. During the middle and later periods of the Ming Dynasty, Dunhuang even devolved into a battlefield of local forces such as Kumul and Turfan. In the 3rd year of Emperor Yongzheng of the Qing Dynasty (1725), the government upgraded the Shazhou Post into Shazhou Guard and garrisoned troops to reclaim the wasteland, reviving the economy of Dunhuang. But because of its remote location far from the frontier defenses, Dunhuang completely lost its strategic military importance.

丝路明珠：敦煌

Dunhuang: Pearl of the Silk Road

敦煌的名胜古迹

Places of Historic Interest and Scenic Beauty in Dunhuang

悠久的历史铸就了敦煌的辉煌，敦煌境内的名胜古迹甚多。敦煌不仅有莫高窟、榆林窟等闻名世界的艺术宝库，还有玉门关、阳关等著名的历史遗迹，而鸣沙山、月牙泉更是大自然赐予敦煌的杰作。正是敦煌拥有上述种种奇妙、独特的风景，才使得其具备了使各国游客流连忘返的魅力。

History produced the splendor of Dunhuang, which is endowed with many places of historic interest and scenic beauty, including world-renowned art treasure houses such as the Mogao Caves and the Yulin Caves, historic ruins such as the Yumen Pass and the Yangguan Pass, as well as natural scenery such as the Mingsha Mountain and the Crescent Moon Spring. It is these great varieties of wonderful and unique scenery that endow Dunhuang with its charm, attracting tourists from all over the world.

敦煌地区的佛教石窟

Buddhist Rock-Cut Architecture in Dunhuang

莫高窟

莫高窟，俗称千佛洞，位于敦煌市东南 25 公里的鸣沙山东麓崖壁上，主要分为南区和北区两大区域(图 58)。莫高窟石窟艺术是融合壁画、彩塑、建筑为一体的综合艺术。莫高窟上下分为 5 层，高低错落，南北长达 1600 米。现在保存有壁画和塑像的洞窟 492 个，壁画面积 45000 多平方米，彩塑 3000 余身，飞天 4000 余身，唐、宋木结构窟 5 座，莲花柱石和铺地花砖数千块。莫高窟是世界上现存规模最宏大、保存最完好的佛教艺术宝库，被誉为“东方艺术明珠”和“墙壁上的图书馆”。20 世纪初，在莫高窟又发现了藏经洞（图 59)。洞内藏有 4 至 10 世纪的文书和文物 5 万余件，引起了国内外学者极大的关

Mogao Caves

The Mogao Caves, also popularly known as the Thousand Buddha Caves, lie at the eastern cliff of the Mingsha Mountain, 25 kilometers southeast of present-day Dunhuang City. They are composed of the northern and southern sections of cave temples (Fig.58). The Mogao Caves are an elaborate form of artwork combining murals, painted sculptures, and architecture. From top to bottom, the caves are divided into five layers; they are 1,600 meters long from north to south. At present, there are murals and sculptures preserved in 492 caves, with over 45,000 square meters of murals, nearly 3,000 painted sculptures, and over 4,000 images of flying apsaras. There are five cave temples with wooden edifices constructed in the Tang and Song dynasties, and thousands of lotus-decorated pillars and patterned floor bricks. Crowned as the “Pearl of Asia” and the “Library on the Wall,” the Mogao Caves constitute the largest and best-preserved existing Buddhist artwork in the world. In the early 20th century, the Library Cave was discovered in the Mogao Caves (Fig.59). More than 50,000 documents, manuscripts, and cultural relics dating from the 4th to the 10th centuries were found in the cave, attracting enormous attention from scholars both in China

图 58 莫高窟南区外景

Fig.58 Panorama of Southern Section of the Mogao Caves

注，并最终形成了国际上著名的显学——敦煌学。敦煌是中国文化、印度文化、波斯文化、古希腊文化四大文化及佛教、道教、袄教、摩尼教、景教等宗教的汇合交流之地，而以莫高窟为代表的石窟艺术及以藏经洞敦煌文献为代表的敦煌文化正是中西方文化交流的结晶。1987 年，莫

and abroad and giving rise to a new discipline in the world: Dunhuang studies. Dunhuang was a place for fusion and exchange among cultures including China, India, Persia, and Hellenistic Greece, and among religions such as Buddhism, Taoism, Zoroastrianism, Manichaeism, and Nestorianism. Thus, the cave art represented by the Mogao Caves and Dunhuang culture revealed by the Dunhuang manuscripts preserved in the Library Cave are the fruits of many years of Sino-Western cultural exchange. In 1987, the Mogao Caves were inscribed on the list of

图 59　藏经洞的发现者——王圆箓

Fig.59　Wang Yuanlu, Discoverer of the Library Cave

高窟被联合国教科文组织列入“世界文化遗产名录”(图 60)。

UNESCO World Cultural Heritage Sites (Fig.60).

根据莫高窟现存唐代碑文的记载，莫高窟始建于前秦建元二年(366 年)。当时一位名叫乐僔的禅师游历到此，忽然看到三危山金光万道，仿佛有千万尊佛显身其间，遂发愿在这里开凿了第一个洞窟。此后，法良和尚效法乐僔在此开凿了第二个洞窟。在随后的短短 30 多年间，莫高窟先后建造了 70 多个洞窟，而且很多洞窟从窟形

According to extant Tang Dynasty records on the Mogao Caves, they were first built in the 2nd year of the Jianyuan Era of the Former Qin Dynasty (366). At that time, a monk named Lezun traveled there; he had a vision of golden lights diffused across the Sanwei Mountain, resembling thousands of Buddhas. Lezun thus vowed to build the first cave there. Later on, Monk Faliang dug the second one following the example of Lezun. During the next 30 years, over 70 caves were built, with many boasting majestic

图 60　著名的莫高窟九层楼(邵如林　摄)
Fig.60　Nine-Storey Tower, Mogao Caves (Photo by Shao Rulin)

到造像都规模宏大，气势雄伟。自此，洞窟开凿和寺院的兴建日盛，历经北魏、西魏、北周、隋、唐、五代、宋、元各代的新建和重修，开窟造像活动共延续了上千年的时间。对于莫高窟名称的由来，目前学术界主要有三种说法：其一，莫高窟修造在鸣沙山东麓的崖壁上，周围是大沙漠。古汉语中沙漠的"漠"与莫高窟的"莫"是可以通用的，所以在沙漠高处开凿的石窟便叫漠高窟，后来演变成为莫高窟。其二，在古代敦煌，鸣沙山又称为漠高山，山下有漠高乡。千佛洞在漠高山下，属漠高乡所管辖，莫高窟是由漠高山、漠高乡演变而来。其三，最早在党河谷开窟的是乐僔和尚，后来的弟子及信众相继也开凿了石窟。但后来者都自认道行"莫高于此僧"，难以超过他，所以将乐僔所开的石窟称作莫高窟，以纪念乐僔开创首窟之功(图 61)。

and magnificent architectural designs and Buddhist sculptures. After that, building cave temples continued and flourished. Through ongoing construction and renovation over several dynasties, continuing through the Northern Wei (386–534), the Western Wei (535–556), the Northern Zhou (557–581), the Sui Dynasty (581–618), the Tang Dynasty (618–907), the Five Dynasties (907–960), the Song Dynasty (960–1279) and the Yuan Dynasty (1206–1368), the construction of caves and the creation of Buddhist sculptures lasted more than a thousand years. In regard to the origin of the name "Mogao" there are three main theories on the part of researchers. First, the Mogao Caves are built at the eastern cliff of the Mingsha Mountain, surrounded by the desert. In ancient Chinese, the character "*mo*" could mean "desert," and "*gao*" means "being high," thus indicating that the Mogao Caves were built "at the high place in the desert." Second, in ancient Dunhuang, the Mingsha Mountain was also called the Mogao Mountain, at the foot of which there was a Mogao Village. The Thousand Buddha Caves were located at the foot of the Mogao Mountain and maintained by Mogao Village, thus leading to the name Mogao Caves. Third, "*mogao*" in Chinese also means "none wiser." Monk Lezun was the first man to cut a cave in the valley of the Danghe River, and later Buddhist disciples also cut caves one after another. But as the followers did not think themselves wiser than Lezun, the

图 61　党河

Fig.61　Danghe River

莫高窟石窟艺术主要分为壁画和彩塑两部分。敦煌壁画在造型手法上以中国传统的线描为基础，采用装饰性构图，工笔重彩的敷色手法，具有强烈的民族特色。在艺术风格上，北朝初期以西域样式为主，人物比例短粗，面相丰圆，以土红色为基本色调，粗犷厚重。自北魏后期开始，江南“秀骨清像”的佛画样式传到了敦煌，与敦煌原有的西域样式同时并存，

caves were called the Mogao Caves in honor of Monk Lezun (Fig.61).

The art within the cave temples is mainly comprised of murals and painted sculptures. Based on Chinese traditional line drawing, Dunhuang murals adopt artwork techniques with strong ethnic features such as decorative composition and fine brushwork color application. In regard to artistic style in the early Northern Dynasties, the figures of people are short and plump and the predominant pigment used is red clay, featuring bold and unconstrained patterns of the Western Regions. During the late Northern Wei Dynasty, the delicate patterns

并逐步开始融合。隋唐时期是敦煌壁画发展的最高峰。经过隋代几十年的统一融合，到初唐阶段，已完全形成了具有中华民族特色的壁画风格。人物比例适度，个性鲜明，形态生动，色彩丰富艳丽。壁画中的形象多采自现实，成为后世的典范。曹氏归义军时期，敦煌设立了画院，创造了规模巨大的洞窟和壁画，形成了统一的院体风格，但日趋僵化，已无唐代生动自然、丰富多彩的繁荣景象。西夏时期显宗、密宗内容同时进入壁画，艺术风格上以继承曹氏院体和唐代的吴道子画风为主，并在图案画中出现了装饰性较强的绿色风格。元代壁画不多，但同时存在着藏密和中原的白描淡彩两种风格，成就十分突出。明、清之后虽有不少增补，但水平低劣，已无艺术性可言。

莫高窟壁画主要分布在石窟前室诸壁、甬道、主

spread to Dunhuang from south of the Yangtze River, merging with the original patterns of the Western Regions, and gradually integrating with each other. The Sui and Tang dynasties marked the peak development of Dunhuang murals. Through decades of unification and integration in the Sui Dynasty, the mural style with Chinese features was completely formed during the Early Tang. The proportion of the figures was more balanced and their personalities were distinct, with vivid shapes and rich colors. The images of the murals were a reflection of the everyday mundane world and became a paradigm for later ages. During the period of the *Guiyijun* regime under Cao's rule, there established an art academy in Dunhuang and created massive cave temples and murals. The overall style was unified but gradually became rigid, losing vividness and richness evident during the Tang Dynasty. In the Western Xia (1038–1227), the contents of both Exoteric Buddhism and Esoteric Buddhism were present on the murals, despite the inheritage of the art style of the *Guiyijun* period and Wu Daozi (a famous art master) from the Tang Dynasty, with use of decorative green tints visible in the patterns. There were a few murals from the Yuan Dynasty, but the styles of Esoteric Buddhism and contour drawing of the Central Plains co-existed prominently on the murals. Although there were quite a few renovations of murals after the Ming and Qing dynasties, they were of little artistic value.

The murals in the Mogao Caves are mainly

室四壁、中心柱四面及窟顶的藻井和四披等部位。莫高窟壁画的题材大致可分为7大类:第一,佛像画。这是佛教壁画中最主要的组成部分,包括三世佛、七世佛、释迦牟尼、多宝佛、药师佛等。此外,还有文殊、普贤、观音、势至等菩萨;以及包括天王、龙王、夜叉、乾达婆、阿修罗、迦楼罗、紧那罗、摩呼罗迦等在内的天龙八部。第二,中国传统神话题材。自北魏晚期开始,在敦煌壁画中出现了东王公、西王母、方位四神、雷公、电母、风伯、雨师以及伏羲、女娲、天人等具有道家思想的神话题材。其中,以莫高窟第249窟最为典型。第249窟顶部,除中心画莲花藻井外,东西两面画阿修罗与摩尼宝珠,南北两面画东王公、西王母驾龙车、凤车出行。车上华盖高悬,车后旌旗飘

located on the antechamber walls, corridors, four walls of the main chamber, four sides of the central pillar, ceilings and slopes. They can be classified into seven categories or types. The first is paintings of the Buddha, the key component of Buddhist paintings. They include the Buddhas of the Three Ages, Buddhas of the Seven Ages, the Sakyamuni Buddha, the Prabhutaratna Buddha, and Bhaisajyaguru, known as the Medicine Buddha. In addition, there are the Bodhisattvas Manjusri, Samantabhadra, Avalokitesvara, Mahasthamaprapta, and so on. Moreover, there are the Eight Classes of Supernatural Beings (*Tianlong Babu* in Chinese): deva, naga, yaksha, gandharva, asura, garuda, kinnara and mahoraga.

The second type is paintings on themes of Chinese traditional mythology. Since the late Northern Wei, there appeared myths with Taoist ideas such as King Father of the East, Queen Mother of the West, gods of Four Directions, the Thunder god, the Lightning goddess, the Wind god, the Rain god, and Fuxi, Nüwa, and Deva as well in caves, of which Cave 249 is the most typical. On the ceiling of Cave 249, apart from the lotus caisson ceiling at the center, there are Asuras in the east, Mani jewels in the west, King Father of the East driving a dragon chariot in the south, and Queen Mother of the West driving a phoenix chariot in the north, both with the canopy and flag flying. In front of the chariots, there are alchemists holding banners and flags, clearing a path for them; behind them, there are dragons with human heads accompanying them. The Vermilion Bird of the south, Black Tortoise of the north, Azure

扬，前有持节扬幡的方士开路，后有人首龙身的神兽随行，朱雀、玄武、青龙、白虎分布各壁（图 62）。道教题材出现在佛教的洞窟内，体现了佛教与中国传统文化的交流和融合。第三，佛经故事画。佛经故事画中既包括主要宣扬释迦牟尼生平事迹的佛传故事画，也包含描绘释迦牟尼生前各种

Dragon of the east and White Tiger of the west are scattered around the walls (Fig.62). The inclusion of Taoist themes in Buddhist caves reflects the cultural exchange and integration of Buddhism and Chinese traditional culture.

The third category of paintings is about Buddhist texts and literature.

图 62　莫高窟第 249 窟　窟顶西披　西魏

Fig.62　Western Slope of Ceiling, Mogao Cave 249　Western Wei

善行，宣扬“因果报应”“苦修行善”的本生故事画。此外,还包括佛门弟子、善男信女和释迦牟尼度化众生的因缘故事画,以及根据佛教圣迹、感应故事、高僧事迹、瑞像图等画成的佛教史迹故事画等。佛传故事中有许多是古印度的神话故事和民间传说，佛教徒经过加工修饰，附会在释迦牟尼身上。在莫高窟中，描写释迦牟尼非凡来历的“乘象入胎”和释迦牟尼离家出走,以修炼正果的“夜半逾城”的佛传故事场面比较流行(图 63)。本生故事在莫高窟早期洞窟的壁画中最为流行,主要有“太子舍身饲虎”“尸毗王割肉救鸽”“九色鹿本生”等。因缘故事主要包括“五百强盗成佛”“沙弥守戒自杀”“善友太

They include the paintings of the Buddha's life, which illustrates events in the life of the Sakyamuni Buddha, as well as paintings of the jataka tales, which depict the deeds of the Buddha in his past life, and serve as moral tales of virtue, selflessness, and generosity. Additionally, there are karma story paintings, known as avadana stories, which are about redemption and salvation, as well as paintings of Buddhist legends and transmission, which illustrate Buddhist history, supernatural scenes, records of eminent monks and so on. Many of the tales of the Buddha's life are from Indian mythology or folk legends, which became embellished by later Buddhist disciples after the historical Sakyamuni's death. In the Mogao Caves, the prevalent paintings of the Buddha's life include “Queen Maya's Dream” and the “The Great Renunciation” (Fig.63). Paintings of the jataka tales are the most popular theme of the early cave murals, mainly including the “Prince Sattva Sacrificing Himself to Tigers,” “King Sibi Cutting his Flesh to Save the Dove” and the “Jataka of the Nine-Colored Deer.” Karma stories mainly consist of the “Five Hundred Bandits,” the “Monk Committing Suicide for Buddist Precepts” and “Prince Friendliness Diving into the Sea to Find Treasure” and so on. The paintings of Buddhist legends and transmission are mainly composed of “Envoy Zhang Qian's Mission to the West Regions,” “Buddha's Footprint in Bactria,” “The Miraculous Tales of Fotudeng,” “Master Tan Yan Being Invited by Emperor Wen of the Sui Dynasty to Pray for Rain” and a variety of other auspiciously supernatural scenes. These kinds of paintings are mostly drawn on secondary architectural

图 63　莫高窟第 329 窟　乘象入胎　中唐

Fig.63　Queen Maya's Dream, Mogao Cave 329　Mid-Tang

子入海取宝"等。佛教史迹画主要有"张骞出使西域""大夏佛迹""佛图澄神异""隋文帝迎昙延祈雨"以及各种瑞像图。这类画多绘于洞窟龛内四披、甬道顶部和角落等次要位置，但有的也绘于正面墙壁。第四，经变画。利用绘画等艺术形式通俗易懂地表现深奥的佛教经典称之为"经变"，又称之为"变相"。这类题材始兴于隋，盛于唐、五代，在宋朝时还继续流行。常见的经变有《法华变》《维摩变》

positions such as the four slopes inside the cave niches, the ceilings of corridors leading to the main hall, and on corners, but some of them are painted on the front walls.

The fourth category is sutra illustration paintings, which are created for illustrating and expounding Buddhist sutras in an intelligible way by means of painting and other art forms. They are known as *jingbian* or *bianxiang* (sutra illustration or sutra transformations) in Chinese. This genre began in the Sui Dynasty, prospered in the Tang Dynasty and the Five Dynasties and still prevailed into the Song Dynasty. The

《药师变》《弥勒变》《阿弥陀变》《劳度叉斗圣变》等(图64)。第五,装饰图案。装饰图案用以丰富洞窟的建筑格式、壁画布局及装饰人物、器物,使整个洞窟和壁画达到令人震撼的艺术效果。装饰图案常画在窟内藻井、龛楣、柱头及画中的华盖、地毯、衣饰、家具器物等部位。主要有植物纹、动物纹、天象纹、几何纹等纹样。第六,山水画。莫高窟壁画中的山水画遍布石窟,内容丰富,在表现形式上也多种多样。第七,供养人画像。供养人就是信仰佛教、出资修建石窟的人。他们为了表示虔诚信佛、留名后世,在开窟造像时,在窟内画上自己和亲眷的肖像,所以供养人画像属于功德肖像画。供养人画像一般画在窟内四壁下部接近地面的地方。早期的供养人画像一般比较小,到晚唐和五代以后逐渐加大,甚至超过真人的大小,并出现了群像和车马出行行列。重要作品有《张议潮

most commonly seen sutra illustrations include the *Lotus Sutra*, the *Vimalakirti Sutra*, the *Bhaisajyaguru Sutra*, the *Maitreya Triple Sutra*, the *Amitabha Sutra*, and the *Illustration of Raudraksa's Battle with Sariputra* (Fig.64).

The fifth category is decorative patterns. Such patterns are used to enrich the architectural styles of the caves and the layout of the murals and to decorate figures and utensils, so that all the caves and murals can achieve a splendid artistic effect. The decorative patterns are usually drawn on caisson ceilings inside the caves, or on niche lintels, both ends of pillars and some parts of the paintings such as the canopies, carpets, clothing, furniture, and vessels depicted in murals. They are floral, animalistic, celestial and geometrical patterns.

The sixth type is landscape paintings. They can be found throughout the murals of the Mogao Caves, which are rich in content and forms of expression.

The seventh type is donor paintings. Donors, also known as sponsors or patrons, refer to pious lay Buddhists who provide financial support for the construction of caves. In order to show their piety to Buddhism and to leave their names behind, when building the caves or constructing the statues, they had their own as well as family members' portraits painted inside the caves. These paintings were considered portraits of merit, lying close to the ground on the four walls inside the caves. The early portraits are comparatively small. After the Late

夫妇出行图》《曹议金夫妇出行图》《于阗国王及皇后供养像》等。

从莫高窟的壁画中，我们可以看到各民族各阶层的社会活动，如帝王出行、农耕渔猎、冶铁酿酒、婚丧嫁娶、商旅往来，使敦煌艺术显得丰富多彩。莫高窟壁画中所描绘的当时的社会生活场景，反映了我国古代狩猎、耕作、纺织、交通、战争以及音乐、舞蹈等生产活动和社会活动各个方面的内容（图65）。壁画中各类人物形象，保留了大量的历代各族人民的衣冠服饰资料。壁画中绘有大量的亭台、楼阁、寺塔、宫殿、城池、桥梁都是研究我国古代建筑图样的宝贵资料。在莫高窟各个时代的壁画中，不仅反映了当时生产劳动场面、社会生活场景，也记录了中外文化交流的历史事实，为研究中国古代社会提供了宝贵资料。莫高窟的壁画具有很高的艺术价

Tang and the Five Dynasties, they gradually became larger, even larger than a real person. What is more, there appeared images of groups of people, vehicles, and horses. Major works include "Procession of Zhang Yichao and His Wife," "Procession of Cao Yijin and His Wife," "Donor Painting of the Khotan King and Queen" and so on.

The murals in the Mogao Caves reflect social activities of various ethnic groups and social classes, for instance, the emperor traveling, peasants farming and fishing, iron-making and wine-brewing, weddings, funerals, and trading, all of which enrich Dunhuang art. The scenes of social life at the time depicted in the murals illustrate production and social activities in ancient China, including hunting, farming, spinning, transportation, battles, music, and dance (Fig.65). A variety of figures in the murals displays profuse costumes of ethnic groups in every dynasty. The pavilions, towers, temples, palaces, fortresses, and bridges depicted in the murals are all invaluable materials for research into the ancient architecture of China. The murals in every dynasty not only reflect the scenes of production and social life at the time, but also record historical events of Sino-Western cultural exchange, thus providing precious materials for research into Chinese history. The murals of the Mogao Caves possess a high artistic value, with those in the High Tang exhibiting the highest standards (Fig.66). Currently, the quintessential

图 64　莫高窟第 9 窟南壁　劳度叉斗圣变　晚唐

Fig.64　Illustration of Raudraksa's Battle with Sariputra, South Wall of Mogao Cave 9　Late Tang

图 65 莫高窟第 249 窟 狩猎图 西魏

Fig.65 Painting of Hunting Scene, Mogao Cave 249 Western Wei

值，其中以盛唐时期的壁画水平最高(图 66)。供游客参观的洞窟较有影响的有第 17、96、130、158、259 等窟(图 67)。

雕塑是莫高窟艺术的重要内容之一。莫高窟现存彩塑 3000 多身，其中圆雕 2000 多身，浮塑 1000 余身。其中基本完好的原作有 1400 余身，其余部分

caves open for tourists are Caves 17, 96, 130, 158 and 259 (Fig.67).

Sculptures figure prominently in Mogao cave art. There are over 3,000 extant painted sculptures, among which there are more than 2,000 three-dimensional sculptures and over 1,000 relief sculptures. More than 1,400 of them are original works and basically intact, and most of others have gone through repainting and reworking in later dynasties. The large number of ancient painted sculptures preserved in the Mogao Caves, their long history, and extraordinary

图 66　莫高窟第 23 窟
未生怨　盛唐
Fig.66　Enemy While Still Unborn, Mogao Cave 23
High Tang

图 67　莫高窟第 96 窟　北大像　初唐
Fig.67　The Northern Great Buddha Statue, Mogao Cave 96　Early Tang

大多经过后代上彩或重塑。像莫高窟这样保存古代彩塑之多、历史之长、技艺之精,在世界上都是罕见的。由于莫高窟开凿在沙砾岩上,不适合雕刻,所以除了南大像、北大像为石胎泥塑外,其他的绝大多数为木架结构。塑匠首先在自然长成的与佛像姿态接近的树枝或人工制成的木架上绑上苇草,在草上敷抹粗泥,然后再敷细泥,压紧抹光塑像成形后,再上白粉,最后进行彩绘,所以被称为彩塑。

敦煌彩塑上起十六国,经北魏、北周、隋、唐、五代、宋、西夏、元,甚至延续到清代,历时1000多年。莫高窟的彩塑主要分为三个时期:早期为北凉、北魏、西魏、北周四朝,彩塑古朴、浑厚、粗犷、庄重,注重人物面部的传神,体现了北方民族的气质特征;中期包括隋唐两代,风格由清瘦秀

workmanship make them rare not only in China but also all over the world. As the soft rock conglomerate of the Mogao Caves is not suitable for fine carving, the sculptures in the caves are mostly created on wood or straw frames, except for the Northern and Southern Great Buddha statues built around stone frames inside. First of all, a wooden frame was made according to the planned size and posture of a Buddha, and then padded over with reeds or straw. Next, it was molded with coarse clay, and refined with fine clay. After the statue took shape, a white base coat was applied. Finally, the statue was finished with pigment painting, thus being called painted sculptures.

Dunhuang painted sculptures first began to appear in the period of the Sixteen Kingdoms, then went through the vicissitudes of the Northern Wei, the Northern Zhou, the Sui Dynasty, the Tang Dynasty, the Five Dynasties, the Song Dynasty, the Western Xia, the Yuan Dynasty, even up until the Qing Dynasty, lasting for a total of over a thousand years. The development of the painted sculptures in the Mogao Caves mainly went through three stages. The early stage included the Northern Liang during the period of the Sixteen Kingdoms, the Northern Wei, the Western Wei and the Northern Zhou dynasties, during which the painted sculptures were simple and primitive. Their styles are bold, unconstrained, and solemn, with a focus on the facial expressions, embodying a northern ethnic flair. The middle stage consisted of the Sui and Tang dynasties. The styles changed from slender figures to plump, elegant ones. They are

丽、潇洒质朴变为丰肌秀骨、精致细腻、绚丽多彩、雍容华贵，体现了唐代社会繁荣昌盛(图 68)；晚期包括五代、北宋、西夏、元 4 个朝代。这个时期人物清淡单调、缺乏活力与生气，标志着敦煌彩塑艺术由唐代全盛逐步走向衰败。

莫高窟现已编号的 492 个洞窟绝大多数集中在南区，而在长约 800 米的北区崖面上，除一个洞窟已编号外，尚有数百个洞窟未予编号。这些不曾编号的洞窟多无壁画和塑像。对于他们的用途，人们最初并不明了(图 69)。为了解开北区洞窟之谜，敦煌研究院的专家从 1989 年起先后多次对北区洞窟进行清理发掘，发现了遗骨、棺木、炕灶、粮仓、塑像等大批遗迹和遗物。出土的重要文物有波斯及西夏的钱币，此外还有汉文、藏

colorful, rich, and magnificent, in which the thriving and prosperous society of the Tang Dynasty are demonstrated (Fig.68). The last stage was from the Five Dynasties to the Yuan Dynasty. In this period, the figures are dull and monotonous, lacking energy and vitality, which symbolizes the decline of Dunhuang painted sculptures from its peak during the Tang Dynasty.

Presently, 492 caves at Mogao have been identified and numbered, most of which lie scattered in the southern section of the cliff. By contrast, on the 800-meter-long cliff face of the northern section, hundreds of caves have not been assigned a number, with the exception of one cave; a majority of these caves are empty and have no murals or sculptures inside. Originally, people were unclear as to the purposes of these unnumbered caves (Fig.69). In order to unveil the mystery of these caves, experts from the Dunhuang Academy have explored the northern section many times since 1989. They have found large numbers of historical artifacts, including osseous remains, coffins, *kang*[1] bed-stoves, granaries, and sculptures. The important cultural relics unearthed include Persian and Tanguts coins, as well as existing scriptures written in Chinese, Tibetan, Tangut, Uyghur, and Mongolian languages, preserved pages of Tangut

① *Kang* is a type of heated, earthen bed used in northern part of China. It is usually made of bricks or other forms of fired clay.

图 68　莫高窟第 45 窟　弟子、菩萨、天王　盛唐

Fig.68　Disciple, Bodhisattva, and Heavenly King, Mogao Cave 45　High Tang

图 69　莫高窟北区外景

Fig.69　Panorama of Northern Section of the Mogao Caves

文、西夏文、回鹘文、蒙古文的写经残页以及西夏文字字典残页，还有木器、陶器、铜器、丝麻织物、木制彩绘俑等。根据已发现的实物资料，学者初步断定，北区是由瘗窟、僧房窟、禅窟、礼佛窟、仓库窟等性质的洞窟组成，也就是僧人、画匠起居生活、坐禅、礼佛、存储粮物、埋葬遗骨的场所，是莫高窟石窟群中不可分割的重要组成部分。

dictionaries, woodenware, earthenware, copperware, silk and linen fabrics, and painted wooden figurines. Based on these unearthed relics, scholars have made a preliminary conclusion that the northern section consists of burial caves, residential caves, meditation caves, worship caves and warehouse caves. That is, this section of caves is where the monks and artisans lived, meditated, worshiped the Buddha, stored grain, and buried their bodies, which are an indispensable part of the Mogao Caves.

在现代敦煌学术研究中，与敦煌石窟艺术研究相并列的是敦煌文献研究。敦煌文献出土自著名的敦煌藏经洞，即莫高窟第 17 窟，原为晚唐敦煌高僧洪䛒的影窟（图 70）。1900 年，藏经洞无意中被住在莫高窟的道士王圆箓发现。藏经洞保存的文物有佛教经卷、社会文书、刺绣、绢画等 5 万余件，其中多数是手写本，此外还有少量雕版印

In Dunhuang studies, Dunhuang document research coincides with Dunhuang cave art research. The documents were discovered in the famous Library Cave, Mogao Cave 17, which was originally a memorial cave commemorating the monk Hongbian in the late Tang period (Fig.70). In 1900, a Taoist priest named Wang Yuanlu living in the Mogao Caves accidentally discovered the Library Cave, in which

图 70　莫高窟第 17 窟　洪䛒像　晚唐

Fig.70　Statue of Hongbian, Mogao Cave 17　Late Tang

刷品和拓本(图71)。从时间上看,敦煌文书上起三国两晋,下迄北宋,历时1000余年。除绝大部分为汉文外,尚有吐蕃、回鹘、粟特、于阗、希伯来等10余种文字,其内容包括政治、经济、军事、历史、宗教、哲学、天文历法、地理、民族、文学、医学、艺术等许多方面(图72)。这些文献包罗万象,博大精

there were over 50,000 cultural relics such as Buddhist scriptures, secular documents, embroideries, and silk paintings. A majority of them were hand-written manuscripts, and there were also a few printed copies of books made from engraved plates or woodblocks as well as copies of rubbings (Fig.71). Chronologically, Dunhuang manuscripts range from the Three Kingdoms and the Jin Dynasty to the Northern Song Dynasty, spanning a thousand years. In addition to Chinese used in the majority of manuscripts, there are over ten other languages used such as the Tibetan, Uyghur, Sogdian, Khotanese, and Hebrew. The content covers politics, economics, military affairs,

图71 藏经洞出土的部分敦煌文书

Fig.71 Dunhuang Manuscripts Discovered in the Library Cave

深，被誉为“中古时代的百科全书”“古代学术的海洋”。藏经洞的发现，也使得敦煌一举名扬世界。

藏经洞发现后不久，英、法、日、俄等国的“探险家”接踵而至，以各种手段掠走藏经洞文物。1907 年，英国人斯坦因掠走写本文书 24 箱

history, religion, philosophy, astronomy, calendars, geography, ethnic groups, literature, medicine, and art (Fig.72). The manuscripts are wide-ranging, profound, and lauded as the "Encyclopedia of Medieval China," and the "Reservoir of Knowledge in Ancient Times." The discovery of the Library Cave catapulted Dunhuang to worldwide fame in the academic world.

Soon after the discovery of the Library

图 72　莫高窟藏经洞出土的观音及地藏菩萨画像

Fig.72　Painted Images of Avalokitesvara Bodhisattva and Ksitigarbha Bodhisattva Discovered in the Library Cave

和绘、绣佛画5箱（图73）。1908年，法国人伯希和骗取写本文书精品约5000件（图74）。1909年，中国学者从伯希和的口中得到敦煌发现大量古代文书的消息。在罗振玉等人的奔走呼吁下，清政府的学部命令陕甘都督毛实君即刻封存藏经洞内剩余的古物，严禁外国人购买（图75）。学部还拨专款，交给敦煌地方政府以尽量收集

Cave, explorers from Britain, France, Japan, and Russia came to compete for the relics and manuscripts, removing them by every means possible. In 1907, Aurel Stein from Britain took away 24 crates of Dunhuang manuscripts and 5 crates of painted or embroidered Buddha images (Fig.73). In 1908, Paul Pelliot of France took away approximately 5,000 pieces of exquisite manuscripts (Fig.74). In 1909, Chinese scholars elicited information from Pelliot that a large quantity of ancient documents had been discovered in Dunhuang. With appeals from scholars such as Luo Zhenyu, the Ministry of Education of the Qing government ordered Mao Shijun, the Commissioner-in-Chief of Shaanxi

图73　斯坦因　英籍匈牙利人

Fig.73　Hungarian-born British Explorer Aurel Stein

图74　伯希和在藏经洞内挑选精品

Fig.74　Paul Pelliot Selecting Dunhuang Manuscripts

图 75 罗振玉与王国维
Fig.75 Luo Zhenyu and Wang Guowei

失散的经卷文物。此后，由新疆巡抚何彦升负责，把封存在藏经洞内的文献全部解送到北京。前往押运的清朝官吏很不用心，并没有把藏经洞文献收拾干净，而且沿途又遗失了不少。而当押运敦煌文书的车队到达北京后，何彦升并没有马上移交学部，而是由亲家李盛铎以及刘廷琛、方尔谦等人将所有敦煌文书翻检一编，将最为精美的部分窃取据为己

and Gansu, to immediately seal up the caves and store the remaining antiques for safe-keeping, banning any further trade with foreigners (Fig.75). The Ministry of Education of the Qing Dynasty also appropriated special funds to the local government of Dunhuang to recover as many lost manuscripts and cultural relics as possible. Later on, under the management of He Yansheng, the Provincial Governor of Xinjiang, all the manuscripts stored in the Library Cave were sent under armed guard to Beijing. However, the officials involved in the

有之后，才将剩余部分交给学部，入藏京师图书馆，总共8000多件。为了不被人发现缺了件数，李盛铎等人竟将较长的卷子截成两段或多段以充数。而在官府前往押运之前，王圆箓早就做过手脚，把许多珍贵的写本都盗取出来。后来，英国人斯坦因再一次从王道士手里获得大量文书。还有一部分在1911年被日本大谷探险队的吉川小一郎和橘瑞超买走，总数约有600多件。

1914年到1915年，俄国人鄂登堡率领的考察队在敦煌进行测绘时，收获更是惊人，一次就弄走敦煌文书3000件以上(图76)。直到1919年，甘肃政府对此有所耳闻，命令敦煌当局查找流失的敦煌遗书时，再次把藏经洞打开，里边居然还埋藏着94捆。1924年，美国人华尔纳也到敦煌淘金(图77)。由于王圆箓手中已经没有可供出卖的敦煌文书，所以华尔纳将目光投

escort were negligent so that they failed to secure all the manuscripts and a number of them went missing along the way. When the wagon train escorting the Dunhuang manuscripts arrived in Beijing, He Yansheng did not hand them over to the Ministry of Education immediately, but delegated his relative Li Shengduo, and friends Liu Tingchen and Fang Erqian to search through all the manuscripts, secretly seizing the most exquisite parts for himself, and then handed in the rest to the Ministry of Education. This left a total of over 8,000 pieces that went to the National Library. In order not to be discovered, Li Shengduo split up some of the relatively longer manuscripts into two or more pieces to make up the original quantity. Actually, before the government's actions, Wang Yuanlu had already stolen many priceless manuscripts from the caves. Later on, Aurel Stein once again obtained a large number of manuscripts from Wang. There was yet another cache numbering more than 600 pieces purchased by Yoshikawa Koichirō and Tachibana Zuichō from the Japanese Otani expedition in 1911.

From 1914 to 1915, during an expedition led by Sergei Olderberg from Russia to survey the Mogao Caves, the loss was even more astonishing. The expedition team took away more than 3,000 Dunhuang manuscripts in one haul (Fig.76). It was not until 1919 that the Gansu government ordered the local government in Dunhuang to seek the lost Dunhuang

图 76 鄂登堡考察队在我国境内考察途中

Fig.76 Sergei Olderberg and Staff in Expedition in China

图 77 华尔纳

Fig.77 American Explorer LangdonWarner

向了洞窟。他用金钱买通王圆箓后,从莫高窟盗走精美的唐代菩萨塑像两身。而更为恶劣的是,华尔纳用特制的化学胶液,从莫高窟粘揭盗走壁画 26 块,给莫高窟造成了无法弥补的损害(图 78)。

从 20 世纪 40 年代初开始,中国学者历尽艰辛,纷纷奔赴敦煌进行考察,对敦煌的古

manuscripts after hearing this news. When opening the Library Cave again, they found 94 bundles of manuscripts still being stored. In 1924, Langdon Warner from the USA also came to Dunhuang to hunt for artifacts (Fig.77). Since Wang Yuanlu had no Dunhuang manuscripts available for sale in hand, Warner turned his attention to the caves. He bribed Wang Yuanlu and stole two exquisite Buddhist sculptures of the Tang Dynasty. To make matters worse, he used a special chemical glue to tear off 26 pieces of murals from the caves, which caused irreparable damage to the Mogao Caves (Fig.78).

From the early 1940s on, Chinese scholars have gone through untold hardships to go to Dunhuang for field investigations, and to collect and collate

图 78 华尔纳粘窃莫高窟第 323 窟壁画的残痕

Fig.78 Defaced Mural Sections after Removal by Langdon Warner, Mogao Cave 323

遗址、遗物和石窟进行了实地调查和资料搜集、整理，对其历史、文物及其价值做了大量细致的研究。尤其是对敦煌壁画的临摹与保护，在这一时期得到了加强。1937年，李丁陇万里跋涉，赴莫高窟临摹壁画（图79）。接着，吴作人、关山月、王子云、张大千等也都先后到莫高窟临摹壁画，并撰文介绍敦煌艺术（图80）。这些成果，进一步向世人展示了敦煌文化无与伦比的历史价值和艺术魅力。张大千等人的作品，引起了国

materials from sites, ruins, and caves. Huge amounts of careful research have been done on its history, cultural relics, and the value. In particular, the copying and protection of Dunhuang murals were strengthened during this period. In 1937, Li Dinglong traveled from afar to the Mogao Caves to make painted copies of the murals (Fig.79), followed by Wu Zuoren, Guan Shanyue, Wang Ziyun, and Zhang Daqian, one after another. They also wrote many articles about Dunhuang art (Fig.80). These achievements further demonstrate to the world the incomparable historic value and artistic charm of Dunhuang culture. The works of Zhang Daqian and others have

图79　第一个临摹敦煌壁画的美术家李丁陇
Fig.79　Li Dinglong, First Painter to Make Facsimiles of Mogao Murals

图 80　1943 年，张大千、谢稚柳、向达等在榆林窟考察

Fig.80　Zhang Daqian, Xie Zhiliu, Xiang Da and Others Surveying the Yulin Caves in 1943

内外的广泛重视。在于右任等有识之士的大声疾呼之下，1943 年 3 月，当时的国民政府教育部委派高一涵、常书鸿为正、副主任，负责筹建敦煌艺术研究所。1944 年 2 月研究所正式成立，结束了莫高窟长期无专门人员进行保护的历史。莫高窟真正得到重视和切实保护，是1949 年中华人民共和国成立之后。1950 年，中央政府接管莫高窟，将敦煌艺术研究所改组为敦煌文物研究所，直隶中央文化部文物

attracted extensive attention from both home and abroad. In March of 1943, with the strong appeal of forward-thinking people such as Yu Youren, the Ministry of Education of the Nationalist government at the time assigned Gao Yihan and Chang Shuhong as the director and assistant director in charge of establishing the Dunhuang Art Institute. The institute was established in February of 1944, ending the period of the Mogao Caves without protection and management by specialized personnel. It was after the People's Republic of China was founded in 1949 that close attention and practical protection were attached to the Mogao Caves. In 1950, the central government took over the Mogao Caves and restructured the Dunhuang Art Institute as the Dunhuang Cultural Relics Research Institute, directly subordinating it to

局，并拨专款于20世纪50年代至60年代对莫高窟的崖体与崖面进行了加固维修。1984年，敦煌文物研究所扩大为敦煌研究院。先后在常书鸿、段文杰、樊锦诗等学者的带领下，敦煌研究院专家在敦煌石窟艺术的学术研究方面取得了令世人瞩目的成就。

在敦煌石窟艺术和敦煌文书的研究领域中，还存在不少的未解之谜。但其中最为人所关注的，莫过于敦煌藏经洞封闭之谜（图81）。晚唐敦煌高僧洪䛒的影窟为什么变成了藏经洞，它是何时封闭的？其原因何在？这不能不引起人们的极大兴趣。由于没有发现详确的文字记载，这一问题就成了一桩历史悬案。中外学者根据各种材料，提出种种假说，试图解开这一千古之

the State Administration for Protection of Cultural Relics under administration of the Ministry of Culture. Moreover, the central government appropriated a special fund to fortify and repair the cliff and cliff face of the Mogao Caves from the 1950s to the 1960s. In 1984, the Dunhuang Cultural Relics Research Institute was expanded into the Dunhuang Academy. Under the successive leadership of Chang Shuhong, Duan Wenjie, and Fan Jinshi, the experts of the Dunhuang Academy made outstanding achievements in the academic research of Dunhuang cave art.

There are still many lingering mysteries in the study of Dunhuang cave art and Dunhuang manuscripts. The one that attracts most of the attention is the closing of the Library Cave (Fig.81). Why did the memorial cave for the monk Hongbian become the Library Cave? When and why was it sealed up? These questions arouse great interest. Since no detailed and valid records have been found, these questions remain unsettled. According to a variety of materials, scholars from both China and other countries have proposed many hypotheses, trying to unveil this deep historical mystery. In regard to the cause and time of the closing of the Library Cave, there are three prevailing theories. The first one is the idea of "taking refuge," which can further be separated into two versions, namely taking refuge from the Western Xia and from the Kara-Khanid Khanate (840-1212). The Western Xia was a regime established by the Tanguts in the early Northern Song Dynasty. In 1036, the Tanguts occupied Dunhuang and the entire Hexi Corridor,

图 81　藏经洞入口

Fig.81　Entrance of the Library Cave

谜。关于藏经洞的封闭原因和时间，目前主要有三种观点:第一,“避难说”。避难说又主要分为避西夏和黑韩王朝两种说法。西夏是我国西北的党项族于北宋初年建立的政权,1036 年西夏占领了敦煌以及整个河西走廊,并统治该地区达 100 多年的时间。藏经洞中出土卷本所题年号，最晚为北宋咸平五年(1002 年)，且藏经洞没有发现西夏文的记载。所以有学者认为，藏经洞的封闭与西夏进攻河西有关，时间在西夏占领敦煌及整个河西之前。莫高窟僧人为保护经卷,故将大批的写经和文物封藏于洞中，并在洞壁外加以装饰。另外,还有学者认为藏经洞的封闭是为了防范黑韩王朝。黑韩亦称大食,为唐宋时期崛起于中亚东部的阿拉伯国家,信仰伊斯兰教。北宋初年,黑韩势力向东扩张,1006 年攻灭于阗，并继续向东进军。因为于阗和敦煌有姻亲关系,当于阗陷没以后,于阗人将黑韩王朝灭佛的消息带

ruling the area for more than 100 years. The last title of the emperor's reign mentioned in the manuscripts from the Library Cave is the 5th year of the Xianping Era in the Northern Song Dynasty (1002), and no manuscripts are in the Tangut language. Thus, some scholars propose that the closing of the Library Cave should be related to an attack from the Western Xia at the Hexi Corridor, which took place before the Tanguts occupied the entire Hexi Corridor. In order to protect the sutras, the monks of the Mogao Caves sealed a large amount of written sutras and cultural relics in the cave, hiding the door by camouflaging it. In addition, some other scholars maintain the closing of the Library Cave was to defend it from the Kara-Khanid Khanate. Kara-Khanid, also called *Dashi* in Chinese, was an Arabian country in the east of Central Asia in the Tang and Song dynasties, which followed Islamism. In the early Northern Song Dynasty, the Kara-Khanid expanded eastward. In 1006, they defeated Khotan and continued their march eastward. Because the Khotanese and the people of Dunhuang were related by marriage, after the fall of Khotan, the Khotanese people brought the news that the Kara-Khanid would destroy Buddhism in Dunhuang. To defend themselves from attack by the Kara-Khanid, and to prevent them from destroying Buddhist cultural relics, the civilians and the soldiers in Dunhuang sealed up the Buddhist sutras and manuscripts and

来敦煌。敦煌的军民为防备以伊斯兰教为国教的黑韩王朝进攻、摧毁佛教文物，故而将其封藏起来。第二，废弃供养说。从佛教本身的理论来讲，佛经是十分神圣的，当其破旧后，不能随意销毁，只能把它供奉起来。从藏经洞中发现的佛经、绢画的形态看，多有损毁。所以，这些物品应该是从敦煌各寺院中搜集来，藏经洞就是堆放它们的处所，时间应在 11 世纪初。第三，末法思想说。在佛教发展历史上，通常将佛教分为正法、像法、末法三个时期。按照佛经的记载，末法时期不仅会出现“水旱不调，五谷不熟，疫气流行，死亡者众”等种种可怕现象，更为严重的是佛法将会灭绝。而按照佛教典籍的推算，1052 年将进入末法时期。为了保护佛法得以永存，所以敦煌当地的僧人将大量佛经封闭在藏经洞，时间应该在 1002 年至 1052 年之间。

finally closed the cave.

The second theory involves preserving obsolete texts. According to Buddhist dogma, sutras and Buddhist scriptures are sacred. After their deterioration, followers should not destroy them casually but maintain and enshrine them. The Buddhist sutras and silk paintings in the Library Cave are mostly old and worn from appearance; they must have been obtained from local temples in Dunhuang, and the Library Cave was a place for their storage. This is estimated to occur in the early 11th century.

The third is the theory of the Age of Dharma Decline. According to Buddhist cosmology, Buddhism usually goes through three ages, namely the Age of the Right Dharma, the Age of Semblance Dharma, and the Age of Dharma Decline. Based on Buddhist scriptures, in the Age of Dharma Decline, there would appear not only destructive phenomena such as “flood and drought, unripened grain, widespread epidemics, and multitudes of deaths,” but also much worse, the decline of the Dharma, and hence the end of Buddhism. Judging from Buddhist documents, the year of 1052 would be the beginning of the Age of Dharma Decline. Thus, local monks in Dunhuang sealed up large amounts of Buddhist scriptures in the Library Cave in order to protect and perpetuate Buddhism. It is estimated that this took place between 1002 and 1052.

榆林窟

榆林窟,亦名万佛峡,位于瓜州县城西南约 70 公里处, 距敦煌市大约 135 公里。榆林窟开凿于榆林河峡谷之中。榆林河又名踏实河, 属疏勒河水系, 源于祁连山的西端野马山和大雪山, 为疏勒河的重要支流。由于受河水的冲刷, 许多地段河床下切很深而形成峡谷, 两岸形成悬崖峭壁, 榆林窟就开凿于万佛峡两岸的崖壁上(图 82)。榆林窟创建于初唐,经中唐、晚唐、五代、宋、西夏、元及清代续建。

榆林窟分为东崖和西崖两个部分,现存洞窟 41 个。其中东崖又分为上下两层。上层有洞窟 19 个,下层有洞窟 11 个。西崖洞窟仅有 1 层,共有洞窟 11 个。从现存的题记和壁画风格来看, 榆林窟中有唐代开凿的洞窟 3 个, 五代时期的 8 个, 宋代的 13 个,西夏时期的 4 个,元代 4 个,清代 9 个(图 83)。由

Yulin Caves

The Yulin Caves, also known as the Ten Thousand Buddha Gorge, is situated approximately 70 kilometers southwest of Guazhou County, and 135 kilometers away from Dunhuang City. The Yulin Caves were constructed in a gorge of the Yulin River, which was also historically known as the Tashi River. As an important tributary of the Shule River, the Yulin River originates from the Yema and the Daxue mountains in the western part of the Qilian Mountains. Due to the erosion by the river, many sections of the riverbed cut out a deep canyon with steep sides. The Yulin Caves are constructed on the cliffs of the gorge (Fig.82). First built during the Early Tang, the Yulin Caves were then expanded in the Mid-Tang, the Late Tang, the Five Dynasties, the Song Dynasty, the Western Xia, the Yuan Dynasty, and the Qing Dynasty.

The Yulin Caves comprise the eastern cliff and the western cliff, with 41 extant caves. The eastern side has two tiers: an upper tier with nineteen caves, and a lower tier with eleven caves; the western side has only one tier, with a total of eleven caves. Judging from the remaining inscriptions and styles of the murals, the Yulin Caves include three caves built in the Tang Dynasty, eight in the Five Dynasties, thirteen from the Song Dynasty, four from the Western Xia, four from the Yuan Dynasty, and nine from the Qing Dynasty (Fig.83). The ruling class of the Western Xia believed in Buddhism. Therefore, they built and remodeled many caves after their occupation

图 82 榆林窟外景(东崖)

Fig.82 Panorama of Eastern Cliff of the Yulin Caves

于西夏统治者崇信佛教,所以在其占领敦煌之后,在敦煌地区新建、重修了不少石窟(图 84)。其中,在榆林窟现存的 41 个洞窟中,至少有10 个洞窟为西夏统治时期所新建,或被重修、重绘、补绘过。榆林窟现存壁画约 25000 平方米,彩塑 200 余身,是敦煌石窟艺术享有盛誉的著名石窟之一。榆林窟壁画的艺术手法多种多样,有铁线描、兰叶描等。由于与莫高窟在内容、艺术风格、绘画形式方面一脉相承,所以榆林窟被学者誉为"莫

of Dunhuang (Fig.84), during which more than 10 existing caves at Yulin were built, rebuilt, or repainted. As a famed part of Dunhuang cave art, the Yulin Caves enjoy a high reputation for their extant murals of approximately 25,000 square meters, and more than 200 painted sculptures. The murals in the Yulin Caves were drawn with various artistic techniques, such as wire-line drawing, orchid-leaf drawing and so on. The Yulin Caves are known as the sister of the Mogao Caves, because their content, artistic style, and form of paintings can be traced to the same origin. Among the caves at Yulin, Caves 2, 3, 6, and 25 have their own uniqueness (Fig.85).

图 83　榆林窟第 16 窟　回鹘夫人供养像　五代

Fig.83　Donor Painting of Uyghur Noblewomen, Yulin Cave 16　Five Dynasties

图 84 榆林窟第 29 窟 童子图 西夏

Fig.84 Portrait of a Boy, Yulin Cave 29 Western Xia

高窟的姊妹窟”。榆林窟的众多洞窟中,第 2、3、6、25 等窟都有自己独具特色之处(图 85)。

榆林窟第 25 窟为唐代开凿的洞窟，前室和甬道在五代时曾被重画，主室四壁保存了唐代的原貌。窟内所绘壁画最为著名的当属南壁的《观无量寿佛经变》和北壁的《弥勒经变》。《观无量寿佛经变》中间画西方极乐世界。极乐世界绘有

Yulin Cave 25 was dug in the Tang Dynasty. The murals on its antechamber and corridors were repainted during the Five Dynasties, while murals on the walls of the main chamber preserved their original appearance from the Tang Dynasty. The most famous murals in this cave are the *Amitayurdhyana Sutra Illustration* on the south wall and the *Maitreya Triple Sutra Illustration* on the north wall. In the middle of the *Amitayurdhyana Sutra Illustration* is painted the Western Pure Land with palaces

图 85　榆林窟第 2 窟　释迦涅槃图　西夏
Fig.85　Painting of the Buddha's Parinirvana, Yulin Cave 2　Western Xia

位于七宝池中的宫殿楼阁，无量寿佛坐于莲花宝座之上，观世音和势至等菩萨分侍左右。无量寿佛面前的平台上有排列成八字形的乐队正在演奏，演奏的乐器有海螺、拍板、琵琶、竖笛、笙等，姿态优美的舞伎随着音乐的节拍翩翩起舞，简直是一幅歌舞升平的盛世图。在极乐世界的侧面则描绘了"未生

and pavilions in a lotus pond. The Amitabha Buddha (Amitayus) sits on a lotus throne, with Avalokitesvara and Mahasthamaprapta attending on each side. In front of the Amitabha Buddha is a stage where a musical ensemble seated in a splay form plays musical instruments such as the conch, clappers, *pipa* (Chinese lute), *sheng* (a reed pipe wind instrument), and vertical flute. The graceful dancers move along to the musical rhythm, creating a peaceful image of a resplendent world. On one side of the Pure Land scene,

怨”等故事场面。所谓“未生怨”也就是说在未出生之前已经结怨。佛经里记载，一个国王年迈无子，无奈之下国王就向相师请教。经相师卜算，国王应该有子，但此人尚在深山修行，等他死后才会前往投胎。国王求子心切，便派人断绝了此人的食物供应，导致此人被饿死。但此人死后，并没有马上去投胎，而是化身为白兔躲藏在国王的花园里。国王得到消息后，就派遣武士将白兔杀死。不久，王后就怀孕，诞下一子。此子长大成人后，某日突生恶念，便与大臣合谋发动了宫廷政变，将国王囚禁起来，而且不给他水和食物。于是，王后韦提希夫人买通狱卒，暗地里给国王送蜜和面以维持生命。王子得知后，持剑欲杀其母，经大臣劝阻后，将王后和国王同时囚禁在深宫。王后在狱中虔诚礼佛，于是佛遣弟子前

narrative paintings depict King Ajatasatru and scenes from his avadana story. The story is also known as “Enemy While Still Unborn,” indicating how grudges were incurred before birth. According to Buddhist records, King Bimbisara, an old king without any children, turned to a fortune-teller for help. The fortune-teller predicted that the King would have a son, but the son was still spiritually cultivating himself in the mountains; after his death, he would be reincarnated as Bimbisara’s son. King Bimbisara was so eager to have a son that he sent soldiers to cut off the man’s food supply with the intention to starve him to death. However, after the man’s death, he chose not to reincarnate immediately as the King’s son, but reincarnated himself as a rabbit hiding in the palace garden. On hearing this news, the King sent his warriors to kill the rabbit. Soon, Queen Vaidehi was pregnant and gave birth to a boy named Ajatasatru. After growing up, Prince Ajatasatru conspired with ministers to launch a palace coup. He usurped the throne by imprisoning his father King Bimbisara without providing any water and food. His mother Queen Vaidehi secretly bribed the guards and brought honey and food to the King to sustain his life, but was discovered. The Prince was so angry that he wanted to kill his mother with his sword, but was stopped by ministers, so he also imprisoned the Queen. The imprisoned Queen called on the Buddha for help. The Buddha first sent a disciple to visit them; then he went to palace to preach for them in person. In Cave 25, from the bottom to the

往探视，并亲自前往为二人说法。第25窟自下而上，共画了王子发动宫廷政变、囚禁国王、王子持剑杀母、王后为国王送蜜面、王后和国王同被囚禁、佛派弟子探视、佛入宫中说法等情节（图86）。

第25窟的弥勒经变以弥勒三会为主体：初会表现了弥勒在龙华树下说法，转轮王向弥勒呈献镇国七宝台，以及转轮王率众落发为僧的情景。第二会和第三会则分别表现了弥勒为比丘和比丘尼说法的场面。在“弥勒三会”主题画的两侧，分别画有人们想象中弥勒世界中的种种美好事物。根据佛经的描写，弥勒世界里“耕种不以力”“一种七收”；寿8.4万岁，临终之前，自诣坟墓；女人500岁才出嫁。对此，第25窟的壁画中一方面绘有农民犁地、播种、收割、打场等场面，真实地反映了唐代农业生产的主要过程（图87）。而对人的临终场面，图中画圆形坟

top, the paintings show the scenes of Prince's palace coup, the imprisonment of the King, the Prince attempting to kill his mother with his sword, the Queen bringing honey and food to the King, the imprisonment of the King and the Queen, the Buddha's disciple visiting them, the Buddha preaching in the palace, and other scenes from the story (Fig.86).

The *Maitreya Triple Sutra Illustration Painting* in Cave 25 mainly depicts the "Three Assemblies of Maitreya Buddha." The first assembly shows the scenes of Maitreya preaching under the Mesuna trees, a Cakravarti-raja (Wheel Turning King) presenting the seven treasures to Maitreya, and Cakravarti-raja and his followers having their hair tonsured to become Buddhist monks. The second and third assemblies respectively represent the scene of Maitreya preaching to the sangha of Buddhist monks and nuns. On both sides of the "Three Assemblies of Maitreya Buddha" are painted a variety of beautiful things in the world of Maitreya. According to the description in the Buddhist sutra, in the Maitreya world, farming requires no force, and sowing seeds once can have seven harvests; people can live up to 84,000 years, and one can go to the grave by oneself before death; women will not get married until they are 500 years old. In this regard, the murals of Cave 25 present the scenes of farmers plowing, sowing, harvesting, threshing and so on, truly reflecting the process of agricultural production in the Tang Dynasty (Fig.87). As for

图 86 榆林窟第 25 窟 南壁观无量寿经变未生怨、观音菩萨 唐
Fig.86 Narrative of Enemy While Still Unborn and Image of Avalokitesvara Bodhisattva from *Amitayurdhyana Sutra Illustration*, South Wall of Yulin Cave 25 Tang Dynasty

墓，墓内置有屏风，有一白髯老人驻杖坐在床上，与家人依依惜别(图88)。而对于“女人五百岁出嫁”的场面，壁画中画青色的帐房；帐房内设有长案，案上陈列着种种美味佳肴，男女宾客列座宴饮，一对青年男女在傧相的主持下正在举行婚礼(图89)。礼拜时，仍然沿袭了武则天时期所遗留下来的“男拜女不跪”的礼仪和风俗。此外，画面上还描绘了树上生衣、路不拾遗、夜不闭户等人间生活的美好想象。

榆林窟第2窟为西夏时期的洞窟，窟内绘有精美绝伦的水月观音及世界上现存最早的唐僧取经图。水月观音，就是世间所绘水中月之观音，是佛教三十三观音之一。最早的水月观音像出现于中唐。榆林窟第2、21、29窟保存有西夏时期所绘的水月观音像，都比较精美。其中尤其是第2窟的水月观音最为精美。该图绘于第2窟

the scene of death, the mural displays a circular grave with a screen, in which a white-bearded old man sits in bed holding a walking stick, saying his farewells to his family members (Fig.88). For the scene of women getting married at the age of five hundred, the mural shows a green tent with a long table inside on which various delicacies are set. Male and female guests are sitting next to the table, witnessing a young man and woman holding a wedding ceremony hosted by a wedding compere (Fig.89). The ceremony follows the etiquette and customs of the period of Empress Wu Zetian that men knelt down while women did not. In addition, the pictures also depict the virtues of this world: trees bearing clothes, no one picking up lost articles on the road, doors unbolted at night, and other beautiful and harmonious scenes.

In Yulin Cave 2 constructed in the Western Xia, murals display the elegant and delicate painted image of Water-Moon Avalokitesvara (*Guanyin*) and the earliest existing painting of *Xuanzang's Quest for Buddhist Scriptures*. Water-Moon Avalokitesvara who watches the moon's reflection in the water is one of the 33 incarnations of Avalokitesvara Bodhisattva. The first portrait of Water-Moon Avalokitesvara appeared during the Mid-Tang. Yulin Caves 2, 21, and 29 all preserve the exquisite paintings of Water-Moon Avalokitesvara from the Western Xia, among which the one in Cave 2 is the most delicate and beautiful. This painting is on the north side of the door of the antechamber, with a height of 148 centimeters and a width of 146 centimeters.

图 87　榆林窟第 25 窟　耕作图　唐

Fig.87　Painting of Farming Scene，Yulin Cave 25　Tang Dynasty

图 88　榆林窟第 25 窟　临终图　唐

Fig.88　Painting of Last Moment Before Death, Yulin Cave 25　Tang Dynasty

图 89　榆林窟第 25 窟　嫁娶图　唐
Fig.89　Painting of Wedding Ceremony, Yulin Cave 25　Tang Dynasty

内前室门北侧，纵148厘米,横146厘米。观音头戴宝冠,长发批于两肩,身着天衣,倚坐在岩石之上。左手自然地放在左腿膝盖上,右手托净瓶，平举于胸前。身体略向后倾斜,凝望着右上角彩云中的一轮弯月。观音所倚坐的山石的前方是绿水,后面为翠竹。在朦胧的月光笼罩之下,观音越发显得楚楚动人(图90)。在观音面前,有一名腾云驾雾的仙童,双手合十礼拜。学者认为此位仙童,应该就是善财童子。

在榆林窟的《唐僧取经图》中,西夏画工大胆地运用我国传统的现实主义与浪漫主义相结合的创作手法,成功地塑造了早期孙悟空的艺术形象。图中的孙悟空人身、猴面、布衣麻鞋,既神话,又拟人化,可爱而有人性。《唐僧取经图》集中出现于榆林窟和东千佛洞的西夏壁画中，有的绘制在《普贤经变》中,有的出现在《水月观音图》中,也有的绘

Avalokitesvara wears a crown, with long hair falling to his shoulders. He sits on a rock with his left hand naturally resting on his left knee and his right hand holding a water bottle in front of his chest. He is staring at the crescent moon on the upper right corner of the clouds, his body slightly tilting back. In front of the rocks is green water, and behind is the green bamboo. In the dim moonlight, Avalokitesvara becomes more delicate and attractive (Fig.90). In front of Avalokitesvara, there is a child standing on clouds, praying with his palms together. Scholars believe that this child represents Sudhana.

In the painting of *Xuanzang's Quest for Buddhist Scriptures* in the Yulin Caves, artists from the Western Xia boldly combined techniques of traditional realism and romanticism, successfully creating the artistic image of an early Sun Wukong. With a human body and a monkey's head, Sun Wukong wears a cloth gown and hemp-soled shoes, both of which portray the myth and personification, thus making it preternaturally charming and strikingly human at the same time. *Xuanzang's Quest for Buddhist Scriptures* mostly appears in the murals from the Western Xia in the Yulin Caves and the Eastern Thousand Buddha Caves, some in the *Samantabhadra Illustration Paintings*, some in *Painted Images of Water-Moon Avalokitesvara*, and some in *Avalokitesvara Sutra Illustration Paintings*. The characters in these paintings consist of only Monk Xuanzang, Sun Wukong, and a white horse carrying the sutras. At the time

图 90　榆林窟第 2 窟　水月观音　西夏

Fig.90　Water-Moon Avalokitesvara, Yulin Cave 2　Western Xia

制在《观音经变图》中，但图中人物仅有唐僧、孙悟空师徒二人及驮经的白马，尚未出现猪八戒和沙和尚的形象，这和南宋时出现的《大唐三藏取经诗话》记载是相符合的。安西榆林窟和东千佛洞的 5 幅西夏时期的《唐僧取经图》

there were no characters of Zhu Bajie (Pigsy) and Sha Wujing (Friar Sand), which is consistent with records in the *Tang Sanzang's Quest for Buddhist Scriptures* of the Southern Song Dynasty. The five paintings of *Xuanzang's Quest for Buddhist Scriptures* from the Western Xia in the Yulin Caves and the Eastern Thousand Buddha Caves are the earliest depictions of the *Journey to the West*, and also serve as precious artistic materials for studying the cause, development, and evolution

是我国描绘有关《西游记》传说的最早的壁画，是研究《西游记》故事成因、发展及演变的珍贵艺术资料。唐僧取经的故事，题材新颖，是画师们颇为喜爱的题材，在榆林窟第2、3、4、29等窟中都绘有《唐僧取经图》。其艺术形象，玄奘合掌做朝拜状，孙悟空是猴像，牵着满载佛经的白马。可见《西游记》中敢于大闹天宫的孙悟空的艺术形象，经过几百年来人民群众的创造，已逐渐形成人民喜闻乐见的美猴王形象了。第3窟的《唐僧取经图》中唐玄奘立于岸边，向水月观音合掌礼拜，而孙悟空则双手合十、憨态可掬地望着水月观音（图91）。这就使得两个部分既独立又相互呼应，人物、景物气势相连贯，显得意境深远。

除了已经拟人化了的美猴王孙悟空的形象外，榆林窟第3窟和第12窟还有两幅有关"猕猴奉蜜"

of this story. The story of the Monk Xuanzang's search for Buddhist sutras was so novel that many painters wanted to portray it, thus Yulin Caves 2, 3, 4, and 29 all contain such pictures. The artistic images in these caves are Xuanzang worshipping devoutly with his palms put together, and the monkey-like Sun Wukong leading the white horse carrying Buddhist scriptures. The artistic image of Sun Wukong, who dares to create a tremendous havoc in the Heavenly Palace in the *Journey to the West*, gradually evolved into the popular image of Monkey King from hundreds of years of artistic creation. In Cave 3, the painting of *Xuanzang's Quest for Buddhist Scriptures* portrays devout Xuanzang, who stands on the riverbank to worship the Water-Moon Avalokitesvara with his palms put together, and charming Sun Wukong, staring at Avalokitesvara with hands together (Fig.91). This makes the two parts both independent and matching, and the characters and the scenery coherent with each other, thus producing a profound artistic conception.

In addition to the personified image of Sun Wukong, in Yulin Caves 3 and 12 there are two paintings relevant to the avadana tale of "The Monkey Who Presented Honey to the Buddha." According to Buddhist legend, at the invitation of a childless Brahmin, the Sakyamuni Buddha goes to visit Brahmin's home with his disciples. On their way, a monkey takes Sakyamuni's bowl away. The disciples want to stop the monkey, but Sakyamuni disagrees. The monkey climbs up the tree, fills the bowl with honey, and then gives it back to

图 91　榆林窟第 3 窟　唐僧取经图　西夏
Fig.91　Painting of *Xuanzang's Quest for Buddhist Scriptures*, Yulin Cave 3　Western Xia

佛经故事的图画。据佛经记载，释迦牟尼应一位还没有孩子的婆罗门邀请，带着弟子一起前往其家中拜访。在途中，有只猴子拿走了释迦牟尼的钵，弟子想要上前阻拦，却被释迦牟尼劝阻。这只猴子拿着钵爬到树上，将蜂蜜装在钵里，然后把钵献给释迦牟尼，但释迦牟尼没有接受。猴子将钵里的虫子取出后，再次把钵献给释迦牟尼，但又被释迦牟尼拒绝。当这只猴子把蜂窝用水洗干净后，再次将钵献给释迦牟尼时，这次释迦牟尼才收下了这个钵。这只猴子非常高兴，欢呼雀跃，但不幸失足掉到井里淹死了。后来，这只猴子托生为婆罗门的孩子。当这个孩子长大后，就皈依了佛教，成为著名的高僧。其中，第 3 窟的壁画表现了猴子在佛陀的脚下奉献蜂蜜的场面，不仅在内容上保存得较为完整，而在色彩上也基本上保持了原貌。而第 12 窟则是以连环画的形式表现了“猴子献蜜”的故事情节，但具体细节已经模糊难辨了。

榆林窟西夏时期的第 3 窟内室东壁南端，还绘有《犁耕图》

Sakyamuni, but Sakyamuni does not accept it. Then the monkey picks a worm out of the bowl, and presents it again to Sakyamuni, but he still refuses. Finally when the monkey washes the honeycomb with water, and once again presents it to Sakyamuni, he takes the bowl. The monkey jumps for joy, but unfortunately falls into a well and drowns. Later, the monkey is reincarnated as the child of the Brahmin. When the child grows up, he converts to Buddhism, and becomes an enlightened Buddhist monk. The murals in Cave 3 show the scene of the monkey presenting honey at the Buddha's feet, which not only preserves the content of the story, but also maintains the original colors. The murals in Cave 12 present the plot of this story in the form of a series of pictures, but the specific details are blurred.

On the southern end of the east wall of Cave 3, the paintings show activities of ploughing, wine making, iron forging as well as dancing, reflecting the agricultural production, skilled trade and the social life of the Western Xia (Fig.92). Some donors from the Western Xia look dignified and devout, embodying their piety to the Buddha for blessing. Commonly used pigments for the murals during that period were red (vermilion), black (lead oxide), and green (malachite or atacamite). Red clay was most frequently used. With its

《酿酒图》《锻铁图》和《舞蹈图》等，反映了西夏农业和手工业生产情况及社会生活（图92）。其中一些西夏供养人神态端庄虔诚，表现了他们向佛祈求保佑的诚挚神态。西夏时期壁画的颜料多用红、黑和石绿三种，且

proper application and distinguishing features, cave art pigments constitute a precious cultural and artistic heritage of China.

Cave 6 is a vaulted cave constructed in the Tang Dynasty, and renovated in the Five Dynasties, the Song Dynasty, the Western Xia, the Yuan Dynasty, the Qing Dynasty, and at the beginning of the Republic of China. On the northern and southern parts of the west wall in

图 92　榆林窟第 3 窟　锻铁、酿造图　西夏

Fig.92　Iron-forging and Wine-making Scene, Yulin Cave 3　Western Xia

以土红色为常用,应用得当,非常具有特色，是我们中华民族宝贵的文化艺术遗产。

榆林窟第6窟是唐代开凿，五代、宋、西夏、元、清、民国初重修的穹隆顶佛窟。此窟前室西壁北侧和南侧绘有蒙古族男女供养人像，他们盘腿坐于一张极低、无腿的长方形坐具上(图93、图94)。此坐具有栏杆式高靠背，坐具后部高靠背两侧有向前延伸的侧围栏，后栏杆式高靠背较高，两侧栏杆较低。高靠背上部呈半椭圆形,椭弧部以连续的小弧纹构成。靠背两端伸出部位向上翻卷,呈灵芝纹似的翘头。坐具座面前沿绘有连续的回纹和小佛。此坐具的形制与蒙元时期设在宫帐中的宝座很相似。从形制来看，榆林窟第6窟蒙古族供养人所坐的坐具很可能是蒙元时期设在各诸王、显贵宫帐中的一种宝座。

除壁画和雕塑外,榆林窟里还保留了大量的供养人题记，而其中以回鹘文题记最为珍贵。在榆林窟现存的41个洞窟中，有25个窟中有回鹘文题

the antechamber, there are donor portraits of a Mongolian man and a woman sitting with legs crossed in a very low, rectangular seat (Fig.93, 94). This seat has a high back, and both sides of the high backrest have lower arms extending forward. The upper part of the backrest has a half-oval shape decorated with arc lines. The ends of the backrest are designed as glossy ganodermas-shaped. On the front of the seat is painted scrolling motifs and small-sized Buddha design. The pattern of this seat is very similar to the throne in the palace during the Yuan Dynasty. Judging from its shape and structure, therefore, the seat in Cave 6 is likely to be a throne in the palaces of Mongolian princes and dignitaries in the Yuan Dynasty.

In addition to murals and sculptures, the Yulin Caves retain a large number of inscriptions regarding the donors, among which the inscriptions in Uyghur are the most precious. In the extant 41 caves at Yulin, there are 25 caves with Uyghur inscriptions: altogether more than 190 terms and more than 590 lines. Yulin Cave 12 has the most inscription terms. These inscriptions were usually written on a cave's corridor in black ink, red ochre, or incised with a sharp stylus. The content of the Uyghur inscriptions for the most part commemorates visitors or Buddhist pilgrims, but there are also some inscriptions created

图 93　榆林窟第 6 窟　前室西壁北侧　供养人　元

Fig.93　Portrait of Donors, Northern Section of West Wall of Yulin Cave 6　Yuan Dynasty

图 94　榆林窟第 6 窟　前室西壁南侧　供养人　元

Fig.94　Portrait of Donors, Southern Section of West Wall of Yulin Cave 6　Yuan Dynasty

记，有 190 余条，590 余行。题记条款最多的石窟为榆林窟第 12 窟。这些题记或写于石窟的甬道上，或墨书或朱书或硬物刻画。回鹘文题记的内容多为游人、香客的题记，以敬佛为主。但也有一些壁画榜题和回鹘供养人题记。题记中一般有时间、人名、从何地因何目的而来、有何功德和愿望等。这些题记多为草书，其时代多在元代。鉴于榆林窟在中国艺术史中所占据的重要地位，张大千在 1941—1943 年间，曾多次前往榆林窟考察(图 95)。

on behalf of Uyghur donors. What can be identified in these inscriptions is the time, the donors' names, origin and rank, their merits and wishes. The writing is mostly cursive and can be dated back to the Yuan Dynasty. In view of the important position of the Yulin Caves in Chinese art history, Zhang Daqian, a famous Chinese traditional painting master, traveled many times to Yulin from 1941 to 1943 (Fig.95).

图 95　1941 年张大千在榆林窟
Fig.95　Zhang Daqian at the Yulin Caves, 1941

东千佛洞

东千佛洞，又名接引寺，大约开凿于西夏时期，是一个以表现密宗内容为主的佛教石窟群。东千佛洞位于莫高窟正东 140 公里的长子山北麓，距今瓜州县城约 90 公里。石窟开凿于河谷两岸，现存洞窟 23 个：河谷东岸有洞窟 9 个；西岸有洞窟 14 个，分上下两层，上层 8 个，下层 6 个（图 96）。在现存的洞窟中，仅为尚存有壁画和塑像的洞窟进行了编号，其中第 1~5 窟在西岸，6~9 窟在东岸。壁画总面积有 486 平方米，窟内原塑均已被毁坏，现存的为清代所塑的 46 身。此外，崖岸上还有数十个安葬僧人遗体的墓穴窟。河谷的河床宽约 100 米，河滩上生长有骆驼刺、红柳等耐旱植物。

东千佛洞两岸的洞窟集中在南北长约 200 米的范围内，崖面坡度较大，都可以直接沿斜坡进出洞

Eastern Thousand Buddha Caves

The Eastern Thousand Buddha Caves, also known as Jieyin Temple, are caves constructed during the Western Xia, with themes and designs based on Esoteric Buddhism. The Eastern Thousand Buddha Caves are located on the northern slope of the Changzi Mountain, about 140 kilometers east of the Mogao Caves, approximately 90 kilometers from present Guazhou County. The Caves are carved on both sides of gorge, with 23 extant caves: 9 on the east; 14 on the west. Caves on the west are divided into two tiers, with 8 caves on the upper tier and 6 on the lower tier （Fig.96）. Only those caves with murals and statues are numbered, among which Caves 1–5 are on the west side, and Caves 6–9 on the east side. The murals cover a total area of 486 square meters. All the original statues have been destroyed, with only 46 statues from the Qing Dynasty being preserved. In addition, there are dozens of burial caves on the slope of cliffs for the remains of the monastic community. The riverbed of the gorge is about 100 meters wide, growing camel thorns, rose willows, and other drought–resistant plants.

The Eastern Thousand Buddha Caves are arranged in a layout 200 meters from north to south. Due to a large slope on the cliff face, one can directly walk into the caves along the slope. The murals in Caves 2, 4, 5, and 7 display a mandala caisson ceiling pattern, Eight–Armed Avalokitesvara, Water–Moon Avalokitesvara, Cintamani Avalokitesvara, Vajrapani Bodhisattva,

图 96　东千佛洞外景

Fig.96　Panorama of the Eastern Thousand Buddha Caves

窟。东千佛洞第 2、4、5、7 窟中的壁画表现的曼陀罗藻井、八臂观音、水月观音、如意轮观音、金刚菩萨以及说法图等密教内容，与安西榆林窟的西夏窟有密切的关系。第 6 窟南北二壁所绘的文殊变与普贤变等壁画，其风格特征也与榆林窟的元代窟中壁画相似。东千佛洞保存了西夏、元代、清代等时期的石窟艺术。东千佛洞西夏和元代洞窟的壁画，系统地表现了佛教密宗的内容，壁画的绘制水平和艺术价值都很高，与榆林窟一起可补敦煌佛教密

Dharma preaching paintings and other content of Esoteric Buddhism, with a close relationship to the caves at Yulin from the Western Xia. The *Manjusri Illustration Painting* and *Samantabhadra Illustration Painting* in Cave 6 are similar in style to the murals at Yulin from the Yuan Dynasty. The Eastern Thousand Buddha Caves preserve cave art from the Western Xia, the Yuan, and the Qing dynasties. The murals in the caves from the Western Xia as well as the Yuan Dynasty present rich content of Esoteric Buddhism, with expert drawing techniques and high artistic value. Together with the Yulin Caves, they provide a strong supplement to the Esoteric Buddhist art in Dunhuang.

宗艺术之不足。

东千佛洞于1993年3月29日被甘肃省人民政府公布为第五批“省级文物保护单位”;1996年11月20日,归入榆林窟,被国务院列入第四批“全国重点文物保护单位”。

On March 29, 1993, the Eastern Thousand Buddha Caves were listed in the fifth group of Historical and Cultural Site Protected at the Provincial Level by the People's Government of Gansu Province. On November 20, 1996, the Caves were reclassified as belonging to the Yulin Caves and designated as a Major Historical and Cultural Site Protected at the National Level in the fourth group by the State Council.

西千佛洞

西千佛洞,位于敦煌市西南约35公里党河北岸的悬崖峭壁之上,坐北向南,东西绵延约2.5公里，现存北魏、西魏、北周、隋、唐、五代、宋、回鹘、西夏、元代洞窟22个,是敦煌石窟的重要组成部分(图97)。西千佛洞因地处莫高窟之西而得名,22个洞窟中有10个洞窟开放,是游客由敦煌至阳关旅游线上重要的参观内容。而从石窟的结构、彩塑、壁画艺术风格等内容上看,西千佛洞与莫高窟体系相近,因而也成为敦煌艺术的一个不可分割的组成部分（图98)。

西千佛洞有9个石窟保存较好,其中央大多有中心座，座四周凿龛，内塑佛像,四壁多绘贤劫千佛、佛涅槃像等。中心座和四壁的佛像下,绘金刚、力士像。北魏时期所开凿的洞窟内绘有“睒子

Western Thousand Buddha Caves

The Western Thousand Buddha Caves are located on a cliff overlooking the north bank of the Danghe River, approximately 35 kilometers southwest of Dunhuang City. Facing south, the caves stretch 2.5 kilometers from east to west, with 22 extant caves from the Northern Wei, the Western Wei, the Northern Zhou, the Sui Dynasty, the Tang Dynasty, the Five Dynasties, the Song Dynasty, the Uyghur regime, the Western Xia, and the Yuan Dynasty. It is considered an important part of the Dunhuang Caves (Fig.97). The caves received their name based on their relative location west of the Mogao Caves, and became an important stopover for tourists going from Dunhuang to the Yangguan Pass. Of the 22 caves, 10 are currently open to tourists. Judging from the art style of the architectural design, painted sculptures, and murals, the Western Thousand Buddha Caves bear strong similarities to the Mogao Caves, and thus remain essential to Dunhuang art (Fig.98).

In the Western Thousand Buddha Caves, nine caves are well preserved. Most of them have a central base with four niches around, and in each niche, a statue of the Buddha being molded. The walls of the caves are painted with images including the Thousand Buddhas of the Bhadrakalpa and the Buddha's Parinirvana, to name a few. On the bottom sections of the central base and below the Buddha images on the four walls, portraits such as Vajrapani are painted. The caves constructed in the Northern Wei display wall paintings of the *Śyāma Jataka* and *Illustration of*

图 97　西千佛洞早春

Fig.97　Early Spring at the Western Thousand Buddha Caves

本生”和“劳度叉斗圣变”等内容，这是同时代的莫高窟中所没有的佛本生故事，具有很高的研究价值和欣赏价值(图 99)。

Raudraksa's Battle with Sariputra. As these do not appear in the Mogao Caves of the same era, they enjoy a very high value for research and appreciation (Fig.99).

图 98　西千佛洞第 18 窟　西壁南侧　未生怨之二　唐
Fig.98　Narrative Painting of Enemy While Still Unborn,
Western Thousand Buddha Cave 18　Tang Dynasty

图 99　西千佛洞第 12 窟　南壁东侧　劳度叉斗圣变(部分)　北周
Fig.99　Section of *Illustration of Raudraksa's Battle with Sariputra*,
Western Thousand Buddha Cave 12　Northern Zhou

敦煌地区城池关隘遗迹
Historical Ruins in Dunhuang

玉门关

玉门关，俗称小方盘城，位于今敦煌市区西北约70公里处。玉门关约建于西汉武帝元封四年（前107年）。当时，汉王朝刚刚取得对匈奴作战的重大胜利，于是在河西走廊“列四郡，据两关”。四郡，即武威、张掖、酒泉、敦煌等四郡，即历史上有名的河西四郡；两关，也即玉门关和阳关。从此，内地通往西域以及欧洲诸国的通路被打开，中西开始了经济、文化交流和友好往来。中国特有的丝绸源源不断运往西方，西方的音乐、宗教以及葡萄、石榴、核桃、苜蓿等也从此传入中国。在汉代，连通中西的丝绸之路自敦煌以西主要分为两路：一条出敦煌向西北经玉门关、鄯善北行，叫天山北路；一条出敦煌向西南经

Yumen Pass

The Yumen Pass, colloquially known as the Small Fangpan Warehouse, is located 70 kilometers northwest of present-day Dunhuang City. It was built around the 4th year of Yuanfeng Era of Emperor Wu （107 BC） when the Han Dynasty had just won a major victory over the Xiongnu. The government set up four prefectures: Wuwei, Zhangye, Jiuquan and Dunhuang, known as the Four Prefectures in the Hexi Area, and two frontier passes: the Yumen Pass and the Yangguan Pass, to guard the security of the region. From that point on, the gateway to the Western Regions and countries in Europe was opened. China began both economic and cultural exchange with the outside world. China's silk was continuously transported to the West, and Western music, religion, and agricultural items such as grapes, pomegranates, walnuts, and alfalfa were brought to China as well. During the Han Dynasty, the Silk Road split into two routes going west from Dunhuang. One was the route north of the Tianshan Mountains, stretching northwest from Dunhuang, and continuing northward via the Yumen Pass and then the Kingdom of Shanshan. The other was the route south of the Tianshan Mountains, stretching southwest from Dunhuang, and continuing

阳关，沿白龙堆、塔克拉玛干大沙漠南行，叫天山南路。因此，玉门关也就成为由敦煌进入西域北道的必经之地、丝绸之路上通往西方的重要关卡。相传西汉时西域和田的美玉，经此关口进入中原，玉门关因此而得名。

提起玉门关，人们总是会想到唐朝诗人王之涣的《凉州词》：“黄河远上白云间，一片孤城万仞山。羌笛何须怨杨柳，春风不度玉门关。”唐朝著名边塞诗人王昌龄《从军行》里也写道：“青海长云暗雪山，孤城遥望玉门关。黄沙百战穿金甲，不破楼兰终不还。”诗中的玉门关并非实指，而是被视作西北边塞雄关的象征。

southward via the Yangguan Pass, Bailongdui Desert and the Taklamakan Desert. Thus the Yumen Pass became a stop along the sole route north from Dunhuang to the Western Regions, and an important checkpoint on the Silk Road. Legend has it that the Yumen (Jade Gate) Pass received its name because Khotan jade from the Western Regions was transported to the Central Plains via the pass during the Western Han Dynasty.

Speaking of the Yumen Pass, many people in China cannot help recalling a famous poem written by Wang Zhihuan. His poem titled "Out of the Great Wall" is as follows: "The Yellow River rises to the white cloud / The lonely town is lost amid the mountains proud / Why should the Mongol flute complain no willows grow? / Beyond the Gate of Jade no vernal wind will blow."① Another poem titled "Army Life" by Wang Changling, a famous frontier fortress poet from the Tang Dynasty, reads: "Clouds on frontier o'er shadow mountains clad in snow / A lonely town afar faces Pass of Jade Gate / Our golden armor pierced by sand, we fight the foe / We won't come back till we destroy the hostile state."② Actually, the Yumen Pass in these poems does not refer to a real pass, but symbolizes the impregnable frontier fortresses in northwestern China.

① The poem is written by Wang Zhihuan (688–742), a poet in the Tang Dynasty. The version here is translated by Xu Yuanchong.

② The poem is written by Wang Changling (698–757), a famous frontier fortress poet in the Tang Dynasty. The version is translated by Xu Yuanchong. "Gate of Jade" refers to the Yumen Pass.

现存的汉玉门关址，坐落在疏勒河下游南岸旁的一处沙岗上。关城呈方形，四周城垣保存完好，为黄胶土夯筑，西、北两面各开一门。城墙高达10米，上宽3米，下宽5米，上有女墙，下有马道，人马可直达顶部(图100)。北距疏勒河南岸约7公里，东南距芦草井子约16公

The site of the Yumen Pass from the Han Dynasty is located on a sand hill beside the south bank of the Shule River. The Pass is square-shaped and surrounded by well-preserved earthen walls rammed with yellow clay, with gates on the north and west sides. The walls are ten meters high: the tops of the walls are three meters wide; the bottoms are five meters wide, with battlements for protection and passageways for horses. Both men and horses could walk onto the top (Fig.100). The Yumen Pass is seven kilometers from the south bank of the Shule River and sixteen kilometers from Lucao Well. It is surrounded by a marsh, with

图100 玉门关遗址

Fig.100 Ruins of the Yumen Pass

里。周围为草滩，北为洋水海子，海子东南侧有跌水泉，是汉代驻扎官兵的饮水水源。关址北面数十米，即是疏勒河下游一大片由河流、碱湖组成的沼泽地。岸边芦草丛生，湖中碧水涟涟，水鸟驼影，若隐若现。关址周围，还有营垒、城郭遗址数处。

玉门关附近的长城和烽燧，是我国汉长城中保存最好的一段。长城基厚 3 米，残高 2~3 米，顶宽 1 米多，由黏土、沙砾夹芦苇或红柳筑成（图 101）。沿着长城，每隔 5 公里左右筑有烽燧一座。而烽燧多以黄土、石块或土坯夹以红柳、芦苇筑成，呈上窄底宽的方柱形。有的残高 10 米左右，底宽 7~8 米。烽燧旁多有房屋、堡台遗迹。烽隧附近还多遗留有芦苇捆扎成束的点火用的“燔炬”和用芦苇、红柳、胡杨枝堆成的“积薪”，这都是当年戍守军士发出报警信

the Yangshui Lake to the north, and Dieshui Spring to the south, where garrison troops in the Han Dynasty obtained drinking water. Less than 100 meters north of the site, there is a large marshland consisting of rivers and alkaline lakes downstream from the Shule River. Around it, there are rich reeds with clear water supporting waterfowl. Around the site, there are the ruins of barracks and the remains of protective walls.

The Han Great Wall with beacon towers near the Yumen Pass is the best preserved section of the wall. It is three meters thick at the base, two to three meters high, and one meter wide on the top. It is made of clay and sand mixed with reeds or rose willows（Fig.101）. Beacon towers are situated every five kilometers along the Great Wall, built from loess and stones, or earth with rose willows and reeds, and shaped in a square column with the top smaller than the base. Some of the remaining beacon towers are approximately ten meters high and seven to eight meters wide at the bottom. Archaeological sites of houses and forts are found next to them. Nearby, there are also torches made of bundled reeds, and fuel piled with reeds, rose willows, and poplar branches. All these were used by garrison soldiers to communicate via smoke signals（Fig.102）. The Danggu Beacon Tower, five kilometers east of the Yumen Pass site, is a microcosm of beacons and the Great Wall. The Yumen Pass lies on the western end of the Hexi Corridor, north of the Tianshan Mountains and south of the Altun Mountains’ foothills. North of

图 101　玉门关附近的西汉长城遗址

Fig.101　Ruins of the Western Han Great Wall near the Yumen Pass

号时所使用的工具(图 102)。东距玉门关址 5 公里的当谷燧,就是这一带长城、烽燧的一个缩影。玉门关地处河西走廊西端,北依天山余脉,南邻阿尔金山麓,疏勒河自东而西流经关北,沿河两岸水草丰足,为天然通道。元封三年(前 108 年),大将赵破奴率骑出玉门关,破车师。西汉太初元年(前 104 年)、太初三年(前 102 年),李广利两度讨伐大宛,均出师玉门关。

王莽篡位后不久,丝路中

the Pass, the Shule River flows from east to west with abundant grasses along its banks. All of these made the Yumen Pass a natural corridor. In the 3rd year of the Yuanfeng Era of Emperor Wu (108 BC), General Zhao Ponu led the cavalry to set out from the Yumen Pass and defeated the Jushi people. In the 1st and the 3rd year of Taichu Era (104 BC and 102 BC), General Li Guangli led the army twice from the Yumen Pass on punitive expeditions against the State of Dayuan in Central Asia.

Shortly after Wang Mang usurped the throne from the Western Han Dynasty,

断，玉门关关闭。东汉建国初期，由于东汉政府忙于内战及内政，所以没有精力去经营西域。光武帝刘秀在建武二十二年(46年)十月，下诏撤销设立在边

declaring himself emperor, the Silk Road was interrupted and the Yumen Pass was closed. In the early Eastern Han Dynasty, the central government was embroiled in its own affairs and distracted by civil turmoil; little attention was paid to the governance and command of the Western Regions. In October of the 22nd year of

图 102　西北地区特有的胡杨树
Fig.102　Desert Poplar Trees in the Hexi Corridor

境的军事设施和戍卒，敦煌郡边塞的宜禾、中部、玉门、阳关四都尉奉诏而罢除，但玉门关作为呵察出入的关卡却继续存在。到建武二十七年(51年)，有官吏上书请求讨伐北匈奴，光武帝不但没有接受这个意见，反而说："现在国家没有好好地实施善政，以至于灾荒不断，百姓惊惶，人不自保，怎么还能再在边地生事呢？"于是，东汉政府就关闭玉门关，以断绝与西域诸国的联系。自西汉武帝以来存在140多年的古玉门关，在建武二十七年(51年)终被罢废。永平十六年(73年)，汉明帝派遣奉车都尉窦固出酒泉，驸马都尉耿秉出居延，骑都尉来苗出平城，以讨伐北匈奴。窦固在天山地区大破匈奴

Jianwu Era (AD 46), when Emperor Guangwu ordered the closure of military installations and withdral of garrison troops at the borders, Commandents of Yihe, Zhongbu, Yumen, and Yangguan in Dunhuang Prefecture were recalled from their positions. However, the Yumen Pass continued to exist as a checkpoint between the Central Plains and the Western Regions. In AD 51, when some officials petitioned Emperor Guangwu for an expedition against the northern Xiongnu, the emperor refused to accept the proposal, saying, "The country hasn't implemented good governance properly, and famines occurred in many places, which made people panic, and unable to protect themselves. So why should we trouble ourselves with the wars in frontier?" Afterwards, in order to avoid contact with the states in the Western Regions, the Yumen Pass was finally closed after being in use for 140 years since the reign of Emperor Wu in the Western Han Dynasty. In the 16th year of Yongping Era (AD 73), Emperor Ming of the Eastern Han Dynasty sent Dou Gu, the Commandant of Charoits, Geng Bing, the Commandant of Attendant Cavalry, and Lai Miao, the Commandant of Cavalry, to set out from Jiuquan, Juyan, and Pingcheng respectively on a campaign against the Northern Xiongnu. Dou Gu defeated Prince Huyan of the Northern Xiongnu in the Tianshan Mountains area, stationing garrison soldiers in Yiwulu Town. In this battle, the Han army crossed the Tianshan Mountains to chase the Northern Xiongnu to the Pulei Lake. In the same year, the Han government established the Commandant of Yihe for land reclamation and garrisoning troops, allowing the

的呼衍王，并留遣士兵屯守天山东部的伊吾卢城。此役，汉军曾越过天山，追击北匈奴至蒲类海。又于同年设置宜禾都尉以经营屯田，于是，东汉政府重新取得了与西域的联系。决心“立功异域”的班超就是在此时参加到窦宪的队伍中，被任命为“假司马”，并奉命出使西域。永平十七年(74年)，窦固大军再次北征，出敦煌昆仑塞，经伊吾、逾白山、过蒲类海、破车师，又在车师前后部署西域都护、戊校尉与己校尉。从此，大汉声威重新在西域得以确立，西域与中原的联系再度密切，在双方联系中充当重要角色的玉门关重新恢复使用。而班超自永平十六年(73年)出使西域，至永元十三年(101年)，近30年的时间未曾返回中原。他离开长安时还是刚过40岁的壮年，此时已经是“头发无黑，两手不仁，耳目不聪明，扶杖乃能行”的七十老翁了。他曾在《求代还疏》中说“臣不敢望到酒泉郡，但愿生入玉门

Eastern Han government to reestablish its contact with the Western Regions. It was at this point that Ban Chao, determined to render meritorious service in the Western Regions, joined the army of General Dou Xian. Ban Chao was appointed as the Acting Commander to launch a military expedition to the Western Regions. In AD 74, Dou Gu led his army to make a second attack against the Xiongnu. He set out from the Kunlun Fortress in Dunhuang, passing through Yiwu, climbing over the Baishan Mountains, and crossing the Pulei Lake, and thereby defeated the State of Jushi, where he then set up the Protector-General of the Western Regions and two colonels: *Wu* Colonel and *Ji* Colonel. After this campaign, the authority of the Han Dynasty was reestablished in the Western Regions; a close relationship was formed between the two. The Yumen Pass was reopened as it played an important role in connecting the Central Plains and the Western Regions. Ban Chao had been in the Western Regions for nearly three decades from the 16th year of Yongping Era to the 13th year of Yongyuan Era (73-101) without returning to the Central Plains. When he left Chang'an, he was over 40 years old with ambition and vigor, while then he was "gray-haired, clumsy, having blurred vision and poor hearing, and unable to walk without a crutch." He wrote in his report to the emperor, saying "I dare not expect to return Jiuquan Prefecture, but if only I could enter the Yumen

关”，表达了希望返回故乡的强烈愿望。在班超的笔下，玉门关也就成了进入汉地的标志。

对于汉代玉门关的关址，唐宋时期的一些古籍，如《括地志》《元和郡县图志》等，均认为在唐寿昌县（今敦煌市南湖乡寿昌故城址）西北59公里。敦煌遗书《沙州图经》《沙州城土镜》《寿昌县地境》等认为在唐寿昌县北80公里。所以，对于玉门关关址问题，学术界一直存在争论。1907年，英国人斯坦因前往小方盘城考察，在关城北面不远的一处废墟中挖掘到多枚汉简，从简的内容判定小方盘城即玉门关。1944年，我国著名考古学家夏鼐、阎文儒也在此地掘得汉简，其中一简比较完整，且文字清晰，墨书“酒泉玉门都尉”等字样，证明小方盘城就是玉门关都尉的驻所。1998年10月，为了配合小方盘城的

Pass while I am still alive," expressing his strong desire to return home. Thus in Ban Chao's writings, the Yumen Pass was regarded as a landmark of the Han Dynasty border.

According to texts from the Tang and Song dynasties including the *Geography of the Tang Dynasty* and the *Yuanhe Maps of Prefectures and Counties*, during the Tang Dynasty, the site of the Yumen Pass in the Han Dynasty was thought to be 59 kilometers northwest of Shouchang County (present-day site of Shouchang of Nanhu Township in Dunhuang City). It was also believed that the site of the Yumen Pass was 80 kilometers northwest of Shouchang County, based on the *Pictorial Records of Shazhou*, the *Geography of Shazhou*, and the *Geography of Shouchang County*. Thus, in the academic field the specific site of the Yumen Pass has been disputed. In 1907, Aurel Stein, a British explorer, went to the Small Fangpan Warehouse where he discovered numerous Han bamboo slips in ruins not far from the north of the Yumen Pass. Judging from the written inscriptions on the Han bamboo slips, the Small Fangpan Warehouse was actually the Yumen Pass. In 1944, Chinese well-known archaeologists Xia Nai and Yan Wenru also found Han bamboo slips there, one of which was complete with clear text engraved on it, reading, "Commandant of Yumen in Jiuquan," proving that the Small Fangpan Warehouse was the seat of the Commandant of Yumen. In October 1998, when reinforcing and repairing the Small Fangpan Warehouse site, archaeologists from Dunhuang

加固和维修工程，敦煌市博物馆在小方盘城汉代遗址南侧的废墟中挖掘清理了一批汉简。其中，7枚汉简所记录的事件都与“都尉府”有关。西汉时，在远离敦煌郡西北90公里的边塞地区，能够称得上“府”之名号的只有玉门都尉府。这次出土木简的地点就在小方盘城南障墙外不到30米的距离，证明小方盘城就是西汉玉门都尉府，也就是玉门都尉日常办公的官署。在小方盘城外围还残存着起保护关城作用的坞墙，只是由于沧海桑田和大自然的长期破坏，已经不甚明显。在小方盘城坞墙外东南角和正东分别有一个属于瞭望哨性质的小坞堡，在城南侧300米处的高地上，有汉代房屋遗址三座。从建筑形制上看，应是三座汉代哨所，既可居高临下保护小方盘城的安全，又可以与小方盘城周围的军事设置呼应。由此可见，小方盘城周围真是守备森严，防守严密，而小方盘城正好处在防御设施的核心位置。经与唐代敦煌当地人的地理著作

City Museum unearthed a number of Han bamboo slips in the ruins south of the Small Fangpan Warehouse site. On seven of these slips, there are contents mentioning “*duweifu*,” the headquarters of Commandant. In the Western Han Dynasty, the word “*fu*” was only used for the Commandant of Yumen in the frontier area 90 kilometers away from northwestern Dunhuang Prefecture. These bamboo slips were unearthed within 30 meters of the south barrier wall of the Small Fangpan Warehouse, showing that the Small Fangpan Warehouse was the headquaters of the Commandant of Yumen in the Western Han Dynasty. Outside the Small Fangpan Warehouse, there are also remnants of the defensive walls, indiscernable for long-term natural erosion. On the southeast corner and due east out of protective walls of the Small Fangpan Warehouse, there are small forts respectively used as watchtowers. On a platform 300 meters south of the warehouse, there are three house ruins from the Han Dynasty. Judging from their architectural form, they are most likely three sentry posts, which must have provided a bird's eye view of the town, and also must have had contact with other military fortifications around the area. Thus, the Small Fangpan Warehouse was well garrisoned as it was situated at the heart of the town's defenses. After the study of geographical works by local writers in Dunhuang from the Tang Dynasty, it can be

进行对比后，可以发现小方盘城距唐代寿昌县故址的距离和方位与玉门关都基本吻合。所以，目前大多数学者均认同小方盘城即汉代玉门关的观点。

小方盘城外围每面宽8丈，城垣坚厚，在6尺以上。小方盘城的外郭虽然被风沙侵蚀得仅剩下不明显的痕迹，但在疏勒河沿岸的地湾城却保存得相当完好。所以，虽然小方盘城本身并不大，不过连外郭算来，仍然可以驻扎不少的军队。古代关城的设置，目的是为了扼守交通要隘，以便盘查行旅、征收商税以及在军事上占据有利位置等。玉门关以西今天的自然景观固然十分荒凉，水草稀少，很难驻军，但在西汉时期，情况却比今天要好得多。今天的疏勒河未至敦煌境内就已枯竭。而在汉代，这条河流的水量远远比今天丰富。当时，疏勒河可以供运粮之用，一直能把军粮运到玉

seen that the distance from the Small Fangpan Warehouse to the site of Shouchang County during the Tang Dynasty and its orientation are basically consistent with that of the Yumen Pass. Therefore, most scholars agree that the Small Fangpan Warehouse is the Yumen Pass in the Han Dynasty.

Each outside wall of the Small Fangpan Warehouse is eight *zhang* wide and more than six *chi*[①] thick. Being eroded by wind and sand, only some unrecognizable ruins of the outside walls remain. However, Diwan Town on the bank of the Shule River is preserved quite well. The Small Fangpan Warehouse itself was not large, but with the outside walls around the town, it was large enough for a large number of troops to quarter themselves there. In ancient times, passes were established for supervising traffic, checking travelers, levying commercial taxes, and holding key strategic locations. At present, the western area of the Yumen Pass is desolate with few plants, unsuitable for a garrison, but during the Western Han Dynasty, the natural conditions were much better. The present Shule River dries up before it reaches Dunhuang, while in the Han Dynasty, it had far greater water volume allowing its use for transportation purpose. Military rations could be shipped to the

---

① *Chi* is a traditional Chinese length unit, equal to 0.3 meters.

门关以东20里左右的昌安仓。该河还继续西流，流出玉门关外，远至今天新疆境内。可以想见，西汉时期，玉门关外必然还有相当面积的水草地，可以供给驻扎此地的士卒们使用。

魏晋南北朝以来战争频繁，丝绸之路呈现出衰颓迹象。隋唐之际，尤其是唐代以后，自安西星星峡通伊吾的道路日益重要。这条道路的开通，使瓜州与伊州直接连通起来，无须再绕行敦煌，缩短了驿程。为了适应这个变化，玉门关自然亦随之东徙瓜州。唐代的玉门关在今瓜州县城东50公里处的疏勒河岸双塔堡附近。与汉代相比，唐代的玉门关东移了240公里左右。这里正处交通的枢纽地位：东通酒泉，西抵敦煌，南接瓜州，西北与伊州相邻，且倚山傍河，形势险要。其四周山顶、路口、河口要隘处今

Chang'an Warehouse 20 miles east of the Yumen Pass. The Shule River previously flowed westward, out of the Yumen Pass, reaching as far as today's Xinjiang. It is conceivable that there must have been plentiful water and grass out of the Yumen Pass for garrison troops in the Western Han Dynasty.

Frequent wars occurred during the period of the Wei, Jin, and the Northern and Southern dynasties, slowing down the development of the Silk Road. During the Sui and Tang dynasties, and particularly after the Tang Dynasty, the road from Xingxing Pass in Anxi to Yiwu County became increasingly important because it linked Guazhou and Yizhou directly, making it unnecessary to pass through Dunhuang. The distance was also shorter. In this way, the Yumen Pass was moved eastward to Guazhou. Thus, the Yumen Pass in the Tang Dynasty is near the Shuangta Fort on the Shule River bank 50 kilometers east of the present Guazhou County. Compared with where the Yumen Pass was in the Han Dynasty, the Pass in the Tang Dynasty was moved 240 kilometers eastward. It formed a transportation hub, with Jiuquan to the east, Dunhuang to the west, Guazhou to the south, and Yizhou to the northwest. There were mountains and rivers nearby, creating an advantageous location. Presently 11 beacon towers remain, located on the top of mountains, at estuaries, and at crossroads, including the Muxu Beacon Tower and seven beacon towers in Luanshanzi. The site

仍存古烽燧11座，如苜蓿烽、乱山子七烽等。唐代玉门关关址于1958年修建双塔水库时被淹，每年冬季枯水时可露出水面。关墙已坍，夯筑，残宽3.5~4米，残高0.3~0.75米，南北160米，东西155米，开东、西二门，四周环以护城河。关墙内外散落大量素面灰陶片、碎砖块、花岗岩石条、残石磨等，均系隋唐时期遗物。

玄奘法师西行求经，于贞观三年(629年)九、十月间抵达瓜州晋昌城，在当地询问西行路程，有人告知他从此北行50余里有一葫芦河，“上置玉门关，路必由之，即西境之襟喉也”。为了顺利通过玉门关，玄奘遂在瓜州找了一位胡人向导，于半夜三更到达河边，遥见玉门关。“乃斩木为桥，布草填沙，驱马而过”。唐边塞诗人岑参曾作《玉门关盖将军歌》:“玉门关城迥且孤，黄沙万里白草枯。南

of the Yumen Pass in the Tang Dynasty was intentionally flooded in 1958 when the Shuangta Reservoir was being constructed, so that currently its ruins can only be seen during the dry season every winter. The rammed walls have collapsed, with the remaining walls 3.5–4 meters wide and 0.3–0.75 meter high. It is 160 meters long from north to south and 155 meters from east to west. There is one gate in the east wall and another one in the west wall, with a moat surrounding the town. At the site numeous relics from the Sui and Tang dynasties, including plain gray pottery shards, broken bricks, granite bars, and stone grinders, have been found scattered all about.

During the Tang Dynasty, sometime between September and October in the 3rd year of the Zhenguan Era of Emperor Taizong (629), Xuanzang, a Chinese Buddhist monk who was travelling to India in search of sacred scriptures, arrived in Jinchang Town in Guazhou Prefecture. When he inquired about the route to India from local people, he was told to travel 50 *li* northward to the Hulu River, where the Yumen Pass was located, the only route and only link to the Western Regions. In order to go through the Pass, Xuanzang found a local guide and reached the river in middle of the night, seeing the Yumen Pass in the distance. Then they chopped down trees for a bridge, stuffed it with reeds and sand, and then crossed the river by horse. Cen Shen, a Tang Dynasty poet, wrote a poem titled “A Song for the Great General of the Yumen Pass,” in which he vividly depicted the important location of the Yumen Pass. He wrote,

邻犬戎北接胡，将军到来备不虞。五千甲兵胆力粗，军中无事但欢娱。”形象地描绘了玉门关的要冲地位。

到五代末宋初，玉门关址继续东移。根据敦煌文书的记载，此时玉门关已东移至今酒泉城西不出百里的地方，已在瓜州县双塔堡东 200 公里。玉门关之所以再次东移，可能有两方面的原因：一是从当时河西走廊一带的政治军事形势来看，石关峡的位置正当东面的甘州回鹘与西面的归义军政权的分界处，自然成为东西交通的要冲；二是与当时瓜州通伊州道路的废弃，以及沙州社会长期稳定，沙州及其以西道路的畅通密切相关。虽由瓜州可直达伊州，驿程较短，但要穿越 400 公里的莫贺延碛，缺乏水草，路况险恶。如果由瓜州绕经敦煌再至伊州，虽路程较远，但沿途戈壁沙漠的规模较小，水草条件稍好，行走较易。这一时期，敦煌、瓜州等地在曹氏归义军政权统治下，社会安定，穿

“The Yumen Pass is far and isolated / With miles of yellow sand without any grass / South to the Rong people and north to the Hu people / The General gets ready for all the unforeseen events / All together five thousand courageous soldiers with great force / There is nothing but joy in the army.”

From the Five Dynasties to the early Song Dynasty, the Yumen Pass continued to be moved eastward. According to Dunhuang documents, during this period the Yumen Pass was moved to a place within 50 kilometers west of present-day Jiuquan and 200 kilometers east of the Shuangta Fort in Guazhou County. There were two reasons why the Pass was moved eastward again. First, considering the political and military situation of the Hexi Corridor at that time, the Shiguan Gorge was a major crossroads connecting the Ganzhou Uyghurs in the east and the *Guiyijun* regime in the west. Second, the road from Guazhou to Yizhou was abandoned at the time, and long-time stability remained in Shazhou, causing the Yumen Pass to lose its importance. There was a more direct, shorter route from Guazhou to Yizhou, but it extended across the vast Moheyan Desert which lacked vegetation and had extremely poor road conditions. By comparison, the road from Guazhou through Dunhuang to Yizhou was comparatively longer but much better, since it passed only a small section of the Gobi Desert so that there was more vegetation

越河西走廊的行旅皆经由敦煌而往。由瓜州通伊州的道路被废弃,设置在这条道路上的唐代玉门关自然也就随之废弃,而被设置于今嘉峪关市石关峡的新的玉门关所取代。西夏占领整个河西走廊后,玉门关就从史籍上销声匿迹了。

and water along the road. At the same time, Dunhuang, Guazhou, and surrounding locations enjoyed social stability under the administration of the *Guiyijun* regime, so travelers preferred to go along the Hexi Corridor through Dunhuang. Thus, the road from Guazhou to Yizhou was abandoned, the Yumen Pass established in the Tang Dynasty became obsolete, and eventually it was replaced by the new Yumen Pass in Shiguan Gorge at present–day Jiayuguan City. After the Western Xia occupied the entire Hexi Corridor, there were no further historical records about the Yumen Pass.

阳关

阳关故址位于今敦煌市南湖乡寿昌故城西10里左右，被当地人俗称为“古董滩”的流沙地带（图103）。提起阳关，人们首先就会联想起唐代诗人王维的千古绝唱《送元二使安西》，诗中言道：“渭城朝雨浥轻尘，客舍青青柳色新。劝君更尽一杯酒，西出阳关无故人。”“元二”，名未详，为王维之友，因奉命前往唐政府设置在西域的安西都护府，所以诗人为其饯行。这是唐代最负盛名的送行诗，曾被誉为唐人绝句中的压卷之作。此诗一经传出，便不胫而走，收入乐府后，更是争唱一时。

Yangguan Pass

The Yangguan Pass is located 10 *li* west of old Shouchang City in Nanhu of present-day Dunhuang City, occupying a dry quicksand zone known by locals as the Gudongtan (Fig.103). Mention of the Yangguan Pass brings to mind an eternal masterpiece by the Tang Dynasty poet Wang Wei. The poem titled “Seeing off Yuan Er on a Diplomatic Mission to Anxi: A Farewell Song” reads, “No dust is raised on the road wet with morning rain / The willows by the hotel look so fresh and green / I would invite you to drink a cup of wine again / West of the Sunny Pass no more friends will be seen.”① There is little information to be found about Wang Wei's friend Yuan Er. When he was dispatched to go to the Protectorate of Anxi established by the central government, Wang Wei saw him off and wrote the poem. The poem has long been known as the most popular farewell poem, being once praised as the most outstanding in *jueju*② during the Tang Dynasty. At the moment the poem came out, it spread like wildfire. After it was added into *yuefu*③ poems it was sung throughout the

① The poem is written by Wang Wei (701-761), a poet in the Tang Dynasty. The version is translated by Xu Yuanchong.

② *Jueju* is a Tang poetic form. It is a four-line poem with five, six, or seven characters per line.

③ *Yuefu* first came into being in the Qin Dynasty. *Yue* means “music,” and *fu* means “bureau”: *yuefu* means “Music Bureau.” *Yuefu* is particularly associated with the Han poetry of the Han Dynasty, and became a royal government-managed organization involving collecting, writing or performing folk songs and ballads in 112 BC. Afterwards, people called poems composed in this folk song style *yuefu*.

图 103　西汉阳关遗址——古董滩(邵如林　摄)

Fig.103　Gudongtan, Ruins of the Western Han Yangguan Pass (Photo by Shao Rulin)

宋人郭茂倩《乐府诗集·近代曲辞》把它题作《渭城曲》,又称《阳关三叠》。此后,“阳关”也便成了离歌的代称而永远留在人们的记忆之中,萦绕不去(图 104)。

汉武帝“列四郡,据两关”之后,阳关和玉门关一起成为内地通西域的必经关口、中外交流的锁钥之地。由于特殊的地理位置和环境,它与玉门关互成掎角之势,南北策应,共同构成了河西走廊西端通往西域的重要门户。阳关设置有阳关都尉。其管辖的范围为阿尔金山主峰以东和阿尔金山脉与祁连山脉结合部

centuries. Guo Maoqian of the Song Dynasty, called the poem “Weicheng Melody or a Parting Tune with a Thrice Repeated Refrain” in his book *Song Verse Collections of the Music Bureau: Modern Music*. Since then, the Yangguan Pass became a code for farewell songs, remaining a lingering memory in the collective consciousness (Fig.104).

After Emperor Wu of the Han Dynasty set up the Four Prefectures and the Two Passes in the Hexi area, both the Yangguan Pass and the Yumen Pass became necessary transits from the Central Plains to the Western Regions, and crucial hubs for exchange between the East and the West. Due to their special geographical locations and surroundings, the Yangguan Pass and the Yumen Pass formed a mutual support system, with one in the south and the other in the north. Together they created an important gateway to the Western Regions at the western end of the Hexi Corridor. The Commandant of Yangguan was established, with jurisdiction over the east side of the main peak of the Altun Mountains, the northern slope of

图 104　阳关遗址附近的水源地(邵如林　摄)

Fig.104　Water Resource Near the Yangguan Pass (Photo by Shao Rulin)

北坡，西起今甘肃阿克塞哈萨克自治县的多坝沟，经敦煌市南湖乡，东到党河口以东的拦河坝附近。由于敦煌郡南境多高山深谷，山中皆是羌人部落，分散游牧，兵力较弱，多归附汉朝政府。所以，在阳关都尉的辖区防守多依靠高山、河流为天然屏障，仅在山口、开阔地等局部地区设置军事防御措施，以盘查道路。自两汉经魏晋迨至隋唐，著名的古丝绸之路到敦煌分为两道。南道从阳关出发，沿着白龙堆沙漠和

the junction of the Altun Mountains and the Qilian Mountains. The area covered Duobagou Township of present-day Aksay Kazak Autonomous County in Gansu Province, to Nanhu Village at Dunhuang, and finally to the dam east of the mouth of the Danghe River. Since there were high mountains and deep valleys in the south of Dunhuang Prefecture with nomadic Qiang tribes living there and governed by the Han government, the area under administration of the Commandant of Yangguan relied on the natural barriers of mountains and rivers for defense, only taking military defensive measures at the entrance of the mountains or conducting a road check at an open place. From the Han Dynasty to the Sui and Tang dynasties, the fabled ancient Silk

塔克拉玛干沙漠的南缘，经鄯善、且末、精绝、扜弥、于阗、莎车，然后翻过世界屋脊帕米尔高原，经阿姆河流域中部再向西，到达安息。399年，65岁的东晋高僧法显大体上就是沿着这条路线越过帕米尔高原的。所以，阳关作为汉唐时期中西交通大动脉——丝绸之路的南大门，在中西交通史上具有重要的战略地位。1977年，甘肃省博物馆文物队（今甘肃省文物考古研究所）在敦煌市西北90公里的马圈湾汉代烽燧遗址发掘出的有关西汉末期和新莽时期的简牍，其中有两件简牍上记载有阳关。

对于阳关关址的规模，P.5034《沙州图经》卷第五记云“东西廿步，南北廿七步”。折合成现代长度单位，则关城东西宽约33米，南北长41米，关城平面面积为1353平方米左右。关于阳关的所

Road split into two routes from Dunhuang. The southern route started from the Yangguan Pass, passing along the southern edge of the Bailongdui Desert and the Taklamakan Desert, via Shanshan, Qiemo, Jingjue, Yumi, Khotan, and Shache, over the Pamirs, across the middle part of the Amu River Basin, finally reaching the Parthian Empire. It was along this route that Faxian, an eminent monk of the Eastern Jin Dynasty, traveled across the Pamirs in 399. Therefore, the Yangguan Pass, as the southern gateway to the Silk Road serving as a traffic conduit in the Han and Tang dynasties, held an important strategic position in Chinese and Western transportation history. In 1977, the Gansu Provincial Museum Heritage Team (the present-day Institute of Archaeology of Gansu Province) excavated Han bamboo slips from the late Western Han Dynasty and the reign of Wang Mang at the ruins of the Maquanwan Beacon Tower 90 kilometers northwest of Dunhuang City. There are two slips bearing records of the Yangguan Pass.

As for the size of the Yangguan Pass, it is recorded in the *Pictorial Records of Shazhou* (Dunhuang manuscripts P.5034) that “the Yangguan Pass measures 20 *bu* long, and 27 *bu* wide.” Converted into modern measurement of length, the Yangguan Pass is about 33 meters from east to west and 41 meters from north to south, covering an area of approximately 1,353 square meters. As for the location of the Yangguan Pass, there are two records in the text: one says it is located 10 *li* and the other 6 *li* west of Shouchang (present-day Pochengzi, Nanhu Township of

在方位，史书中有寿昌城（敦煌市南湖乡破城子）西“十里”及“六里”两种记载，而 P.5034《沙州图经》卷第五阳关在“城西十里”的记载与《新唐书·地理志》的记载相同，由于出自本地人之手，所以更为可信。

阳关建成后，始终未曾迁移。后魏时，曾在此设置阳关县，北周时废弃。由于阳关是中原人士进入西域的最后关隘，所以人们多把它视作即将迈入西域的象征。而最早将阳关写入诗歌，以抒写故国乡关之思的是南北朝诗人庾信。其《燕歌行》云：“属国征戍久离居，阳关音信绝能疏。愿得鲁连飞一箭，持寄思归燕将书。”作为汉朝控扼西部边塞门户的阳关，便被庾信用作典故。诗句言良人远戍边地，离居久之，音信断绝，闺中思妇怨旷，辗转忧思中忽发奇想，思得鲁连飞箭，驰射边地唤回亲人。“阳关”已

Dunhuang). The first opinion can be found both in the *Pictorial Records of Shazhou* and in the *New Book of Tang*: *Treatise of Geography*, both of which were compiled by local residents, making it more credible.

The Yangguan Pass has remained in one location since its completion. In the Later Wei (the Northern Wei Dynasty), Yangguan County was ever set up there, but was abandoned in the Northern Zhou. Since the Yangguan Pass was the last pass for people from the Central Plains to the Western Regions, people always regarded it as a symbol of the gateway to the Western Regions. Yu Xin from the Northern and Southern Dynasties was the first poet writing about the Yangguan Pass in poetry to express people's homesickness for their motherland or hometown. The poem titled "A Song of the Yan Country" reads, "My husband has been fighting in the Garrison for many years / No letter can be exchanged because the Yangguan Pass is so far away / How I wish I could have Lu Lian① shoot an arrow to the Western Regions / Holding my letter saying how much I miss him and hoping he can soon return home." The poet vividly depicts a wife pining for her husband who garrisoned a remote place. Since she had not received news from her husband for a long time, she wished she could shoot an arrow like Lu Lian's to call her husband back home. As the portal of frontier

① Lu Lian was a tactician in the Warring States Period.

从实际意义上的汉代关塞抽象化为普遍意义上的边塞。庾信还有一首《重别周尚书二首》,诗中言道:"阳关万里道,不见一人归。唯有河边雁,秋来南向飞。"诗歌开篇即以一条遥遥万里、空空荡荡的阳关大道展现出一个寥廓的境界,极写南北阻隔、诗人被羁束于西北一隅有乡难回的惆怅之情。诗人以汉人出塞必经之地阳关,比喻自己羁留长安,犹如在阳关之外。诗人笔下的万里阳关道,已不是写实性描述,而是泛指通往边塞的漫漫长途。

而经过悠悠岁月,作为汉代时通往西域的雄关,到唐代时已被废弃。据撰于武周时期的《沙州图经》卷五的记载,此时阳关已仅存遗址。敦煌文书 P.3929《敦煌廿咏》中有一首《阳关戍》,从文学角度描述了当时阳关的废弃:"万里通西域,千秋

fortress to the Western Regions, the Yangguan Pass became an allusion in Yu Xin's poem, changing in meaning from a frontier fortress of the Han Dynasty to a symbol of any frontier fortress. Another poem by Yu Xin is titled "Farewell to Minister Zhou," which reads "The way to the Yangguan Pass lasts tens of thousands of miles / No one can be seen going back / There are only the wild geese by the riverside / Flying south when autumn comes." The poem describes an empty and boundless area to create a forlorn atmosphere of the poet's sadness at being unable to return home. Since the Yangguan Pass was a compulsory stop when people went to the Western Regions in the Han Dynasty, the poet compared his detention in Chang'an to staying outside of the Yangguan Pass. "Tens of thousands of miles to Yangguan" is not an accurate description, but rather a reference to the long distance required to reach a frontier fortress.

As an impregnable fortress for the Western Regions during the Han Dynasty, the Yangguan Pass had already been out of use in the Tang Dynasty. According to the *Pictorial Records of Shazhou*, compiled during the reign of Empress Wu Zetian of the Tang Dynasty, only the base site of the Yangguan Pass remained by that time. There is a poem called "Garrison in the Yangguan Pass" in *Twenty Poems of Dunhuang* (Dunhuang manuscripts P.3929), describing the abandonment of the Yangguan Pass from a literary point of view: "Tens of thousands of miles to the Western Regions / And famous for thousands of years / Now the sands

上有名，平沙迷旧路，眢井隐(引)前程。马素(色)无人问，晨鸡吏不听。遥瞻废关下，昼夜复谁扃。”到唐代，汉时的西域雄关阳关已经不存在了。此时的阳关已无昔时军事、交通上的意义，而只是人们发思古幽情的凭藉对象了。

在古董滩沙丘之间的砾石平地上，散布着许多古代的钱币、兵器、装饰品、陶片等古遗物，分布广泛，随手可捡。所以，当地人有“进了古董滩，空手不回还”之说。1943年，我国著名学者向达到这里考察，记载道：“今南湖西北隅有地名古董滩，流沙壅塞，而版筑遗迹以及陶片遍地皆是，且时得古器物如玉器、陶片、古钱之属，其时代自汉以迄唐宋皆具，古董滩迤逦而北以迄于南湖北面龙首山俗名红山口下，南北可三四里，东西流沙湮没，广阔不甚可考。”又说：

cover the old path / And the parched well leads to no future / No one cares about the drab horses / And the officials do not listen to the morning crow / Looking up from the abandoned Yangguan Pass / I wander what will be the gateway in years to come.” The Yangguan Pass no longer existed and it had lost its importance in a transportation and military sense, but was still an object that people remembered in the literary arts.

On the flat gravel ground among the dunes on Gudongtan are scattered ancient relics including coins, weapons, ornaments, and pottery shards. Therefore, the locals say, “Once one enters Gudongtan, one will not return empty-handed.” In 1943, Xiang Da, a well-known Chinese scholar, went there for archaeological research and noted, “Here is Gudongtan, located in the northwest of the present Nanhu Township. Despite sand congestion, relics of rammed walls and pottery shards are available everywhere; antiques such as jade, pottery, and coins made in the dynasties from Han to Tang and Song can be found. Gudongtan stretches northward to the Longshou Mountain (commonly known as the Hongshan Mountain) located in northern Nanhu. The area covers approximately three to four *li* from north to south, but is uncharted from east to west because it is covered by quicksand. Two mountains meet at the Hongshan Mountain entrance and a river flows north. Travelers moving between the two passes must go through this area. The Yangguan Pass is located here to connect the two roads, with one stretching west and the other north. On the peak of

"红山口两山中合，一水北流,往来于两关者在所必经,阳关适在口中,可以控制西、北两路。口西山峰上一汉墩翼然高耸，自敦煌赴南湖未至四十里,即见此墩。阳关设于口内,而以此墩为其眼目,盖可想而知也。"向达先生所说的"阳关眼目",即当地人所说的墩墩山烽火燧（图105)。据考古专家考察,墩墩山烽火燧系汉代建筑，现残高4.7米，上宽南北8米,东西6.8米，底宽南北8.8米，东西7.5米(图106)。登上墩墩山烽火燧四目望去，尽是茫茫无际的沙漠，让人顿生苍凉之感。据史书记载,西汉时阳关设有都尉。阳关都尉的管辖范围为汉代敦煌南塞，大体上在今南湖至党河口间以及阳关至玉门都尉管辖南段。由于这一段特殊的地貌环境，塞防多依赖于高山、河流、沙漠等天然屏障。所以墩墩山烽火燧应为古阳关瞭望之地无疑。

此外，李并成先生在1983年至1992年间,曾先后

the west mountain stands a mighty tower of the Han Dynasty used as the 'Yangguan Eye.' It is visible within 40 *li* on the way from Dunhuang to Nanhu." In fact, the Yangguan Eye mentioned by Xiang Da is the beacon tower on the Dundun Mountain named by local people (Fig.105). According to archaeologists, this beacon tower was built in the Han Dynasty. The remaining part of it measures 4.7 meters high, 8 meters wide from north to south and 6.8 meters wide from east to west on the top, and 8.8 meters wide from north to south and 7.5 meters from east to west at the base (Fig.106). From the top of the beacon tower, one can see the vista of the boundless desert, instantly giving a sense of desolation. From historical records, the Western Han Dynasty set up the Commandant of Yangguan with jurisdiction over the southern fortress of Dunhuang, roughly covering the area from the Nanhu to the estuary of the Danghe River, and to the southern area governed by the Commandant of Yumen. Due to its unique geographic conditions, barriers such as mountains, rivers, and desert provided it with natural defenses. There is little doubt that the beacon tower on the Dundun Mountain served as a lookout for the ancient Yangguan Pass.

Li Bingcheng surveyed the Gudongtan five times from 1983 to 1992. Based on his findings, the landscape of Gudongtan is a curved formation of sand dunes in a chain running northeast to southwest, due to the

5次前往古董滩考察。据他考察所见，古董滩地貌景观为一片新月形沙丘地带，由于受当地盛行的西北风的影响，新月形沙丘链呈东北、西南方向排列。沙丘一般高3到5米，沙丘之间有50多米宽的间隔，暴露出大片古代的耕

impact of frequent northwest winds. The sand dunes are three to five meters high, between which there are gaps more than 50 meters wide. Many traces of large tracts of arable land from the past lie exposed. Scattered among the sand dunes are a large number of plain gray pottery shards, gray pottery shards with rope patterns, remnants of red clay pottery, broken bricks, bronze and iron debris, potter's wheels, iron adzes, stone grinders, stone mortars, and other tools. One can

图105 墩墩山远眺（邵如林 摄）
Fig.105 View of the Dundun Mountain (Photo by Shao Rulin)

地痕迹。沙丘上散落有大量的素面、绳纹灰陶片、红陶片、夹砂红陶片、碎砖块、铜器铁器残片，此外还有陶纺轮、铁锛、石磨、石臼等器具，还可以找到五铢钱、半两钱、开元通宝等古钱币，所以当地人才会把此处称为古董滩。1972 年酒泉地

also find ancient coins including Wuzhu coins, Banliang coins and Kaiyuan Tongbao coins. Because of this, local people have called it Gudongtan (*gudong* meaning antique). In 1972, when a survey on cultural relics was done in Jiuquan, the local administration in charge of cultural relics found the ruins of rammed wall bases in Gudongtan. It has a clearly discernable outline, with an area of more than 10,000 square meters. There were broken and shattered wall

图 106　阳关眼目

Fig.106　Yangguan Eye

区文物普查时，当地文物部门曾对古董滩进行过探测，在沙梁后发现了大量版筑墙基遗址，经发掘和测量，房基排列整齐清晰，面积有上万平方米。附近有断续的城堡垣基，证明这里应就是汉代阳关的遗址。汉唐之际，古董滩一带是一片兴旺的绿洲，东西长约4公里，南北约5公里，总面积约20平方公里。古绿洲呈一盆地形，比今天的南湖绿洲要低20米左右，所以容易遭受洪水和风沙的侵袭。据当地人描述，这里不止一次遭受过洪水的侵扰。早在中华人民共和国成立之前，曾有人在此筑坝提水，就遇到过洪水暴发、土坝被冲毁的事件。而1967年7月，古董滩附近更是曾经爆发过大洪水，洪峰的水头高达丈余，将拦河土坝冲毁。洪水过后，沟岸纷纷塌陷，河谷加宽，大量泥沙顺流而下，遂在下游沉积下来；后来泥沙又被强风吹扬搬运，从而形成条条沙垄。阳关故址正是在类似的状况下，经过洪水的不断冲刷和强风的掩埋，而最终演变成一片沙漠地带。

bases nearby, indicating that it is the site of the Han Dynasty Yangguan Pass. During the Han and Tang dynasties, Gudongtan was a thriving oasis, being about five kilometers from north to south and four kilometers from east to west, with a total area of 20 square kilometers. The ancient oasis was a basin, 20 meters lower than the present-day oasis in Nanhu Township, and thus it was vulnerable to floods and sandstorms. According to locals, the oasis suffered flooding more than once. Before the founding of the People's Republic of China in 1949, when people were constructing the dam in the area, some witnessed floods destroying the dam. In July 1967, a great flood broke out near the Gudongtan. The water rose more than three meters high, washing away the dam completely. After the flood, the channel banks collapsed and the river valley became wider. Large amounts of sand and mud sediment were washed and deposited downstream. Later, the sediment was blown by strong winds, and thus the sand dunes came into being. It is the same case with the Yangguan Pass which eventually evolved into a part of desert due to constant floods and strong winds.

昌安仓

昌安仓,俗称"大方盘城", 长期被误认为是河仓城遗址,在敦煌西北 80 公里,又在小方盘城即玉门关故址东北 11 公里。大方盘城北面为汉长城遗址,南侧为丝绸古路,有古代车马通行所留下的痕迹。从大方盘城特殊的建筑形制来看,其本是汉晋时期敦煌郡西部边塞的一座军用仓库。遗址大体为正方形,坐北朝南,四面城垣皆已坍塌,残基可见。南北长 150 米,东西长 155 米,周长 610 米。城内稍靠北部有一座横亘东西的自然土台,高约 1 米。台上土筑仓库一座,东西长 132 米,南北宽 17 米,中筑隔墙两道,间隔成三大间,每间均南面开门。顶盖早

Chang'an① Warehouse

The Chang'an Warehouse, colloquially known as the Big Fangpan Warehouse, has long been mistaken as the ruins of the Hecang Warehouse. It is located 80 kilometers northwest of Dunhuang, and 11 kilometers northeast of the Small Fangpan Warehouse, the site of the Yumen Pass. To the north of the Big Fangpan Warehouse is the site of the ruins of the Han Dynasty Great Wall, and to the south is the ancient Silk Road with vestiges of vehicles from ancient times. Judging from its distinctive architectural shape, the Chang'an Warehouse was used as the military depot in the frontier fortress west of Dunhuang Prefecture in the Han and Jin dynasties. Generally speaking, the ruins are square-shaped with a southern orientation; they are surrounded by collapsed walls. The relic site is 150 meters long from north to south, and 155 meters from east to west with a total perimeter of 610 meters. On the north section inside the warehouse is a naturally raised base about one meter high, on which an earthen depot was built measuring 132 meters from east to west and 17 meters from north to south. Two walls partitioned the warehouse into three rooms, with the door of each facing south. The roof has caved in, and the

---

① Chang'an (prosperous and peaceful) refers to the name of a military warehouse providing provision for garrison troops in frontier fortress. It is different from Chang'an (perpetual peace), an ancient capital of more than ten dynasties in Chinese history, today known as Xi'an. Both names have the same spelling in English, but different Chinese characters, therefore they refer to two places.

已坍塌，四壁除南壁多处塌毁，仅存残壁数段，其余东、北、西三面墙壁均尚在，残高平均 6 米，最高处 6. 7 米(图 107)。南北壁上部和下部整齐排列着三角形的通风孔两排。墙厚 1. 5 米。仓库外12 米处原有围墙一周，今存东、北二面残基，四面各筑墩台一座，西南墩台犹存，高约 7 米，其余三墩均已塌毁，仅见基址。西南墩台建在一个较大的自然土台之上，另外，还有房屋残基。城北至东北 100 米外为湖滩，西至东南为高起坡地，东南高坡上有汉代残烽火台一座。20 世纪 40 年代初，夏鼐、阎文儒在此考察时，曾于大方盘城东面土台内掘得晋泰始十一年（275 年）石碣，石刻文曰：“泰始十一年二月廿七日甲辰造乐生。”晋武帝泰始仅有十年，十一年乃咸宁元年(275 年)。因为敦煌距离中央较远，所以得到中央改元的消息较晚。

south wall has collapsed, with only some sections of it remaining. The other three walls in the north, west, and east still stand with an average height of 6 meters, the highest point being 6.7 meters (Fig. 107). The north and south walls, with a thickness of 1.5 meters, contain two rows of triangular holes for ventilation. Another four walls together serving as a fence originally stood 12 meters outside the warehouse. Only a few vestiges of the north and east walls remain. Raised watchtowers extending in the four directions were originally built, and the watchtower in the southwest built on a larger natural earthen base still remains, with a height of 7 meters. Other watchtowers, however, have collapsed and only their foundations are left. Over 100 meters to the north and northeast of the warehouse is the lake shore, and the area running from the west to the southeast is a high hillside, on the slope of which are the ruins of a Han Dynasty beacon tower. In the early 1940s, when Xia Nai and Yan Wenru were on an archaeological expedition there, they dug out a stone tablet of the Jin Dynasty inscribed with the words, “February 27th of the 11th year of the Taishi Era of Emperor Wu” from an earthen base east of the Big Fangpan Warehouse. The Taishi Era (265–274) of Emperor Wu of the Jin Dynasty, however, lasted for only 10 years. The 11th year of the Taishi Era written on the tablet should have been the 1st year of the Xianning Era (275). Since Dunhuang was so remote and far away from the Central Plains, people had not been informed of the news that the Emperor had

图 107 昌安仓遗址(邵如林 摄)

Fig.107 Ruins of the Chang'an Warehouse (Photo by Shao Rulin)

在汉代设立边塞之初，这里既靠近前线，便于供应；又在长城和玉门关以内，安全得到了充分的保障。从大方盘城的规模、形制及配套设施看，都表明这里是汉代西部边塞的一个重要军事物资储备仓库。因为这里储存了大量的粮食和武器装备，所以既需要有较大的仓库，又需要保证它的安全。所以在玉门关以内的大道北侧修建了这座仓库，并为库房加修内外两道围墙，内围墙的四角修建了 4 个高

changed his reign title.

In the early years of the establishment of the Han Dynasty frontier fortresses, the Big Fangpan Warehouse was close to the frontier, making it easy to supply provision for the army, and security was ensured since it was within the Great Wall and the Yumen Pass. Judging from its size, shape and facilities, the Big Fangpan Warehouse served as an important military fortress storehouse during the Han Dynasty. During that time, a more spacious warehouse was necessary for the large quantities of food and weapons requiring storage. In order to keep it safe, the warehouse was built north of the avenue within the Yumen Pass; protective inner and outer walls were then built around it. The tall watchtowers for guards were built at four corners of the inner wall, and a beacon tower was constructed on a slope 500 meters southeast of the outer wall to

大的警戒台，又在外围墙东南1里的高坡上专门修筑了一座烽火台，为库藏提供了充分的安全保障(图108)。

据遗址考察和出土的汉简来看，大方盘城始建于西汉。而据大方盘城内出土石碣“泰始十一年二月廿七日甲辰造”的记载，可知西晋时又曾对其进行重修。西晋的时候，中央政府还要重修囤积军储之需的昌安仓，证明玉门关此时仍在发挥着作用，中央政府经营西域的活动仍未停止(图109)。其后，

provide adequate security (Fig.108).

Based on information from site surveys and unearthed Han bamboo slips, the Big Fangpan Warehouse has been dated back to the Western Han Dynasty. From records engraved onto the stone tablet, it can be determined that the warehouse was rebuilt in the Western Jin (265–317), which proves that the Yumen Pass was still playing its role at that time; the central government continued its governance in the Western Regions (Fig.109). Thereafter, the Five Liangs were successively set up in the Hexi area. From the Former Liang to the Later Liang, many expeditions to the Western Regions were launched. Zhang Jun

图108　昌安仓通玉门关的古道(邵如林　摄)

Fig.108　Ancient Path from Chang'an Warehouse to the Yumen Pass (Photo by Shao Rulin)

图 109　昌安仓内景(邵如林　摄)

Fig.109　Inner View of Chang'an Warehouse (Photo by Shao Rulin)

五凉政权先后崛起于河西，自前凉至后凉，都有出征西域的举措。前凉张骏曾以武力威慑西域，以敦煌、晋昌、高昌、西域都护、戊己校尉、玉门大护军三军三营为沙州。东晋孝武帝太元七年(382 年)，前秦派遣大将吕光征伐龟兹。龟兹臣服后，吕光被任命为使持节散骑常侍、都督玉门以西诸军事安西将军西

of the Former Liang once fought off the states in the Western Regions. He merged prefectures of Dunhuang, Jinchang and Gaochang with military jurisdictions under the command of the Protector-General of the Western Regions, *Wuji* Colonel and Grand Commandant of Yumen, naming it Shazhou. In the 7th year of Taiyuan Era of Emperor Xiaowu (382), General Lü Guang of the Former Qin went on a punitive expedition against Qiuci. After Qiuci surrendered, Lü Guang was appointed the Cavalier Attendant-in-Ordinary commissioned with special authority, Commander-in-Chief managing military affair west of Yumen, *Anxi* General and Colonel of the Western Regions. In 385, Lü Guang occupied Guzang, appointing his son the *Zhenxi* General commissioned with special authority,

域校尉。太元十年(385年),吕光据姑臧,就曾以其子为使持节镇西将军都督玉门以西诸军事西域大都护,镇高昌。而北魏时期,为了经营西域,阻断柔然的西部势力,敦煌曾一度废郡置镇。虽然北周和隋建立后,与西域地区都保持了较为稳定的关系,但敦煌一带仍为边地。至唐贞观四年(630年),唐政府设置伊州。贞观十四年(640年),唐太宗派遣侯君集平定高昌,设立西州。显庆二年(657年),平定突厥,置濛池、昆陵二都护府,“分种落置州县,西尽波斯国,皆隶安西”。至此,唐朝疆域远远越过敦煌而达中亚。敦煌成为后方,玉门、阳关等汉代旧塞已失去边防作用。大方盘城,这座边塞仓库也随之失去继续存在的价值。

Commander-in-Chief managing military affair west of Yumen and Grand Protector-General of the Western Regions to guard Gaochang. During the Northern Wei Dynasty, in order to manage the Western Regions and repress the Rouran forces, Dunhuang's status as a prefecture was abolished and it became Dunhuang Garrison. Although both the Northern Zhou and the Sui governments maintained a relatively stable relationship with the Western Regions, Dunhuang remained a frontier area. In the 4th year of Zhenguan Era (630), the government of the Tang Dynasty established Yizhou. Emperor Taizong of the Tang sent General Hou Junji to pacify Gaochang in 640, establishing Xizhou there. In the 2nd year of Xianqing Era (657), the Tang government defeated the Turks and established two protectorates named Mengchi and Kunling. Based on these tribal groups, the central government established prefectures and counties under the administration of Protectorate of Anxi. Therefore, the territory of the Tang stretched to the border of Persia in the west, indicating that the territory of China in the Tang Dynasty extended beyond Dunhuang to Central Asia. Dunhuang shifted its position as a frontier town to one east of the frontier, with the Yumen Pass and the Yangguan Pass losing their functions as frontier defenses. The Big Fangpan Warehouse accordingly lost its value.

Like the Small Fangpan Warehouse, Big Fangpan Warehouse is not its original name, but a name given by new migrants during the reign of Emperor Yongzheng of the Qing Dynasty. In the 54th year of Emperor Kangxi (1715), troops from the

"大方盘城"和小方盘城一样，都不是其本来的名称，而是清代雍正年间新移民到来后给其所起的新名。清康熙五十四年(1715 年)，清军进军嘉峪关外，收复瓜、沙二州。雍正三年(1725 年)，清政府于沙州故城置沙州所。自本年起至雍正七年（1729 年)，清政府从西北 56 州县迁徙民户 2405 户。而新来移民多不知当地古迹本名，或沿用明代吐鲁番蒙古占领者的旧名，或另起新名。大方盘城最初被称为"塔尔布津"，稍后，又写作"跌烈半金"，都是蒙古语"都尔伯勒津"的音译，意思就是方形城。随着移民文化日趋成熟，对蒙古语译名词语开始改为意译，于是，塔尔布津就被改为方盘城。乾隆十六年(1751 年)儿月立于敦煌的《青墩峡之碑记》记载："青墩为黄墩营迤北之要隘，东接瓜州，西抵方盘城"，这是方盘城之名第一次出现。后为了和小方盘城进行区别，所以最终被改称为大方盘城。

1907 年，斯坦因来到这里

Qing Dynasty entered the Jiayu Pass and captured Guazhou and Shazhou. In the 3rd year of Emperor Yongzheng (1725), the Qing government established the Shazhou Post in the place of Shazhou. From 1725 to 1729, approximately 2,405 households were ordered to move there from 56 counties in northwest China. Most of these new residents had no idea about the original names of the local landmarks, so they either followed the names used by the Mongols who occupied Turfan in the Ming Dynasty or gave the places new names. The Big Fangpan Warehouse was originally called "Ta'erbujin," and later was written as "Dieliebanjin," both of which are transliterations of the Mongolian word "Du'erbolejin," meaning a square area. With the development of the migrant culture, people began to translate the old Mongolian names quite liberally, so "Ta'erbujin" was changed to Fangpan Warehouse (*fang* meaning square). Records on the Qingdun Pass Stele in Dunhuang erected in September of the 16th year of Emperor Qianlong (1751) read that "Qingdun is an important pass north of Huangdun camp, connecting Guazhou in the east and the Fangpan Warehouse in the west." It was the first time that the name "Fangpan" was recorded. Later, in order to distinguish it from the Small Fangpan Warehouse, it was eventually renamed the Big Fangpan Warehouse.

In 1907, Aurel Stein came to the Big

考察，根据城内主体建筑为高墙大屋，且屋内有上下两排通风孔这一特殊形制，推断这里应是储存军用物资的仓库。斯坦因在遗址内坞墙内西北角和第二仓库西北角，采集到汉简340余枚，其中有很多从敦煌输送粮食及储存衣物的记载，证明了他的推测。对于大方盘城的本名，斯坦因根据敦煌文书中“河仓城，州西北二百三十里，古时军储在彼”的记载，认为大方盘城就是河仓城。此后，中国学者向达、阎文儒等均撰文支持斯坦因的观点（图110）。由此，“大方盘城即敦煌文献中所载河仓城”的观点遂成定论。

而经过著名敦煌学家李正宇先生的考察和勘测，指出大方盘城并非传统观点所认为的河仓城。他的理由主要有4条，下面我们主要列举前三点：其一，大方盘城距沙州的里程与史书记载不符。对

Fangpan Warehouse on an expedition. Based on its special architectural structure consisting of a main building with high walls with two rows of ventilation holes, he deduced that the site was a warehouse for military supplies. Stein collected more than 340 artifacts of Han bamboo slips from the northwest corner of the protective wall and from the second storehouse. The slips contained records about deliveries of food and storage of clothing from Dunhuang, which proved his hypothesis. Based on records he found in the Dunhuang manuscripts, Stein believed that the Big Fangpan Warehouse was actually the Hecang Warehouse. The records state that “the Hecang Warehouse, 230 *li* northwest of Dunhuang, was a warehouse for military supplies in the past.” In the following years, Chinese scholars including Xiang Da and Yan Wenru agreed with Stein （Fig.110）. Thereafter, it was universally held that the Big Fangpan Warehouse was indeed the Hecang Warehouse recorded in the Dunhuang manuscripts.

However, based on the archaeological work and research, renowned Dunhuang scholar Li Zhengyu concluded that the Big Fangpan Warehouse was not the Hecang Warehouse. There are four main reasons for his conclusion, and only the first three are listed here. First, the distance from the Big Fangpan Warehouse to Shazhou is not consistent with relevant records in history. According to the *General Introduction to the Comprehensive Institutional History*, a political book written by Du You from the Tang

图 110 向达、夏鼐在敦煌考察
Fig.110 Xiang Da and Xia Nai on Archaeological Survey in Dunhuang

于河仓城距沙州城的里程，按照唐人杜佑《通典》及敦煌文书《沙州都督府图经》《沙州城土镜》的记载，大约在 230 里至 240 里左右。而经李正宇先生实地考察测算，大方盘城距唐代沙州城的距离在 160 里左右，与史书记载相差较多。其二，从大方盘城与河仓城二者规模对比看，大方盘城要远远大于河仓城。据《沙州都督府图经》的记载，河仓城“周回一百八十步”，

Dynasty, as well as certain Dunhuang documents such as the *Pictorial Records of Superior Prefecture of Shazhou*, and the *Geography of Shazhou*, the distance between the Hecang Warehouse and Shazhou was about 230 to 240 *li*, while Li Zhengyu, after his survey of the site, held that the actual distance was around 160 *li*. This is quite different from historical records. Second, judging from the size of the Big Fangpan Warehouse and that of the Hecang Warehouse, the former is much larger than the latter. In the *Pictorial*

即周长为180步。按照唐朝的制度,1步为5尺,1唐尺合31.1厘米,则河仓城周长为280米左右。而大方盘城周长为610米,要远远大于河仓城。其三,从两座仓库的破坏程度上看,也可以看出大方盘城并非河仓城。据敦煌文书的记载,初唐时河仓城的地面建筑已经毁坏殆尽,仅能从残留的墙基的痕迹上推测它昔日的雄姿。而现存至今的大方盘城除了屋顶塌毁外,四壁大部分仍巍然耸立,甚至连房屋上下两排三角形通气孔仍然基本保持原貌,这不得不使人产生怀疑。而斯坦因在第二次中亚探险中,曾于1907年3月至5月间,对大方盘城等遗址进行发掘(图111)。斯坦因在上述遗址中发掘出很多汉简,其中有一枚记载了昌安仓一名官员于某年某月十一日支付物品的记录。此外,1979年9月,甘肃省文物工作队在玉门关外的马圈湾遗址进行考古发掘时,也曾发掘出两枚与昌安仓相关的汉简。在大方盘城能出土关于昌安仓物资支付的汉简,这就证明这座仓城应该就

Records of Superior Prefecture of Shazhou, the perimeter of the Hecang Warehouse is 180 *bu*. As a length unit in the Tang Dynasty, one *bu* equaled five *chi*, and one *chi* was 31.1 centimeters. The Hecang Warehouse's perimeter is about 280 meters long, whereas that of the Big Fangpan Warehouse is 610 meters. It's much larger than the Hecang Warehouse. Third, judging from the extent of its damage, the Big Fangpan Warehouse is not the Hecang Warehouse. According to the Dunhuang manuscripts, the buildings in the Hecang Warehouse had been wiped out during the Early Tang, with only traces of wall foundations left. By contrast, except for its roof, most of the walls of the remaining Big Fangpan Warehouse are still standing, and the two rows of triangular ventilation holes in the walls have remained intact. Additionally, during his second expedition to Central Asia, Stein excavated many Han bamboo slips in relic sites including the Big Fangpan Warehouse between March and May of 1907 (Fig.111). On one of the slips was recorded that an official from the Chang'an Warehouse paid for some items on the 11th of a certain month in a certain year. Moreover, in September 1979, the Gansu Provincial Archaeological Team unearthed two fragments of Han bamboo slips associated with the Chang'an Warehouse

是西汉时期建成的昌安仓，而非传统观点所认为的河仓城。至此，对于大方盘城本名的争论终告一段落。

in the Maquanwan site outside of the Yumen Pass, which illustrates that the warehouse should be the Chang'an Warehouse built in the Western Han Dynasty, rather than the Hecang Warehouse. Thus, there was finally a clear and definitive conclusion about the real name of the Big Fangpan Warehouse.

图 111　斯坦因到中国探险之护照

Fig.111　Aurel Stein's Passport

锁阳城

锁阳城，原名苦峪城，为唐代瓜州治所所在地晋昌城，位于甘肃省瓜州县城东南约 40 公里的戈壁滩上。锁阳城虽已成废墟，但城垣仍在。城分为内城和外城，外城在北，内城居南，此外还有 4 个瓮城。主城平面大致呈方形，南北长 470 米，东西长 430 米。城内布满断垣残壁，由此可以想见当年

Suoyang City

Suoyang City, formerly called Kuyu City, was actually Jinchang City, the seat of the Guazhou government during the Tang Dynasty. Located in the Gobi Desert about 40 kilometers southeast of Guazhou County in Gansu Province, most parts of Suoyang City is in ruins now, with some original walls remaining. The city ruins consist of two parts, the inner part in the south and the outer part in the north, as well as four enclosure-like structures for defense outside the gate. The main city is essentially square in layout, 470 meters from north to south and 430 meters from east to west. Considerable numbers of ruins and artifacts

图 112　锁阳城内城(邵如林　摄)

Fig.112　View of Inner Part of Suoyang City (Photo by Shao Rulin)

规模的宏大(图 112)。

锁阳城在唐高祖武德五年(622 年)以后不仅为瓜州治所，而且同时还是瓜州都督府所在地，设有总管府，管理瓜、沙、肃三州。瓜州处于河西走廊西部，是丝绸之路上非常重要的一站。其西与安西四镇衔接，在军事上形成互相呼应之势。另外，瓜州紧靠祁连山，山南即为吐蕃所占领。而吐蕃为了切断西域与唐朝的联系，常常越过

can be seen scattered around the city, indicating its grand size in the past (Fig.112).

After the 5th year of the Wude Era of Emperor Gaozu of the Tang Dynasty (622), Suoyang City was not only the seat of the local government of Guazhou, but also the headquarters of the Area Command of Guazhou, having jurisdiction over Guazhou, Shazhou, and Suzhou. Located in the west of the Hexi Corridor, Guazhou enjoyed an important position along the Silk Road. It connected the Four Garrisons in Anxi in the west, facilitating communication with each other in military matters. In addition, Guazhou was close to the Qilian Mountains, the

祁连山进攻瓜州和沙州。由于其地理位置重要，所以，唐政府在瓜州设置墨离军，统兵多达5000人。

传说，唐初名将薛仁贵曾带兵在此与敌军作战，由于弹尽粮绝，被围困在城内。在此危难之际，有人献上一种称作“锁阳”的植物，其状如萝卜，味道甘美，且食后很快就精力充沛。由于锁阳遍布城周围，于是士卒纷纷取以为食。薛仁贵所率的唐朝军队士气大振，并最终大获全胜。所以，此地也就被命名为锁阳城。

史书中并没有记载薛仁贵食锁阳击败敌军的记载，不过薛仁贵确曾赴西北边陲作战。其一是唐高宗龙朔年间，薛仁贵随郑仁泰到天山一带讨伐叛乱的九姓铁勒。薛仁贵身先士卒，三箭射死敌军三人，威慑敌胆，九姓铁勒纷纷下马请降。这一战使得九姓铁勒从此一蹶不振，失去了侵扰唐朝边境的能力，也就是后人所歌颂的“将军三箭定天山，战士长歌入

southern part of which lived the Tubo. In order to disrupt contact between the Western Regions and the Tang Dynasty, the Tubo would cross the Qilian Mountains to attack Guazhou and Shazhou. Due to its important geographical location, the Tang government established the Moli Army in Guazhou, commanding as many as 5,000 soldiers.

A legend had it that Xue Rengui, a famous general of the Early Tang, engaged in a battle with enemy troops there. When his troops were trapped in the city because of a dwindling food supply, they were presented with an edible rhizome plant called cynomorium (*suoyang* in Chinese). It looked like a Chinese radish and had a sweet flavor, making one refreshed. Since cynomorium was widely available around the city, the soldiers fed on it. They regained their fighting spirit and ultimately achieved victory. The place was then named Suoyang City.

There is no such record about this legend in history books, but Xue Rengui did fight on the northwestern border. One record is that sometime during the Longshuo Era of Emperor Gaozong of the Tang Dynasty, Xue Rengui, led by General Zheng Rentai, suppressed the rebellion of the nine branches of Tiele tribe. Xue took the lead with killing three fierce warriors on the battlefield by shooting three arrows, which intimidated the enemy troops. The soldiers from Tiele tribe dismounted from their horses and surrendered; afterwards, the

汉关”。但此场战役，战场远在大碛以西、伊吾以北，而战斗结束得如此迅速，所以与传说中薛仁贵据锁阳城抗御敌军的记载不符。其二是在唐高宗咸亨年间，为了救援吐谷浑，唐高宗任命薛仁贵为逻娑道行军大总管，携将军阿史那道真、郭侍封等率领大军攻打吐蕃。但由于各路军队配合失当，结果薛仁贵在大非川被吐蕃击败，薛仁贵也因此遭到唐高宗的贬斥。而此次战事的行军路线应是从陇右节度使衙鄯州到大非川，战场则在青海，所以也与锁阳城无关。而据《旧唐书·薛仁贵传》，由于唐高宗开耀元年(681 年)之前，吐蕃连续攻击河西一带，导致中原和敦煌、瓜州之间的道路被阻断，大非川之败后被贬斥的薛仁贵重新得到重用。唐高宗首先任命薛仁贵为瓜

Tiele tribe was no longer a threat to the border of the Tang. Xue Rengui was lauded in verse: “The general is able to pacify the Tianshan Mountains with three arrows / The warriors sing their songs as they enter the boundaries of Han.” This battle, however, was fought in the west of Lingbei Desert and north of Yiwu, and it ended rather quickly. It was not consistent with the legend that Xue Rengui resisted enemy troops in Suoyang City. Another record is that during the Xianheng Era of the Tang Dynasty, Emperor Gaozong appointed Xue Rengui as the Regional Commander-in-Chief of the Luosuo Circuit to counterattack the Tubo, along with generals Ashina Daozhen and Guo Shifeng for the purposes of aiding the Tuyuhun. However, due to improper coordination of troops, Xue Rengui was defeated by the Tubo in Dafeichuan, causing him rebuked by Emperor Gaozong and relieved of his post. Xue’s troops marched from Shanzhou, the seat of Military Commissioner of Longyou, to Dafeichuan, where they fought against the Tubo. The site of battlefield had no connection with Suoyang City. However, according to the *Old Book of Tang*: *Biography of Xue Rengui*, before the 1st year of Kaiyao Era (681), the Tubo continuously invaded the Hexi area, cutting off the road from the Central Plains to Dunhuang and Guazhou. Xue Rengui was thus entrusted once again by Emperor Gaozong and was appointed as the Chief Official of Guazhou. Not long after, he was promoted to the General of the Right Imperial Army and Acting Commander-in-Chief of Daizhou. Therefore, the legend that Xue Rengui was under siege in

州长史，此后不久，薛仁贵就被提升为右领军卫将军，检校代州都督。所以，薛仁贵兵困锁阳城的传说很可能就发生在薛仁贵担任瓜州长史期间。而正是因为薛仁贵在抗击吐蕃的过程中立有大功，所以其才得以由瓜州长史提升为右领军卫将军。

唐玄宗开元十五年（727年），吐蕃攻陷锁阳城，对城防建设进行了大肆的破坏，整个河西地区都笼罩在惶恐的气氛之中。为了巩固唐朝在河西尤其是在瓜州的统治，唐玄宗任命张守珪出任瓜州刺史、墨离军使。张守珪到任后，带领军民重新修筑被破坏的锁阳城。在修复工作尚未完成之时，吐蕃再次兵临城下。瓜州军民惊慌失措，虽然都登上城头，但并没有守御吐蕃的决心和勇气。幸赖张守珪足智多谋，上演了一出空城计，在城头大摆宴席并演奏音乐，以招待将领。吐蕃怀疑城中设有埋伏，最终不敢攻城而退却。张守珪趁机率军追击，结果大败

Suoyang City likely emerged during the period when he was the Chief Official of Guazhou. It was precisely because of his great victories in the fight against the Tubo that he was promoted to the General of the Right Imperial Army.

In the 15th year of the Kaiyuan Era of Emperor Xuanzong of the Tang Dynasty (727), the Tubo occupied Suoyang City and destroyed buildings on a large scale, leaving the entire Hexi area in a state of panic. In order to consolidate the rule of the Tang Dynasty in the Hexi area, especially in Guazhou, Emperor Xuanzong appointed Zhang Shougui as the Prefect of Guazhou and Military Commander of Moli Army. After his arrival, Zhang led soldiers and civilians in rebuilding Suoyang City. Before the repairs were completed, the Tubo besieged the city again. Losing morale in panic, the soldiers did not have the determination or courage to fight back against the enemy. Fortunately, resourceful Zhang Shougui came up with a stratagem to hold a large banquet on the top of the city wall, playing music to entertain the generals and officers. The Tubo misunderstood it as an ambush and then retreated. Taking this opportunity, Zhang led his troops to chase the Tubo in a rout and defeated them. Thereafter, he continued to mobilize the civilians to repair the houses inside the city, and called back those who had fled from fear of war. Together they joined forces so as to restore normal life. In 728, Ximolang, a Tubo general, led his troops to

吐蕃。此后，张守珪率众修复城内的房屋，召集因惧怕战火而逃到外地的居民，恢复了原来的生产。开元十六年(728年)，吐蕃大将悉莫朗率兵进攻瓜州城，结果再次被张守珪击败。次年，张守珪和贾师顺率领瓜、沙军队，驱逐了吐蕃常驻沙州西南一带的大同军。

“安史之乱”之后，河陇地区的精锐被唐政府抽调以平叛，吐蕃乘虚而入，在先后占领凉州和甘州后，唐代宗大历十一年(776年)，瓜州最终沦入吐蕃之手。吐蕃占领瓜州后，仿照唐朝的节度使制度，在瓜州也设置了节度使，管辖瓜、沙、肃、伊等州。瓜州节度使不仅管理辖区内的军事事务，此外还着手处理当地百姓中的房屋、土地纠纷，进行户口、土地登记并制定赋役标准等，将军事、行政、经济等职能合而为一。而在大中二年(848年)张议潮收复瓜州后，恢复了唐朝原来的州县建制，阎英达、索勋、李弘定等人曾先后

attack Guazhou, but was defeated by Zhang Shougui once more. In the following year, leading the army of Guazhou and Shazhou, Zhang Shougui and Jia Shishun expelled the Datong Army of the Tubo which had been stationed long-term in the southwest of Shazhou.

After the An Lushan Rebellion, when elite soldiers in the Helong area were charged with pacifying the rebellion, the Tubo took advantage and successively occupied Liangzhou and Ganzhou. In the 11th year of Dali Era of Emperor Daizong of the Tang Dynasty (776), Guazhou eventually fell into the hands of the Tubo. After the occupation of Guazhou, the Tubo followed the system of the Tang, setting up the Military Commissioner of Guazhou in charge of Guazhou, Shazhou, Suzhou, and Yizhou, who was not only in charge of military affairs within his jurisdiction, but also tackled issues among local people with administrative matters including housing and land, birth and land registration, and setting standards for taxes. This meant the Military Commissioner played military, administrative, economic, and other roles simultaneously. After Zhang Yichao recovered Guazhou in the 2nd year of Dazhong Era (848), the original administrative system of prefectures and counties from the Tang Dynasty was restored. Yan Yingda, Suo Xun, and Li Hongding all served as the Prefect of Guazhou successively. There are scant historical records of Guazhou from the Western

出任瓜州刺史。西夏时期,史书对瓜州的记载很少，但从锁阳城附近的榆林窟所反映的情况看，这一带仍比较繁荣。西夏在瓜州驻有军队,并设立了监军使。此时,瓜州地区的畜牧业、手工业生产也有一定发展，并且还创造出了独具特色的西夏文化。但是到了西夏以后，瓜州地区风沙为害，自然条件不断恶化。一遇天旱,就“赤地数千里,牛羊无所食”,所以居民不得不向东迁徙。元朝至元二十八年(1291 年),政府曾将瓜州的居民迁徙到肃州，并于甘州和肃州的西界划分出田地,让移民耕种。无力耕种的人户,政府还给予耕牛、粮种及农具。元以后,明朝的西部边防退缩到嘉峪关,嘉峪关以西弃置不守。小股的流徙和大规模的政府移民，导致唐朝天宝年间曾管辖1477 户、人口 4987 人的锁阳城成为荒滩上的一座空城，逐渐沦为废墟(图 113)。

除了被称为锁阳城的瓜州城外，瓜州县西南还有另

Xia. However, judging from art depicted in the Yulin Caves near Suoyang City, the area was still relatively prosperous at the time. During the Western Xia, troops were stationed in Guazhou with an Army Supervisor appointed. In addition, animal husbandry and skilled trades in Guazhou developed further; a unique Western Xia culture came into being. After the Western Xia, sandstorms caused great ecological damage to the Guazhou area, and natural conditions continued to deteriorate. When drought occurred, dry and sandy land extended thousands of miles, causing sheep and cattle to lose pasture for grazing, and forcing local residents to migrate eastwards. In thc 28th year of the Zhiyuan Era (1291), the government of the Yuan Dynasty relocated residents in Guazhou to Suzhou, allocating the land along the west border between Ganzhou and Suzhou for them. For those who could not afford to farm, they were offered cattle, grain seeds, and tools. During the Ming Dynasty, the Jiayu Pass was set as the western border, indicating the area west of the pass had been abandoned. As a result, due to these events, Suoyang City, once a prosperous city with 1,477 households or 4,987 people in the Tang Dynasty, became an empty ghost city standing on a wasteland, and was gradually reduced to ruins (Fig.113).

Besides this Guazhou City known as Suoyang City, there was yet another Guazhou

图 113 锁阳城外的佛塔(邵如林 摄)

Fig.113 Ruins of Buddhist Pagoda out of Suoyang City (Photo by Shao Rulin)

外一个瓜州城。这个瓜州城坐落在一片绿洲之上，城墙很薄，有城垛。此城建于清雍正十三年(1735 年)，为旧安西卫的治所，《大清一统志》上称它为"新瓜州城"。这已是清朝统一全国后，重新着手这个地区的管理，选择临水之地而另建的瓜州城了。

City, southwest of Guazhou County, situated on an oasis, with narrow walls and battlements. It was built in the 13th year of Emperor Yongzheng of the Qing Dynasty (1735), and was used as the seat of the old Anxi Guard. It was named New Guazhou City in the *Comprehensive Geography of the Qing Dynasty* since it was built in another locale for the management of Guazhou after the Qing unified China.

悬泉置

悬泉置遗址，位于敦煌甜水井东南3公里的三危山山前沙砾冲积扇上。该遗址在今敦煌、瓜州交界处，东距瓜州60公里，西去敦煌市64公里。遗址东南的吊吊沟内1.4公里处，就是汉唐时著名的悬泉，现在当地人俗称吊吊水（图114）。据史书记载，西汉武帝时派遣贰师将军李广利征伐大宛，在返回长安途中路经此山。由于所携带之水用尽，而附近又没有水源，众将士口渴难耐。于是李广利以掌击山，仰天悲誓，拔佩剑刺山，甘甜之山泉随之喷涌而出。悬泉最为灵异之处在于，如果前往取水的人多，那么涌出的泉水也就多；如果人少，涌出的泉水也就少。因为此泉是从悬崖一侧涌出，故名悬泉（图115）。

悬泉置因悬泉而得名。自汉代以来，悬泉置为酒泉至敦煌的必经之地，所以汉、晋、唐、清各代，均在此或附近设置有驿站。悬泉置

Xuanquan Posthouse

The ruins of Xuanquan Posthouse are located on a fan-shaped tract of alluvial gravel in front of the Sanwei Mountain three kilometers southeast of Tianshuijing at Dunhuang. The site is situated at the junction of present-day Dunhuang City and Guazhou County, 60 kilometers east of Guazhou and 64 kilometers west of Dunhuang. At a depth of 1. 4 kilometers inside the Diaodiao Ravine (*diao* means hanging) southeast of the ruins, there is the Xuanquan Spring, well-known in the Han and Tang dynasties. It is now colloquially known as the Diaodiao Spring (Fig.114). According to legend, General Li Guangli was dispatched by Emperor Wu of the Western Han Dynasty to launch a military expedition against Dayuan. On their way back to Chang'an, the troops were nearly dying of thirst and no water source could be found. When they passed the Sanwei Mountain, General Li Guangli slapped the mountain, swore to the sky, and stabbed the mountain with his sword. Sweet water then gushed forth. What is most notable about Xuanquan Spring is that the more people fetch water from it, the more water comes out; conversely, the fewer people, the less water. Since this spring flows out from a side of the cliff, it was named the Xuanquan Spring, meaning Hanging Spring (Fig.115).

The Xuanquan Posthouse was named after Xuanquan Spring. From the Han Dynasty, it was necessary to pass through the spot when people

图 114　悬泉水(邵如林　摄)

Fig.114　Site of the Xuanquan Spring (Photo by Shao Rulin)

图 115　悬泉谷口(邵如林　摄)

Fig.115　Entrance of the Xuanquan Valley (Photo by Shao Rulin)

由坞、传舍、厩、仓等部分组成。经考古工作者利用科学手段探测，坞近正方形，边长50米，面积2300平方米，东北、西南各有一角墩。坞门位于东坞墙正中。传舍位于坞内，分为上、中、下三等。沿北坞墙的一组传舍，有4个院落，每个院落前都有长廊，中为客堂，后有寝室、洗手间，内有蹲式厕所、净手瓮和排水设施，是接待高级官员、外国使者和贵人的高级住所。沿西坞墙有一组一字形排开的土质平房，应该是接待一般官员和驿站办公所在。马厩位于南坞墙外，为棚式建筑。仓位于东坞墙外东南侧，为一长方形大型土木建筑。在悬泉置遗址，曾出土大量的汉简，最早的纪年汉简为西汉武帝太始三年（前94年），最晚为东汉安帝永初元年（107年）。由此可知，此遗址始建于西汉武帝后期，废弃于东汉中期。魏晋时期，在汉代废址

were traveling between Jiuquan and Dunhuang. Therefore, a posthouse was built there or in surrounding vicinities during the Han, Jin, Tang, and Qing dynasties. The Xuanquan Posthouse consists of a small fort, houses, stables, storehouses and other sections. The fort is square-shaped, with a 50-meter-long wall and a total area of 2,300 square meters, and raised piers in the northeast and southwest corners. The door is set in the middle of the east wall. Inside the fort are houses divided into upper, middle, and lower classes. A set of houses along the north wall have four courtyards each with a corridor. The main living room is in the center of the courtyard, with a bedroom and bathroom in the back equipped with a toilet, a wash basin, and drainage facilities. It was a place where senior officials, foreign messengers, and distinguished guests were received. Along the west wall there is a row of earthen bungalows which seem to have served as reception rooms for ordinary officials and offices of the posthouse. Outside the south wall there are stables in the barn. In the southeast area outside the east wall there is a large rectangular wooden storehouse. A large number of Han bamboo slips were unearthed from the site of the Xuanquan Posthouse. The earliest slips date back to the 3rd year of Taishi Era of Emperor Wu of the Western Han Dynasty (94 BC), and the latest to the 1st year of the Yongchu Era of Emperor An of the Eastern Han Dynasty (AD 107). It can be assumed that the Xuanquan Posthouse was built during the late reign of Emperor Wu of the

西南角重建驿站，筑有石块所垒砌的烽燧、坞墙、房屋等。遗址前后历经多次整修和改建，延续近400年时间。据甘肃省文物考古研究所统计，遗址出土汉简23000余枚，此外，还出土有麻纸、帛书、印章、生产工具、车具、丝织品残片等大量物品，为研究悬泉置遗址及汉代西北地区的历史提供了丰富的实物资料(图116)。

Western Han Dynasty, and was abandoned in the Mid-Eastern Han Dynasty. During the Wei and Jin dynasties, a post was reconstructed with watchtowers, defensive walls, and houses—all made of stone. For nearly 400 years, the site went through several renovations and alterations. More than 23,000 fragments and pieces of Han bamboo slips were unearthed there. In addition, there were pieces of silk, hemp paper, silk manuscripts, seals, farming implements, cart parts, and other items excavated, which offers a wealth of data for the study of the Xuanquan Posthouse site as well as the history of the northwest area of China in the Han Dynasty (Fig.116).

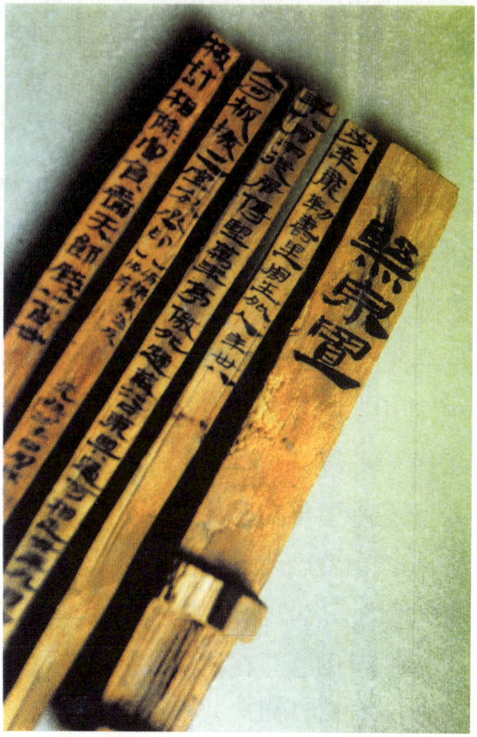

图116　悬泉置出土的汉简(邵如林　摄)
Fig.116　Han Bamboo Slips Unearthed in Xuanquan Posthouse (Photo by Shao Rulin)

敦煌地区的著名自然景观

Natural Landscapes in Dunhuang

鸣沙山、月牙泉

鸣沙山，位于敦煌市南5公里，东西长40公里，南北宽20公里，古名沙角山，又名神沙山。各沙山都向外延伸出几条沙垄，每两条沙垄之间，都有一个弧形滑动面，在其坡度较陡处下滑，时常能听到沙鸣之声。

鸣沙山平均山高（相对高度）100米左右，最高处为后山之西南峰，高587米。砾石基座之上流沙聚为重重峰峦，山形弯环，山脊如刃，十分壮丽。因游人登山下滑其沙随足滑落，轰鸣作响，故名“鸣沙山”。鸣沙山沙粒有红、黄、绿、黑、白5色，又名“五色沙”。早在唐代以前，鸣沙山就已经成为敦煌当地的著名自然景观。《元和郡县图志》在记述敦煌的名胜古迹时，就记

Mingsha Mountain and Crescent Moon Spring

The Mingsha Mountain, located 5 kilometers away from the south of Dunhuang, is actually a group of sand dunes 40 kilometers long from east to west, and 20 kilometers wide from north to south. In early times, it was known by such names as the Shajiao Mountain or the Shensha Mountain. Each sand hill consists of several longitudinal dunes, between which there are arc–shaped surfaces where the singing of sand can be heard if one slides down the steep slope of a sand hill.

The average height of the Mingsha Mountain is about 100 meters, with the highest peak standing at 587 meters. Drifting sand gathers together at the gravel base to form sand hills with curved landforms and blade–shaped ridges. It received its name Mingsha or “Singing Sand” Mountain because the rolling sand grains can produce sound when people slide down the dunes. In addition to the singing of sand, the sand grains are known as “five–colored sand” for their five colors: red, yellow, green, black, and white. Hence, the Mingsha Mountain has been a well–known natural landscape in the local area as early as the Tang Dynasty. In the *Yuanhe Maps of Prefectures and Counties*, the mountain was recorded like this: “The mountain is formed by sands, having steep

载鸣沙山“积沙为之，峰峦危峭，逾于山谷，四面皆为沙垅，背如刀刃，人登之即鸣。随足颓落，经宿风吹，辄复如旧。”而修撰于唐和五代时期的敦煌地理书《敦煌录》对鸣沙山的描写也甚为详细：“鸣沙山去州十里，其山东西八十里，南北四十里，高处五百尺，悉纯沙聚起。此山神异，峰如削成。其间有井，沙不能蔽。盛夏自鸣，人马践之，声振数十里。”

根据唐代敦煌当地的风俗，每年到端午节，敦煌城中士女都要登上鸣沙山峰顶，一并从山上奔下。这时沙声吼如雷，而“至晓看之，峭崿如旧”。鸣沙山因沙鸣而得名，但沙山前后鸣沙声并不相同，是其另一大特色：其后山有人滑动时，声震如巨雷轰鸣；而前山发出的声响却如锣鼓般洪亮。而更为神奇的是不管在游人步履的扰动下有多少

cliffs and blade-like ridges. When someone slides down the sands, a drum-like sound is made. Even if footprints are left on the dunes, they will vanish the next day.” The *General Records of Dunhuang* compiled during the Tang and Five Dynasties gives further detailed description: “The Mingsha Mountain, formed by sand, is situated 10 *li* away from Shazhou. It is 80 *li* from east to west, 40 *li* from north to south, with a height of 500 *chi* at the peak. The mountain is miraculous for its blade-like ridges. Among the dunes is a spring, which cannot be covered by sands around. The sands can sing by themselves in mid-summer and the sound produced when people or horses are walking down the dunes can be heard dozens of *li* away.”

According to the local customs of Dunhuang in the Tang Dynasty, on the Dragon Boat Festival, young men and women in the city would climb onto the top of the Mingsha Mountain and then ran down. At this moment, the sand would roar as loudly as thunder. The next morning, however, no any trace could be found on the sand dunes. The Mingsha Mountain is thus named after the sand's “singing.” Another feature of the mountain is that the sound will change when people slide down from different parts of it. If people walk down the back of the mountain dunes, the sand roars and rumbles like thunder, but if people run down the front slopes, the sand sounds like the playing of gongs and drums. Moreover, it is amazing that no matter how many sand grains pour down the mountain because of people walking around the

沙粒从山上滑下，经过大自然一晚上的鬼斧神工，当我们第二天再去看时，却发现山峦陡峭如故，高度丝毫不减。正因为鸣沙山有这样的种种神异之处，所以人们才会把它敬称为神沙，并在山上设祠祭拜。

鸣沙山年降雨量低于40毫米，年蒸发量却高达2400毫米。蒸发量高出年降雨量60多倍，属典型的极端干旱气候。此外，鸣沙山一带全年多风，这样的气候状况为沙山的形成提供了基础条件。鸣沙山附近多戈壁滩，西部100公里外还有库木塔格沙漠，它们为沙山的形成准备了充足的沙源。鸣沙山的沙源主要来自东北方、西方、西北、西南方。有了气候和沙源条件，沙山能否形成还要看地面是否具备风沙沉降和积存的条件。鸣沙山之所以成为高耸挺拔的沙山，雄踞于周围戈壁绿洲之上，正是因为鸣沙山所在地区具有特殊的风沙沉降和积存条件。张梅先生指出，鸣沙山一带东

top, the next day the dunes are the same as those in the previous day, with the same steep ridges. Hence, people in ancient times regarded it as a sacred mountain and built a temple there for worshipping.

The annual precipitation in the Mingsha Mountain is less than 40 millimeters, while its annual evaporation is 2,400 millimeters, making it classified as an extreme arid climate. Additionally, it is windy throughout the year. These factors provide ideal conditions for the formation of sand dunes. The Gobi Desert is near the Mingsha Mountain, and the Kumtag Desert is 100 kilometers away as well, which supplies a sufficient sand source to the formation of a sand mountain. The sand of the Mingsha Mountain comes mainly from four directions: northeast, northwest, southwest, and west. The sedimentation and stockpile of the sand blown by the wind are necessary for sand mountains. And the Mingsha Moutain is blessed with such conditions. According to Mr. Zhang Mei, to the east of the Mingsha Mountain is the Sanwei Mountain and to the south is the Heishi Mountain. These two mountain formations block the wind from the north, northeast, northwest, and west, which helps to reduce the wind speed or cause vortex of wind, leading to sedimentation of the sand carried by the wind near the ground. As the area where the Mingsha Mountain is located possesses special conditions of sedimentation

有三危山，南有黑石山，东北、北、西北、西等几个来向的风受到阻挡，使风速降低或发生涡流，导致近地面气流所挟带的风沙沉积下来。所以，三危山和黑石山的阻挡，为风沙的沉降创造了条件。鸣沙山以东有西水沟，以西有党河，而鸣沙山区域内没有规模较大的河流。沙粒一旦沉降到地面，既不会被水流冲走，也不会被洪水冲积物掩埋。地面一旦出现积沙，就将出现小的沙丘，对近地面气流产生减速作用，加速风沙的沉降。积沙地面由于相对较软，使跃起的沙粒落到地面后产生的反弹力降低，也增加了近地面风沙流的沉积作用。而经过千百万年的沉积之后，就形成了今天世界闻名的沙山。

对于鸣沙山沙粒鸣响的原因，学者经过长期的实地考察和查阅大量历史资料后，发现沙鸣大体分为自鸣和人马践踏出声两种。自鸣是指沙漠在没有人为因素的干预下，自行发出响声。另一种就是人马行走，或从沙山滑下造成声

and stockpile of sand, the Mingsha Mountain can grow into a high and steep sand mountain standing proudly at the oasis in the Gobi Desert. Although the West Shuigou is to its east and the Danghe River is to its west, there is no relatively large river in the area where the Mingsha Mountain stands. Once sand grains fall on the ground, they can neither be washed away by currents nor be buried by alluvial deposits from floods. If sand accumulates, a small sand dune will form, reducing the airflow speed near the ground and then speeding up the sedimentation of sand blown by the wind. Meanwhile, the soil where sand grains gather is relatively soft, so it lowers the bounce force of sand grains when they fall on the ground. As a result, it accelerates the sedimentation of sand. After millions of years, the world-renowned Mingsha Mountain has been formed.

As for the sand singing of the Mingsha Mountain, after the long-term survey and much references from historical documents, two sources of sound are found—the sound from the sand itself without any person's intervention, and the sound from people and horses walking, sliding or treading on it. There are various explanations from scholars about the sand singing phenomenon. The first one is the theory of electrical charge. This view holds that electrical charges attach onto the sand grains. When the temperature of the sand grains increases sharply by extended sun

响。学术界对沙鸣的成因有若干解释:其一为电荷说。这种观点认为砂粒表面有电荷。当阳光长时间照射沙粒,其温度急剧上升,石英砂粒就会产生静电。电荷遇到风和气流等外力因素时，与之产生摩擦,顿时发出轰鸣之声。其二为共鸣放大说。这种观点认为鸣沙山群峰环绕一周形成壑谷,是天然的共鸣箱,流沙下泻时发出的摩擦声或放电声,及滑沙时引起的气流活动而产生的呼啸声,引起共振,经过“共鸣箱”的共鸣作用,放大了音量,于是形成巨大声响。其三为碰撞说,认为沙粒相互碰撞即可发出声响。其四为切力说,认为当沙粒向下崩泻时,砂粒之间产生切力运动,也促使沙漠出声。此外,还有学者支持吐气说，认为夏日炎热阳光烤灼,沙层增温后,内部空气因膨胀排出,导致声响。最近,中国科学院兰州沙漠研究所的屈建军教授对鸣沙成因又有新解释。他认为外国学者发现的砂粒表面非晶体二氧化硅凝胶体的存在,是一种普遍现

exposure, the quartz sand grains will produce static electricity, producing friction with wind or airflow, and thus making a roaring sound. The second one is the theory of resonant amplification. It holds that the sand dunes of the Mingsha Mountain form a circular valley like a natural resonator, which can amplify the sound from resonance produced by the sound of friction and the roaring sound of air movement when grains of sand flow down. The third is the theory of collision, that is, sand grains collide with each other to produce sound. The fourth is the theory of shear force. It holds that when sand grains slide down from the hills, there occurs shearing movement between sand grains, which produces sound. There is also the theory of “breathing” in which the temperature of the sand bed increases under the burning sunlight, causing the internal air of the sand bed to erupt and make a rumbling sound. Recently, Qu Jianjun, Professor of Lanzhou Desert Research Institute of Chinese Academy of Science, pointed out a new explanation on the sand singing. He maintains it is a universal phenomenon that there exists amorphous silicon dioxide gel on the surface of sand grains. The natural environmental conditions are also necessary for sand singing, such as the proper qualities of the sand, the gradient of the sand dunes, the moisture content in the atmosphere around the sand hills and so on. Therefore, a desert that is rich

象，沙粒发声必不可少的条件还有自然环境条件，如适合的砂粒度、沙丘环境的坡度、周围大气中所含的水分等。在存在较丰富的地下水的沙漠，沙丘周围有水洼和湖泊的沙漠，都是鸣沙的多发区。他经研究后发现鸣沙的最佳坡度为32度，水分含量临界值为0.3%，掌握住这些关键因素后，人类还可制造鸣沙自然景观。而鸣沙山所处的环境及其本身形态特点与屈教授的观点基本吻合，所以他的观点得到了很多学者的支持。但鸣沙山沙鸣之谜的神秘面纱并没有被完全揭开，仍然吸引着全世界探索的目光。

在均由流沙堆积而成的鸣沙山，在四周都是100多米高的沙山怀抱中，竟有一泓明镜般宛如新月的月牙泉。月牙泉形似月牙，东西长约250米，南北宽约50米。南侧平台高出泉水面，其上曾建有古建筑群，但均已在“文革”中被破坏。1986年，国家拨款重新修复，使名列敦煌八景之一的“月牙晓彻”的奇妙景色得以

in underground water, or a desert in which there are puddles of water or lakes are areas where sand can frequently sing. He found that the best gradient of a sand hill for singing sand is 32 degrees, and the critical value of moisture content is 0.3%. If such key factors can be recreated, people can produce sand singing by themselves. The natural environment of the Mingsha Mountain and its landforms closely accord with Professor Qu's view, and his opinion has been supported by many scholars. However, the mystery of the Mingsha Mountain has not been completely unveiled, and it still attracts attention from all around the world.

Located among the Mingsha Mountains' layers of sand dunes is, miraculously, a crystalline body of water named the Crescent Moon Spring. It is a crescent-shaped spring within an oasis, measuring 250 meters from east to west, and 50 meters from north to south. On the platform south of the spring had been a collection of ancient buildings, which were damaged during the Cultural Revolution. In 1986, the archaistic buildings were constructed again, making it one of the famous scenic spots in Dunhuang. The sand and water, two polar opposites, have co-existed harmoniously there for thousands of years, which people have always found fascinating. As early as the Eastern Han Dynasty, the Crescent Moon Spring was one of the most well-known landscapes in

重现。神奇的是这原本相克的一沙一水，却相辅相成，千百年来共生互映。早在东汉时期，月牙泉就已是敦煌胜景之一。《元和郡县图志》中所记载的“绵历古今，沙填不满，水极甘美”的沙井泉，正是我们今天所看到的月牙泉。古诗中则曾这样描写：“银沙四面山环抱，一池清水绿涟漪。”（图 117）

月牙泉虽环以流沙，却恒久生存，与它所处的特殊地貌和气象因素有着密切的联系。今天我们所见到的月牙泉是党河改道后遗留在沙漠上的一处古河湾，河湾基底为灰色和紫红色的粉砂质泥岩。以前，鸣沙山中还有几个储水湖，但都和党河古道一起被流沙所掩埋，唯有月牙泉这个残留的古河湾的地势低洼，由于受到周围地形保护而得以幸存。其水源来自鸣沙山下含水层位置较高的地下潜流和河流渗漏的地下水。所以，水面面积虽然有限，但底部水路却畅通无阻。水不足时，风沙将干涸的河

Dunhuang. In the *Yuanhe Maps of Prefectures and Counties*, it was recorded that there had been a Shajing Spring with sweet water for many years, which could not be overwhelmed by sand. That spring was the present-day Crescent Moon Spring. It was described in the poem that “surrounded by the silver-like sand dunes, ripples undulate on the green water” (Fig.117).

Such a wonderful phenomenon is closely related to special land configurations and weather. The Crescent Moon Spring is in fact a river bend in the desert after the diversion of the Danghe River; the base of the river bend is gray or purplish red silty mudstone. In the past there were several reservoir lakes among the Mingsha Mountain, but together with the ancient watercourse of the Danghe River, they all were buried by sand. Only the Crescent Moon Spring survived because of protection from its unique land location. The source of water for the Crescent Moon Spring was from underground currents in aquifers and underground water coming from the river below the Mingsha Mountain. Therefore, it formed an unimpeded water route beneath the spring, in spite of the limited surface area. When water was insufficient, sand nearly covered the riverbanks; when water was ample, it could wash out the sand. Later, the river became an enclosed residual lake mainly for one of the three reasons: the river water receded, the river diverted its route, or

图 117 鸣沙山 月牙泉

Fig.117 Mingsha Mountain and Crescent Moon Spring

滩掩埋,水来时又将沙地冲开。现在月牙泉大、小泉湾的地形是典型的平原沙质曲流型河谷残留湖地型。后来由于河水退去，或由于河谷改道，或由于南北沙山在月牙泉西部相连，堵塞了古河道,使原来的小河形成了封闭式的残留湖。它千百年来未被蒸发消失,是因为地下水仍能向被封闭的古河槽积水洼地补给水分,于是就形成了如今沙山环抱中的一汪清水,而且形状宛如月牙一般。

the north and south sand dunes joined together at the west end of the Crescent Moon Spring. The present large and small spring bays of the Crescent Moon Spring are typical landforms of residual lakes of meander-type sand river valleys found in plains. It is due to the underground water supply for this enclosed low-lying land that the crescent-shaped spring surrounded by sand hills came into being.

渥洼池

渥洼池，也称寿昌海，即汉武帝得天马之处。汉武帝元狩三年(前120年)秋，匈奴的浑邪王杀休屠王，率众4万余人归附西汉。河西地区正式成为汉朝的统治区域。于是，汉武帝就在河西设置了武威和酒泉郡。为了经营新获得的领土，汉朝调遣内地的刑徒前往屯垦。其中，有一个来自南阳新野名叫暴利长的罪犯被派往敦煌地区屯田。当时，有人多次在渥洼池旁看见野马，其中有一匹长得神异非凡。于是，暴利长在水边做了一个手持马笼头的土人。等到马对这个土人习以为常的时候，暴利长就将自己装扮成土人的样子，趁马饮水不备之时将它套住。而在献给汉武帝的时候，为了使这匹马的来历显得更加神异，暴利长就宣称马是从渥洼水中擒获的天马。此时，好大喜功的汉武帝正致力于开拓西域，以宣

Wowa Pool

The Wowa Pool, also known as the Shouchang Lake, is the location where Emperor Wu received a "Heavenly Horse." In the 3rd year of the Yuanshou Era (120 BC), Prince Hunye of the Xiongnu led his troops to surrender to the Western Han Dynasty after killing Prince Xiuchu, indicating the Hexi area was officially under the control of the central government. The government then set up Wuwei and Jiuquan prefectures. Aiming at managing the new land, the government assigned gangs of convicts from the Central Plains to reclaim the wasteland in the Hexi Corridor. A criminal named Baolichang from Nanyang was sent to Dunhuang. At that time, some people saw wild horses near the Wowa Pool several times, among which one horse stood out from the rest. In order to catch it, Baolichang first made a clay figurine holding a bridle, and placed it standing in the river. When the horse became accustomed to the clay figurine, Baolichang disguised himself to be the clay figurine and caught the horse unprepared when it was drinking water. Later, when the horse was presented to Emperor Wu, who was engaged in his expedition to the Western Regions, it was given the magical backstory that it was a "Heavenly Horse" from the waters of the Wowa Pool. The legend pandered to the needs of the emperor, who desired to boost the prestige of the Han Dynasty. Therefore, Emperor Wu first established Longle County in Wowa, which had been a small remote village of Dunhuang. He then composed "Ode to the Heavenly Horse I," which

扬汉朝的天威。而渥洼水出天马一事，恰巧迎合了汉武帝的需要。渥洼水附近本来只是敦煌境内一个边远乡村，在暴利长擒获天马后，汉武帝在此地设置了龙勒县。此外，为了张扬此事，汉武帝还亲自作《太一之歌》，歌曲曰："太一贡兮天马下，沾赤汗兮沫流赭。骋容与兮跇万里，今安匹兮龙为友。"这首歌首先宣扬神马来自天赐，意味着上天对武帝眷顾深厚；接着夸赞此马体貌不凡，不远万里而来，投效王廷，意味着大汉帝国地广万里，宝物时出。汉武帝通过夸赞天马，炫耀了汉朝凭天之助，得地之宜，所以成为天子之国。此外，汉武帝还将渥洼水所得的天马和元鼎四年（前 113 年）六月在后土祠附近所得到的宝鼎相提并论，在元鼎五年（前 112 年）十一月昭告天下，以制造皇权神授的舆论。为了顺应渥

reads "The god of Oneness granted the heavenly horse come to the earth; His red brown sweat is like the blood flowing. It is so easy for him to gallop about ten thousand miles; The friend of the dragon in the sky becomes the horse on the earth." The song first depicted the horse bestowed by heaven, indicating that Emperor Wu had received the mandate of heaven, and then praised the extraordinary horse for offering its service to the court from thousands of miles away, showing the Han Dynasty was large in territory and rich in treasure. By exaggerating the Heavenly Horse's characteristics, Emperor Wu showed off the favor he received from heaven and earth, proving he was the Son of Heaven. In addition, in November of the 5th year of Yuanding Era (112 BC), Emperor Wu equated the Heavenly Horse from the Wowa Pool with the *ding* (an ancient bronze cauldron) from the Earth-God Temple in June of 113 in his imperial edict so as to influence public opinion into accepting that his imperial power was granted by heaven. In March of the 2nd year of Taishi Era (95 BC), Emperor Wu even claimed in his edict that when he offered sacrifices to heaven, he received in return a white *qilin*, a mythical auspicious beast, as a gift to sacrifice in the ancestral temple. The Heavenly Horse from the Wowa Pool and gold from the Taishan Mountain then appeared, indicating it would be proper to change the previous names. Previously, gold currency was cast in a pie shape. After this event, they were cast in the shape of a *qilin*'s foot, or a horsehoof. His edict was to inform people that

洼水出天马的祥瑞，汉武帝还在太始二年(前 95 年)三月下诏，宣称："往者，朕郊见上帝，西登龙首，获白麟以馈宗庙；渥洼水出天马，泰山见黄金，宜改故名。"在此之前，黄金货币皆铸成饼形，自此开始改铸成"麒趾"和"马蹄"形。诏书告诉人们，铸造马蹄金是为了顺应上天所赐的祥瑞，把渥洼水出天马事件的影响扩展到了经济生活领域。而汉武帝改铸马蹄金的做法，成为后世金银元宝的雏形，对我们的货币形制的发展带来了重要的影响(图 118)。

由于汉武帝的鼓吹和宣传，渥洼水的神奇色彩越来越浓厚。自从汉朝开始，渥洼水就被视为出产龙种之地。唐代所修的《寿昌县地境》中也记载到渥洼水："寿昌海，源出县南十里。方圆一里，深浅不测，即渥洼池水也。汉得天马之所。"在晚唐归义军文人记载敦煌当地名胜古迹的《敦煌廿咏》中有《渥洼池天马咏》一首：

horsehoof-shaped gold conformed to the propitious omen from heaven. Such changes demonstrated that the Heavenly Horse from the Wowa Pool had a great impact on the economy at the time. In addition, the horsehoof-shaped gold had great influence on the shape of currency, for it became the prototype for the later shoe-shaped gold or silver sycee ingots (Fig.118).

Due to the propaganda efforts from Emperor Wu, the Wowa Pool became increasingly mysterious and miraculous. Since the Han Dynasty, the Wowa Pool had been considered a birthplace of auspicious dragons, a symbol of the emperor. In the *Geography of Shouchang County* compiled in the Tang Dynasty, it records, "The Shouchang Lake, known as the Wowa Pool, is originated from 10 *li* south of Shouchang County. It's a bottomless lake with a radius of one *li* where the Heavenly Horse in the Han Dynasty was found." In the *Twenty Poems of Dunhuang* compiled during the *Guiyijun* regime to record scenic spots in Dunhuang, there is a poem titled "Ode to Heavenly Horse from Wowa Pool." It says, "Wowa is a lake where the Heavenly Horse was presented / It runs as light as soft silk among the flowers, as fast as white silk in the clouds / The horse gallops in palace like a wind without traces / Jumping into the lake, even a good fortune cannot buy." During the *Guiyijun* regime, Tang Wuzhen, an eminent monk in Dunhuang, wrote the

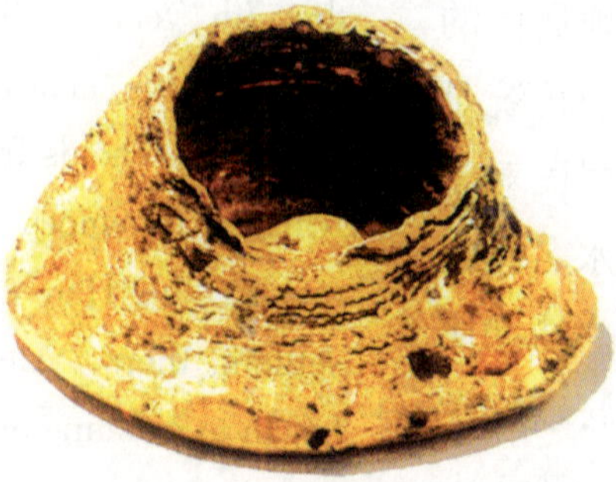

图 118　西汉马蹄金
Fig.118　Horsehoof-shaped Coin in the Western Han Dynasty

“渥洼为小海，伊昔献龙媒。花里牵丝去，云间曳练来。腾骧走天阙，灭没下章台。一入重泉底，千金市不回。”而在敦煌当地的著名僧人唐悟真在为归义军节度使张议潮撰写《河西节度公德政及祥瑞五更转兼十二时并序》时，就宣扬张议潮为“渥洼龙种，丹穴凤雏，禀气精灵，生便五色”，为张议潮的出身制造神奇色彩，以便其更好地统治从吐蕃手中新收复的河陇地区。可见在唐朝的时候，当地人还非常清楚渥洼水的具体位置。由于元、明两朝政府经营西北策略的转变，敦煌居民曾

Achievements of the Military Commissioner of the Hexi Area for Zhang Yichao, the Military Commissioner of the *Guiyijun* Force, in which Zhang Yichao was described as the son of auspicious dragon and phoenix from the Wowa Pool and was born with five colors and extraordinary spirit. The Wowa Pool was used to create mystery for the birth of Zhang Yichao so as to support his management of the newly-recovered Helong area. All of the aforementioned show that local people were certain about the exact location of the Wowa Pool in the Tang Dynasty. But due to different policies for controlling the Hexi area in the Yuan and Ming dynasties, local residents migrated from Dunhuang to other places several times, which caused a loss in the transmission of local culture over the generations. The new settlers did not know much about the original names of fortresses, beacon towers, watchtowers, or scenic spots in Dunhuang. In the 54th year of the Emperor Kangxi of the Qing Dynasty (1715), the area outside the Jiayu Pass resumed habitation. In

经多次迁出。随着本地居民的外迁，本土文化的历史传统难以传承，而新迁入的居民对敦煌当地城堡、烽燧、山水名胜的固有之名已不甚了解。清朝康熙五十四年(1715 年)，嘉峪关外之地开始逐渐收复。雍正七年(1729 年)，清政府从陕、甘、宁等地迁徙了 2405 户农户前来敦煌，汉人重新成为敦煌的主体居民。移民到来之后，一些文人雅士开始对敦煌当地的遗址进行考订和命名。清朝的文人曾将敦煌城南 10 里的月牙泉误定为渥洼池。宣统二年(1910 年)，敦煌县令还特地为月牙泉题写对联：

活水巧回环，问那如许清光，可曾有姮娥误奔；

灵沙常拥护，念此摩诃妙谛，还须望天马重来。

1944 年，北京大学西北考察团考古组的阎文儒先生到敦煌南湖考察，在收集和研究敦煌出土的当地地志资料基础上，推断今天南湖乡黄水坝水库就是汉朝渥洼池遗址。而 P.

the 7th year of the Emperor Yongzheng (1729), the central government relocated 2,405 households from Shaanxi, Gansu, and Ningxia provinces to settle in Dunhuang, making the Han ethnicity the majority of settlers there. After that, some scholars began to examine and rename some sites. At the time, they even mistook the Crescent Moon Spring lying 10 *li* south of Dunhuang for the Wowa Pool. In the 2nd year of Emperor Xuantong (1910), the Magistrate of Dunhuang County wrote a couplet for the Crescent Moon Spring specially:

Running water circulates tactfully, asking the bright water whether the goddess Chang'e took it as the Moon;

Miraculous sand embraces it frequently, considering the intelligent essence and hoping the Heavenly Horse revisits the spring.

In 1944, when Yan Wenru, member of the northwestern archeological expedition of Peking University, was investigating the Nanhu area in Dunhuang, he deduced that the present Huangshuiba Reservoir in Nanhu was the site of the Wowa Pool in the Han Dynasty based on collections and research on the local topography. In the *Pictorial Records of Superior Prefecture of Shazhou* (Dunhuang manuscripts P.5034), it was recorded that the Wowa Pool was located in

5034《沙州都督府图经》记载渥洼池位于寿昌故城东南10里，“方圆一里”。唐代10里相当于今天的5.4公里。所以，李正宇先生认为汉唐的渥洼池应该在南湖水库南边1里，而此处的大泉应就是渥洼池的水源（图119）。不过，汉唐时代深不可测的渥洼池，由于时过境迁、沧海桑田，已经淤积成平滩，不复昔日的风采了。

a site 10 *li* (5.4 kilometers) southeast of Shouchang City and had a radius of one *li*. Mr. Li Zhengyu concluded that the Wowa Pool should be 500 meters south of the Nanhu Reservoir with the Daquan River as its water source (Fig. 119). However, the bottomless Wowa Pool in the Han and Tang dynasties has since evolved into a flat shoal without its original characteristics.

图119 渥洼池遗址

Fig.119 Ruins of the Wowa Pool

三危山

三危山，也称卑羽山、升雨山，位于敦煌市东南30里。三危山海拔1800米左右，绵亘数十里，主峰在山脉西端，和大泉河与鸣沙山相望(图120)。对于三危山，唐太宗之子李泰编撰的《括地志》中曾有记载："三危山有三峰，古曰三危，俗亦名卑羽山，在沙州敦煌县东南三十里。"明朝所修的《都司志》的解释更为详细："三危山为沙州望山，俗名升雨山。在今城东南三十里，三峰耸峙，如危欲堕，故名。"据史书记载，三危山也就是《尚书·舜典》所载的"窜三苗"的"三危"之地。"三苗"为我国上古时代的民族之一，也称"有苗"或"苗民"，活动地域大体在今河南南部、湖北西部及湖南和江西的北部，活动中心在今洞庭湖和鄱阳湖一带。三苗的部落组织很发达，经常与中原诸族

Sanwei Mountain

The Sanwei Mountain, with an altitude of 1,800 meters and spanning dozens of kilometers, are colloquially known as the Beiyu Mountain or the Shengyu Mountain. Located 15 kilometers southeast of Dunhuang, the mountain faces the Daquan River and the Mingsha Mountain (Fig.120). In the *Geography of the Tang Dynasty* compiled by Li Tai, the son of Emperor Taizong, it recorded, "the Sanwei Mountain, also named the Beiyu Mountain, was located 30 *li* southeast of Shazhou. It had three peaks, so named *sanwei* in ancient time." The *Records of Dusi* compiled in the Ming Dynasty had record in detail that "the Sanwei Mountain, known as the Shengyu Mountain, is situated at southeast of Shazhou and it was given such a name because of its three cloud-kissing peaks (*san* meaning three and *wei* meaning danger)." According to the *Book of Documents*: *Canon of Shun*, the first record about this mountain said that the Sanwei Mountain was the same Sanwei area where the Sanmiao ethnic group was expelled. Sanmiao, also known as the Youmiao or Miaomin, was one of the ethnic minorities before the Xia Dynasty, who settled mainly in the southern part of present-day Henan Province, the western part of present-day Hubei and the northern part of present-day Hunan and Jiangxi provinces. The area around present-day Dongting Lake and Poyang Lake was the focus of their activities. They had an advanced tribal organization and frequently contacted or even fought with ethnic groups in the Central Plains.

发生交往和战争。在尧舜时代，三苗曾长期与中原冲突，屡起战端。在舜的建议下，尧在击败三苗后，“迁三苗于三危，以变西戎”。关于三苗被迁三危之事，最早的记载是《尚书·舜典》所载的“窜三苗于三危”。《左传·文公十八年》也记载：“舜臣尧，宾于四门，流四凶族。”这说明当时被流徙的有四族，三苗为其中之一，统称为“四凶”。此外，《左传》还记载：“允姓之戎，居于瓜州。”杜预的注释说：“允姓，阴戎之祖，与三苗俱放三危者。瓜州，今敦煌。”学者根据此条记载，再结合当时的历史形势，多认为流放三苗的“三危”当在中原之西的古雍州境内，进而将三危地望最终定在今天敦煌市东南的三危山。但近年来，除“敦煌三危山说”之外，学者们还提出“甘青说”“西裔说”“云南说”“康藏卫说”“四川说”等多种说法，使得《尚书》中的“三危”所指显得扑朔迷离。但我们有理由相信，随着学术研究的进一步深入，历史的迷雾终究会被揭开。

During the rule of Emperors Yao and Shun, the Sanmiao had been fighting against the Central Plains for a long time. After defeating the Sanmiao, Yao accepted Shun's suggestion and expelled the Sanmiao westward to the Sanwei area. In *Zuo Qiuming's Chronicles*, it was also recorded that Yao, the minister of Shun, exiled four malevolent, fierce tribes in four directions, the Sanmiao being one of them. Another record showed that one branch of an ethnic minority, whose family name is Yun, was living in Guazhou. Annotation given by Du Yu explained that Yun, the ancestor of Yin enthnic group, was expelled and exiled to the Sanwei area with the Sanmiao, and Guazhou was present-day Dunhuang. Based on such records and historical situation at the time, scholars agreed that Sanwei area where the Sanmiao were exiled was within the territory of ancient Yongzhou in the west of the Central Plains, and finally they concluded that it is today's Sanwei Mountain southeast of Dunhuang City. In recent years, however, in addition to the story about the Sanwei Mountain of Dunhuang, there are many other versions such as those involving Gansu-Qinghai, western origins, Yunnan, the Tibetan areas, and Sichuan, which makes Sanwei area a mystery. Undoubtedly, it is believed that the mystery will be clarified with further research.

图 120　三危山朝霞

Fig.120　Dawn Breaking at the Sanwei Mountain

疏勒河

疏勒河，西汉名籍端水，东汉六朝名冥水，唐朝时名独利河，元、明时名布隆基勒河，清以来名疏勒河，又名苏赖河，为跨瓜、沙二州之河流。疏勒河属于内陆河流域，发源于祁连山脉最高峰团结峰(海拔5808米)。河水全长约1000公里，年总径流量为14.66亿立

Shule River

The Shule River, the second longest river in the Hexi area flowing through Guazhou and Shazhou, was known as the Jiduan River in the Western Han Dynasty, the Mingshui River in the Eastern Han Dynasty, the Duli River in the Tang Dynasty, the Bulongjile River in the Yuan and Ming dynasties, and the Shule River or Sulai River since the Qing Dynasty. As an inland river, it starts from Tuanjie Peak (with an altitude of 5,808 meters) in the Qilian Mountains and stretches for 1,000 kilometers, with an annual runoff of 1.47 billion cubic meters. Originating in the Qilian

方米，在河西是仅次于黑河的第二大河。由于发源自祁连山地，疏勒河上游多峡谷陡壁，中下游比较平缓，形成广阔的绿洲。《沙州都督府图经》这样记载疏勒河："源出瓜州东南300里，流至敦煌县东北界，雨多即流，无雨竭涸。"疏勒河流经祁连山西段疏勒南山与陶勒南山之间的大纵谷间，即汉代羌人所居的"南羌中"和唐代吐谷浑人所居的"吐谷浑界"，向西北、北流，至昌马盆地以北出山，分为数支。其主流侧向东北，流至玉门市黄闸湾乡，折而向西北流，又流至瓜州县桥湾附近折而向西流，经安西县城北、西湖乡、敦煌黄墩子北、小方盘城北、榆树泉盆地，而终止于罗布泊哈拉湖。据《汉书·西域传》的记载，东汉政府为了利用疏勒河运送军粮，曾动用大量的人力疏浚疏勒河的河道。而到了唐代开

Mountains, the Shule River flows out of deep, precipitous gorges into a gentle basin where a vast oasis forms. It is recorded in the *Pictorial Records of Superior Prefecture of Shazhou* that "the Shule River starts from 300 *li* southeast of Guazhou, stretching to the northeast border of Dunhuang. It flows with heavy rain and dries up without rain." The Shule River flows through the valley between the Shulenan Mountain and the Taolenan Mountain, which was known as the region where Qiang tribes lived in the Han Dynasty and the Tuyuhun area in the Tang Dynasty. Then it continues northward to north of the Changma Basin, where the river bifurcates into several branches. Its main branch flows northeast to Huangzhawan Township in Yumen City, then turns northwest to Qiaowan Township in Guazhou County, continuing westward through the northern part of Anxi County, Xihu Township, Huangdunzi Village, the Small Fangpan Warehouse and Yushuquan Basin, finally ending in the Hala Lake in Lop Nor. Based on the *Book of Han: Traditions of the Western Regions*, the Eastern Han government once dredged and broadened the Shule River in order to deliver army provisions. During the Kaiyuan Era of the Tang Dynasty, Zhang Shougui, the Prefect of Guazhou, transported timber for building dams via the river. In the 7th year of Dade Era (1303), the Yuan government continued to dig the watercourse of the Shule River, aiming at shipping army provisions and other materials. In the 4th year of the Emperor Yongzheng of the Qing Dynasty (1726), Yue

元年间，出任瓜州刺史的张守珪还曾利用疏勒河运送修造水堰的木材。元朝大德七年(1303 年)五月，元朝政府为了沿途运送兵粮及其他物资，继续开挖疏勒河古河道,引水渡舟。清雍正四年(1726 年),川陕总督兼甘肃巡抚岳钟琪议开疏勒河西流之水，与党河尾合，以通舟运。于是造船兴工,终因河水渗漏过甚，水势不能通流而罢。所造之舟,亦沉于安西双塔堡河。20 世纪 60 年代以后,在汛期和冬春季节，疏勒河常有尾水流入敦煌境内，并向西注入罗布泊。之后，安西建成双塔水库,疏勒河下游基本断流,河道干枯。

Zhongqi, the Governor–General of Sichuan and Shaanxi, and Provincial Governor of Gansu, advised river naviagtion by combining the west fork of the Shule River with the tail of the Danghe River. People began ship–building and construction work, but the work had to be suspended because water could not flow smoothly due to serious river leakage; also, the ships sank in the Shuangtabao River in Anxi County. After the 1960s, during flood season or winter and spring, the tail waters of the Shule River flowed into Dunhuang and reached farther west to Lop Nor. After the construction of the Shuangta Reservoir, the lower reach of the Shule River downstream dried up.

党河

党河属疏勒河系内陆河流，为敦煌境内最主要的河流，覆盖敦煌城周绿洲，是绿洲的命脉。党河源于祁连山疏勒南山和党河南山东部的冰川群，经肃北蒙古族自治县注入敦煌。党河在西汉时名氐置水，唐宋时名甘泉水，而今名是蒙古语“党金果勒河”译名的简称。据说党河一名是以元代驻领沙州的贵族党金洪台吉的名字命名的。党河全长390公里，年平均径流量约为2.9亿立方米。党河的支流有大清水沟、大水河、野马河等。党河水由源头流出峡口后，向西北进入漫土滩，下渗形成潜流，至乌兰窑洞后溢出地表形成径流，经过融汇多股水流，最终汇成巨流。此后，党河经大别盖、桥头子，出水峡口，再经党城湾、浪湾流、沙枣园，折向东北流，注入敦煌市境。

Danghe River

The Danghe River, the most important river in Dunhuang, is an inland river of the Shule River system. It functions as the lifeblood for oases around the city. Originating from a glacier group in the Qilian Mountains, it flows through Subei Mongol Autonomous County into Dunhuang. In the past, the Danghe River was known as the Dizhi River in the Western Han Dynasty, and as the Ganquan River in the Tang and Song dynasties, but the present name is short for transliteration of the Mongolian name, Dangjinguole River (*guole* in Mongolian meaning river). It was said that the river was named after a Mongolian nobleman, Dangjin Hongtaiji, who was in charge of Shazhou in the Yuan Dynasty. The Danghe River is 390 kilometers long, with an average annual runoff of 290 million cubic meters. Its branches include Daqingshui Creek, the Dashui River, and the Yema River. The Danghe River flows from its source through the valley northwestward into Mantutan, where the water infiltrates the soil to form an undercurrent. From there it goes past the Wulan Caves, where the water flows onto the earth, and finally it becomes a mighty current integrating with other currents. Then the river passes Dabiegai, Qiaotouzi, out from Shuixiakou, through the Dangcheng Bay, Langwanliu, and Shazaoyuan, flowing northeast and eventually into Dunhuang City.

参考文献(原文)
Work Cited

[1] 郑炳林.敦煌地理文书汇辑校注[M]. 兰州:甘肃教育出版社,1989.

[2] 敦煌市志编纂委员会. 敦煌市志[M]. 北京:新华出版社,1994.

[3] 甘肃省敦煌市对外交流协会,张仲. 敦煌简史[M]. 兰州:甘肃文化出版社,1995.

[4] 荣新江. 归义军史研究——唐宋时代敦煌历史考索[M]. 上海:上海古籍出版社,1996.

[5] 吴廷桢. 河西开发史研究[M]. 兰州:甘肃教育出版社,1996.

[6] 杨铭. 吐蕃统治敦煌研究[M]. 台北:新文丰出版公司,1997.

[7] 李明伟. 丝绸之路贸易史[M]. 兰州:甘肃人民出版社,1997.

[8] 薛宗正. 安西与北庭——唐代西陲边政研究[M]. 哈尔滨:黑龙江教育出版社,1998.

[9] 陆庆夫. 丝绸之路史地研究[C]. 兰州:兰州大学出版社,1999.

[10] 杨秀清. 敦煌西汉金山国史[M]. 兰州:甘肃人民出版社,1999.

[11] 杨秀清. 华戎交会的都市——敦煌与丝绸之路[M]. 兰州:甘肃人民出版社,2000.

[12] 荣新江. 敦煌学十八讲[M]. 北京:北京大学出版社,2001.

[13] 萧默. 敦煌建筑研究[M]. 北京:机械工业出版社,2003.

[14] 殷光林. 丝路明珠——敦煌[M]. 西安:三秦出版社,2003.

[15] 中国公路交通史编审委员会. 中国丝绸之路交通史[M]. 北京:人民交通出版社,2000.

[16] 吴礽骧. 河西汉塞调查与研究[M]. 北京:文物出版社,2005.

[17] 余太山. 两汉魏晋南北朝正史西域传要注[M]. 北京:中华书局,2005.

[18] 赵汝清. 从亚洲腹地到欧洲——丝路西段历史研究[M]. 兰州:甘肃人民出版社,2006.

[19] 敦煌文物研究所. 中国石窟·敦煌莫高窟[M]. 北京:文物出版社,东京:

平凡社,1984.

［20］敦煌研究院. 中国石窟·安西榆林窟［M］. 北京:文物出版社,1997.

［21］邵如林. 丝绸之路古遗址图集——河西走廊段［M］. 兰州:甘肃人民美术出版社,1998.

［22］敦煌研究院:敦煌图史［M］. 上海:上海古籍出版社,2000.

［23］樊锦诗. 世界文化遗产·敦煌石窟［M］. 北京:中国旅游出版社,2004.

参考文献(译文)
Translation References

[1] 姜秋霞. 敦煌文化关键词. 北京:外语教学与研究出版社,2019.

[2] 罗常培. 语言与文化. 北京:北京大学出版社,2017.

[3] 吕宗万. 中国历代官制大辞典(修订版). 北京:商务印书馆,2015.

[4] 丝绸之路文化大辞典. 北京:红旗出版社,1995.

[5] Charles O. Hucker. *A Dictionary of Official Titles in Imperial China*. Stanford University Press, 1985.

[6] Rong Xinjiang. translated by Imre Galambos. *Eighteen Lectures on Dunhuang*. Leiden·Boston: Konin-klijke Brill NV, 2013.

[7] Xu Yuanchong. *300 Tang Poems*. Beijing: Dolphin Books, 2013.